'An Animated Son of Liberty'
A Life of John Witherspoon

After a brief career in accountancy, the author, J. Walter McGinty, prepared for the ministry of the Church of Scotland at the University of Glasgow, then spent thirty-five years as a Parish Minister. A 'late-developer', he went on to acquire a B.A. in History, at the Open University, in 1975, and a Ph.D. at the University of Strathclyde, in 1995. In 2003, his *Robert Burns and Religion*, was published by Ashgate. It was during a twelve year stint as a lay-governor at the University of Paisley (now the University of the West of Scotland), that he became more aware of the significance of John Witherspoon, and began the research that led to this book. Research both in Scotland and at Princeton revealed the huge contribution of Witherspoon to education, politics and the church. This book examines in detail his lectures on Eloquence (Rhetoric), Divinity, and Moral Philosophy at the College of New Jersey, considers his work as an Educationalist, and as a Congressman, and also looks at the contribution he made to encouraging emigration from Scotland to America. It analyses the pamphlets, speeches, sermons, newspaper articles and personal papers that reveal much about this man. It shows how Witherspoon helped create the ecclesiastical structures for the Presbyterian Church in America, and most importantly, how he helped lay the political foundations for the young Republic as it made its way towards Independence.

By the same author –

Robert Burns and Religion

'An Animated Son of Liberty'
A life of John Witherspoon

J. Walter McGinty

Arena Books

First published in 2012 by Arena Books

Arena Books
6 Southgate Green
Bury St. Edmunds
IP33 2BL

www.arenabooks.co.uk

McGinty, J. Walter
'An Animated Son of Liberty' A Life of John Witherspoon
1. Witherspoon, John, 1723-1794. 2. Church of Scotland -
Clergy – Biography. 3. Princeton University – Presidents -
Biography. 4. Statesmen – United States – Biography.
5. United States. Declaration of Independence – Signers -
Biography.
    I.   Title
    973.3'092-dc23

ISBN   978-1-906791-93-3

BIC categories:- BG, BGH, BGX.

Printed and bound by Lightning Source UK

Cover design
by Jason Anscomb

Typeset in
Times New Roman

Dedication

*To my wife, Lois, for
all her encouragement
and loving support over the years*

Acknowledgements

The inspiration for this book came from a visit to the studio of Sandy Stoddart, Sculptor in Residence, at the then University of Paisley. As a member of the University Court, I had been invited to view the clay model of John Witherspoon from which would be cast the twin statues for the campuses at Paisley and Princeton. My research into the life of John Witherspoon began shortly afterwards.

I am indebted to staff at the following libraries: The Mitchell, Glasgow, the University of Glasgow, the University of Paisley, now the University of the West of Scotland and Paisley Public Library. I must especially mention Firestone Library at the University of Princeton, where research facilities were made available, and where Meg Rich and her colleagues in the Rare Books Room were particularly helpful. My thanks are also due to the staff at Princeton Public Library where I had the use of the beautifully appointed Witherspoon Room and its Local Collection. I also benefitted from time spent at the Princeton Historical Society.

I was hugely assisted in the final work of checking the manuscript by my wife Lois, who patiently endured the painstaking business of trying to eliminate textual errors. In conclusion, I thank James Farrell of Arena Books for his kind attention and co-operation.

Contents

CHAPTER 1

Parish Minister

Identical statues of the Reverend John Witherspoon stand in the University of the West of Scotland's Paisley Campus and that of Princeton University. On the face of it, these two universities would not seem to have much in common. After nearly one hundred years as a College of Technology, Paisley University emerged in 1993 as one of Scotland's new universities. In 2009 its further growth saw it adopt the title The University of the West of Scotland.[1] Princeton can trace its foundation to the College of New Jersey chartered in 1746, which in its one hundred and fiftieth year assumed the title of University and is now in the Ivy League of American institutions of higher education.[2] The present educational establishment in the United Kingdom in its obsession with league tables, would certainly see the university at Paisley as the poor relation of Princeton. But it could be said with some justification that if it had not been for Paisley, Princeton would not have attained the prestigious position that it occupies today, and for this, John Witherspoon, the man who went from Paisley to Princeton in *1768* to become President of the College of New Jersey, must take a share of the credit.

John Witherspoon was born in the Manse of the Parish Church of Yester in the village of Gifford, East Lothian in Scotland on February 5, 1723. His father, the Reverend James Witherspoon, a minister of the Church of Scotland, was inducted at Gifford in March 1720, and it was there that John was baptised on February 10, 1723. John was the eldest of six children to be born to Mary and James who had been married in that same church some six months after James had been installed as its minister.[3]

James Witherspoon was born in 1691, graduated from Edinburgh University in 1709 and went on to study Theology. The period between his theological studies and coming to Gifford is unrecorded, but he served there for forty years until his death in 1759. The little that we can glean of James's character is obtained from rather doubtful sources and often seems to be largely anecdotal. Even Varnum Lansing Collins, whose 1925 biography of John Witherspoon at times borders on hagiography, is cautious about their veracity. He seems to have been a capable minister who performed his parish and congregational duties diligently. He was appointed to a Royal Chaplaincy, served on several General Assembly committees and on one occasion was invited to preach before the Lord High Commissioner, the King's representative at the General Assembly.[4] The positive comments are sourced to John Witherspoon's son-in-law, Dr

Samuel Stanhope Smith, and the negative ones to the autobiography of the Reverend Alexander (Jupiter) Carlyle, John's contemporary, who was writing towards the end of a long life that had been full of ecclesiastical controversy and politicking.

Alexander Carlyle recalls visiting the Gifford Manse in the summer break from Edinburgh University where he and John were fellow students, and how they would fish all day to keep out of the way of James Witherspoon, who was:

> very Sulky and Tyrannical, But who being much Given to Gluttony, fell asleep Early, and went always to Bed at 9, and Being as Fat as a porpus [*sic*], was not to be awak'd, So that we had 3 or 4 hours of Liberty every night to amuse ourselves, with the Daughters of the Family, and their Cousins who Resorted to us from the Village when the Old Man was Gone to Rest.[5]

Carlyle remembers how in 1744 he was sent to James Witherspoon to be examined as part of his trials for license to preach, but asserts that Witherspoon senior had very few things to ask in examining a divinity student, and comments:

> How to Eat and Drink and Sleep being his Sole Care, tho' he was not without parts, if the Soul had not been buried under a Mountain of Flesh.[6]

In listening to such a character assassination, it should be kept in mind that the writer was looking back upon a person he had met some sixty years previously. James Witherspoon was also the father of a man who had been an anti-establishment, indeed a revolutionary figure, both ecclesiastically and politically, whereas Carlyle himself had been aligned with the ruling parties in both Church and State.

Trying to find evidence from a source that has no bias, the Kirk Session records show James Witherspoon's habit of preaching for several Sundays on the same text. For example, he preached for eight successive Sundays on *Romans* 8.33, 'Who shall lay anything to the charge of God's elect', and for seven Sundays on *Ephesians* 5.15, 'See then that ye walk circumspectly, not as fools but as wise'.[7] The first text is full of the self-satisfied assurance of those who have made it into the select band of 'the elect', those who are saved from damnation and destined for heaven, and who know that nothing can now prevent them from getting there. The second text urges people to walk carefully through life, to refrain from acting foolishly and to seek to be wise.

To spend such time on texts like these perhaps tells us something about the man that is more accurate than what has been said in the funeral oration of a friend or written by the acid pen of an old rival. I suspect that James Witherspoon was content to proclaim and believe what were at the time the orthodox doctrines of the church, and that he was convinced that he was one who was assured of his place in heaven. This might in some way go to substantiate Carlyle's insinuation of laziness, in that if one is convinced that one has already made it into God's favour, without any effort of one's own, then what further activity is called for? However, if this attitude is adopted, it does raise the question, did James continue to care for the souls of others, now that his own was safe? Again this strengthens Carlyle's case against James. The second text's caution to his hearers, to walk carefully through life and not to act foolishly, would seem to be encouraging a very restricted form of living. There seems to be no place for spontaneity or fun, and the over-riding sense is of the utterly serious nature of life. But the positive aspect of his character and what has been said of his diligence at congregational level and participation in the Presbyterian government of the Church is also attested by his sermon methods. The thoroughness with which it is necessary to approach the exposition of a text must have been tested to the limit by the practice of preaching for several weeks on the same text, and this counters the charge of slothfulness levelled by Carlyle.

One very significant omission from any account of John Witherspoon's family life is the role of his mother in his upbringing. The only mention made of her is that she was responsible for his earliest education that enabled him to be able to read the *Bible* by the age of four. He also acquired a knowledge of the text of the *Bible* through learning by rote. Legend has it that he could recite large portions of the *New Testament* and *Watt's Psalms* and *Hymns* by heart.[8] Perhaps Carlyle's epithet 'tyrannical' tells of a household dominated by a father and one in which a mother had but little input, although for her son John, her contribution, in teaching him to read at an early age, was significant.

I have perhaps dwelt overlong in speculating on the character of James Witherspoon but when I go on to consider the remarkable life of John Witherspoon it might be possible to see how he was to a certain extent in reaction to his father, and also how much of his influence remained with him.

John Witherspoon, like John Knox two centuries before him, began his formal education at the grammar school in Haddington, some four miles from his home. He followed a curriculum that included English, Mathematics and the Classics, and by the time he completed his studies there, was proficient in Latin, Greek and French. He entered the University of Edinburgh when he was only thirteen years of age (not uncommon for the times) to begin a degree in Arts. Witherspoon's fellow students at Edinburgh included Hugh Blair, later Professor of Rhetoric at the University, John Home, the author of the play *Douglas*, and Alexander Carlyle, a Moderator of the General Assembly of the Church of Scotland. All of them were to become prominent leaders of the Moderate party, that from the 1750s was to dominate the ecclesiastical, university and political scene in Scotland for the next thirty years, while Witherspoon was to become a leader of the opposition, the Popular party, until he left for America in 1768.[9]

At Edinburgh, a university that was undergoing reform of its academic curriculum and teaching structure, Witherspoon came under the tutelage of John Stevenson, Professor of Logic and Metaphysics. Stevenson was an innovator, who, like Francis Hutcheson at the University of Glasgow, lectured largely in English. The Classics, that had previously dominated the curriculum, continued to be taught, but were given a new relevance by Stevenson who used them effectively as models in his lectures on English composition. Stevenson also lectured on contemporary English and French literary criticism, and was one of the first to encourage the study of John Locke's *An Essay Concerning Human Understanding* (1690). But basic to his teaching was the study of the civic rhetoric of Aristotle, Cicero and Quintillian. It is significant that John Witherspoon's Latin M.A. thesis written and defended in 1739, three years after he matriculated, 'includes more references to Cicero than any other source'. Cicero was to become a life-long influence on John Witherspoon, providing not only apt quotations but at times, perhaps as we shall see, a role model. Having successfully defended his thesis and graduated M.A. in 1739, Witherspoon went on to study Divinity at Edinburgh for the next four years.[10]

The detail of what John Witherspoon was taught in his theological studies is difficult to discern. There were only three professors in the faculty at that time, Divinity or Theology, Church History and Hebrew. Divinity was the only required course and was taught by Professor John Goldie or Gowdie (1682-1762). He specialised in expounding the work of the Swiss theologian, Benedict Pictet (1655-1724) whose *Theologia Christana* is similar to the covenant theology of the *Confession of Faith* drawn up by the Westminster Divines and approved by the General Assembly of the Church of Scotland in 1647. Pictet deals with the same themes as the *Confession*: the Authority of Scripture, The Trinity, Creation, Providence the Fall of Man, Sin, Christ the Mediator, the Covenants, Election, Sanctification, Sacraments, and Judgement.[11] It is perhaps significant that on the reading list of theological books compiled for his students by Witherspoon in 1773, Pictet's, *Theologia Christiana* is in a prominent fourth place. Witherspoon's early sermons also attest to his continued interest in and exposition of those themes found in Pictet. The reading list is headed by John Calvin's *Institutes of the Christian Religion* (1536) which had preceded both the Confession and the work of Pictet and upon whose theology both drew. John Witherspoon would continue to express an interest in French theologians throughout his life, and in this he was perhaps showing the influence of his father who had a similar taste for their works.

Witherspoon completed his theological studies at Edinburgh in 1743 and on September 6 of that year was Licensed to Preach the Gospel by the Presbytery of Haddington, thereby achieving the status of a Probationer of the Church of Scotland. He assisted his father at Gifford until April 11, 1745, when he was ordained and inducted to the charge of Beith, a parish in Ayrshire in the West of Scotland. But before he was even installed as minister at Beith he had met up with controversy, in that his orthodoxy was at first challenged, before his ordination and induction was allowed to proceed.

The matter that seems to have caused concern to the Presbytery of Irvine in which the parish of Beith was set, was Witherspoon's M.A. thesis of 1739, whose subject was *De Mentis Immortalitate* (On the Immortality of the Mind). Witherspoon again successfully defended his thesis whose subject had possibly been taken as an indication that he believed in the pagan philosophy of the immortality of the soul, as against the Christian orthodox belief in the Resurrection of the Body.[12] But although Witherspoon won their acceptance of the fact that his thesis was not in contradiction of Christian doctrine, any examination of Witherspoon's sermons would incline one to believe that he was closer to the Greek philosophy than to the orthodox Christian belief in the Resurrection. But I will return to this subject later when I come to look at Witherspoon's Christology.

A more likely cause of the Presbytery of Irvine's zealousness in testing Witherspoon's orthodoxy is to be found in the theology of his predecessor at Beith, the Reverend William Leechman, who had demitted his charge the previous year in order to take up the post of Professor of Divinity at the University of Glasgow. Leechman was already known as an ally and friend of Francis Hutcheson, Professor of Moral Philosophy at Glasgow, who had been instrumental in helping Leechman to obtain the Chair. The Presbytery of Irvine was probably glad to be rid of the liberal Leechman, and would be trying to make sure that any successor was more orthodox than he had been.[13]

There are conflicting views of the parish of Beith. Varnum Lansing Collins holds it up as a desirable charge and gushingly describes it as:

> A parish that dated back to the Reformation, in a neighbourhood full of romance and historic interest, yielding an annual stipend of seventeen pounds twelve shillings and sixpence and seventy-nine bols of meal and a glebe of thirty-one acres hard by the village.[14]

In a letter of August 5, 1743, recommending William Leechman to the Belfast congregation who had invited him to be their minister, Francis Hutcheson gave a more sanguine account of the parish and the people of Beith:

> Leechman is well as he is and happy, tho' preaching to a pack of horse copers and smugglers of the rudest sort. He would do nothing hard or disagreeable to any worthy man and has no desire of change. But, if the field be clear, it would be *peccare in publica commoda*, not to force him out of that obscure hole, where he is so much lost. ... He was the man I wished to be, in the first place, our Professor of Theology.[15]

The truth about Beith and its people surely lies somewhere between these two descriptions. However Witherspoon would soon find out for himself, for on November 23, 1743, the Reverend Michael Potter, the incumbent of the Chair of Divinity died, the way for Leechman to succeed him opened up, and subsequently, for the twenty-two year old John Witherspoon to obtain the vacant charge of Beith.[16]

John Witherspoon had only just established himself in his new parish when the first in what were to be a series of national or even international events was to take a hand in shaping the course of his life. On July 25, just three months after his Induction to Beith, Prince Charles Edward Stuart anchored off the shore of Arisaig in Loch nan Uamh and was to raise his standard on August 19, 1745, at Glenfinnan, Loch Sheil.[17]

The Church of Scotland was united in opposition to the threat posed by the rebellion led by Charles. The Church was a wholehearted supporter of the Hanoverian government which was pledged to maintain the Protestant religion in the country, and saw Charles as representative of the Roman Catholic religion by which it perceived it had been oppressed prior to 1688, and from which it had been delivered by William of Orange and his successors down to the present King George II. In January 1746, in response to the Presbytery of Irvine's instruction, John Witherspoon organised the recruitment of fifty men from the parish and helped raise the money to equip them for one month's service in a Militia. He duly led his men to the muster point at Glasgow, but there the authorities informed him that his little band of militia men were not required. Dismissing his men, he and his beadle set off to the scene of an expected battle at Falkirk.[18]

Prince Charles had already defeated government forces at the Battle of Prestonpans on September 21, 1745, and had gone on to invade England, reaching as far as Derby before turning back to Scotland. They were not a defeated army retreating, and in the course of their returning journey they had inflicted severe punishment on the government troops at Clifton, near Penrith. On their return to Scotland, they captured Glasgow, and were on course to encounter General Hawley's forces at Falkirk.[19]

It is indicative of the nature of warfare at that time, that a number of non-combatants had gone to be spectators of the battle at Falkirk. However, the Jacobite Army was not amused by this, as two contemporary letters to Lord Kilkerran show. The first, from Alexander Moore on February 4, 1746, tells of how after the battle, the Highlanders 'had sent away about a hundred prisoners to the Castle of Doun[e] who were spectators at the battle near Falkirk'. Another letter of the same date, from a Captain John Dalrymple of the Inniskillin Dragoons, confirms this and gives further details in a jocular tone:

> They have taken with all the prisoners they had among which are Mr Muirhead the Doctor's Chaplain [and] Mr Simpson the minister of Falla - both these gentlemen seem to be unlucky in the choice of their trade. Witherspoon of Beith too is a prisoner.[20]

The prisoners were held at Doune for a short time, and among them was one of Witherspoon's future opponents, John Home. Varnum Collins tells of how some of the prisoners escaped by the classic 'Boys Own Paper' method of tying their blankets together to make a rope and making their way over the battlements to the ground below, but Witherspoon thought it too risky and waited out his time until he was released.[21] Another source relates how John Home, having been an officer serving in a volunteer force who had fought and been captured at the Battle of Falkirk, was likely to have been the leader of the escape. Home was later to be the author of *Douglas* and to have a major part to play in the controversies involving the Moderate literati in Edinburgh. Collins makes much of this incident of Witherspoon's experience as a captive, and claims that Witherspoon's nerves were affected by the stress of it for the rest of his life. But I am inclined to think that the account that he gives has suffered from too little information and too much interpretation.

Upon his release, Witherspoon returned to Beith in time to be present at the Presbytery of Irvine and to support its forming a committee to 'wait on the Duke of Cumberland' and to convey to him, 'how joyful it is to the presbytery that His Grace is come to our country to oppose the present Rebellion'. Witherspoon settled into the life of a parish minister in Beith. On September 2, 1748, he married Elizabeth Montgomerie by whom he was to have ten children, five of them born in Beith and five in Paisley. Only five of these children survived to accompany John and Elizabeth to America in 1768.[22]

Witherspoon continued to study, if only to produce the weekly sermons, but he seems to have made time for a number of leisure pursuits. Apart from his reading, he enjoyed riding, fishing and golf, and, during the cold Scottish winters, developed a reputation as a keen curler. *The Cairn of Lochwinnoch Manuscripts*, a collection of local anecdotes compiled between 1827 and 1837, hand-written by a Dr Andrew Crawfurd, shed some light on the character of Witherspoon. Dr Crawfurd tells of a challenge match between Witherspoon's Beith team of curlers and that of the neighbouring village of Lochwinnoch:

> The Beith heroes seemed apparently to be vanquished. In the course of the important day there came a thaw that garrit the ice to be dauchie and covered it with water. [Witherspoon] drew all his loyal Beith partizans to a point. Their weight pressed the ice down and made the water overflow the rink more and deeply. This reckless trick not suitable to the character of a Christian minister was the cause of the ending of the sport as a draw game and it threatened to make the Beith horse cowpers food for the geds, Anglice, pikes and Braizes at the bottom of the loch, (all for the empty honour of a vain boast).[23]

Crawfurd has an interesting footnote on this incident:

> When the news of the turbulent priest of Beith being elected as Representative of New Jersey, for the Congress arrived at Lochwinnoch, his antagonists remembered his dangerous prank near Beith and they were red that he was in a far wider field than the Lochwinnoch bonspiel and he wants to play a more dangerous game, and they concluded that, 'he would spill a horn or make a spur to make a republic, or cause many men hing in a wuddie'.

Perhaps this little incident on the ice is an indication that Witherspoon was willing to take a calculated risk when the conditions were right. The reaction of the Lochwinnoch folk to his being elected to Congress also indicates that they thought that this risk-taker might well put other people's lives at risk, even as far as to put them in danger of swinging on a gallows.

One last incident from Witherspoon's social life in Beith tells of a man who enjoyed the gregarious atmosphere of the pub. On his visits to Lochwinnoch for the curling, Witherspoon was a regular at the Strand's Inn. Dr Crawfurd tells of how:

> One Saturday night after a tench bonspiel he was dining with his friends and at eleven o'clock at night Strand's wife, Janet Orr, a douce, and serious Christian, patted him and whispered into his lug a hint about his public duty, the next day being the Lord's day. Witherspoon replied loudly, 'A minister who could not shake a sermon out of his coat sleeve is a silly cuif'.

Witherspoon, according to this anecdotal evidence is a bit of a puzzle. He goes bravely off to do battle, and is then afraid of the risks involved in an escape. He is willing to engage in what today would be called 'gamesmanship', or, more plainly, 'cheating', in order to avoid defeat, even at the risk of a ducking in the freezing waters of Lochwinnoch, while no doubt he had been advocating honesty in all things in his preaching. He displays a brashness and a cockiness to the landlady that is a very good example of one of the ironically critical 'Maxims' of his *Ecclesiastical Characteristics*, of what makes a Moderate minister: 'A moderate man must endeavour as much as he handsomely can to put off any appearance of devotion'.[24] These are not carping criticisms but are merely noted here as an indication that Witherspoon combined in his nature both piety and a touch of devilment. He was no impetuous, thoughtless combatant who rushed off to war, but a man who also knew the anxiety of uncertainty, yet for all that, he was prepared to take a risk when he judged that it was the right time to do so.

Before going on to consider in more detail John Witherspoon's perhaps best known early foray into ecclesiastical pamphleteering and politics with the publication of *Ecclesiastical Characteristics* in October 1753, I want to explore some of the reasons why he aligned himself with the Popular party, those who were in opposition to those known as the Moderate party who were at that time beginning to achieve positions of power and influence within the Church of Scotland and the Scottish Universities. These men who were emerging to become known in a few years time as the Edinburgh literati: William Robertson and Adam Ferguson, and those who had been his fellow students, Hugh Blair, John Home and Alexander Carlyle had all benefited from a similar education, all of them became part of the ecclesiastical establishment, while Witherspoon was for all the years of his Scottish ministries, its constant critic. All of these men had proceeded to become ministers of the Church of Scotland by very similar routes, sharing similar forms of early education, and engaging in study at Edinburgh or Glasgow Universities and coming into service in the same presbyterian church system. All of them had actively supported the government in opposing the Rebellion of 1745, all of them serving in volunteer support units. But the times in which they lived and worked threw up several major issues that clearly divided the two parties: Patronage, the propriety of stage plays, and later, after Witherspoon had gone to America, the American Revolution, and Roman Catholic Relief. On all these issues Witherspoon found himself on the opposite side from the Moderates.

Yet when Witherspoon's writings are examined they bear many of the hallmarks of the ideals held by Moderate ministers such as Hugh Blair. The language is similar, the style and balance of his sentences closely resemble theirs.[25] There seems to be the same concern for society's betterment and the means by which to achieve it through the inculcation of sound belief. But undoubtedly there were deep divisions of opinion as to how the Church should be organised in order to achieve the betterment of society, and there were huge theological differences as to what constituted sound belief, or real religion.

In the early biographies of Witherspoon, he is portrayed as the upholder of orthodox Christianity as against the deviant and watered down version of the Christian Faith that was said to be proclaimed by the Moderates. This is a gross oversimplification that does little to the credit of either party. I would like to turn the thing on its head and to question the orthodoxy of Witherspoon's proclamation, and to see whether or not the much maligned Moderates might not have been nearer to the gospel proclamation. This I will come to when I look at the sermons of Witherspoon and the Christology that emerges from them. But before I attempt to look at these matters, I would like to put forward the view that this champion of the Popular party and castigator of the Moderates was much more of a Moderate than has been hitherto acknowledged.

When I was following up a reference to Blaise Pascal, whose *Provincial Letters* are included in Witherspoon's book-list for his students at the College of New Jersey, I came across a comment about Pascal that seemed to shed some light on what might be called Witherspoon's ambiguous attitude to the Moderates. T. S. Eliot writes of Pascal's great interest in Montaigne:

In every way the influence of Montaigne was repugnant to the men of Port Royal [the Jansenists]. Pascal studied him with the intention of demolishing him. Yet in the *Pensees* at the very end of his life, we find passage after passage, and the slighter they are the more significant, almost 'lifted' out of Montaigne down to a figure of speech or a word ... .[26]

Eliot expresses the judgement that, 'by the time a man knew Montaigne well enough to attack him, he would already be thoroughly infected by him'. Perhaps by the time Witherspoon had got to know the Moderates well enough to attack them, he had become thoroughly infected by them.

While casting around for an understanding of why this man, who shared so many of the educational experiences, parental influences, occupational, Christian and humanitarian concerns with the Moderates, should turn out to be so opposed to them, I tried to see if I could find any possible model for his satirical writing. An observation made by J. M. Cohen in his Introduction to *The Histories of Gargantua and Pantagruel* by Francois Rabelais, again seemed to apply to Witherspoon's attitude to the Moderates. Cohen writes:

For Francois Rabelais, like all true satirists, was more than half in love with the objects of his satires. As Cervantes setting out to mock the ballads and stories of chivalry, in fact composed a book more romantically adventurous than the material he parodied; ... so Rabelais clearly delighted most in that curious learning at which he directed so much of his rumbustious artillery.[27]

Was Witherspoon more than half in love with the objects of his criticism? That is a question to which the answer might be revealed as we pursue our enquiries into his relationship with the Moderates and his alignment with the opposing Popular party.

It is not my intention to rehearse in detail the complex history of the issues that were brought to a head by the *Patronage Act of 1712*. But it will be necessary to sketch in the background to the events prior to the Act, and the consequences of it that in time prompted the emergence of the Moderate and Popular parties into whose ideological and ecclesiastical disputes John Witherspoon entered as a protagonist.

The *Patronage Act of 1712* was in flagrant breach of the *Treaty of Union of 1707*, which had pledged to uphold the independence of the Church of Scotland from any state interference. Passed by a Tory administration, the Act returned power to the patrons by restoring to them the right to present a minister to a congregation. The *Act of Security of 1707*, which was an integral part of the *Treaty of Union* had clearly stated:

> Her Majesty with advice and consent foresaid expressly Provides and Declares that the foresaid True Protestant Religion contained in the abovementioned Confession of Faith with the form and purity of worship presently in use within this Church and its Presbyterian Church Government and Discipline, that is to say the *Government of the Church by Kirk Sessions, Presbyteries, Provincial Synods and Generall Assemblies*, all established by the foresaid Acts of Parliament to the Claim of Right shall Remain and Continue Unalterable, and that the said Presbyterian Government shall be the only Government of the Church within the Kingdom of Scotland.[28]

Despite the Church protesting against the legislation at the ensuing General Assembly, and thereafter each year until 1784, as a standing annual instruction to its Commission, the *Patronage Act* remained in place.[29]

The *Acts Establishing Presbyterian Government of 1690*, approved by William III, had given power to the local landowners and elders as follows:

> The heretors of the said parish (being protestants) and the elders are to name and propose the persone to the whole congregatione to be either approven or disapproven by them, and, if they disapprove, that the disapprovers give in their reasons to the effect the affair may be cognosced upon by the presbytery of the bounds ... .[30]

The *Patronage Act of 1712* gave this power to the patron. No longer were elders or local heritors to have the power to nominate a minister. Even the role of Presbytery was reduced to that of an executor: requested and expected to act in fulfillment of a patron's wishes. In the early years following the *Patronage Act*, some patrons did not at first assert their right. But by the 1730s there was an increasing conflict between patrons and the people of the congregations.

The people's right to choose their minister had been established in 1560, when John Knox's *First Book of Discipline* had declared that 'It appertaineth to the people and to every several congregation, to elect their Minister'.[31] This was confirmed in even stronger terms in 1578, in the *Second Book of Discipline* which bluntly states:

> III. 5. In the order of election it is to be eschewit that na person be intrusit in ony of the offices of the kirk contrar to the will o the

congregation to whom they ar appointed, or without the voce of the elderschip ... .[32]

The Church's autonomy was confirmed by an *Act of Parliament in 1649*, when patronage was abolished and the right to call a minister was vested in Kirk Sessions, with the proviso of a congregation's right to appeal to presbytery if they did not approve of the choice.[33] However, the *Acts Rescissory of 1661*, and the *Act Restoring Episcopal Government of 1662*, again took away the power from Kirk Sessions, Congregations and Presbyteries, and restored Patronage.[34] Troubled years followed for the Presbyterian Church in Scotland, and it was not until 1690, that government of the Church by the Church was restored, with one qualification, that the heritors, usually local landowners (who had to be protestant), had a say in the choice of a minister.[35] It is against this one hundred and fifty year old struggle for its freedom to govern its own affairs that the impact of the *Patronage Act of 1712*, upon the Church of Scotland is best be understood.

By 1732, the confusion as to who had the right to choose a minister became more of an issue. A charge at Kinross had been vacant for six years because the congregation would not accept the patron's candidate and the Presbytery of Dunfermline had refused to induct him. The General Assembly of 1732 ruled that the induction should proceed and the patron's nominee was inducted by a 'riding committee', the Presbytery still being unwilling to take part in the service. At the General Assembly, the minister, Ebeneezer Erskine, who had initially been the people's choice, but who was now in Stirling, asserted the right of the congregation to choose their own minister and cited the authority of the early Reformation documents: the *Books* of *Discipline*. Following his defeat in the Assembly, Erskine continued his protest from his own pulpit, at the Synod and at the following year's Assembly, during which he was censured. But, continuing to protest, he brought upon himself the wrath of the Assembly, who ordered the next Commission to exact a withdrawal of his protest and those of three colleagues, or to face suspension from their ministerial functions. In August 1733 they were suspended, and in November the Commission decided to remove them from their charges. Although in 1734, and again in 1736, the General Assembly attempted a reconciliation, perhaps because it feared further defections, by 1737, the four ministers had been joined by another four and had formed themselves into a Presbytery. The unwillingness of the General Assembly to fully implement the decision to suspend and remove these men from their charges is seen in that they were allowed to receive their Stipends and to live in their Manses until finally being removed in 1740. It could be said that Ebeneezer Erskine's protest was more about the people's rights than about the *Patronage Act* but it brought about the formation of the Original Secession Church.[36]

A series of cases between 1740 and 1750, involving a patron's presentee being found unacceptable to a congregation and a presbytery's unwillingness to preside over his induction, led to a concern that the law of the church was being flouted. However unpalatable the *Patronage Act* was, even to the General Assembly, it had been passed and was the law of the land, and for individual ministers or lesser courts of the Church to refuse to implement it, was to refuse to acknowledge the authority of both Church and State. For the ecclesiastical establishment, the issue had become less one of the rights and wrongs of patronage but of the authority of the most senior Court of the Church, the General Assembly.

In 1751, matters were brought to a crisis point. In 1748, Lord Torphichen had exercised his right as patron in presenting his candidate James Watson who did not win the acceptance of the congregation. So poor was his reception that only five or six heads of households out of about a thousand would sign his call. The Presbytery of Linlithgow referred the case to the Synod who ruled in favour of the induction of Watson. Yet the Presbytery still refused to induct him. Even after the General Assemblies of 1749 and 1750 had ordered the Presbytery to do so, they still refused on the ground of conscience. At the General Assembly of 1751, a 'riding committee', including the Moderates, Hugh Blair, William Robertson and John Home, was appointed to carry out the Assembly's order to induct James Watson, which was duly performed on May 30, 1751.[37]

Alexander Carlyle, who was then a minister at Inveresk, and was to become a leading member of the Moderate party, gives his interpretation of these events in his *Anecdotes and Characters of the Times*:

> It was in this Year 1751 that the Foundation was laid for the Restoration of the Discipline of the Church the next Year, in which Dr. Robertson and John Home and I had such an active Hand.

He goes on to tell of how:

> A select Company of 15 , were Call'd together in a Tavern, a night or two before the case [Linlithgow Presbytery's disobedience] was to be Debated in the Assembly.

The group included several ministers, among them, Blair, Robertson, Home and Carlyle, the lawyers Gilbert Elliot and Andrew Pringle, and Lord Provost Drummond of Edinburgh. They were not concerned with the rights of patrons but as Carlyle writes:

We were confirm'd in our Opinion that it was necessary to use every Means in our Power, to Restore the authority of the church, otherwise her Government would be Degraded and everything Depending on her authority would fall into confusion.

It was agreed that in the ensuing Assembly, John Home seconded by William Robertson would propose that Mr Adams who had been nominated but had refused to preside over the ordination at Torphichen should be suspended for six months and the Presbytery of Linlithgow censured for its disobedience. The proposers knew that they would be defeated in the Assembly, but by causing a debate they would 'keep the object in view'. They were heavily defeated but they had made their point and when in March 1752, a further case came before the Commission of the General Assembly, their point of view as to the seriousness of the flouting of the authority of the Assembly was again made and was to lead to action in the Assembly in May. Alexander Carlyle records his opinion: 'It was in the Assembly of 1752 That the Authority of the Church was Restor'd by the Deposition of Gillespie'.[38]

The Presbytery of Dunfermline had refused, on the ground of conscience, to induct the Reverend Andrew Richardson who had been presented to Inverkeithing by the patron in 1749. In November 1751, they were warned of serious consequences if they did not obey the Commission's instruction. At the March 1752 meeting they still had not complied but the Commission did not carry out its threat. Robertson and Home had entered a complaint about the Commission's inaction and registered their dissent. On 11 March in collaboration with Carlyle, Blair and Pringle they produced a paper, *Reasons of Dissent* which set out the case for the absolute necessity of discipline in the Church and the recognition of the authority of the General Assembly over its subordinate courts.[39]

By recording their dissent from the Commission's decision not to censure in the Inverkeithing case, Robertson and Home were permitted to appear at the bar of the Assembly in May 1752. A few days before the Assembly a counter pamphlet, *Answers to Reasons of Dissent* had been produced by John Witherspoon, but it failed to persuade the Assembly which fell into line with the thinking of Robertson and Home's argument and voted to depose the minister of Carnock, Thomas Gillespie, who had refused to participate in the induction at Inverkeithing.[40] The infant Moderate party, despite its humble birth in a tavern the year before, had achieved its first major success in its attempt to restore the discipline and authority of the Church. But as far as the Popular party was concerned, this had been achieved at the cost of the devaluation of conscience.

Reasons of Dissent had skillfully avoided any discussion of the rights or wrongs of the *Patronage Act of 1712*.[41] It concentrated on the need to restrict individual freedom for the sake of society's good. It asserted that those who are part of society, especially those who benefit from it, have a responsibility to abide by its rules. Further it held that to allow disobedience to go unpunished is to invite civil disorder, and declared that such conduct is 'an offence against the nature and principle of society'. It went on to declare that the Church as a society has to abide by the same principles that govern society and equally has a need for discipline and the recognition of authority. It went on to assert that although an individual member may disagree with its laws and policies it does not give that person the right to defy them on the grounds of conscience. It pointed out that in the presbyterian form of church government where all ministers are of equal rank it was even more important to recognise the Courts of the Church as having authority over them, that the General Assembly was the supreme authority and that as its Commission was set up to implement the General Assembly's authority in the interim period between Assemblies, it was vested with the same authority and ought therefore to be recognised as such and have its authority respected.

But when all the principled arguments of the Moderates had won the day at the General Assembly of 1752, there was one equally principled person, Thomas Gillespie, who was made the scapegoat of the Assembly's decision. Although a campaign was begun immediately after the Assembly and a pamphlet was issued, at the next General Assembly in May 1753, a move to reinstate Thomas Gillespie was defeated and his deposition confirmed. However the argument for the primacy of the individual conscience would not go away and continued to be taken up by those who like John Witherspoon had *Answers to Reasons of Dissent*.[42]

CHAPTER 2

Ecclesiastical Characteristics

In October 1753 John Witherspoon anonymously published a pamphlet that is ever to be associated with his name: *Ecclesiastical Characteristics or The Arcana of Church Policy, Being an Humble Attempt to open up the Mystery of Moderation wherein is shewn: A plain and easy way to the Character of a Moderate Man, as at present in repute in the Church of Scotland.*[1] Almost immediately Witherspoon was suspected of being the author of this sixty-two page document, which sets out thirteen 'Maxims' by which 'moderate men' conduct themselves. At first glance the style adopted seems to be similar to that of a playful senior pupil writing for the school magazine. But as the work progresses it takes on a more mature, ironic and whimsical tone. The satire is delivered in mock heroic prose such as was used by Jonathan Swift in *Gulliver's Travels* (1726) or later by Laurence Sterne in *The Life and Opinions of Tristram Shandy, Gentleman* (1759).[2] At first it seems so gently satirical that it makes a present day reader wonder what all the fuss was about, but its effect is cumulative, and by the time the reader has reached Maxim 13, the true nature and importance of the satirical method and the points made by it are more fully appreciated. Taken as a whole, the work is an extended criticism of the stance of the Moderates within the Church of Scotland at the time.

Witherspoon dedicates his work: 'To the Departed Ghost or Surviving Spirit of the late Reverend Mr.—, Minister in—', and writes:

> I was fully resolved to have sent it abroad by itself and not to have dedicated it to any person in the world: and indeed in a confined sense of the word, World, you see I have kept my resolution.

He then muses on how he might present a copy of his work to the one to whom it was dedicated, but he confesses: 'I did not find in myself any inclination to depart this life in order to transport it'.[3]

Having set the tone of whimsicality, Witherspoon then proceeds to outline his 'Maxims upon which moderate men conduct themselves'. He cautions that he shall 'make very little use of scripture because that is contrary to some of the maxims themselves'. Then in thirteen maxims, each with an accompanying commentary, he makes mockery of what he perceives to be the stance adopted by the Moderates within the clergy of the Church of Scotland:

ECCLESIASTICAL CHARACTERISTICS

Maxim I
> All ecclesiastical persons of whatever rank, whether principals of Colleges, professors of divinity, ministers or even probationers that are suspected of heresy, are to be esteemed men of genius, vast learning and uncommon worth and are by all means to be supported and protected.[4]

In 'Maxim I', Witherspoon is attacking what he sees as an over willingness among Moderates to rush to the defence of anyone who is suspected of heresy. He alleges that all moderate men have a 'kind of fellow feeling with heresy'. He might have cited the tolerance extended to Frances Hutcheson and William Leechman.[5] He then goes on in Maxim II to attack the Moderates tolerance of immorality:

Maxim II
> When any man is charged with loose practices or tendencies to immorality he is to be screened and protected, as much as possible, especially if the faults laid to his charge be, as they are incomparably well termed in a sermon preached by a hopeful youth, that some noise lately, good humoured vices.[6]

Witherspoon criticises the leniency of treatment accorded to Moderate sinners who are treated as if they were artistic geniuses who are allowed to break the rules, and for whom allowances have to be made because of their special talents. Whereas if any of the orthodox similarly offend they will be hunted down and punished, viz. the recent cases of orthodox ministers being suspended for not implementing the instruction of the Church's supreme court, The General Assembly.[7]

Maxim III
> It is a necessary part of the character of a moderate man never to speak of the *Confession of Faith* but with a sneer; to give sly hints that he does not thoroughly believe it; and to make the word orthodoxy a term of contempt and reproach.[8]

With this, Witherspoon opens up another issue of the day, the authority of *The Westminster Confession of Faith*, mocking the Moderates who in his estimation do not give the *Confession* the authority which it deserves. He alleges that they dismiss it because it was:

framed in times of hot religious zeal and therefore it can hardly be supposed to contain anything agreeable to our sentiments in these cool and refreshing days of moderation.

It is in his commentary on Maxim III that Witherspoon's satire loses its school-boyish tone and becomes more bitingly satirical, thereby becoming a source of offence to the thin skinned, or to those who perhaps find it uncomfortably near the truth.

Witherspoon then turns the spotlight on how the Moderates evaluate a good preacher:

Maxim IV

A good preacher must have the following special marks as signs of a talent for preaching. 1) His subjects must be confined to social duties. 2) He must commend them only for rational considerations viz. the beauty and comely proportions of virtue, and its advantages in the present life, without any regard to a future state of more extended self-interest. 3) His authorities must be drawn from heathen writers, NONE or as few as possible from scripture. 4) He must be very unacceptable to the common people.[9]

In Maxim IV and its accompanying commentary, Witherspoon develops his attack on the Moderates seeming concern only for the present life and their unwillingness to deal with the possibility of an extension of that life to include an afterlife in which there might be a 'judgement, heaven and hell'. He accuses them of avoiding the subjects that most concern ordinary people, making little use of scripture and when they do, distorting its meaning to make it conform to their moderate views. He refers to an earlier *Biblical* scholar, John Taylor of Norwich, whom he blames for 'altering Christianity to reconcile it to moderation and common sense'. This last comment seems strange coming from one who is now often credited with being at least one of the sources who helped introduce the common sense philosophy of Thomas Reid into America. At this stage in Witherspoon's development, common sense seemed to be debarred from scriptural interpretation.

There is a brief pause in Witherspoon's serious criticism in his next maxim:

Maxim V

A minister must endeavour to acquire as great a degree of politeness in his carriage and behaviour, and to catch as much of the air and manner of a fine gentleman as he possibly can.[10]

He immediately follows this with the suggestion that to achieve this they should keep the company of young army officers and rich young men. This in an era when the army was notorious as being the place of last resort of the criminal and the talentless, and when the dissoluteness of 'young men of fortune' was a feature of society.

Witherspoon offers more words of commentary upon the subject of education in his next maxim:

> Maxim VI
> It is not only unnecessary for a moderate man to have much learning, but he ought to be filled with a contempt of all kinds of learning but one, which is to understand Leibnitz's scheme well; the chief parts of which are so beautifully painted, and so harmoniously sung by Lord Shaftsbury and which has been so well licked into form by the late immortal Mr. H—n.[11]

In the commentary that follows, Witherspoon severely criticises what he perceives to be the Moderates' attitude to education and in particular, education in preparation for the ministry. He reveals his antagonism to the philosophies of Leibniz, Francis Hutcheson, Lord Shaftsbury and David Hume. He sees Leibniz as the main culprit in setting the trend for a more optimistic perception of the world, a perception that is in direct opposition to the scriptural account of Adam's disobedience and fall, the consequence of which is the tainting of the human race with sin, which in turn creates the need for redemption, if the human race is to escape the fires of Hell. He lists Shaftsbury and Hutcheson as those who have refined and advanced the ideas of Leibniz and therefore share the responsibility for creating a false picture of the world. In his commentary, he constructs what he calls 'The Athenian Creed' made from some of the ideas of these philosophers, thereby revealing that he himself is familiar with the books of those whom he is mocking, if not condemning:

> I believe in the beauty and comely proportions of Dame Nature, and in almighty Fate, her only parent and guardian, for it hath been most graciously obliged, (blessed be its name) to make us all very good. I believe that the Universe is a huge machine wound up from everlasting to everlasting by necessity, and consisting of an infinite number of links and chains ... That I myself am a little glorious piece of clockwork ... that my soul (if I have any) is an imperceptible number of exceedingly minute corpuscles ... I believe that there is no ill in the universe nor any such thing as virtue absolutely considered; that those things called *sins* are only errors in

the judgement ... that the whole race of intelligent beings, even the devils themselves (if there are any) shall finally be happy; so that Judas Iscariot is by this time a glorified saint, and it is good for him that he has been born. In fine, I believe in the divinity of L. S—, the saintship of Marcus Antonius, the perspicuity and sublimity of A—e, and the perpetual duration of Mr. H—n's works, notwithststanding their present tendency to oblivion. Amen.[12]

As I looked again at the elements of Leibniz's ideas to see more precisely why Witherspoon singled him out for such criticism, one rather odd fact emerged. It seems that Leibniz had a reputation for being mean with money. So when any of the young ladies at court got married he gave them a 'wedding present' consisting of useful maxims. Bertrand Russell writes that Leibniz used to conclude his maxims with the advice to the lady 'not to give up washing now that she had secured a husband'.[13] The Moderate reader would probably have reacted as angrily as any lady of the court to Witherspoon's 'Maxim VI'. Witherspoon's present of maxims for Moderates, in *Ecclesiastical Characteristics*, often have a similar 'edge' to them, and his adoption of Leibniz's habit perhaps shows an even more intimate association with his work than he cares to acknowledge.

In the next Maxim, Witherspoon takes up the subject of public and private worship:

Maxim VII
    A moderate man must endeavour as much as he handsomely can, to put off any appearance of devotion, and avoid all unnecessary exercises of religious worship, whether public or private.[14]

In this Maxim and his commentary upon it, Witherspoon attacks what he deems to be the complacent attitude of the Moderates towards public and private worship, and also what he sees as their seeming disdain for any reputation of piety. He accuses the Moderates of doing as little as they can get away with in the performance of their religious offices. He asserts that they have such a large majority in the Church courts that they can stifle the aspirations that others might have for special days of prayer or fast days. He alleges that they even offer up an economic argument against fast days by claiming that 'a fast day in Scotland loses 50,000 pounds to the nation'. As for family worship, he claims that if Moderates conduct it at all, that it is done in such a way as to make it nonsensical, and instances the head of a family praying, 'O Lord, we thank thee for Mr Bayle's Dictionary, Amen'.[15]

With heavy irony, Witherspoon returns to the concern that had initially prompted the writing of *Ecclesiastical Characteristics*: the dispute over the respective rights of patrons and congregations in relation to the choice of a minister:

> Maxim VIII
> In church-settlements which are the principal causes that come before ministers for judgement, the only thing to be regarded is, who the patron, and the great and noble heritors are for; the inclinations of the common people are to be utterly despised.[16]

As a preface to his argument, he asks that it be recognised that 'there is an original and essential difference between the gentry and the common people'.[17] Having established this, he then goes on to give his reasons why the patron (who is always of the gentry) should be allowed to determine the choice of a minister. Because the gentry seldom attend church this signals their disinterestedness and impartiality of judgement, therefore they are the best judges of a minister's preaching; and because they are undemanding of a minister's services except:

> Perhaps talking of the news at a private visit, or playing a game of backgammon it is but fair that in view of the edification of the common people, they should have the honour of conferring the benefice.[18]

With this satirical and quasi-logical argument, Witherspoon exposes the illogicality and nonsense of granting the power of patronage to people who are unlikely to attend the church, who do not seem to need a minister for other than social reasons, and who will not be in relation to him as their pastor and preacher.

In Maxim IX, Witherspoon attacks the fickleness of patrons who seem to be always in opposition to the people of a congregation no matter what attitude is adopted by them.

> Maxim IX
> While a settlement is carrying on, the candidate against whom there is a strong opposition from the people, must be looked upon, and everywhere declared to be, a person of great worth, and remarkable abilities; provided always, that if ever the same person, after he is settled, be at pains, and succeed in gaining the people's affection, he shall then fall as much below the ordinary standard in his character, as before he was raised above it.[19]

Witherspoon, in this Maxim, does not seem to be adopting a satirical pose but is instead accurately portraying the attitude of patrons who quite naturally present their candidate in the best light possible so that he may gain the acceptance of the people. But he cannot resist a sly dig at the petty attitude of a patron who is discomfited when a candidate whom he has forced on a people wins their favour, and cites a case in which this happened.[20] It is in his commentary on the maxim that the satirical note returns:

> The people being against a man, is a certain sign of his being a good preacher … it is also a pretty good sign of his being of moderate principles.

Witherspoon uses a phrase that clearly aligns the Moderates with heretical beliefs, when he writes of candidates who fail to live up to their patron's expectation, as those who 'apostatize to orthodoxy'.[21] He also accuses the patrons of cynically appointing in order to strengthen the moderate party.

The Moderates are next accused of being vindictive:

Maxim X

> Whenever we have got a settlement decided over the body of perhaps the whole people in the parish, by a majority in the General Assembly, the victory should be improved, by appointing some of the orthodox opposers of the settlement to execute it, especially those that pretend to have a scruple of conscience at being an active hand in any such settlement.[22]

The gloves are now off as Witherspoon makes an allusion to a very specific case in which this actually happened, namely that of the Reverend Thomas Gillespie, Minister of Carnock, who had refused on grounds of conscience to take part in the induction of the patron's presentee to the charge of Inverkeithing, thereby defying the authority of the General Assembly, which resulted in his being deposed in 1752.[23] But a remark in the commentary reveals an aspect of Witherspoon's own character that seems to indicate that were he in the same position of power as the Moderates, he would do the same. He betrays the ruthless streak in his own nature, one that was later to show itself as he engaged in the pursuit of the war against the British, when he writes: 'They do not deserve victory who know not how to push it or to improve the advantage they have gained'.[24]

Witherspoon next attacks the Moderates for their unreasonableness towards those who oppose them:

Maxim XI

The character which moderate men give their adversaries of the orthodox party must always be that of knaves or fools; and as occasion serves, the same person (if it will pass) may be represented as a knave at one time and as a fool at another.[25]

Witherspoon is here criticising the attitude of the Moderates who are so convinced of the reasonableness of their case that they impute either foolishness or knavery to those who oppose them. They do not seem to be able to acknowledge that there is just the possibility that they are being opposed on grounds of conscience: 'we cannot suppose that such as are against us can be so from conscience'.[26] This passage also relates to the conflict with authority on the grounds of conscience which had been so in evidence in the Gillespie case, when the General Assembly of the Church of Scotland ordered those whom it knew to be in opposition on grounds of conscience to comply with its instruction.[27]

Witherspoon's resentment at the attitude taken by Moderates towards what he calls 'the world', and to those such as Atheists, Deists, and those who are careless in their living, is made clear in:

Maxim XII

As to the world in general, a moderate man is to have great charity for Atheists and Deists in principle, and for persons that are loose and vicious in their practice, but not at all for those that have a high profession of religion, and a great pretence to strictness in their walk and conversation.[28]

It is difficult not to interpret his words as betraying a certain meanness of spirit. Hidden within the satire there seems to be a rather petty attitude being taken towards those who extend a charitable judgement to those who do not share theirs or his religious views. In addition, Witherspoon is adopting such a judgemental attitude towards those whom he deems to be 'loose and vicious', that it begs the question as to what conduct came under that category in his mind. I suspect that at this time, some very ordinary aspects of human frailty would be termed by Witherspoon to be 'loose' behaviour. At this stage in his life, Witherspoon had a very narrow and gloomy view of 'the world', but as we shall later show, the widening of his experience and the development of his working life into areas other than the parish ministry brought about a change of attitude towards much of which he had been so dismissive.[29] As for his half-hearted tilt at the tolerance extended by the moderates towards 'Atheists and Deists', he does not lay specific charges, but like many would be upholders of orthodoxy, he tended to ascribe such labels, without a great deal of thought, to those who did not subscribe to his own strict views.

From Maxim IX, Witherspoon's arguments have become more carping and the satirical element of his writing less imaginative and effective. It is as if he has run out of ideas for satire and has resorted to a mere complaining. In Maxim XIII he somewhat revives his attack:

> Maxim XIII
>   All moderate men are joined together in the strictest bond of union and do never fail to support and defend one another to the utmost, be the cause they are engaged in what it will.[30]

Here speaks the defeated outsider. The Moderates had won a total victory over the Popular party at the previous General Assembly and appeared now to be able to do what they liked, regardless of any issues of principle or conscience raised by the opposition in which Witherspoon had played a prominent part. Witherspoon takes a last bite at the Moderates:

> O what noble, sublime and impenetrable sermons shall be preached! What victories and triumphs shall be obtained over the stupid populace, by forced settlements, which never have such a beautiful and orderly form as when finished by soldiers, marching in comely array: with shining arms, a perfect image of the church militant![31]

Something of the original sparkle has returned in this passage. In his commentary he attacks Francis Hutcheson, whose ideas have influenced the Moderates' philosophy and in Witherspoon's view weakened their moral stance. He accuses them of suspending 'all the rules of conduct … when they seem to interfere with the general good'. He cannot resist reminding the Moderates of the one area in which they have not been successful, the augmentation of stipend. But he comforts them with the thought that when they have brought moderation to perfection and:

> driven away the whole common people to the Seceders, who alone are fit for them and captivated the hearts of the gentry to a love of our solitary temples they shall have nothing to do but spend their stipends.[32]

Yet, *Ecclesiastical Characteristics* ends 'not with a bang but with a whimper'. What had started out as a light-hearted yet vigorous attack upon the attitudes that Witherspoon saw as the dominant and driving forces of the Moderate party within the Church of Scotland, ends in a feeble and slightly petulant tone. Inevitably his critics focused in on the person who had written this criticism of the Moderates rather than attempting to answer or refute the allegations made. The pamphlet sold well, going through three editions between October 1753 and May 1754.[33] But it did not change anything, nor did it cause any slowing down of the progress of Moderatism. Although the pamphlet became a talking point and caused a stir among the clergy even to the point of reaching the floor of the Synod of Glasgow and Ayr, Witherspoon, still not admitting to being its author, nevertheless made a speech in his defence in which he expressed his resentment at being represented as: 'a firebrand, as violent and contentious, unfit to be a member of any quiet society'.[34] Ironically, in this speech to Synod and in the later *A Serious Apology for the Ecclesiastical Characteristics* (1763), Witherspoon much more cogently and effectively criticised some of the Moderates' practices and attitudes and argued ably in defence of the points made by the Author of the earlier pamphlet. Free from the need to be humorously satirical, his arguments become more direct, succinct and convincing. But by the time he was writing the *Apology* it was as if he was acknowledging that although he was not giving up the war, he had lost the battle. Witherspoon ruefully concludes what the publication of *Ecclesiastical Characteristics* has taught him:

> This has afforded me one observation, not very honourable to human nature, *viz.* That the rage of enemies is always more active and lasting than the affection of friends.[35]

CHAPTER 3

The Stage

On December 14, 1756, the tragedy *Douglas* opened at the Canongate Theatre in Edinburgh. Its author, the Reverend John Home, Minister at Athelstaneford in the Presbytery of Haddington, could not have anticipated the huge controversy that it would provoke, nor that it would end eventually with his resigning from his charge.[1] John Witherspoon had shared both student life with Home at Edinburgh University, and later, the adventure of their being captured after the battle of Falkirk and taken as prisoners to the castle at Doune. His familiarity with Home had been furthered by the fact that Home's charge was in the same Presbytery as that of Witherspoon's father, James, and also because they both had been members of General Assemblies in the immediately preceding years. Witherspoon was one of those who immediately entered into the debate that ensued following the first performance of the play. In the 'Advertisement' to his treatise: *Serious Enquiry into the Nature and Effects of the Stage: Being an attempt to show that contributing to the Support of the Public Theatre is inconsistent with the Character of a Christian*, Witherspoon tells what prompted it:

> The Reader will conjecture, therefore I do readily acknowledge, that what gave occasion both to the writing and publishing the ensuing treatise, was the new tragedy of *Douglas* lately enacted in the theatre at Edinburgh.[2]

The arguments at the time focused on the propriety of the stage, whether attendance at a theatre was compatible with being a Christian, and especially, whether a Minister should be engaged in the writing and production of a play.

Published in the spring of 1757, Witherspoon's treatise is a document that reveals as much about the author, as it contributes to the issues at stake. Witherspoon was still Minister at Beith when he wrote this 72 page and 23,000 word (approx.) pamphlet. He was already under call to The Laigh Kirk, Paisley but the Presbytery at Paisley had delayed the processing of the call because of objections raised by some presbyters who accused Witherspoon of being the author of *Ecclesiastical Characteristics*. Despite the instruction of Synod, the call was further delayed, and his Induction to Paisley did not take place until June 16, 1757.[3] Other events in his life were also making it a difficult time for him. At the General Assembly in May 1757, he had again suffered defeat at the hands of the

Moderates, failing in his attempt to thwart their achieving the appointment of Commissioners to the General Assembly, who in Witherspoon's opinion were but 'place-men' who would vote for the Moderate cause.[4]

In addition to this, his family life had been, to say the least, eventful, at times bringing him and his wife and children to the extremes of experience. His wife Elizabeth had given birth to three children: Robert in April 1753, Barbara in February 1756, and John in July 1757. Within those years, Robert had died in July 1754, aged 15 months, and his second daughter Christian died in December 1756, aged six years. These were years of great emotional upheaval, and perhaps when we read his pamphlet against that background, we might begin to better understand how some of the views expressed in it were formed.[5]

The subject of this essay might have made it an ideal foil for Witherspoon's satire, but instead he eschews this method of dealing with it for a much more serious approach. Gone is the schoolboy flippancy of *Ecclesiastical Characteristics* and in its place are the pessimistic, dark grumblings of a man in danger of becoming a misanthropist. On page three he bemoans that:

> such a levity of spirit prevails in this age, that very few persons of fashion will read or consider anything that is written in a grave or serious stile [*sic*].

Yet he proceeds to write in the manner that he has already judged will not be read by the very people that he is setting out to reach. Perhaps he has grown so used to failure and disappointment that he is not expecting his pleas to be listened to.

Revealed in this essay is a grim, no room for fun attitude, a meanness of spirit, a bitterness against his fellow men, a lack of understanding of the nature of humanity, a narrowly theological view of man's state that will brook no argument, and a pessimism that sees no hope for society, save in the personal salvation of the elect within it. In addition to these personal traits and predilections that affect his judgement, the quality of argument is poor, statements are made that are unsupported by evidence, the structure as laid out at the onset is not adhered to, and an attitude toward the *Bible* is displayed that favours a literalist view and makes no attempt at a scholarly interpretation.

The natural seriousness of Witherspoon which had been in evidence from his earliest years might have been increased if not exacerbated by the personal trauma of the deaths of two of his children, the defeats in ecclesiastical courts, the hurt at the vilification of his writings, and the vindictiveness of his fellow presbyters. Whether or not the understanding of the tone of this essay lies in the events as outlined above, what is certain is that his *Serious Enquiry into the Nature and Effects of the Stage* is one of the poorest of Witherspoon's contributions to the controversies of the times in which he lived.

Witherspoon writes from the standpoint of one who sees religion in:

> a declining state and that the cause of the dispute as to whether or not stage plays are right or wrong is because of a division in society as to the nature of religion.

He claims:

> I will endeavour to shew that PUBLIC THEATRICAL REPRESENTATIONS either tragedy or comedy are, in their general nature, or in their best possible state, unlawful, contrary to the Purity of our religion; and that writing, acting or attending them is inconsistent with the character of a christian.[6]

He then tries to meet the challenge that there is no express prohibition of the stage in scripture by citing 'the late Mr. Anderson', whom he says:

> has good reason to believe that the apostle Paul in his *Epistle to the Ephesians* 5th chap. 4th ver. By 'filthiness, foolish talking and jesting' intended to prohibit stage plays that were then in use.

He says that Anderson goes on to suggest that 'the [Greek] word *komoi* is used in more places than one and translated "revelling", points to the same thing'.[7] Checking this out, one discovers that a form of the word is used only twice in the *New Testament* (*Galatians* 5.21 and *1 Peter* 4.3) and on neither occasion is there any hint of its being associated with stage plays.[8] Further, in using the phrase 'more than once' instead of the more simple and accurate 'twice', Witherspoon's source is being less than honest, for the first phrase implies a more frequent usage. Witherspoon is guilty of a too easy acceptance of another person's exegesis, and does his reputation as a scholar no good by dragging a *Biblical* text in to support a very tenuous argument.

Witherspoon attempts to make a case for the 'unlawful' nature of the stage: 'If it be considered as an amusement, it is improper and not such as any Christian may lawfully use'. He sees recreation as 'an intermission of duty' that is 'only necessary because of our weakness'. He goes on to assert: 'the truth is, the need for amusement is much less than people commonly comprehend, and where it is not necessary it must be sinful'. He then returns to the idea of equating 'improper' with 'unlawful'; this time giving another reason: 'the stage is an improper that is to say an unlawful recreation to all without exception, because it consumes too much time'.[9] Witherspoon is here being extremely hypocritical, for it is very likely that in the long hard winters at Beith, he had spent many more hours at his favourite sport of curling followed by a visit to the local tavern than anyone might have spent attending a theatre. He adds another reason for the improper, and in his opinion, unlawful nature of the stage, by asserting that: 'it agitates the passions too violently'. That is a somewhat strange remark from a man who was a passionate debater and controversialist and who frequently went 'over the top' in a passion driven polemic. Yet Witherspoon was at heart afraid of passion, and tries to distance himself from it as he continues:

> He [the Christian] ought to set bounds to and endeavour to moderate his passions as much as possible instead of voluntarily and unnecessarily exciting them. The human passions since the fall, are all of them but too strong and are not sinful on account of their weakness, but their excess and misapplication.[10]

I will return to Witherspoon's ideas on the passions when I later consider his understanding of his fellow men and women, as I believe that there might be a connection between that and his apparent fear of them. But to complete the examination of his arguments regarding the unlawful nature of the stage, it is remarkable that it is not until the last page of the seventy-two page pamphlet that he produces a legal justification for the illegality of the stage:

> Is it not also flying in the face of a clear and late act of Parliament, agreeably to which the Lords of Council and Session not long ago found the stage contrary to the law, in this country. And although the law is eluded and the penalty evaded, by advertising a concert after which will be performed *gratis* a tragedy etc.[11]

In presenting this argument, Witherspoon nevertheless is not precise in his citing of the law to which he is referring, which was probably the *Licensing Act of 1737*. This act was passed in England, partly in reaction to Henry Fielding's satirical play *Tom Thumb*, which had attacked the Walpole Government. The Act of 1737 had been adopted by the Court of Session and applied in Scotland. In England, it had resulted in the closure of theatres. Allan Ramsay's theatre was closed by the act in 1737, and although he tried to reopen it in 1738 and again in 1739, he failed. But in 1739, the ruse referred to by Witherspoon was first successfully engaged in, as Adrienne Scullion relates in *A History of Scottish Theatre*:

> On 18 December 1739 a group of actors initiated a ruse that was to prove an effective and quite legal subterfuge for theatre in Edinburgh and elsewhere. On that night *The Provok'd Husband* was played free as an afterpiece to a concert.

When a theatre opened in the Canongate, Edinburgh in 1747, it was called the Canongate Concert Hall, and successfully worked the same deceit by charging for admission to a concert and signalling that this would be followed by a free performance of *Hamlet*.[12]

Witherspoon's argument asserting the illegality of the stage was very ill-considered, in that the local council was already tacitly admitting the legitimacy of the stage by not attempting to prosecute those who had found what they thought to be a legal loophole. His use of language in connection with his citing of the law is imprecise, and gives the impression that a very recently passed piece of legislation is being ignored, whereas, he is actually referring to a law that had been in place for nearly twenty years. Further, the doubtful status of such a hastily put together piece of legislation that was based on an earlier *Act for Reducing the Laws relating to Rogues, Vagabonds, Sturdy Beggars and Vagrants* (1713), when it was clearly contrived by a self-protecting government, is hardly a good foundation for any legal argument.[13] When examined, Witherspoon's legal argument against the stage fails. It is more of a moral than a legal argument but even that moral argument is based on the very shaky premise that what is not necessary is sinful.

Witherspoon goes on to consider the nature of those who attend the theatre:

> For whatever debate there be, whether good men *may* attend the theatre, there can be no question at all, that no *openly* vicious man is an enemy to it, and the far greater part of them do *passionately* love it.[14]

Here is a judgement not based on a careful examination of evidence, but born of preconceptions engendered by an understanding of humanity derived from his then theological beliefs, and perhaps to some extent by his own experience of personal relationships within the context of the more recent occurrences in his family and professional life. It is as if at this point

Witherspoon's mind was closed to all reasonable argument. This irrationality is further illustrated as he attacks the plays themselves:

> The stage is not only an improper method of instruction, but that all or the far greatest number of pieces there represented, must have, upon the whole, a pernicious tendency. This is evident, because they must be to the taste and relish of the bulk of those who attend it.[15]

This circular argument adds nothing to the debate and only betrays the weakness of Witherspoon's case. Witherspoon then goes from one ill-founded generalisation to an even more sweeping one that betrays his misanthropic and pessimistic view of humanity. He starts off by alleging that the stage is 'an improper method of instruction', that it is 'persuasive and hurtful' because 'it is drawn from life', and he goes on to assert:

> Are not the great majority of characters in real life bad? Must not the greatest part of those represented on the stage be bad? And therefore must not the strong impression which they make upon the spectators be hurtful in the same proportion?[16]

I cannot escape the feeling that these are the writings of a man hurting from the blows of life, unable to see anything good in his fellow men and women, lashing out at all around him, and in danger of losing his hold on rationality. He has at this point in his life become like a cat that is in spitting reaction to the prolonged twisting of its tail.

Witherspoon's dark vision of the world seems to be derived from his concept of God. He sees the stage play as an improper imitation of God's activity, and in the course of describing this activity, he reveals the God in whom he believes. He writes:

> There are many things which are proper and competent to God, which it would be the most atrocious wickedness in man to imitate. Because it is good and just in God to visit us with sickness, or to take us away by death, when he sees it proper, would it therefore be lawful in us, to bring any of them upon ourselves at our own pleasure? ... While it is true that God allows evil to take place within his providential plan - it is wrong to imitate evil [on stage] as we don't have the control of the outcome - we are not as powerful as God who is able to bring good out of evil by his over-all plan. Therefore it is wrong to enact evil on stage - they are a mockery of divine providence.[17]

THE STAGE

The Stage is for Witherspoon a pernicious activity of those:

> who are not content with seeing the world as it is ordered by a wise
> and holy God, but must see it over again, in a vile imitation by sinful
> man.[18]

The previous arguments have, in my opinion, been easy to challenge on the
basis of their weak premises and lack of real evidence. Here we come to the
bedrock of Witherspoon's objection to the stage and all that happens on it.
It is an argument based on his concept of God, a concept with which we
might disagree or think it wrongly arrived at, but which we cannot deny
was for him the firmest of grounds for his objection to the stage.

At this point in the pamphlet, Witherspoon digresses, citing the stage
as analogous to the recording of history, but then he lets history off the
hook, commenting: 'the knowledge of history is, in many respects
necessary for the great purposes of religion'. But he qualifies this, as if he
is wishing that certain events had never happened:

> Perhaps, even as it is, it had been better for the world that certain
> ancient facts and characters, which now stand upon record had been
> buried in oblivion.[19]

But he quickly retreats from the argument, perhaps realising that if he were
to pursue that line it would undermine his stated belief in providence and
the ability of God to turn evil to his over-all purpose. But by even
considering the analogy of the stage with history, he has revealed a further
weakness in his argument against the stage.

Witherspoon then turns to his final argument against the stage,
saying:

> No person can contribute to the encouragement of the stage without
> being partaker in the sins of others - by attending the theatre [he] is
> not only faulty of his own proper conduct but is further chargeable
> with the guilt of seducing others.[20]

He sees two ways in which even the occasional attending of plays can
contribute to the sins of others: the supporting of the actors themselves in
an unchristian occupation and encouraging by example others who will be
in danger of infection. Witherspoon then makes a telling statement about
his description of both the content of theatre and its attenders. 'I pretend to
no knowledge of these things but from printed accounts and public bills of

what plays are to be acted'.[21] Similarly, he has no first-hand knowledge of actors, but feels nevertheless able to comment on their effect upon others:

> Nay if I am rightly informed, that variety of characters which they put on in the theatre deprives them of common sense and leaves them in a manner no character at all of their own.[22]

But not content with pointing at the possible negative effects of acting upon the actors themselves, Witherspoon goes much further and sees their profession as having a malignant effect upon others:

> What foul polluted minds must these be, which are such a receptacle of foreign vanities, besides all their own natural corruption, and where one system of folly is obliterated only to make way for another. But the life of players is not only idle and vain, and therefore inconsistent with the character of a Christian, but it is still more directly and grossly criminal ... [they] portray the vicious ... therefore [are] in danger of becoming in truth what they are in appearance.[23]

Witherspoon here is at his most splenetic. His critique is not based on an accumulation of fact or a personal observation, but is entirely speculative and uncorroborated in any way by empirical evidence.

In the concluding pages, he grudgingly admits that there might be some merit in some plays, but that one good play is not enough to cause any value to be placed in the stage. He briefly refers to the play *Douglas* that had sparked off his pamphlet. He does not display any knowledge of its content, but instead tartly remarks:

> There is an old saying, that a man is known by his company. If this be true of the play, which one would think it should, as it must be chiefly to the taste of congenial minds, by those who have appeared in defense of Douglass [*sic*], it is a work of very little merit.[24]

It is hugely revealing of Witherspoon's contemptuous tone and total disregard for the work that caused him to write the pamphlet, that he cannot even correctly spell the title of the play. Indeed, his snide remarks might with greater truth be applied to his own attempt at offering a critique of the Stage.

CHAPTER 4

Theology

Just before he sailed for America, John Witherspoon prepared a collection of sermons for publication: *Sermons on Practical Subjects to which is added A Farewell Discourse delivered at Paisley in April and May 1768.*[1] In the Preface he claims that: 'The following sermons were published just in the manner in which they were delivered'. He was leaving behind his printed work so that he might 'speak while absent and continue to instruct those whom it is so much my duty to love and serve'.

If John Witherspoon had chosen to publish these particular sermons so that his instruction to his people might be continued after he had left for America, it would seem to me that these sermons can be regarded legitimately as typical examples of his preaching work, if not indeed what he deemed to be the best of that aspect of his work. The sermons certainly must be considered as those that contain themes that he held as important and representative of his theological stance.

Before examining some of these sermons in detail, a preliminary look at the sermon titles and *Biblical* texts is revealing of Witherspoon's theological predilections. Excluding Sermon IX 'A Farewell Discourse', because of the special event that occasioned its preaching, an examination of Sermons I to VIII reveals that six out of the eight are from *Old Testament* texts, and of the other two, one is from *Hebrews*, the most Jewish of the *New Testament* books and the other is from *Revelation*, the most obscure of them. None of the texts in this group of sermons are from the Gospels.

The sermon titles signal the subjects that seem to most concern Witherspoon:

I   The security of those who trust in God.
II.   The object of a Christian's desire in religious worship.
III.   The glory of Christ in his humiliation.
IV.   The deceitfulness of sin.
V.   The believer going to God in his exceeding joy.
VI.   The Christian's disposition under a sense of mercies received.
VII. A view of the glory of God humbling to the soul.
VIII. Of the happiness of the saints in heaven.

All of the above sermons are concerned with the state of mind of the believer and his relationship with God. They are concerned too with the nature of faith. But none apparently are concerned with the teaching of Jesus Christ. This is further revealed when the *Biblical* texts are examined:

I. 'The name of the lord is a strong tower, the righteous runneth into it and are safe' (*Proverbs* 18.10).

II. 'And he said, "I beseech thee, show me thy glory"' (*Exodus* 30.18).

III. 'This that is glorious in his apparel, travelling in the greatness of his strength' (*Isaiah* 63.1).

IV. 'But exhort one another daily while it is called today, lest any of you be hardened through the deceitfulness of sin' (*Hebrews* 3.13).

V. 'Then will I go unto the altar of the Lord, unto God my exceeding joy' (*Psalm* 43.4).

VI. 'Return unto thy rest, O my soul, for the Lord hath dealt bountifully with thee' (*Psalm* 116.7).

VII. 'I have heard thee by the hearing of the ear, but now my eye seeth thee. Wherefore, I abhor myself, and repent in dust and ashes' (*Job* 42.5,6).

VIII. 'Therefore are they before the throne of God, and serve him day and night in his temple' (*Revelation* 7.15).

The cumulative impression made by these texts is that they are used by one who has a concern for the state of a person's soul. However this is a pietism that seems unrelated to the human ministry of Jesus or the model of Jesus as an ethical figure. There is no evidence of a Christian philosophy, that is, one that is extrapolated from the character and activity of Jesus, built up from the *New Testament* evidence, and that gives substance to any ethical imperatives that might apply to ourselves.

There is an irony of which John Witherspoon must have been totally unaware, that despite such obvious omissions, he announces the title of his *Farewell Discourses*: *Ministerial Fidelity in declaring the whole counsel of God*, based on the text: 'Wherefore I take you to record this day, that I am pure from the blood of all men: for I have not shunned to declare unto you all the counsel of God' (*Acts* 20.26,27). A judgement based on this selection of sermons would have to admit that there are huge gaps in the 'Gospel' that John Witherspoon proclaimed. By no stretch of the imagination can he be said, in these sermons, to have declared, 'all the counsel of God'. Right at the heart of these proclamations is a hole where the Jesus of the *Gospels* might have been but is not, as an examination of these sermons will reveal. Instead of delineating the way of Jesus, he proclaims the efficacy of Jesus Christ as the means of God's plan of redemption. The accuracy or not of this judgement can be judged as the detail of these sermons are examined.

When Sermon I, 'The security of those who trust in God', based on the text, 'The name of the Lord is a strong tower' (*Proverbs* 18.10), is examined, it reveals a preacher who deals only indirectly with Jesus. He contends that:

> There are three principle ways by which God hath discovered himself to mankind; namely the visible creation, his written word, and the daily administration of his providence.[2]

He only illustrates the first from scripture, as something that attests the work of a creator. It is noticeable that he does not introduce any personal example or opinion, or theories of contemporary writers like Isaac Newton, or William Derham, both of whom asserted in different ways that the structure of the natural world, indeed of the known universe, attested the work of a Creator.[3] It is also noticeable that he does not claim that Jesus Christ is a revelation of God, but that the written word of scripture is the bearer of the revelation: 'he hath in his word clearly revealed himself as infinitely gracious to sinners through Jesus Christ'. In his third point he turns to the ever recurring theme of his work: 'the revelation of the providence of God that is discovered in the day to day events of life'. By the 'daily administration of providence, God reveals his name'. He claims that a 'personal application of the truths relating to divine providence would reveal as it were a new world to you'.[4] In other words if you will but reflect upon your life, you will see it as revealing the hand of providence.

All of Witherspoon's illustrations are from scripture. There is not a breath of the outside world in the sermon. The version I read extended for thirty-five pages, and by my calculation ran to approximately 10,500 words, which at a delivery rate of say one hundred words a minute, with appropriate pauses for breath, would have lasted for nearly two hours. *The Scots Magazine* of June 1768, reviews this collection of Witherspoon's sermons in its 'New Books' section, and confirms the length of these sermons:

> This book consists of nine sermons, *some of them very long*, particularly the last entitled 'Ministerial Fidelity in declaring the whole counsel of God' of which we insert the introduction, the last three heads entire.

There follows seven pages (300-306), each including two columns of closely printed text. *The Scots Magazine*, perhaps remembering

Witherspoon's pamphlet on the stage, mischievously follows this review with an article purporting to be by Voltaire on 'A Dispute between the Play Houses and the Church' (translation from the French, Dodsley, 1s).[5]

In Sermon II 'The object of a Christian's desire in religious worship,'[6] Witherspoon sets out his structure: '(1) To explain the object of a saint's desire, when he saith in the words of Moses, "I beseech thee shew me thy glory". (2) To improve the subject - particularly by pointing out what is the most proper preparation for such a discovery'. Witherspoon's development and extrapolation of the text reveals a vivid imagination rather than an exposition of the *Biblical* text. Making the legitimate point that Moses desired to be able to physically see a sign of God's presence, he goes on to speculate that when Christians desire to see the glory of God it seems to imply that:

> They desire to see the glory of an independent God; [and] they desire to see the glory of a gracious and reconciled God, not infinitely glorious in himself but infinitely merciful to him.

Witherspoon at this point is blatantly taking the opportunity of putting across his own view of the *Old Testament* and is departing from the exposition of the *Biblical* text. He does have a point to make:

> My brethren we are now come to the very substance of practical religion. The glory of an all sufficient God, appears as more than a balance to all that pretends to reveal him in our affections; to all that we are called to give up for his sake.

He then goes on in part (2) 'to make some practical improvement'. He begins 'the application of the text'. At this point Witherspoon is clearly seeking to over-awe his audience: 'Let us admire the divine condescension in admitting his saints to the discovery of his glory'. The sermon then becomes an impassioned appeal in which he confronts his hearers with the challenge:

> Do you know in any measure what it is to see the glory of the true God? Hath he appeared before you in his terrible majesty? Have your very souls been made to bow down before him and to give him the glory that is justly due to his name? Have you seen the glory of a reconciled God? Have you chosen him in his Christ as your portion?

Witherspoon having laid down a barrage intended to create a state of unease in his hearers, then goes on to exhort them to 'diligence in seeking after your communion with God'. It is at this point he makes the only reference to the outside world, when he briefly contrasts the experience of 'the Protestants abroad who are lying under persecution' with 'the season which we now enjoy', claiming that the Protestants abroad would think it so wonderful that they would live with a sense of gratitude in their hearts and show their great appreciation of it. He acknowledges how difficult it is to be perfectly free of sin in this life, but offers the opinion that:

> A real Christian will have it as the great object of his daily study to cleanse himself of all the filthiness of the flesh and spirit that he may perfect holiness in the fear of God.

Then in a passage that must have caused many to see the hopelessness of their condition, he says: 'To bring sinful dispositions, indulged in, and still suffered in the heart, to the worship of God, and to expect acceptance in such a state, is implied blasphemy and the greatest dishonour we can possibly do to him'. The sermon, having seemingly closed the door to sinners, then opens it a crack by inviting those present to win through to the state of being in which they can say: 'I have heard of thee by the hearing of the ear; but now mine eye seeth thee' and urges that anyone coming to church should engage in preparatory prayer.

In Sermon III, 'The Glory of Christ in his humiliation',[7] Witherspoon uses a text from *Isaiah* 63.1, and applies it to Jesus Christ. *Isaiah* had been painting a picture of the messianic figure who would one day arise to be the redeemer and the bringer of salvation to his people, the Hebrews. Again Witherspoon does not give the context of the text. He does not say what it meant to those who had first heard it from *Isaiah* himself, or as the scroll containing his words was read to them. He simply uses the text as a tag on which to pin his thoughts of Jesus Christ. He explains:

> I shall not spend time in assigning the reasons why interpreters generally apply these words to Christ, but only observe that in this supposition they contain a mixed representation of glory and suffering, of strength and abasements, which is the very substance and meaning of a Saviour on the Cross.

Witherspoon sets out to explore:

> In what respects the glory of our Redeemer was apparent even in his sufferings and shone through even the dark cloud that covered him in his humiliations.

That last quote from Witherspoon demonstrates clearly the literal manner in which Witherspoon dealt with the scriptural text: For him, 'glory' is associated with the physicality of light and therefore can be expected to be still visible in the 'darkness' referred to by the writers of the *Synoptic Gospels Matthew*, *Mark* and *Luke*. With Witherspoon, a literal understanding of *Scripture* is preferred to any metaphorical interpretation, even if as on this occasion it leads to a speculative idea that is quite unnecessary, and that does not add to the understanding of the text. But in a way, my digression to comment on his method of interpretation of scripture is almost made irrelevant, as Witherspoon reveals that his purpose: 'is chiefly and directly designed for heightening the devotion, for quickening the love and increasing the faith and comfort of believers'.

The Christology that emerges from Sermon III is enlightening and says much about Witherspoon himself and the things that he admired and held dear. His Christ, and I use the term advisedly, isolating the title that was at a later stage given by the Church to Jesus, was a functionary that betrayed few traces of humanity. Witherspoon's Christ 'had a clear and perfect knowledge of every event that was to befall him ... his affections were constant and perpetual without interruption'. He goes on to quote from an unnamed source that, 'Jesus was never observed to laugh, but frequently seen weeping', and uses this as a fulfillment of the prophesy in *Isaiah* 53.3, that the coming messiah would be 'a man of sorrows and acquainted with grief'. He then goes on to make use of other *Old Testament* texts which he alleges describe Jesus. He again uses the texts in a literal way as applying to Jesus, and so from *Isaiah* 52.14 we learn that, 'his visage was so marred more than any man'; from *Psalm* 22.14 that Jesus is aware of his self-giving so that he declares: 'I am poured out like water and all my bones are out of joint', and from *Job* 16.8, he even makes Jesus describe himself: 'thou hast filled me with wrinkles'. Before quoting these texts Witherspoon writes:

> It is probable from several passages in the prophetical writings that he [Jesus] was of a very tender and sensible frame, and therefore his affections had a great and powerful effect upon him. They deeply touched him, so that his body was wasted and his strength melted and decayed, which is the usual effect of lasting and continued sorrow.

Witherspoon is using texts at random, with total disregard for their context, in order to present his figure of Christ. So indiscriminate is his use of texts to support *Isaiah* 52.14, which he interprets as a portrayal of Jesus Christ, that there can be no justification for using them, as against any number of other texts that also describe physical characteristics. This is an astounding piece of writing from a man who went on to achieve so much in his later career in America. It betrays a gullibility, and a naivety, and gives an impression that is so out of keeping with all that we now know was accomplished by Witherspoon in the years after 1768.

It would seem as if Witherspoon has been so taken over by the concept of Christ being the instrument used by God in the task of man's redemption, that he has forgotten the human nature of Jesus who became the Christ. The obvious places to look for a filling in of the physical and mental characteristics of Jesus are the *Gospels* of *Matthew, Mark, Luke* and *John*. From these books a more accurate picture of Jesus can be obtained, but then what might emerge might question the concept of the necessary functionary who brings about man's redemption; and that, would not have suited Witherspoon's purpose.

Witherspoon then goes on to try to describe the suffering of Christ:

> Let us imagine what must be the anguish of a pious and affectionate parent, on the death of a wicked child, who apparently trode [*sic*] in the path of the destroyer, and of whom he hath the greatest reason to fear, that he no sooner closed his eyes in the light of this world, than he lifted them up in the torment of hell.[8]

Here the stark literalness of Witherspoon's understanding of the concepts of death and hell are clearly seen. The sentiment expressed above is similar to that of James Hervey, author of *Among the Tombs*, who similarly speculated:

> How must the wretches scream with wild amazement and rend the very heavens with their cries when the aiming thunderbolts go abroad - go abroad with a dreadful commission to drive them from the kingdom of glory and plunge them not into the sorrows of a moment or the tortures of the hour but into all the reckless agonies of unquenchionable fire and everlasting despair … so must we warn – 'to seek the Lord while he may be found'.[9]

Witherspoon once wrote to James Hervey in appreciation of his work, in a letter prefixed to an *Essay on the Connection between the Doctrine of Justification by the Imputed Righteousness of Christ etc.* (1756)[10] Here in this sermon Witherspoon is likening the suffering of Christ to the anguish of the pious parent, when the parent believes that his 'wicked child' will be going to hell. Something is being said here about the mindset of

Witherspoon as someone who can talk coldly of a 'wicked child' and the dreadful consequences of that wickedness.

Witherspoon moves towards the conclusion of this part of the sermon by asserting:

> Without question every part of his [Christ's] humiliation was satisfactory to appease the wrath of God. This cup was put to his mouth as soon as he assumed our nature - he continued to drink of it daily and was therefore justly stiled [*sic*] a man of sorrows. He sees the glory of Christ in that by submitting to all these sufferings he nevertheless achieved, the everlasting salvation of elect sinners.

Notice the narrow concept of salvation. The work of Christ is not for the whole world but for 'elect sinners' for those predestinated by God to share in life eternal. This graceless theology is put across with such vigour that Witherspoon even makes Jesus appear to be smug in successfully accomplishing his mission by putting *John*'s words into Jesus's mouth: 'I have glorified thee on earth, I have finished the work which thou hast given me to do'. There is no way that such sentiments can be put into the mouth of the much more human Jesus that emerges from the earlier texts of the first three *Gospels*. Clearly, Witherspoon is not interested in the human aspects of Jesus, but only in his function as an instrument in the hands of God.

The sermon concludes with a threat to the congregation: 'If he punished sin so severely in the person of his own Son, how shall he punish it in the persons of the finally impenitent? There is a terrible fierceness in his words as he asserts:

> Every drop of that blood which was spilt on behalf of sinners shall be as oil to the flames that consume the impenitent … and make them burn with greater fierceness, to all the ages of eternity.

Finally Witherspoon states the basis of his condemnation of his fellow men and women:

> Here is a truth, which not only the word of God everywhere teaches, but which every part of his providence towards us is intended to satisfy, *that in us dwelleth no good thing*.

This belief in the utterly corrupt nature of man since the fall of Adam is at the heart of Witherspoon's theology and colours all his outlook, forcing him to conclude that: 'This world was plainly designed as a place of trial and discipline and not of complete rest to the children of God'.

Reading the concluding words of this sermon for the first time, in the early stages of my research into the life and work of John Witherspoon, I was amazed that they had come from the same man that had gone on to achieve so much in America. It is not that Witherspoon was alone in adopting such beliefs, for in so doing, he was perfectly in accord with the doctrine of the *Westminster Confession of Faith* to which every minister of the Church of Scotland was expected to subscribe, and can also be said to be fairly representative of the Presbyterian and reformed theology of the time.[11] But the contrast between these beliefs, and the forward and positive thinking that Witherspoon displayed when in any of his roles as an educationalist, an administrator of a college, a politician, or an entrepreneur in emigration schemes is difficult to reconcile.

I shall attempt to put aside, for the present, these perhaps too-soon-arrived at conclusions, and further explore this set of specially selected sermons to ascertain whether or not there is justification for holding to this opinion, or whether a fuller understanding will emerge. Perhaps there is one clue to the understanding of why Witherspoon was able to hold on to such a definite and fixed scenario of man's total depravity, judgement and eventual salvation or damnation, is his belief in a Providence that ultimately overrides all human reasoning and logic.

Sermon IV, 'The Deceitfulness of Sin', is based on the text in *Hebrews* 3.13: 'But exhort one another daily while it is called Today; lest any of you be hardened through the deceitfulness of sin'.[12] Witherspoon returns to the theme of the corrupt nature of human beings:

> We see many mysterious things in the frame of nature, and the course of providence, but nothing can be more mysterious and wonderful than what we may often see in the state of our own hearts.

Witherspoon could then have gone on to expound the good qualities that can be discovered within the human heart, but instead he chooses to dwell on the evil that he sees within:

> When we speak of sin's being deceitful, it is not so much anything without us, taking advantage of our weakness, but it is the effected evidence of the strength of corruption *within us*, which makes us see things in a wrong light, and draw unjust and pernicious consequences from them.

Again, most of the illustrations are *Biblical*, apart from a reference to the Inquisition and a brief mention of Philip of Macedon, but none are drawn from the current world scene.

In Sermon V, 'The believer going to God in his exceeding joy', whose text is taken from *Psalm* 43.4: 'Then will I go unto the altar of God, unto God my exceeding joy', Witherspoon displays an utterly dismal attitude to life, and counsels patience and acceptance of it.[13] He writes: 'But so long as we are here, let us patiently content ourselves with what is necessary to support our weary steps in this desolate wilderness; with this ordinance, instituted for enlivening our faith, supplies us for our comfort and joy'. This sermon was preached at the Sacrament of the Lord's Supper, which is the 'ordinance' to which Witherspoon refers. On this occasion of the celebration of Holy Communion, which is spoken of as if it was an oasis amidst the desert of the world, Witherspoon uses a curious phrase when he describes God as 'your offended Maker'. In portraying God in anthropomorphic terms, he inadvertently makes God occupy the same moral level as the human being who harbours a grudge against another human being because of some sleight suffered in the past. Witherspoon is of course referring to the offence caused to God by Adam's sin, but by the use of this phrase he creates an image of a small minded, petty God. He tries at the end of his sermon to offer comfort to his hearers, but in reality it must have been cold comfort, as he pictures a God who has deliberately created a world difficult to live in:

> This life has been expressly designed in providence as a scene of difficulties and trials. We are here in exile from our father's house. Yet he does not leave us altogether desolate but has given us this as a token and a pledge of his love before the full manifestation of it.

This theology of a satisfaction deferred, and a glory withheld, is a far cry from the invitation later issued to would be emigrants, to come and enjoy a greater freedom, and a healthier and more prosperous life in America.

Sermon VI, 'The Christian's Disposition under a sense of mercies received', uses the text from *Psalm* 116.7: 'Return unto thy rest, O my soul; for the Lord hath dealt bountifully with thee'.[14] Witherspoon acknowledges that, 'it is the language of nature, as well of grace, to cry to God in distress', but having acknowledged that, he suggests a better way. He advocates an acceptance of the concept of the sovereignty of God as a means to bringing peace to the troubled mind. He writes:

> But what a mercy is it, when it pleaseth God to reconcile our minds to the will of his providence, to set home upon the conscience his

right of sovereignty, his title to dispose of our persons, our reputation, our substance, our relations without exception and without condition, even as he will.

Before Witherspoon left Paisley in 1768, he had suffered the deaths of five of his children, and although I cannot pinpoint the date of this sermon, it does sound as if he is indeed speaking from the personal experience of bereavement. There is a kind of sad grandeur in his words as he continues: 'One affliction, truly sanctified, prepares the mind for others to follow and makes them more tolerable and more useful'. However admirable the fortitude displayed by Witherspoon, it still takes a huge effort of the mind to empathise with the sentiments expressed. His attitude becomes even more singular and isolated from what might be called the natural human reaction to suffering, when he writes: 'How happy, my brethren, to have our corruptions mortified by suffering!' (Witherspoon's exclamation mark, not mine). In this sermon Witherspoon reveals just how strongly he believes in the sovereignty of God and in the all-encompassing power of providence and its ability to bring good out of evil. But it also reveals an attitude that demands a total acceptance of the afflictions that come to us as God's way of dealing with our corruption.

Sermon VII, 'A view of the glory of God humbling to the soul', is supported by a text from *Job* 42.5,6: 'I have heard of thee by the hearing of the ear; but now my eye seeth thee. Wherefore I abhor myself, and repent in dust and ashes'.[15] He had already quoted the first verse of this text in Sermon II and Witherspoon uses it again to emphasise the need for a close personal experience of God.

Witherspoon begins the sermon with a flight of fantasy:

My brethren, we can have no experiental [*sic*] knowledge; and indeed we have not much distinct knowledge at all of the nature of religion as it takes place among angels and other intelligent beings, who have kept their first estate and never were polluted by sin … .

Then, turning away from the angels as if on cue from the word 'sin', he gives his attention to man in his fallen state:

We ought never to forget that every instance of the favour of God to men is *not* to be considered as the exercise of goodness to the worthy, nay not merely as bounty to the needy, but mercy to the guilty. For this reason repentance is necessary to every sinner in order to his reconciliation to God.

45

In his opening speculation on angels, Witherspoon reveals an acceptance that such creatures exist, even if, as he says, that we do not have experience of them. But he also seems to indicate that there are 'other intelligent beings' who have not been affected by sin. This is hardly an orthodox belief, but he does not indicate who or what these beings are. He is much more definite and firm in his opinion of the state of ordinary people whom he sees as 'polluted by sin'. It is as if he wants to indelibly impress upon his hearers how sinful they are. He shuts the door firmly on any hopes that they might have that there are signs of God rewarding the good because of their goodness, or giving succour to those in need of help because they deserve it. No, says Witherspoon, all that the goodness and bounty and help of God means is that he is showing mercy to the guilty. Witherspoon gives another example of his naivety in his interpretation of scripture when he admits that: 'it is not improbable ... that it pleased God to give Job some visible representation of his glory and omnipotence'. Then as if to counter his hearers' question, 'but why does God not do these things now?' he adds, 'This was not unusual in ancient times before the canon of scripture was closed'. As if by a human declaration of the canon of scripture it could be determined that God would cease to give a visual assurance of his presence. Witherspoon takes a step back from this position by saying: 'But no doubt the discovery which chiefly affected him [Job] was inward and spiritual'. Witherspoon seems to want it both ways. He accepts the possibility of the visual experience of Job's perception of the glory of God, but because of the difficulties that this creates he wants to retain the fall back position of the experience being only an 'inward and spiritual' one. He then again quotes the text to re-enforce his claim that: 'seeing gives a man a more distinct, full and satisfying knowledge of anything, than hearing of it only by the report of others'. But the result of this seeing experience of Job, brings Job to say, 'I abhor myself', and so the text brings Witherspoon back to one of the fundamental beliefs of his Credo, and, as is his intent, brings his hearers to consider their state, and 'repent in dust and ashes'.

The sermon has reached a pivotal point and hinges on the next sentence:

> That discovery of the perfection, glory and majesty of God, has a powerful influence on leading us to repentance, and the clearer this discovery is, the more sincere will be our repentance, and the deeper our humiliation.

The sermon then develops this thought of the different levels of understanding, and tries to show how there is a knowledge that remains in the head and that does not lead to action, while there is a knowledge that is effectual knowledge that results in action. He writes:

> There is a common distinction to be met with in almost every practical writer, between knowledge merely speculative that swims in the head, and practical knowledge, that dwells in and governs the heart.

Witherspoon in his sermons is trying to instill the latter kind of knowledge, the knowledge that will govern the activity of a life.

As he works his way through this very long sermon, which fills pages 203 to 234 in the Glasgow version I read, Witherspoon reveals again his belief in the *Old Testament* as a document that provides a historical record of the activities of God in relation to his people, and his own acceptance of this record as literally true. He writes:

> When God swept away a polluted world by an universal deluge: when he overthrew Sodom and Gomorrah by fire and brimstone from heaven, when the earth opened her mouth and swallowed up Korah, Dathan and Abiram. These were the terrible proofs of his hatred of sin, of the justice and holiness of his nature.

Here in all its rawness is an expression of Witherspoon's trust in the *Old Testament* as a document that contains an accurate description of historical events, events that to his mind, prove certain things about God, such as his hatred of sin and of the justness and holiness of his nature.

After his exhortation to repentance, Witherspoon then points out that repentant sinners have a responsibility for their children and servants. His own paternalism is imparted as he urges:

> I must also entreat all heads of families whom God has enabled to have the labour of others, to think of the obligation that lies upon them to entrust their servants on the principles of religion, and not to suffer any under their roof to perish for lack of knowledge. Do not think you have done enough when you have given them food and wages, if you wholly neglect their precious souls.

In Sermon VIII, 'The Happiness of the saints in heaven', is based on the text from *Revelation* 7.15: 'Therefore are they before the throne of God, and serve him day and night in his temple; and he that sitteth on the throne shall dwell among them'.[16] It is ironic that this sermon should focus on heaven, when it comes from the lips of a preacher who was to go on to engage in the world of politics and education and business to such an extent that his activities a preacher only occupied a small proportion of his working life. It is noticeable that Witherspoon does not hold up the human life of Jesus as a guide to anyone that wished to end up in heaven, and that the sermon is drawn from a *New Testament* book that is not at all concerned with expounding and commenting on that life.

Witherspoon opens on the note that has so often been struck in these specially selected sermons, that of the corrupt state of humanity:

> My brethren, however great a degree of corruption prevails at present in the visible church, the very profession of every Christian, implies a renunciation of the world, and a fixed hope of a better state.

The concern of Witherspoon the preacher was to instill 'a fixed hope of a better state' in his hearers, but the state of which he was thinking then, was the state in which they would be after death. Soon after leaving Scotland in 1768 he was to go on to act in such a way as would have enabled any reader of this text to think that he had a more earthly state in mind. From his arrival in America in 1768 it was that earthly state that seemed to concern him more, as he worked through education, and politics to achieve a better life for the people under his care.

The final sermon in the collection, is one that was preached over two Sundays as Witherspoon's final words to his congregation in Paisley, to whom he had ministered for eleven years. Sermon IX, 'Ministerial fidelity in declaring the whole counsel of God', is based on the text in *Acts* 20.26,27: 'Wherefore I take you to record this day, that I am pure from the blood of all men. For I have not shunned to declare unto you all the counsel of God'.[17] The slight ambiguity of the word 'all' in the *King James Bible's* translation is cleared up by the twentieth century texts of the *New English Bible* and *The Good News Bible*, where the word 'all' is clearly related to the advice offered, and not to the people. The first translates: 'I have kept back nothing; I have disclosed to you the whole purpose of God'; and the latter: 'I have not held back in announcing to you the whole purpose of God'.[18]

In his opening remarks, Witherspoon says that he wants to concentrate on the main thrust of the text of St. Paul, *viz.* that he had declared to them, 'all the counsel of God', and that he had not shunned to do so. He outlines the structure of the sermon:

> (1) To consider the fidelity of a minister, as consisting in a full and complete declaration of the counsel of God.

(2) To consider the difficulties which may lie in his way, or tempt him to shun any part of his work.

(3) To make a particular improvement of the subject, by giving you any parting advices in the spirit of this passage, and in a way to the best of my judgement suited to your salvation.

In the opening passage Witherspoon sets out his stall, putting on display what he deems to be the most important topics of his preaching. He writes:

> If we look into the scriptures of the *Old and New Testament* we shall find certain leading truths which are of so great moment that they ought hardly ever to be out of view; such as: the lost state of man by nature; the absolute necessity of salvation through Christ; the suffering of the Saviour in the sinners room and the free forgiveness through the blood of the atonement; the necessity of regeneration; and the gift of the Holy Ghost to enlighten, sanctify, and comfort his people. These truths are of such unspeakable moment, in divine revelation that they ought to be clearly explained, strongly inculcated, and frequently repeated. They are the doctrines of the reformation; they make the substance of all the Protestant churches; and have been sealed by the blood of thousands of suffering martyrs.

These powerful words cannot be bettered in putting forward the truths that John Witherspoon considered to be the substance of 'the whole counsel of God', or as contemporary versions translate: 'the whole purpose of God'. However what a present day theologian might want to question is the incompleteness of the topics listed by Witherspoon. There are a number of very significant omissions that a theologian of today might have seen as having just as great a claim to be on the list. For example, Witherspoon makes no mention of the love of God; the gracious coming toward us of God in Jesus Christ; the compassion both shown to us and urged upon us; the ethics of the new way of Jesus as against the *Old Testament* morality. None of this gets any mention in the theology of John Witherspoon, and begs the question as to whether or not he did indeed present to his people 'the whole counsel of God'. What we do know, is that he was not alone in his perception of what these counsels were, and much of what he has to say in his sermons can be found in the sermons of his contemporaries.[19] What is summarised in Witherspoon's list has its roots in the theology of Paul and the developing Church, and is heavily dependent on the images of God gained from the *Old Testament*. It seems to draw little from the *Gospels* of *Matthew, Mark, Luke* and *John*, while the language is redolent of the *Westminster Confession of Faith*. Further speculation on these matters is not especially relevant in the present context. For the present I want to return to the claim made by Witherspoon that those listed above are the salient topics that ought to be preached by any faithful minister, and that had been preached by him in his years as a minister at Beith and Paisley.

Opening up the subject Witherspoon takes a sideswipe at the Moderates and their preaching:

> What poison to the souls of men, for any to speak, as if they were speaking to Adam before the fall, and to sing those sinners asleep in security, whom they should endeavour to alarm, that they may be persuaded to flee from the wrath to come.

He then sets about to establish that, 'To declare all the counsel of God is to preach all the truths of God in their proper order and connection'. Witherspoon urges this sequential treatment of what he calls 'the truths of God' and suggests that:

> The necessity of salvation by Christ is founded upon the lost state of men by nature. Unless the one is established, the beauty and the meaning of the other will wholly disappear; unless we are now in a corrupt and guilty state; unless man has, indeed lost the knowledge of the true God, the kindness of God to his peculiar people, the promises in the prophetic writings of light to the gentiles, and the victories of divine grace in the gospel, spoken in such magnificent terms, must all appear inconsiderable and unworthy of regard. Unless you convince men of their sins, and make them sensible of the holiness and justice of God, in vain will you preach the gospel to them; in vain will you call it 'glad tidings of great joy to all people'. They do not understand the terms, they will deride the message, and spurn the offered mercy.

Witherspoon then urges that having got the people to the recognition of their sins and an acceptance of Jesus Christ, the preacher has to preach: 'the necessity of regeneration and sanctification or it will be turned into licentiousness'. As well as preaching the truths in proper and logical order, there is a need to preach 'the truth in its proper season'. It is essential to be aware of the times through which the church is passing and to preach appropriately. He cites the case that:

> When times are easy and the profession of the gospel is at any rate safe and in some degree profitable, the church is always encumbered

with a dead weight of customary Christians who receive religion from their fathers and continue to tread as it were in the beaten path.

He confesses that 'it is no easy matter to shake their security when every outward circumstance conspires to encrease [*sic*] it'. He sees it as the role of the preacher to disturb this kind of complacency by preaching the truths in their season. He sees a danger in neglecting these truths and opines that:

> Societies crumble because they run away from the corruption of human nature, and shall never be quit of it, because they carry it within them.

This was the theme to which he would return in his lectures at the College. He concludes the first part of his 'Farewell Discourse' with what is his fifth point: 'In the last place declaring the whole counsel of God implies preaching the truths of the gospel honestly and boldly, without respect of persons'. He offers the opinion that 'There are few temptations more dangerous to a minister, than the fear of man'. With this pugnacious statement from a man who was forever displaying his willingness to enter into contentious argument with his fellow ministers and elders in Church Courts the first part of his 'Farewell Discourse' ends.

Witherspoon on his last Sunday, preaching as the minister of his Paisley congregation, opens the sermon with this statement of intent: 'I proceed now to the second thing proposed which was to consider the difficulties which may lie in a minister's way'. He lists three: '(1) sloth or worldliness in ourselves; (2) the prejudice of our people; (3) the opposition of our enemies'. With reference to (1) Witherspoon offers a keen insight that is as relevant today as it was then, when he observes of persons of considerable abilities that 'instead of being excited to improve their talents, they are inclined to trust them'. He must have observed among his contemporaries men of considerable ability, who instead of trying to improve or add to their understanding were more inclined just to rely upon it, or, as he continues: 'finding by experience they can do tolerably with but little pains, they soon come to content themselves with next to none'. Expanding on the second difficulty that lies in the way of a minister, Witherspoon refers to the attitude sometimes taken by parents seeking baptism for their child when they themselves had not been admitted to the Lord's Supper (which is today's equivalent of being admitted into the church through Confirmation). Witherspoon writes: 'The chief complaint is that it is a pity the child should suffer for the fault of the father'. Witherspoon sees this attitude as arising 'from the remaining degree of

Popish superstition to look upon the sacraments as spells or charms received'. He explains:

> The sacraments, my brethren are not grace, but the means of it, they are not faith, but are appointed for confirmation and growth of it.

At this point Witherspoon is firmly upholding the doctrinal stance of the reformed church and particularly of the Presbyterian branch of it. Without doubt, reflected in his words, is the experience of having to explain to parents who are seeking the baptism of their child, that some commitment is demanded of them and that this act of baptism is not like some magical ritual that confers blessing by the power of the medium. Witherspoon deals briefly with the last difficulty, 'the opposition of our enemies'. No doubt he had in mind the many confrontations he had experienced or witnessed in Kirk Session, Presbytery, Synod and General Assembly, or the private disagreements between parishioners, fellow ministers or the more public opposition that he met up with following the publication of works like his pamphlets: *Ecclesiastical Characteristics* and *A Serious Enquiry into the Nature and Effects of the Stage.*[20]

The sermon moves on to the practical application of the text, or as it is called 'the improvement of the subject'. Witherspoon leads off by urging:

> Every sinner in this assembly to hearken to the message of the gospel and to believe in the name of the Son of God, that believing they may have life through his name. This is the substance of the counsel of God. That Christ died on the cross to save sinners and that there is no salvation in any other.

Witherspoon then becomes very direct and personal, and one can imagine a tense silence after these words were spoken:

> After a few more turns in this world, the body must be laid to the dust, and the spirit must go to its own place, that is to say, either the mansions of glory, or the place of torment … . It is wonderful, indeed that sinners are able to sleep in quiet, and to indulge themselves in worldly pleasure, while they are suspended by nothing but the frail thread of life over the bottomless pit … .

Then with a touch of macabre humour he adds, 'Many are hearing a farewell sermon though not to the minister, yet to themselves, when they little think of it'.

THEOLOGY

Witherspoon, well aware that the majority of the people in his congregation were God-fearing and in earnest in their profession of faith and in their conduct of a Christian life, nevertheless uses the occasion to have a last strike at those who came to church, but who flouted its ways. He deliberately singles them out:

> Notwithstanding this general address, I have a few words to say to the loose and the profligate. I am sorry to think that in a place like this, of no great extent, there should be so many sinners; who set everything at defiance.

He then mentions drunkenness and lust and alludes to 'scenes of riot and dissipation' and utters a final warning: 'Think then, I beseech you, on your condition, and pray that God, for Christ's sake, may grant you repentance unto life'. Then having duly warned the wicked he ends on a quieter note by scattering a few last words of advice:

> Understand the gospel well, but let it always be accompanied by practice and applied to promote the spiritual life. Guard against speculative religion. Guard against the introduction of a worldly spirit.

Witherspoon then makes a specific reference to Paisley, possibly sparked by his last warning:

> This place, engaged in commerce, and traffick, growing in numbers and I suppose growing in wealth, is in great danger of a worldly spirit, and of importing, if I may speak so, fashionable vices instead of real improvements.

He does not specify, but counsels temperance:

> I will dispose a truly pious person to be rather late than early in adopting new ornaments; rather sparing than excessive in dress, furniture and equipage.

But at the last, he becomes more specific, and has a final ride on his old hobby-horse, 'The Stage', against which he had written a pamphlet in 1757, eleven years before this final sermon:

> However not to keep entirely to generals, I must once more give my publick testimony against what was lately attempted to be brought in

here equally contrary to the law of the land and the precepts of the gospel, the pernicious entertainments of the stage. The best and wisest men in all ages have born witness against them, as the great means of corrupting the morals of a people; and I am certain that they must be of all others most hurtful to the inhabitants of this place, the far greater part of whom live by daily labour.[21]

He concludes his warning against adopting a worldly spirit by condemning those who break the Sabbath by 'that most pernicious refinement of gadding abroad paying private visits upon the Lord's day'.

In part four of this sermon Witherspoon urges the importance of 'a conscientiousness in family government'. Family worship is extolled as he writes: 'Personal religion is the foundation of all family and relative duties', and he claims that 'family worship strengthens personal religion and re-enforces the message and the sanctions against sin'. This seems to bring to mind one particularly vicious sin and he cites drunkenness. His fifth point is to emphasise the need for practical religion. 'Let religion be incorporated in your lawful employments. True religion will shew its influence in every part of your conduct'. There is a further reference to the economic climate in Paisley, in which Witherspoon reveals his attitude towards poverty:

> Oh my brethren! How often hath it grieved me to see that many persons, formerly of a decent character, when they lost their substance, lost their religion with it; and indeed, to consider how few, when were reduced in their circumstances, could satisfy the publick, that they had acted fairly.

Witherspoon would appear to be siding with those in his society who blamed poverty on people's laziness and indolence, but in his case, he sees a link between poverty and their lack of what he calls 'real religion'. This surmise is confirmed as he follows up those words with the injunction to his congregation: 'Make it the daily subject of your prayer to God, that he would either keep you from the shame of poverty or at least the sin of it'.

These are some of Witherspoon's farewell words to Paisley. They are lacking in any warmth and they are an indication of the formal relationship that he had with his congregation. It is a disappointing note on which to finish my comments on the *Sermons on Practical Subjects*.

Four years before the publishing of his *Sermons on Practical Subjects* John Witherspoon wrote *A Practical Treatise on Regeneration*. Although first published in 1764 the thesis was republished in 1824 within a volume entitled *Treatises on Justification and Regeneration* for which

William Wilberforce wrote an Introductory Essay.[22] Witherspoon begins his *Treatise on Regeneration* by stating that a great change is called for, and that it is necessary for 'every child of Adam before he can become an heir of life'. He asserts that:

> He that is born again considers the favour of God as absolutely necessary to his comfort. He sees the emptiness and inherent vanity of all things else. He considers the favour of God as full and sufficient for his comfort and happiness. The effect of people being born again will be, if they are parents, that they will love their children more.

Witherspoon then makes a peculiar use of this conclusion by making an observation on the society in which he lived, a society where the families of poor people almost invariably went to work as servants in the houses of the richer people:

> What then shall we think of those parents who, from the single prospect of gain, without scruple, place their children in houses deeply infected with the leprosy of sin and expose them without the least necessity to the most dangerous temptations.[23]

In this observation Witherspoon displays a lack of social awareness of the state of the ordinary working people and even more so of the unemployed poor of his time. Wages were, at most, at a subsistence level, and it was an economic necessity for the children of such parents to 'go into service'. The parents had little choice as to where their children might go for employment. The harsh economic facts made it difficult for them to make a choice based on their judgement of the level of morality of any would-be employer. Witherspoon is clearly out of touch with the actual circumstances of the lives of the working people who were barely above the poverty line, and even less in touch with the desperate situation of the unemployed poor. He seems to be more concerned for the state of their souls than for any physical hazards and suffering that might befall their children through an immoral employer.

The violence of Witherspoon's language when he talks of 'the leprosy of sin' shows the strong feelings that he had on that subject. Witherspoon spends a considerable wordage (pages 221-298) on 'The steps on the way to change' section of the *Treatise*. He begins by asserting that for change to take place:

> There must be a discovery of the real nature of God, and the infinite glory of God. … There must be a conviction of sin and danger.

He considers and tries to measure, 'the degrees of sorrow for sin in true penitents', and asserts that there must be 'acceptance of salvation through the cross of Christ'. Witherspoon then tries to assure the would-be 'born again' person: 'There is no guilt so deep but this precious blood will wash out'. In dealing with the post-conversion experience, Witherspoon asserts that, 'the believer recovers peace of conscience', and how 'the love of God is shed abroad in his heart' and he is 'under the constant influence of gratitude to God'.

The language Witherspoon uses is typical evangelical jargon. There is no trace of originality in his description of the transformed life of the 'born again' person. He appeals:

> Judge, O Christian! Will any cold reasoning on the nature and beauty of virtue have such an effect in mortifying corruptions as a believing view of a pierced Saviour?[24]

Here Witherspoon is continuing to attack the Moderates whom he perceives to be preaching on the life-changing merits of attempting to pursue a virtuous life. It is also noticeable that he attaches the epithet, 'cold' to reasoning, thereby giving it a pejorative flavour. He then returns to expound the substitutionary theory of the atonement:

> None can see the form or comeliness of a Saviour standing in the room of sinners, and purchasing forgiveness from a holy God, till the glory of this God is discovered, till the guilt of sin lays hold upon the conscience, and its power is both felt and lamented.

From this passage the theological predilections can be observed. His emphasis is upon the need for a person to become aware of the glory of God, to be overwhelmed by the sense of God's presence in the world and of themselves standing before that presence. It is only after becoming aware of the glory of God that a person's eyes are opened to their own sinfulness and to the work of Christ as God's emissary and functionary. Witherspoon's words conjure up a picture of Christ buying man's salvation from God at the cost of his own life. Witherspoon is so consumed by the idea that God's holiness and justice demands satisfaction for man's disobedience in Adam, that he sees Christ as having been contrived by God as the means of making things right between himself (God) and man. Witherspoon is contending that only by becoming aware of the glory of

God can man then see the value of Christ, and appreciate the need to accept him as the means by which he will be saved. The result of this emphasis, is to diminish the figure of Jesus to the point where he hardly seems to exist as even a person in whom God dwelt. Jesus is not mentioned in this treatise, which features only Christ.

From an examination of this *Treatise on Regeneration* it would appear that Witherspoon's God is constructed more by the *Old Testament* and the theology of the Pauline epistles, than by the *Gospels* of the *New Testament*. Witherspoon's Jesus has been dehumanised to become the Christ. The way through to salvation is not via the following of Jesus and the acceptance of him as a Saviour, but it is by means of becoming aware of the glory of God and consequently of our own sinfulness and the need for a Saviour, who in Witherspoon's scenario is not Jesus, but the Christ, the means determined by God to be our Saviour.

Witherspoon ends this section by asserting:

> Regeneration or the new birth, we are warranted to say, after the manner of our Saviour, is absolutely necessary to salvation, 'Except a man be born again, he cannot see the kingdom of God'.

Witherspoon concludes his treatise in the manner of a sermon, speaking his words directly and in a personal manner:

> Answer this question in seriousness. Whether do you belong to one class or another? We are dropping into the grave day by day, and our state is fixed beyond any possibility of change? What astonishing folly to continue in uncertainty whether we shall go to heaven or hell, whether we shall be companions of angels or associates with blaspheming devils to all eternity? Nothing therefore can be more salutary, than that you make impartial search into your present character and state ... Be persuaded therefore, to fly to the blood of Christ, the precious blood of Christ, 'Who loved you and gave himself for you'.

Although I am beginning to form ideas as to the main elements of Witherspoon's theology, it is difficult to come to a definite evaluation because of the paucity of the quantity of his public sermons that are still extant. But although it might be difficult to reach a final verdict on the extent of his theological interest, there is, I think, a sufficient body of his work still available to us to enable us to identify the dominant themes, or at least those to which he returned again and again. A further clue as to his theological stance is provided by a 'list of sermons [22] being prepared for publication' found in a collection of Witherspoon's notes in his *'Almanack and Memorandum of 1768'*.[25] It contains the dates that the sermons were preached and their texts, and covers the period from July 24, 1757, to January 31, 1768. Fifteen of the texts are taken from the *New Testament* and seven from the *Old Testament*. Five of the *New Testament* texts are from the *Gospels*, four from the letters of *Paul*, four from the later letters of *John* and *Peter* and two from *Revelation*.

Whereas the collection of *Sermons on Practical Subjects*, published at Glasgow in 1768, shows that three quarters of sermons were from the *Old Testament* and only a quarter from the *New Testament*, the list in the *Almanack and Memorandum* shows the proportions reversed. But, only five out of the fifteen *New Testament* texts are from the *Gospels*. This again shows a tendency of Witherspoon to draw from the other parts of the *New Testament* than the *Gospels*. Now I appreciate that one has to be careful in drawing too many firm conclusions from such a small sample of Witherspoon's sermons, but it does seem significant that there is such scant attention paid to the *Gospels* as against other *New Testament* texts, most of which are heavily weighted towards the theology developed by the emerging young Church. Or to put it another way, and perhaps more strongly, the voice of the Church is much more prominent than the voice of Jesus. Perhaps Witherspoon is drawn more to the concern of the Church for order and the establishing of a system of government, of practice and an agreed set of beliefs, than the more existential behaviour of Jesus and the less formal teaching that can be derived from what he is reputed to have said, or for that matter left unsaid. It is noticeable that Witherspoon seems to omit preaching about the Jesus who was born in Bethlehem, lived and worked in Nazareth, preached and taught and healed in the district of Galilee, confronted the religious and secular authorities in Jerusalem, was tried for blasphemy and sedition, found guilty scourged and crucified, died, was buried and then was proclaimed by his followers to have risen from the dead. When the five texts of the sermons taken from the *Gospels* are examined, they are found to contain either the words of the Church, or the remarks that other people make about Jesus. For example, in the sermon dated July 23, 1758, the words of Jesus according to *Mark* 16.15, 'Go ye into all the world and preach the gospel', are more likely to be the words of the Church, put into the mouth of Jesus, than the words of Jesus himself. Many scholars now think that verses 9-20 of *Mark*, is a new ending, grafted on to the text by the Church at a later date. All the other four texts are from *John*'s *Gospel* and three of them are spoken by people other than Jesus: John the Baptist says, 'Behold the Lamb of God' (*John* 1.29); Thomas makes the declaration of his faith, 'My Lord and my God' (*John* 20.28); and Peter says, 'Lord, thou knowest all things' (*John* 21.17). The only words of Jesus used are those taken from the incident of Jesus being given 'vinegar' to drink just prior to his death. While there is no record in the *Synoptic Gospels* of these words being used, John records Jesus as saying, 'It is finished' (*John* 19. 30). Again these words might well be the words of the Church which had the benefit of hindsight. In all his use of the *Gospels* the living human voice of Jesus does not come through. He is the one whose message he commands to be preached; he is the Lamb of God, he is Lord and God, he is the one who knows all things and the one who has completed a mission. Nothing is communicated by the texts that show us the Jesus of the parables, the Jesus of the beatitudes, or the Jesus who questioned and challenged the orthodox religion of his day. Instead we have a picture presented to us of one who wanted his message to be continued, one who accomplished God's purpose, one who was a sacrifice made for the sins of the world, one who was both Lord and God, and the one who knew all things. The Jesus presented by these texts is the Jesus constructed by the doctrines of the Church, rather than the living, breathing, challenging and controversial Jesus that can be met in the *Gospels* by any reasonably diligent perusal of them, in particular the accounts of Jesus given by *Matthew, Mark* and *Luke,* the earliest of the texts. Even the later *Gospel according to John,* although it bears the mark of a later overview of the significance of Jesus, still contributes to an understanding of him as a person rather than a functionary.

Many of the other texts reflect the previously demonstrated interests and favourite topics of Witherspoon: the need for a relationship with God and his Christ; the soul that searches to be with God; the sacrificial death of Christ; the joy of worship; the providence of God; and the invitation to come to God who is all sufficient. But all of this is done without reference to Jesus as a person. If and when Witherspoon does feature Jesus, it is as the instrument of God, the means by which God achieves his satisfaction for the offence of man's sinful disobedience, and whose sacrifice opens up the way for man's redemption.

If we can only glean Witherspoon's theology from his sermons, we might hope to come to a more firm conclusion as to his beliefs from an examination of the more formal *Essay on the Connection Between the Doctrine of Justification by the Imputed Righteousness of Christ and Holiness of Life,* published at Glasgow in 1756, while he was still minister at Beith.[26] In his Preface, Witherspoon writes:

> What follows was first delivered in two sermons, but it is now thrown into the form of an essay, lest the despised title of sermon should offend some and that it might admit of several additions, both in the body of the piece and in the notes which could not have been

so properly delivered from the pulpit. Some of these regard the philosophical principles, which of late have been published among us.

The essay begins with a sentence that betrays an occasional tendency in Witherspoon's theology to hide behind the mystery of God: 'All the works and ways of God have something in them mysterious, above the comprehension of any finite understanding'.[27] Therefore, he concludes, why should the method for the redemption of the world be any different. Witherspoon then shows his dependence upon the apostle Paul in his letter to the *Romans* who:

> at great length establishes the fundamental doctrine of the gospel, that sinners are justified by the free grace of God through the imputed righteousness of a Redeemer.

It is highly debatable that this is indeed the fundamental doctrine of the *Gospel*, but for Witherspoon it clearly is. He then goes on to paraphrase the passage in *Romans* 3.23 that begins: 'For all have sinned and come short of the glory of God'. This passage of Witherspoon's writing is worth quoting in full:

> That every intelligent creature is under an unchangeable and unalienable obligation, perfectly to obey the whole law of God; that all men proceeding from Adam by ordinary generation, are the children of polluted parents, alienated in heart from God, transgressors of his holy law, inexcusable in this transgression and therefore exposed to the dreadful consequences of his displeasure; that it was not agreeable to the dictates of his wisdom, holiness and justice to forgive their sins without an atonement or satisfaction, and therefore he raised up for them a Saviour Jesus Christ, who is the second Adam, perfectly fulfilled the whole law and offered himself up a sacrifice upon the cross in their stead; that his righteousness is imputed to them as the soul foundation of their justification in the sight of a holy God, and their reception into his favour; that the mean of their being interested in this salvation is a deep humiliation of mind, confession of their guilt and wretchedness, denial of themselves, and acceptance of pardon and peace through Christ Jesus, which they neither have contributed to the procuring, nor can they contribute to the continuance, by their own merit, but expect the renovation of their nature to be inclined and enabled to keep the

commandments of God, as the work of the Spirit, and part of the purchase of the Redeemer.[28]

That is the breathtakingly simple and thoroughly orthodox for the time statement of Witherspoon's understanding of what he considered as, 'the fundamental doctrine of the gospel'. It is a totally enclosed system. The person outside it cannot pick and choose which parts of it to believe; to accept all of it, or none of it, is the only way to deal with it. Undoubtedly it takes Paul's words in a very literal way, but its roots are deeply embedded in Paul's words in the letter to the *Romans*.

Enclosed in this paraphrase of Paul's teaching, is God's scheme of redemption, the substitutionary theory of the atonement, the doctrine of original sin and the inevitable consequences of that sin, and therefore the necessity of adopting Jesus Christ as Saviour. All of these ideas are strongly held and preached upon by Witherspoon and bring about the emphasis that we have already observed in his sermons. This very complete system makes no allowances for speculative theories: for example was Paul really intending that his words should be taken literally? Was the metaphor that Paul used of Jesus, as the perfect sacrifice made for the redemption of our humanity, made into a concrete physical occurrence - a blood sacrifice to appease a just and wrathful God? But this system of belief allowed for no such dangerous speculation, it ruled out any metaphorical interpretation of Paul's words, and followed entirely in the tradition of the literal acceptance of them as they had been understood for centuries by the Church.

Yet Witherspoon sometimes does speculate, and when he does he demonstrates that naivety that sometimes shows through his work. A few pages after making this 'blockbuster' of a statement, Witherspoon deals with an incident in Jesus life that is recorded in *John*'s *Gospel*, when Jesus is being questioned by some Jews who say, 'Thou art not yet fifty years old, and hast thou seen Abraham?' On which Witherspoon comments: 'The meaning of this is hardly obvious unless we suppose that his [Jesus] natural beauty and bloom was so wasted and decayed by sorrow, that he seemed to strangers nearly twenty years older than he really was'. This strange speculation seems to fly in the face of the more obvious explanation that all that the Jews were saying was that Jesus had not yet reached fifty years of age and therefore could not have known Abraham. This slant on the text was used in Sermon III of the *Sermons on Practical Subjects* that we looked at earlier.[29] Occasionally Witherspoon displays a strange naivety in his exegesis and interpretation of a scriptural text.

Then, perhaps anticipating some Christian challenging his assertion of what he claims to be the fundamental doctrine of the *Gospel*, Witherspoon rather bitterly writes in opposition to:

> Those Christians, if they deserve the name, who disguise or explain away or give up the satisfaction of Christ, or even those who have a strong tincture of a legal spirit, and are for contributing somewhat toward their acceptance with God by their own merit and defective obedience.

He will not tolerate any deviation from this doctrine that he has laid down as fundamental. He then turns to the subject of love, and in particular to the obligation of the Christian, and begs the question: 'Is not the love of God, I mean the supreme love of God precisely what is meant by holiness?' Consequently he sees:

> All sins of whatever kind, may be easily reduced to this, and shown to be nothing else, but the alienation and estrangement of our heart and affection from God to whom alone they are due.

He sees the foundation of virtue in the precept: 'Thou shalt love the Lord thy God with all thy heart, with all thy strength and with all thy mind'. Witherspoon engages in this theorizing in preparation for criticising David Hume, 'who hath excelled all that went before him in an extraordinary account of the nature of virtue'. Witherspoon mocks Hume:

> That man must be beyond the reach of conviction by reasoning, who is capable of such an insult upon reason itself and human nature, as to rank all natural advantages, mental and corporeal among the virtues; and their contraries among the vices. Thus he has expressly named, Wit, Genius, Health, Cleanliness, Taper Legs and Broad Shoulders among his virtues; diseases he also makes vices and consistently enough indeed, takes notice of the infectious nature of some diseases, which I suppose he reckons is an aggravation of the crime.

Witherspoon rather coarsely attacks Hume, and describes what he thinks is an appropriate answer to this 'infidel', in a mocking cartoon. But Witherspoon makes it clear that there is only one way to virtue, and that is by practise of the love of God.[30]

Witherspoon then attempts to deal with the charge that believing in a doctrine of imputed righteousness will encourage abuse, e.g.

antinomianism, but shrugs off the charge by admitting that although some who don't really understand the doctrine might abuse it, but insists that 'all those who believe it upon *real* and *personal* conviction, must be most conscientious in the practise of every moral duty'.

Witherspoon then quotes *John* 3.36 to show the danger of not believing it upon a '*real* and *personal* conviction': 'He that believeth on the Son hath everlasting life; and he that believeth not shall not see life; but the wrath of God abideth on him'. He lashes out at the Socinians and the Pelagians and to a certain extent the Arminians:

> The application of these passages of scripture to the particular principles above maintained will perhaps be thought to include in it a very severe and uncharitable condemnation of many Christians who differ in judgement upon the points of justification ... as to Socinians and Pelagians, who are the greatest opposers of the truths above defended. *I never did esteem them to be Christians at all*, so the consequences with regard to them may be easily admitted. But it will be thought hard to say the same about the Arminians. However if the righteousness of Christ is the only ground of our justification and the reception of him in this character the true principle of sanctification, I do not see how we can avoid concluding the danger of those who act upon any other.[31]

Witherspoon's unshakeable conviction of the necessity of accepting the Pauline doctrine of Justification is seen here with all its stark consequences for unbelievers. He concludes after this statement: 'It is the duty of all ministers of the gospel to make it [justification through the imputed righteousness of Christ] the main and leading theme of their sermons'. Witherspoon certainly followed his own precept in making it a theme to which he ever returned in his sermons. The closing words of his *Essay on the Connection between the Doctrine of Justification by the Imputed Righteousness of Christ and Holiness of Life* sound a sombre note:

> There are none who set the strictness and obligation of the law, the holiness and justice of God in so awful a light as those who believe there is no shelter from the sanction of the law, and the wrath of an offended God, but in the blood of Christ.

In 1785 the Synod of New York and Philadelphia appointed John Witherspoon to be chairman of a committee to examine the constitution of the Church of Scotland and other Presbyterian Churches, with a view to drawing up a constitution for the Presbyterian Church in the United States of America.[32] This exercise led in 1787 to his being appointed by the Synod to prepare a book of discipline and church government for use within the Church. In 1788 he presented to the Synod a document that contained a draft *Constitution, Confession of Faith, Longer and Shorter Catechisms, The Form of Government and Discipline and The Directory of the Worship of God*, for the Presbyterian Church in the U.S.A. All of these were based on similarly titled documents drawn up by the Divines at Westminster in 1643 and approved by the General Assembly of the Church of Scotland in 1647, and ratified and established by Acts of the British Parliaments of 1649 and 1690. There are of course significant amendments and omissions in the American document that reflect the quite different relationship between Church and State in the two countries, but the American document remains firmly within the theological framework of the Westminster statements.

In 1787 the American Presbyterian churches agreed at Synod level, a set of principles to be approved before any *Book of Church Order* was prepared. They then instructed their committee to draft the *Book of Church Order* based on these Preliminary Principles. These Preliminary Principles had emerged from the Synod of New York and Philadelphia and seem to show the influence and theological position of John Witherspoon whose committee had produced them.[33] Albeit, set firmly within the protestant and reformed Church of Scotland tradition, but qualified by the quite different relationship between Church and State, and taking into account that there was complete freedom to draft these documents in such a manner as would allow them to restate the structures of the Church in a fresh way, they still recognise the value of the Westminster documents upon which they are founded. Varnum L. Collins in his biography of Witherspoon writes in support of Witherspoon's significant contribution in the drafting of the new constitution:

> Dr. Ashbel Green is authority for the statement that most of the published acts of the Synod of New York and Philadelphia had been from Witherspoon's pen, and that in framing the constitution of the Church his opinions were all but dominant. He had suggested that the publication of the principles of the Synod in forming that constitution and the draft he brought in was adopted with scarce an alteration, if we believe Dr. Green, who was present.[34]

The introduction to these documents, probably written by Witherspoon himself, states:

The Synod of New-York and Philadelphia, judging it expedient to ascertain and fix the system of union and the form of Government and Discipline of the Presbyterian Church in the United States under their care, have thought proper to lay down, by way of introduction, a few of the general principles, by which they have been hitherto governed, and which are the groundwork of the following plan. This, it is hoped, will in some measure prevent those rash misconstructions, and uncandid reflections, which usually proceed from an imperfect view of any subject; as well as make the several parts of the system plain, and the whole plan perspicuous and fully understood.[35]

Declaring that 'The Synod are unanimously of the opinion' the first of the Preliminary Principles upholds the importance of the conscience of the individual:

That 'God alone is Lord of the conscience; and hath left it free from the doctrines and commandments of men, which are in anything contrary to his word, or beside it, in matters of faith or worship:' Therefore they consider the rights of private judgement in all matters that respect religion, as universal and unalienable: they do not even wish to see any religious constitution aided by the civil power, further than may be necessary for protection and security, and, at the same time equal and common to all others.[36]

The quotation at the beginning of the paragraph is from *The Confession of Faith agreed upon by the Assembly of Divines at Westminster* (1643), Chapter XX, Section II, 'Of Christian Liberty, and Liberty of Conscience', which *Confession* had been adopted by the General Assembly of the Church of Scotland in 1647.[37] Its inclusion shows clearly how that *Confession* was still set at the very heart of the thinking of the American Presbyterians who nevertheless went on to separate themselves from one of the aspects of it, namely that pertaining to the Church's relationship to the State in the matters relating to the proclamation of the *Gospel*. The document produced for the Presbyterian Church in the United States of America in 1788, and passed at its first General Assembly in 1789, wholeheartedly adopted the doctrinal matters of the earlier *Confession* which it regarded as a faithful record of the substance of the faith.

The second 'Principle' is concerned to establish the rights of 'every Christian Church, or union or association of particular Churches' to determine its own regulations for admission of members and ministers, and its own internal government, but warning of the need to ensure that these rules do not 'infringe upon the liberty, or the rights of others'. The third 'Principle' was concerned that discipline should be maintained by 'the rules contained in the Word of God'. The fourth 'Principle' sets out the importance of truth and urges that any opinions held by the Church should conform to truth. The fifth 'Principle' relates to the fourth and seeks to underline the need for 'Teachers who are sound in the faith', but tolerant and of good character. The sixth 'Principle' makes the point that although the 'character, qualifications and authority of those in office is laid down in scripture', their election is in the hands of the people. The seventh 'Principle' seeks to assert that 'the Holy Scriptures are the only rule of faith and manners' and to ensure that 'no church judicatory ought to pretend to make laws to bind the conscience, or in virtue of their own authority'. The eighth 'Principle' claims that:

> If the preceding scriptural and rational principles be steadfastly adhered to, the rigour and structures of its discipline will contribute to the glory and happiness of any church. Since ecclesiastical discipline must be purely moral and spiritual in its object, and not attended with any civil effects, it can derive no force whatever, but from its own justice, the approbation of an impartial public and the countenance and blessing of the great Head of the Church universal.[38]

The eight 'Principles' were adhered to and the resulting *Book of Church Order* is in line with these principles and the documents compiled at Westminster in 1643, with only a few exceptions in style language and presentation, barring one significant area, which reflects the new freedom as exercised in a new republic as against the ethos of an ancient monarchy. D. G. Hart and John R. Muether of the present day Orthodox Presbyterian Church in America claim that:

> The substance of the revision was to reformulate the Westminster Divines' teaching on the civil magistrate. The Westminster Assembly had been called by Parliament, and its affirmations about the role and functions of government, especially in ecclesiastical matters, reflected a situation in which the state exerted control over the church as part of the price of religious establishment. The American revision of 1787-1789 took into account the new situation in the United States, where the state had no authority over the church.[39]

THEOLOGY

The Westminster *Confession of Faith*, Chapter XXIII, 'Of the Civil Magistrate', Section III, gave the power to the civil magistrate to call a meeting of synods:

> For the better effecting whereof, he hath power to call synods, to be present at them, and to provide that whatsoever is transacted in them be according to the mind of God.[40]

The American '*Confession*' curbed the power of the Civil Magistrate, denying him any role in calling its synods, and in its version of the section, asserted that the magistrate only has a duty to:

> protect the church of our common Lord, without giving preference to any denomination of Christians above the rest, in such a manner, that all ecclesiastical persons whatever shall enjoy the full, free, and unquestioned liberty of discharging every part of their sacred functions without violence or danger.

Further revision was made to Chapter XXXI, 'Of Synods and Councils', Section II of which again referred to the power of the magistrate to call a synod and this was again deleted.[41] The magistrate only gets a mention in an innocuous way in the new section IV (old V) of Chapter XXXI which states that the church is 'not to handle or conclude', any matter of civil polity except for 'cases extraordinary' to satisfy the conscience of the Church, or to comply with the request from the civil magistrate. Hart and Muether conclude:

> The 1789 revision of the Westminster standards stripped the state of any authority over the church beyond that of seeking its freedom from hostile interference ... the clear meaning of the revised *Confession* was to remove the powers of the civil magistrate over the church that had been previously granted by an ecclesiastical establishment.[42]

Apart from what has been noted above, the *Confession and Catechisms* are unchanged and adopt the same forms as those of Westminster. The language used in *The Form of Government* in its sections on the Church, I, II and III is much less formal than that used in the Westminster version. The section on the Calling and Election of a Minister bears the imprint of Witherspoon's thinking and experience and seeks to legislate for the primacy of the people's voice in the choosing and election of a minister.[43] When he assisted in the drafting of this legislation, Witherspoon must have remembered the unhappy battles long ago in Scotland when patrons attempted and sometimes succeeded in forcing their nominee upon an unwilling congregation or even a presbytery. This section is explicit in its support of the right a congregation to choose and elect its minister. One other piece of evidence of Witherspoon's influence is seen in the drafting of the legislation for the commissioners to the General Assembly, when it is asserted that they 'shall always be appointed by the presbytery from which they come'.[44] This reflects the practice, prevalent in the Scotland he had left, of the 'establishment' choosing a known supporter from another part of the country to represent a presbytery, thereby denying the possibility of opposition, and being assured of a vote.

In *The Directory for the Worship of God*, the American version strikes a modern note in its advice on the singing of hymns:

.I.   It is the duty of Christians to praise God by singing psalms or hymns publicly in the Church, as also privately in the family.

II.   In singing the praises of God, we are to sing with the spirit, and with the understanding also; making melody in our hearts unto the Lord. It is also proper that we cultivate some knowledge of the rules of music; that we may praise God in a becoming manner with our voices as well as with our hearts.

III.   The whole congregation should be furnished with books and ought to join in this part of worship. It is proper to sing without parceling out the psalm, line by line. The practice of reading the Psalm line by line was introduced in times of ignorance, when many in the congregation could not read: therefore it is recommended that it be laid aside as far as convenient.

IV.   The proportion of time of public worship to be spent in singing is left to the prudence of the minister, but it is recommended that more time be allowed for this excellent part of divine service, than has been usual in most of our churches.[45]

There is a lightness of touch in the drafting of these words that reveals, regardless of how strictly the theology of the *Confession* adheres to the Westminster version, that here is a Church that is willing to try new forms, forms that are in keeping with the new freedoms being experienced in their separateness and independence. Although Witherspoon does not seem to display any particular fondness for music, it would appear that he is willing to go along with the modernisers in their advocacy of the value of singing in church.

In the section 'Of Public Prayer' it is possible to discern an outline of a structure for a service of worship, and to see the divisions into which prayers were set: Prayer / Psalm or Hymn Singing / Prayer of adoration, thanksgiving, confession, supplication, and intercession / Sermon / Prayer related to sermon subject / Psalm / Collection for the Poor or for the Church / Benediction. On the subject of extempore or set prayers a freedom is given to choose, but with a warning to the minister to prepare well for prayer that 'he may not disgrace that important service by mean, irregular or extravagant effusions'. This advice is in keeping with Witherspoon's distaste for extravagant or flowery language.[46]

This thorough revision of the organisation and scrutiny of the doctrine of the Church was approved by the first General Assembly of the Presbyterian Church in America in May 1789. When its proceedings began on the third Tuesday of May 1789, in the Second Presbyterian Church in Philadelphia, presiding over its proceedings was the Reverend Dr John Witherspoon, no doubt in recognition of the huge part he had played in bringing the Church to this stage in its history. It is worth noting that the sermon he preached that day at the opening of the General Assembly was from the text, *I Corinthians* 3.7, the same one that he had preached from when he first spoke from his Princeton pulpit. Its theme was 'humility'. We do not know what differences there were between the two sermons but the passage certainly lends itself to a preacher wanting to make a very humble personal statement. Starting from the preceding verse:

I have planted, Apollos watered but God gave the increase. So then, neither is he that planteth any thing, neither he that watereth, but God giveth the increase.

The preacher can adopt a very humble stance as he applies the words to himself. Yet for all that Witherspoon could have felt a legitimate pride in being either one 'that planteth' or one that 'watereth', despite being compelled to proclaim that at the end of the day it is God who 'giveth the increase', for most certainly he had played a part in bringing the Presbyterian Church in America to its unification in its first General Assembly. At this same Assembly he was appointed to present an Address to President George Washington, surely a sign that at that time he was regarded by his peers as *primus inter pares*.

The same General Assembly set in motion a plan to issue an American edition of the *Holy Bible* and appointed Witherspoon to chair a committee and to meet with other denominations to choose the text and correct the proofs of the proposed work.[47] Princeton Public Library's Witherspoon Room, houses the Joseph J. Falcone Collection, one volume of which, New Jersey Books 1698-1800 contains the details of the *Bible* that was produced and Joseph J. Falcone's description of the book:

The Holy Bible, containing the *Old and New Testaments* translated out of the original tongues and with the former translations compared and revised. Trenton: Printed and sold by Isaac Collins MDCCXCI. The first *Bible* printed in New Jersey, the second quarto edition of the King James Bible printed in America, and the most ambitious project of Isaac Collins, printer.

Falcone notes:

> Collins and his editor, John Witherspoon reject the traditional dedication to King James as 'Wholly unnecessary for the purpose of edification and perhaps on some accounts improper to be continued in an American edition', and substituted a brief introduction, 'To the Reader' by John Witherspoon. Witherspoon's authorship was not so identified until the second edition, printed by Collins' firm in New York in 1807.[48]

In a way it is fitting that one of John Witherspoon's final literary productions was in seeing through an edition of the *Holy Bible*, and to know that in its second edition published thirteen years after his death, his name was disclosed as the author of its Introduction. The anonymity of the Introduction to the first edition bears testimony to the sincerity of his proclamation on the theme of humility at the General Assembly of 1789.

In Chapter 9, I will examine two of Witherspoon's best known sermons: *Christian Magnanimity* (1775) and *The Dominion of Providence* (1776), and claim that both of these are political in their nature.[49] *Christian Magnanimity* indeed could be said to be the least religious of Witherspoon's sermons that I have been able to examine, and remembering its context as having been preached in College to a largely student audience, this is understandable. Witherspoon himself seems to realise this, as after spending a considerable time on outlining the nature of magnanimity he writes: 'Let me run over and apply to religion the above mentioned ingredients of magnanimity'. But his application only provides a thin veneer of religiosity before he returns to his mainly secular and humanistic address as he writes:

> Religion calls us to the greatest and most noble attempts whether in private or public view. In private it calls us to resist and subdue every corrupt and sinful passion. In public every good man is called to live and act for the glory of God.

But in the next sentence he reverts to the secular theme when he suggests that, the good man is permitted 'to hazard his life in his Maker's service or his country's cause'. Witherspoon drags religion into it again when in his next sentence he writes:

> Nor am I able to conceive any character more truly great than that one, whatever be his station or profession, who is devoted to the public good under the immediate order of Providence.

In this sermon Witherspoon's patriotism is more to the forefront of his thought than his commitment to his theological belief in Providence.

'*The Dominion of Providence*' sermon, although highly political, is firmly rooted in a theology that strongly defends: the orthodox Presbyterian and Reformed Church doctrines of original sin and the necessity of redemption through the sacrifice of Christ; and most importantly, it reflects the need for an undergirding commitment to the all-embracing Providence of God, a God who is capable of bringing good out of evil. Of these two sermons from his period in Princeton, *The Dominion of Providence* is much more firmly rooted in his theological beliefs than *Christian Magnanimity*, which could more accurately be classed as a political address than a sermon. In the latter sermon there is evidence that Witherspoon at this stage in his life is being drawn more and more towards politics, and perhaps is wanting to cast off some of the inhibiting strictures of religion. In *The Dominion of Providence* his theology is more in evidence, but apart from the outburst against Thomas Paine, during which he engages in an ardent defense of the doctrine of original sin, it still does not dominate. These two sermons from his American period are indicative of a change that seems to be gradually taking place in the life of John Witherspoon. Further evidence of this change I hope to put forward when I attempt a sketch of his character in a later chapter.

CHAPTER 5

President of the College of New Jersey

Although written in March 1772, almost four years after John Witherspoon's arrival at Princeton, his pamphlet, *Address to the Inhabitants of Jamaica, and other West-India Islands, on behalf of the College of New-Jersey*, is the fullest statement now available from which can be discerned the organisation, curriculum and mores of the institution of which he had become President.[1]

After an opening passage in which he extols education as something that 'promotes virtue and happiness, as well as arts and industry', Witherspoon goes on to declare:

> Education is therefore of equal importance, in order either to enjoy life with dignity and elegance, or employ it to the benefit of society in offices of power or trust.[2]

He then suggests that it would be much more convenient for the gentlemen of the West Indies to send their young men to an American college than to one of the universities of Great Britain. He is careful not to criticise the ancient universities that are found there, and indeed particularly commends those of 'North Britain', confessing that he, 'the author', was educated at Edinburgh, and also had had a 'great intimacy with the members of the University of Glasgow'. But, he suggests:

> it would be more to the advantage of the gentlemen of the West Indies, to give their children their grammar school and college education, at least to their first degree in the arts, in an American seminary.

He is willing to admit that:

> if any gentleman of fortune, who would give the last and highest polish to the education of a young man of promising parts, would do well to send him, after his principles are fixed, and his judgement a little matured, for a year or two, to some of the universities of Great Britain.[3]

Witherspoon makes his claim for the merits of the College of New Jersey, which is of course, the main purpose of the pamphlet that is virtually an advertising gambit extolling the virtues of the College, and that has as its aim, the enrollment of new students. He begins by citing the established reputation of the ancient universities, and points out how the new American colleges are eager to build their reputation. The older universities don't need to care whether some of their students are not diligent and consequently fail. Whereas in attempting to build its reputation, a new American College such as New Jersey offers an environment that encourages, indeed almost enforces, diligence among its students.[4] The old university is so long established that it doesn't need to care about some of its students who 'come out of college almost as ignorant as they went in', or as Robert Burns was later to write in his first 'Epistle to J. Lapraik':

> What's a jargon o' your Schools,
> Your Latin names for horns and stools;
> If honest Nature made you *fools*,
> > What sairs your Grammars?
> Ye'd better taen up *spades* and *shools*,
> > Or knappin-hammers.

> A set o' dull conceited Hashes,
> Confuse their brains in *Colledge-classes*!
> They *gang in* stirks, and *come out* asses,
> > Plain truth to speak;
> An' syne they think to climb Parnassus
> > By dint o' Greek![5]

I border on digression with the above quote, but hope like Laurence Sterne that the reader might benefit from it, for in a way Burns was mocking those who in his view were made no wiser by their formal education because having already the nature of a fool or a dilettante, they didn't apply themselves to learning industriously so that they might benefit themselves, and came out of college with only a patina or varnish of learning upon them, but with their basic nature and attitude unaffected.[6] Witherspoon's system at Princeton sets out to ensure that such a thing would not happen. He claims that he has built into the life-style, schemes that will secure for the students a greater security of their instruction, and the preservation of their morals. On 'Instruction', he writes:

> The colleges in Britain have by no means that forcible motive that we have, not only to teach those who are willing to learn, but to see that every one be obliged to study, and actually learn, in proportion to his capacity.

On morals, he claims that whereas in Britain, where most universities are in the cities, where there is a 'constant succession and variety of intoxicating diversions, such as balls, concerts, plays, races and others', the American College setting by contrast is more conducive to learning.[7] In regard to the moral benefits to be gained by a student at Princeton, Witherspoon defers outlining these immediately, but says that he will leave it 'till I come to speak of the constitution and situation of the College of New Jersey'. When a few pages on he does this, it is in a way that implies that the moral welfare of the students has been a concern from the days of the granting of the charter to the Trustees of the College:

> They … raised a noble building, called Nassau Hall, at Princeton, New-Jersey. This they chose to do, though it wasted their capital, as their great intention was to make effectual provision, not only for the careful instruction, but for the regular government of the youth. There all the scholars are lodged, and also boarded, except when they have express license to board out, in the president's house or elsewhere.[8]

Witherspoon had earlier remarked that:

> all the scholars with us, as soon as they put on the gown, are obliged to lodge in college, and must of necessity be in their chamber in study hours; nor is it in the least difficult to discover, whether they apply carefully or not. The teachers also live in college, so that they have every advantage, not only for assisting the diligent, but stimulating the slothful.[9]

He later writes of how discipline is maintained, pointing out that 'no correction by stripes is permitted', and adds rather proudly, 'Such as cannot be governed by reason, and the principles of honour and shame, are reckoned as unfit for residence in a college'.[10] He even speaks of the geographical location of the College as conducive to the moral tone:

> The place where the College is built is most happily chosen for the health, the studies and the morals of the scholars. All these were particularly attended to when the spot was pitched upon … Princeton is on a rising ground … sheltered by a range of hills covered with woods … and has been found one of the healthiest places … . It is upon the great post road, almost equally distant from New York and Philadelphia, so as to be a centre of intelligence, and have an easy conveyance of everything necessary, and yet to be wholly free from

the many temptations in every great city both to the neglect of study and the practice of vice.

He cites the greater freedom of young scholars in the cities that makes the disciplining of them difficult to manage, and contrasts this with Princeton, where:

> with us, they live all in College, under the inspection of their masters; and the village is so small, that any irregularity is immediately and certainly discovered, and therefore easily corrected.[11]

However restricting this might have seemed to any young lad reading this prospectus, to parents it must have sounded very attractive indeed.

Witherspoon describes the structure and the curriculum of a four year course, where the four classes are named: Freshman, Sophomore, Junior and Senior:

> In the first year they read Latin and Greek, with the Roman and Grecian antiquities and rhetoric. In the second, continuing the study of the languages, they learn a complete system of geography, with the use of the globes, the first principles of philosophy, and the elements of mathematical knowledge. The third, though the languages are not wholly omitted, is chiefly employed in mathematics and natural philosophy. And the senior year is employed in reading the higher classics, proceeding in the mathematics and natural philosophy, and going through a course in moral philosophy. In addition to these, the President gives lectures to the juniors and seniors, which consequently every student hears twice over in his course, first upon chronology and history, and afterwards upon composition and criticism. He has also taught the French language last winter, and it will continue to be taught to those who desire to learn it.[12]

Witherspoon then goes on to explain one of the distinguishing features of the student life at Princeton:

> During the whole course of their studies, the three younger classes, two every evening formerly, and now three because of their increased number, pronounce an oration on a stage erected for that purpose in the hall, immediately after prayers, that they may learn,

by early habit, presence of mind, and proper pronunciation and gesture in public speaking.

This is a practice he claims, that has been kept up almost from the first foundation of the College. He also indicates that:

the senior scholars every five or six weeks pronounce orations of their own composition to which persons of note in the neighbourhood are invited or admitted.

He claims that the library 'contains a very large collection of valuable books', and illustrates the important part of science in the curriculum by telling that the lessons on astronomy are assisted by the College possessing an orrery constructed by David Rittenhouse. He also hints that a further apparatus that will assist in the teaching of mathematics and natural philosophy is currently under construction.[13] Witherspoon stresses that the College is 'altogether independent - It hath received no favour from government but the charter, by the particular friendship of a person now deceased'. The consequence of this is its freedom to go its own way without fear of government or patronal interference. Something of the politically concerned Witherspoon that we shall see gradually beginning to emerge is evident as he claims:

But surely a constitution which naturally tends to produce a spirit of liberty and independence, even though this should sometimes need to be reined in by prudence and moderation, is infinitely preferable to the dead and vapid state of one whose very existence depends upon the nod of those in power.[14]

The same Witherspoon who led the Popular party in its battles against the Moderates and their patrons within the Church of Scotland is also coming to the surface here. Following this, Witherspoon distances himself from any particular religious denomination, and quotes the Charter in support of this: 'That every religious denomination may have free and equal liberty and advantage of education in the said college'.[15]

Witherspoon concludes this section of the pamphlet by restating one of the principles upon which the College works: 'It has been, and shall be our care to use every mean in our power to make them good men and good scholars'. He concludes that the matter as to which denomination of the Church a person belongs, will be of no account as long as they become good men and good scholars. But he cannot help betraying his allegiance to the reformed tradition within the Church when he says: 'I shall hear of their future character and usefulness with unfeigned satisfaction, under every name by which a real Protestant can be distinguished'.[16] This last statement is quite revealing of the character of John Witherspoon. It is a deeply layered character, and every time you think that you have reached to its depths, a further level is revealed that has still to be explored. In his *Address to the Inhabitants of Jamaica* both the credo and the curriculum of the College are revealed. (It was written nearly four years after he arrived at Princeton.) During that time there were changes in the curriculum and in the personnel who helped implement it, and changes too in the facilities and in the physical properties of the buildings, but despite all these changes, the credo remained the same; it was this constant that caused so many men who later achieved distinction to emerge from it in the years during which John Witherspoon was President.

Immediately following Witherspoon's acceptance of his election, he set about getting ready for his taking up of his teaching duties. He wanted to re-start the Grammar School which had ceased to function following the death of the previous President, Dr Finley. There were at least two good reasons for seeing to it that the Grammar School should be re-established: firstly as a 'feeder' for the College, and secondly, and not unimportantly, as a financial perquisite for the President.

Varnum Lansing Collins records that Witherspoon went to London in February 1768, where he visited 'eminent teachers and get hints as to methods and textbooks', and reports that Ashbel Green had seen a memorandum book that contained the notes of his itinerary, although Green did not quote from the book which had since disappeared.[17] It is possible that the book seen by Green has resurfaced. In the Firestone Library at Princeton University I examined the *Almanack & Memorandum Book of Dr John Witherspoon, 1768*, which contains among other things some details of Witherspoon's preparations for going to take up his new position, and among them is an itinerary for his London visit of February 1768. Between Wednesday 2 and Monday 14 February, 1768, fourteen appointments are recorded.[18] Among these are two with a 'Mr. Dilly'. This is very likely to have been Charles Dilly (1739-1807), or his brother Edward Dilly (1732-1779) booksellers. *The Concise Dictionary of National Biography* records of Charles, that he was 'noted for the hospitality that he extended to the writers of the day'; and of Edward, that he 'exported works of Dissenting theology to America'. When one considers the timing of Witherspoon's trip to London, the nature of the work that had to be prepared for, and the kind of books that the Dilly's traded in, the fact that his itinerary records: 'Friday 4, breakfast with Mr. Dilly. Visit Dr. Gibbons, dine with Mr. Dilly' seems to substantiate the claim made by Green and Collins as to the reasons for the visit to London. The 'Dr. Gibbons' referred to is likely to have been Thomas Gibbons (1720-1785) who is listed in *The Concise Dictionary of National Biography* as, 'Dissenting minister and author; Independent minister of Haberdasher's Hall, 1743; tutor of Mile End Academy, 1754; D.D., Aberdeen, 1764; M.A., New Jersey, 1760'. Witherspoon's visit to Dr Gibbons is significant, because he is a clergyman with current teaching experience and in addition, someone who was also a graduate of the College of New Jersey.[19]

Witherspoon's London Itinerary within the *Memorandum* also indicates two appointments with the Reverend George Whitefield, the evangelical preacher who had spent many years in the American Colonies. Whitefield was at that time involved in the establishing of Lady Huntingdon's College at Trevecca in that very same year of Witherspoon's departure. He was to leave again for the American Colonies in 1769 to found Bethesda College.[20] Here again is Witherspoon meeting with people who were already involved in Education and who were knowledgeable of the country to which he was heading, and who might be a help to him as he sought to anticipate the needs of the Grammar School and College and equip himself for the new tasks.

During that London visit, it is interesting to note that his first engagement was with Mr Nisbet, minister of Montrose, who had been Witherspoon's suggested candidate for the Presidency of the College at the time when he had declined the offer of the Trustees. He also met Benjamin Franklin, who at that time was still of the opinion that the American Colonies should continue to be part of the British Empire.[21] Franklin did not seem to fully appreciate the feelings of many of the Colonists over the imposition of the *Stamp Act*, and after its withdrawal, the further offensiveness to the Americans of the Townsend legislation. The month before Witherspoon met with him, Franklin had written an article in the London *Chronicle* (January, 1768), called, 'Causes of the American Discontents'. His biographer, Walter Isaacson, comments that this article was:

> Written from the perspective of an Englishman, it explained the Americans' belief that their own legislatures should control all revenue measures, and it added in a squirrelly manner, 'I do not undertake here to support these opinions'. His goal, he averred, was to let people 'know what ideas the Americans have'. In doing so, Franklin tried to have it both ways: he warned that America's fury at being taxed by Parliament could tear apart the empire, then pretended to lament these 'wild ravings' as something 'I do not pretend to support'.[22]

It is ironic that Witherspoon was to meet up with Franklin when he was in that frame of mind, and yet go on later to entrust him with some of the most delicate negotiations in trying to secure the *Peace Treaty* with Britain.

The entry that immediately follows the itinerary of the London visit in the *Memorandum*, records the expenses of Witherspoon for his trip to Holland. Collins suggests that this visit had been undertaken as a follow up to an earlier consideration by the Trustees of the College of New Jersey in 1766, of the possibility of inviting a Professor of Divinity from Holland to take up office in the College. But the proposal fell through then and Witherspoon's visit did not result in success other than as a seed-sowing exercise reminding the Dutch of the existence of the College and its ability to provide an education for young Dutch candidates for the Church in the American Colonies.[23]

The *Memorandum* also records that immediately following his return from the visits to London and Holland, Witherspoon wrote letters of thanks and sent gifts to some of the people in London and Holland who had been helpful, including 'Mr. Dilly and Dr. Gibbons'. This note is followed by a list of 'Persons to be noted for their labours for the College'. Immediately following this note is the first indication that Witherspoon's labours at Princeton are being rewarded with success as he records the enrollment of a pupil: 'John Denton, shoemaker, entered to the Grammar School, Thomas Denton, 10 years of age'. The fact that Witherspoon records this in his personal notebook is indicative of the significance of the addition of one pupil to the roll of the Grammar School. It is as if he is telling himself that his endeavours have paid off.[24]

The curriculum of the Grammar School had 'consisted chiefly of the elements of Latin and Greek, arithmetic, penmanship, reading and declamation'. Pupils who graduated from the Grammar School were automatically guaranteed admission to the College. On August 25, 1768, Witherspoon placed an announcement in the local papers that the Grammar School would re-open on November 7, 1768. Witherspoon relates in the article that after a long vacancy, 'the chair being now filled by the arrival of the Gentleman last chosen from North Britain'. The announcement included the information that a new teacher had been hired and placed in charge of the school but makes it very clear that he will be under the direction of the President and will be working to a plan devised by the President. The advert indicates the importance that is to be given to language studies which will facilitate 'easy, pleasant and successful' subsequent studies at College. It also states that provision can be made for boarders in local homes, or that pupils can enter as day scholars. Witherspoon proudly announces that 'there is a Terrestrial Globe provided for the school that they may be taught Geography at some Hours of

Leasure'; and indicates that pupils will have 'an hour a day appropriated to Writing and Arithmetick without any additional Expense'. The advert urges that those parents who expect their children 'to begin the Latin' should ensure that they should be sent 'upon the very day above mentioned that they may neither suffer any loss themselves nor be the means of retarding others'.[25]

No major changes in the College curriculum were made immediately, but one practice that had fallen into disuse, Witherspoon vigorously tried to restore and promote: the provision of graduate courses. By these he sought to re-establish the aims of the original trustees to provide not just for the training of those who wished to enter the ministry of the church, but for all the professions. An announcement made at the same time as that concerning the Grammar School gave details of this provision. It so clearly states the vision of Witherspoon for the widening of the scope of the College from being merely a seminary for students for the Church, into becoming a more broadly based educational establishment where young men could both begin their basic preparation for any profession, then go on to more specialised studies that would help equip them for their chosen profession, or entry into some form of public service. I quote it in full:

> The Trustees further give Notice that they have made Provisions for the Encouragement of young Gentlemen, who have finished the ordinary Course of Philosophy, to return and pursue their Studies at College, and fit themselves for any of the higher Branches, to which they shall think proper chiefly to devote their future application, whether those called learned Professions, Divinity, Law and Physic, or such liberal Accomplishments in general, as fit young Gentlemen for serving their country in public Stations. For this purpose, the Professor of Divinity, besides what Attention he may give to the Instruction of the Senior Class will give regular Lectures upon the System. The President also has engaged to give Lectures twice in the Week, on the following Subjects (1) On Chronology and History, civil as well as sacred; a Branch of Study, of itself extremely useful and delightful, and at present in the highest Reputation in every Part of Europe, (2) Critical Lectures on the Scripture, with the Addition of Discourses on Criticism in general; the several Species of Writing, and the Fine Arts, (3) Lectures on Composition, and the Eloquence of the Pulpit and the Bar. The President will also endeavour to assist every Student by Conversation according to the main Object, which he shall chuse for his own Studies; and will give Lists and Characters of the Principal Writers on any Branch, that Students may

accomplish themselves, at the least Expence of Time and Labour. For the Attainment of their Ends, a very valuable Addition to the Public Library was brought over with the President, another large collection of the most standard Books, is newly arrived; and a Third is very soon expected from London. So that this College, which had before all the Advantages for Study, that a retired healthful Place could possess, is now well furnished with a valuable Public Library, which will be improved by continual Additions. It is to be observed that from those, who after their ordinary Courses, shall return to the College, in order to pursue their Studies with those Advantages, no Tuition Money will be required, except that the French language will be taught, if desired, for a very reasonable Gratuity.[26]

Witherspoon had got off to a very good start in the promotion of the institutions to which he had been called.

Witherspoon, ever aware of the need to be pro-active in promoting the Grammar School and the College, returned to the Press some six months later. On March 2, 1769, he had an advert published in the *Pennsylvania Journal* that was in effect a progress report on the Grammar School. Witherspoon reports that as promised, it is functioning as per the previous advert, under his personal direction, assuring his readers that the teacher he has appointed 'receives his whole directions from me and has hitherto given the greatest satisfaction by fidelity and diligence in the execution of them'. He claims that the methods of teaching Latin have drawn upon the experience of one who was 'long Rector of the public grammar school in Glasgow' and that the teacher is well provided with teaching aids. He emphasises that religious instruction has been given 'every Lord's day evening' since the school began, and claiming that this was done because so many of the young people's parents live at a distance.[27]

Both the Grammar School and the College were growing under Witherspoon's leadership, and by September 1770, there were one hundred and fifteen pupils and students being taught at Nassau Hall: the Grammar School pupils in the basement and the College students on the ground floor while above there were forty-nine rooms or suites each capable of accommodating three boarders, and capable of providing for one hundred and forty-seven scholars and staff. That Witherspoon's drive and out-going energetic policies were appreciated by the Trustees is evidenced by the minute of the Board in September 1770, which records that: 'The President of the College is invested with the sole direction as to the Methods of Education to be pursued by this Seminary'. This minute is significant in that it indicates the Trustees' backing not only of Witherspoon's methods, but in the light of the significant changes he had made, it can be taken as signalling their approval of his ideology.[28]

When Witherspoon had first arrived at Princeton in 1768, he discovered that the prevailing views among the tutors were largely those of the Ideal philosophy of George Berkeley. Berkeley's philosophy had also been adopted to a certain extent by one of his Presidential predecessors, Jonathan Edwards, who had imbibed Berkeley's ideas through the Reverend Samuel Johnson who had been his tutor at Yale. Sharing the idealist position, was Jonathan Edwards Jnr, who was a tutor on the staff of the College. Ashbel Green, Witherspoon's first biographer recalls:

> The Berklean [sic] system of Metaphysics was in repute when he [Witherspoon] entered his office. The tutors were zealous believers in it, and waited on the President, with some expectation of either confounding him, or making him a proselyte [sic]. They had mistaken their man. He first reasoned against the system and then ridiculed it, till he drove it out of the College.[29]

Jeffry H. Morrison asserts that at this time the idealist philosophy that pervaded Princeton at the time of Witherspoon's arrival 'probably owed more to Jonathan Edwards and Samuel Johnson, Edward's tutor at Yale, than to Bishop Berkeley'.[30] But whatever the cause, Witherspoon was naturally inclined to counter the prevailing idealist views and replace them with his own blend of common sense realism and Old Side Calvinism. The basis of Witherspoon's opposition was both theological and philosophical.
Jonathan Edwards along with the English clergyman George Whitefield, had been one of the preachers who had helped initiate and foster what became known as the First Great Awakening. Born in 1703 in Connecticut, he graduated from Yale in 1720 where his tutor was Samuel Johnson. From 1727 to 1750, he was Pastor to a congregation in Northampton, Massachusetts. The Great Awakening of the 1730s was characterised by fiery revivalist meetings with congregations being stirred by sermons that emphasised the dreadful fate that awaited the unconverted, and were then urged to seek salvation. This often resulted in semi-hysterical, mass emotional conversion experiences. Some time in 1734, Edwards preached one of these 'terror' sermons, *Sinners in the Hands of an Angry God*. It demonstrates the extremes to which this brand of evangelical Calvinism had taken Edwards. Walter Isaacson, in his biography of Benjamin Franklin, records that Edwards told his congregation that the only thing that kept them from eternal damnation was the inexplicable grace of 'the God that holds you over the pit of Hell, as one holds a spider or some loathsome insect over a fire'.[31]

Edwards so emphasises the doctrine of the Sovereignty of God that it colours all the rest of his theology. As is often the case with theologians, when they give one doctrine a central place in their scheme, they then have to revise their view of all the other doctrines so that they will articulate organically with it.[32] Each one of the commentators on Jonathan Edwards that I have read has emphasised the importance that he gave to the doctrine of the Sovereignty of God. It is in this context that we can best understand his favouring of the idealist stance of George Berkeley, and to a certain extent, Berkeley's theories as they were mediated through Edwards's former tutor at Yale, Samuel Johnson. Both Edwards and Johnson being totally committed to the idea of the Sovereignty of God and also to the inability of man to do anything to effect his own salvation, caused them to be attracted to and grasp at Berkeley's immaterialist view that the source of man's ideas is the mind of God - that literally, God puts ideas into man's head. The appeal of this aspect of God's activity would be strong, for it would account for the religious conversion of man, who by himself was incapable of achieving it. The idea of God being the sole agent in effecting religious conversion, chimed in with their Calvinistic view of man's total depravity and therefore his total inability to bring about his conversion because he lacked the moral will to do so.[33]

Another of Berkeley's views that would appeal to Edwards and Johnson's Calvinist perception of the world, was his attack on Sir Isaac Newton and John Locke for their mechanistic views of the universe. The sheer physicality of Newton's system and John Locke's wholehearted philosophical endorsement of the work of the 'incomparable Mr. Newton', could easily have been understood as likely to displace God from the minds of men.[34] Berkeley perceived the Newtonian view of the universe as a threat to the belief in God's existence and his function as a Creator God. In his Introduction to George Berkeley's, *The Principles of Human Knowledge*, G. J. Warnock writes:

> In Locke's 'material' world, that supposedly self-sufficient machine, God's tenure was that of a precariously tolerated outsider; in Berkeley's world, from which matter is totally banished, every natural event, every object that we perceive, 'the whole choir of Heaven and furniture of the earth', are immediate effects and evidences of the will of God. God does not dwell remotely outside, but incessantly and everywhere sustains in existence the material world, whose existence in fact cannot be coherently conceived without Him.[35]

Berkeley's findings were not all accepted by Samuel Johnson as Johnson's letter to Berkeley of September 10, 1729, clearly shows. But what was accepted and passed on to students such as Jonathan Edwards were aspects of Berkeley's philosophy that seemed to support his Calvinistic beliefs. For example: Johnson is prepared to allow for the compatibility of Berkeley's theory of immaterialism with Sir Isaac Newton's scheme: 'for the laws of nature which he so happily explains are the same whether matter be supposed or not'. He objects to God being portrayed as forever active in creation as he thinks that this is not as 'impressive as the concept of God as the First Cause'. He sees immaterialism as lowering the status of the 'means of perception' e.g. the eye which he calls 'this fine apparatus'. He has difficulties with 'Death', and quibbles: 'if our bodies are nothing but ideas ... what room is there left for any resurrection, properly so called?' Yet he capitulates to Berkeley, and speculates on 'the usefulness of your doctrine' and suggests that there might be 'further application of it to the arts and sciences'. Johnson concludes his letter in a way that indicates the very favourable impression that Berkeley's work has made upon him:

> May we not hope to see logic, mathematics, and natural philosophy, pneumatology, theology and morality, all in their order appearing with a new luster under the advantages they may receive from it? [36]

Unlike Johnson and Edwards, who seemed willing to accommodate the views of Berkeley into their own system of belief, John Witherspoon met them head on, and dealt with them dismissively.

Witherspoon perceived that Berkeley's views were an attack on common sense and a denial of the reality of the world. In *Lecture 6* of his course on *Moral Philosophy* he writes:

> It is easy to raise metaphysical subtleties, and confound the understanding on such subjects. In opposition to this some late writers have advanced, with great apparent reason, that there are certain first principles, or dictates of common sense, which are either simple perceptions, or seen with intuitive evidence. These are the foundations of all reasoning, and without them, to reason is a word without meaning.[37]

Now, although these words of Witherspoon had as their immediate target David Hume, they constitute the same argument as could be used against the metaphysical arguments of Berkeley. Witherspoon had a natural suspicion of metaphysical argument, and sought always to bring things down to earth with what he judged was common sense. Berkeley's denial of the existence of a material world and his insistence that it was all in the mind was dismissed by Witherspoon on the basis of what he took to be the 'dictates of common sense, which are either simple perceptions or seen with intuitive evidence'. Berkeley's attack upon Newton and Locke's conception of the universe as a mechanical, physical and material entity and their acknowledgement of God as the first cause of its coming into being seemed to Witherspoon to allow him a proper praise to a Creator. But unlike Samuel Johnson, he did not find Berkeley's assertion of the ongoing creativity of God in any way offensive, indeed it is compatible with what he says in *Lecture 4* of his *Moral Philosophy* course: 'It seems to me absurd that infinite perfection should exhaust or limit itself by a created production'.[38] However, his admiration for Newton caused him to yearn for the day when Moral Philosophy would be written with the same precision as Natural Philosophy. He saw Newton's work as a further confirmation of the Universe as the material creation of God, and as something that further enhanced the wonder of that creation and its creator.[39]

Witherspoon was not in outright opposition to Jonathan Edwards or his school of thought, but although he shared their belief in the Sovereignty of God, there was a difference in his attitude as to man's capabilities even in his fallen state. Williston Walker, a former Professor of Ecclesiastical History at Yale, Edwards's Alma Mater, writes of him:

> A Calvinist, emphasizing the absolute divine sovereignty in conversion against all Arminian modifications, in his *Enquiry into...Freedom of Will* of 1754 he held that while all men have natural ability to turn to God, they lack moral ability - that is the inclination - so to do.[40]

Witherspoon always acted on the premise of the overall sovereignty of God but allowed for the freedom of men to choose to do or not to do in response to God's promptings by means of the persuasive powers of men or by the inner voice of conscience or by the movings of the holy spirit. He therefore could not go along with the teaching of those who followed Edwards's belief, that had been strengthened by Berkeley's understanding of the mind of God controlling man's perception and activity, as that would have been a denial of man's freewill.

Edwards too had attacked the moral sense theories to which Witherspoon had become attached through his gradually coming to see the value and truth of the teachings of Francis Hutcheson. Edwards's adoption of the spiritual metaphysics of Berkeley's theories, also sat uncomfortably with Witherspoon, who had an almost built in aversion to metaphysics, and certainly was suspicious of the display of feelings that often accompanied what were claimed by others as spiritual experiences. He was never one to encourage admiration or support for those who were enthusiastic about revivalist preachers, or meetings where there were displays of emotional behaviour. For him passion was something that must be controlled, and the religious fervour that accompanied the preaching of the followers of Jonathan Edwards was not something of which he approved.

Witherspoon's opposition to Jonathan Edwards and his followers was not based on petty animosity or academic rivalry towards one who had pre-eminence in American theological circles, or even towards one who had previously occupied the President's Chair at the College, for that had been a very brief sojourn. He opposed the views represented by Edwards's name and that of Berkeley and Johnson, because he saw them as pernicious and as obstructions to the way forward for a College that was entering into a new era with the intention of attracting students who wanted a broad and mainstream educational environment, not one linked to the past and to a rather esoteric brand of Calvinism tinged with a peculiar metaphysic.

Jonathan Edwards Jnr had been on the College staff as a Tutor when Witherspoon took over as President, but followed a modified version of his father's theology, that allowed for a more liberal approach. He believed that Christ died for all and not just for the elect only. But by the summer of 1769, he resigned, apparently without engaging in any conflict with the President. Witherspoon's brand of common sense philosophy, and Calvinism had brought to an end the influence of George Berkeley, Samuel Johnson and Jonathan Edwards.[41]

Witherspoon's personal background and education gave him a natural bias towards the Arts as against the Sciences, but he made it his business to see that the College was as thorough as it could be in the provision of a scientific education. Right from his encouragement of the importance of a firm grasp of Arithmetic through to his admiration for the rigorous methods of Natural Philosophy, science was given a prominent place in the curriculum. John Adams records in his diary, his first visit to what he described as 'Nassau Hall Colledge' in August 1774. He recalls that when walking in the grounds with one of the students they 'met Mr. Euston [Houston] the Professor of Mathematicks who kindly invited us to his Chamber'. Houston, clearly enthusiastic about the College, then gave Adams the grand tour, as the diary records:

> Mr. Euston shewed us the Library. It is not large, but has some good Books. He then led us into the Apparatus. Here we saw a most beautifull Machine, an Orrery, or Planetarium, constructed by Mr. Writtenhouse of Philadelphia. It exhibits almost every Motion in the astronomical World. The Motions of the Sun and all the Planetts

with all their Satellites. The Eclipses of the Sun and Moon &c. He shewed us another orrery which exhibits the true Inclination of the orbit of each of the Planetts to the Plane of the Ecliptic. He then shewed us the electrical Apparatus, which is the most compleat and elegant that I have seen. He charged the Bottle and attempted an Experiment, but the State of the Air was not favourable. By this time the Bell rang for Prayers. We went into the Chappell, the President soon came in, and we attended.[42]

Adams's detailed description of the visit suggests that Mr. Houston was an enthusiastic and well informed advocate for his subject. Not only that, Houston had been with Witherspoon as a colleague from the time that Witherspoon appointed him as teacher of the Grammar School in 1768. Houston might also have been influential in the development of Witherspoon's political opinions as they moved towards realizing that the way forward for the American Colonies lay in their independence from Great Britain. It is no coincidence that on the same page of Adams's diary that records the meeting with Houston and Witherspoon, Adams notes that after attending prayers in the chapel:

> we went into the President's House and drank a glass of wine. He is as high a Son of Liberty, as any man in America.

Adams was not only impressed by the facilities as demonstrated by the Professor of Mathematics, but clearly came away with a favourable understanding of the President as an activist and propagandist for Independence. He obviously thinks highly of Witherspoon's ideas when he takes the trouble to remember and notes:

> He [Witherspoon] says it is necessary that Congress should raise Money and employ a Number of Writers in the Newspapers in England, to explain to the Public the American Plea, and remove the Prejudices of Britons. He says also We should recommend to every Colony to form a Society for the Encouragement of Protestant Emigrants from the 3 Kingdoms.

Adams also notes that Witherspoon is a member of the Committee of Correspondence, and had been in the Provincial Congress that appointed Delegates to the general Congress. Adams records too that Witherspoon had spoken of his part in encouraging the ban on paying duty on tea. Adams's references to Witherspoon continue to be positive as the diary reveals him listening to Witherspoon preach and meeting with him socially to share a coffee and later with friends at dinner. The entry for Saturday, September 3, 1774, notes:

> Dr. Witherspoon enters with great Spirit into the American Cause. He seems as hearty a Friend as any of the Natives - An animated Son of Liberty.

The day's entry ends with a description of a very convivial supper in which Witherspoon again shares:

> Spent the evening at Mr. Mifflins with Lee and Harrison from Virginia, the two Rutledges, Dr. Witherspoon, Dr. Shippen, Dr. Steptoe, and another Gentleman. An elegant supper, and we drank Sentiments till 11 O Clock.

The 'Sentiments' are then listed:

> Harrison gave us for a Sentiment 'a constitutional Death to the Lords Bute, Mansfield and North'. Paine gave us 'May the Collision of british [sic] Flint and American Steel, produce that Spark of Liberty which shall illumine the latest Posterity'. Wisdom to Britain and Firmness to the Colonies, may Britain be wise and America Free. The Friends of America throughout the World. Union of the Colonies. Unanimity to the Congress. May the Result of the Congress, answer the Expectations of the People. Union of Britain and the Colonies, on a Constitutional Foundation - and many other such Toasts.[43]

The toasts reflect the range of opinions still prevailing in the Colonies at the time, and the different stages that people were at in their thinking about the best way forward. But the picture of Witherspoon that emerges from these pages of Adams's diary, is of a man so thoroughly immersed in the American political scene that the topic of Mathematics first engaged in by Adams, does not seem to have been returned to. Instead the conversation ranges over the major concerns of the day, the ongoing dispute between America and Britain. In a way it tells us something about the relative importance to Witherspoon of Education and Politics. At that period in his life politics seems to have eclipsed education.

It might have been difficult for Witherspoon to have supplied Adams much further information on Mathematics or Science in any case for these were subjects about which he had but a superficial knowledge, and relied upon others to teach. Collins agrees with Dr Ezra Stiles's assessment of Dr

Witherspoon's mathematical and scientific training as 'inferior', and 'judges that the President's acquaintance with the higher mathematics, with astronomy and with physical science in general, was little more than elementary'.[44] This judgement is attested by the very few references to the subject that are to be found in his writings.

Surprisingly, despite the numerous historical references in Witherspoon's writings, the subject of History was not well taught by him. At the outset, let me say that I suspect that this might well have been because he had stretched himself too far in his attempt at providing a full and rounded curriculum on the meagre resources available to him at the time.

A set of notes by Abel Johnson of the Class of 1784, on the *History Lectures of John Witherspoon*, reveal a course of six lectures that would be better described as Lectures on Chronology.[45] The lack of real historical content in the lectures is signalled by two quotations from *Lecture I*: 'We cannot go far into history without being led to the Creator', and secondly: 'There is a clearer view of Rome in Horace's satire than in the history of these times'. *Lecture II* purports to deal with the dating of Creation, and offers a theory of the flood without attempting any explanation: 'Some have suggested that the earth's motion before the flood was irregular, the axis parallel to the plane of the eclipse'. In dealing with the dating of Creation, Witherspoon writes: 'Historical chronology is deduced from the beginning of the world only in the sacred writings'. He asserts that

> So far as profane writing goes, it agrees perfectly well with … [indistinct] and the state of the world … this is a strong collateral proof of the truths of the scripture, and [if] we receive them as inspired we have a basis for scriptural Chronology from the Creation of the World.

In *Lecture III* Witherspoon seems to follow the then accepted date for the Creation of the World (BC 4004) given in the *King James Bible* of 1611. He bandies about figures such as:

> Period from the creation of the world according to the Hebrew text 1656 years; Summarian Pentateuch 1302 and Septuagint according to two editions 2,240 and 2260.

The significance of these figures is as difficult to ascertain now, as seems to have been the experience of the student taking the notes at the time. In fairness to Witherspoon the scrappiness of these lectures might be attributed to the student's slipshod work, but even allowing for that, their content can hardly merit being described as history. In the final part of *Lecture III* Witherspoon offers his students three different theories of how the world was created: '(1)That it is in form and substance eternal. (2) That it was made of pre-existent matter. (3) That it was created out of nothing'. He says of (3) that 'it is most rational as well as scriptural'. He also muses on 'the short history of the antediluvian world', considering its longevity and temperature, and throws in the opinion that 'moral and immoral habits increase inconceivably by time'.

    Lecture IV returns to the subject of dating, estimating that 'the second period of general history is from the Deluge to the death of Jacob which contains about 657 years'. He treats the Babel story literally: as God creating the different languages, and offers evidence of his still holding to the understanding of providence that undergirded his sermon in 1776, *The Dominion of Providence*. He sees the significance of the Babel incident, as 'probably the occasion was in providence to effect the dissention that immediately took place'. In this lecture he seems to wander along, spraying his theories indiscriminately in just one long ramble through the past, as he sees it. In *Lecture V* he deals with the origins of the early practices of bread-making, wine-making, weaving, agriculture and ploughing, all in a vague way. This is followed by excursions into the development of building, metalwork and coinage; while writing's evolvement is dismissed: 'that it was like all the other discoveries, the work of providence'. *Lecture VI*, the last in the course, attempts to deal with the origins of Arithmetic, Astronomy, and manners and customs.

    Even allowing for a possible lack of diligence on the part of Abel Johnson, the student who took the notes of them, Witherspoon's *History Lectures* lack structure, coherence, and do not in any way seem to have a discernible teaching aim other than to assert that all that has happened has happened according to the will and the purpose of providence. They do not merit the title of lectures on history and perhaps should be treated as one of John Witherspoon's experiments that failed. But like his early venture into lectures in Divinity, these lectures are perhaps evidence of the fact that John Witherspoon was trying to cope with too many tasks at the College with too small a staff and in doing so stretched his own resources and revealed that for all his undoubted talent, in some areas he was decidedly lacking both in experience and understanding. These lectures in history do him no credit whatsoever. Varnum Lansing Collins's judgement is perhaps more kind than mine, but even he has to admit that 'the fragmentary notes on his lectures would indicate that his outlines were more curious than well formulated'.[46]

    On John Adam's first visit to Nassau Hall, he said of the library: 'It is not large, but has some good books'.[47] The building up of a well-stocked library was one of Witherspoon's aims from the very time of his acceptance of the appointment as President, and work towards that was begun with his approaches to friends for help in providing books, and his visit to London in February 1768. He already had a good personal library because of his own love of books, and this had been augmented by those acquired from his father's collection for he too was widely read, especially in the Calvinist authors of the continent. Witherspoon's *Moral Philosophy* course in its concluding lecture provides a list of books which he commends to his students and it is significant that included in these are some of these Calvinist writers known to both himself and his father. The provision of the list also signals that his *Moral Philosophy* course was but an introduction to the subject. Further evidence of the width and depth of Witherspoon's own reading is given by L. Gordon Tait in *The Piety of John Witherspoon*. Tait reproduces a 'List of Books of Character as Collected by Dr. John Witherspoon 1773', and writes of the document:

> The original is bound with William Beekman Jr.'s student copy of Witherspoon's, 'Lectures on Moral Philosophy' and the title on the cover page reads, 'A list of books of Character as collected by Dr. Witherspoon - 1773 - Transcribed at Nassau Hall by William Beekman Junr.'. The title on the first page of the list is, 'List of Books of Character in different Branches of Science to direct Students, especially in Divinity, either in the Course of their Reading or furnishing their Libraries'.

Two hundred books are listed either by title or author and the list is clearly not just another version of the one appended to the final lecture of Witherspoon's *Moral Philosophy Course*, which includes just thirty-three references. It is a reasonable assumption to make that in the furbishing of the College Library, the titles and authors in the 'List of Books of Character' would have featured.[48]

The Reverend Samuel Davies, the fourth President, produced the first printed Catalogue of the College's library. William S. Dix in his book, *The Princeton University Library in the Eighteenth Century* quotes from the Preface compiled by Davies:

> A large and well sorted collection of Books on the various Branches of Literature is the most ornamental and useful Furniture of the College and the most valuable Fund with which it can be endowed. It is one of the best helps to enrich the Minds both of the Officers and Students with Knowledge, to give them an extensive Acquaintance with Authors, and to lead them beyond the narrow limits of the

> Books to which they are confined by their stated Studies and Recitations that they may expatiate at large thro' the boundless variegated Fields of Science.[49]

Davies was only thirty-six when he was appointed President, but at the first meeting of the Trustees, he made it clear how important the Library's place in the College was, as the Minute of September 27, 1759, records:

> That Pres. Davies be desired as soon as he conveniently can to take a Methodical Catalogue of Books in the College Library and order the same to be printed at the Expense of the College.

On January 29, 1760, the Catalogue was completed and printed. Dix writes of Davies's Preface: 'Its emphasis upon independent study, intellectual freedom, and the integration of the library with the teaching program seems thoroughly modern'.[50]

Davies had been involved in promoting this aspect of the College even before he became its President. In 1752, a promotional pamphlet was prepared by the Trustees for a Fund Raising trip to Britain to be undertaken by Davies and another minister the Reverend Gilbert Tennent.[51] Tennent had been called to Philadelphia by the New Side or evangelical faction of the Presbyterian Church in 1749. This congregation developed under Tennent and a new church building to house the Second Presbyterian Church of Philadelphia was designed and built by the Scottish born Architect/Builder Robert Smith and was opened in December 1751. Smith was later to be responsible for designing and building Nassau Hall. The planning of the new College building at Princeton was begun in 1753, through the collaboration of Robert Smith and Dr William Shippen, Trustee of the College and a member of Tennent's congregation. The vision of the trustees was realised when in the autumn of 1756, the new building was occupied by President Aaron Burr and seventy students.[52]

But the vision of the Trustees shared by Davies and Tennent was much more than to have a splendid new building; it was to contribute and implement new ideas on education. The Teaching Method described in the 1752 promotional pamphlet, produced in expectation of the planned trip to Britain by Davies and Tennent, is one that amongst other things would require to be supported by a well-stocked library. It claims:

> The governors of this college have endeavoured to improve upon the commonly received plans of education. They proceed not so much in the method of dogmatic instruction by prolix discourses on the different branches of the sciences, by burdening memory and

infusion of heavy and disagreeable tasks, as in the Socratic way of free dialogue between teacher and pupil or between the students themselves, under the supervision of their tutors. In this manner, the attention is engaged, the mind entertained and the scholar animated in the pursuit of knowledge.[53]

If the above ideals were to be upheld then a library representing a wide range of scholarship would be essential. This was certainly the aim of the then President, Aaron Burr, who occupied the post from 1748 to 1757, and whose correspondence with Philip Dodderidge of Northampton later reveals an admiration for the then radical scholar John Taylor of Norwich who addressed his students at Warrington Academy in 1757:

(1) I do solemnly charge you … in all your studies … you do constantly, carefully, impartially, conscientiously attend to evidence as it lies in Scriptures or the nature of things and dictates of reason. (2) That you admit, embrace or assent to no principle or sentiment, by me taught or advanced, but only so far as it shall appear to you to be supported and justified by proper evidence from Revelation or the reason of things.

Dix comments: 'It is my impression that this enthusiastic insistence that students make up their own minds declined at Princeton with the arrival of Witherspoon'.[54] I suspect that Dix might be right about this but I shall return to further consider this when I try to assess the personality of Witherspoon. But the drive of this attitude adopted by Burr and later pursued by Samuel Davies, necessitated the provision of a compendious library.

Later, in the Catalogue of 1760, Davies draws attention to a particular area of need when he points out that 'few modern authors adorn the shelves. This defect is most felt in the study of Mathematics and the Newtonian philosophy'. The Catalogue of 1760 lists '789 titles in 1281 volumes,' nearly all gifts - one third of them from Governor Joseph Belcher after whom the new building was nearly called. He declined the original suggestion that it be named Belcher Hall and suggested that it be called Nassau Hall:

as it will express the honour that we retain, in this remote part of the Globe, to the immortal memory of the Glorious King William the Third who was a branch of the illustrious House of Nassau.[55]

Witherspoon's arrival at Princeton initially augmented the library with the books he had collected from friends and those that had been ordered on his London trip. Although his numerous fund raising trips throughout the colonies in the years before the open conflict with Great Britain began had helped increase the library stock, his efforts were defeated by the wartime occupation of Nassau Hall at different times by the opposing armies. On November 29, 1776, Witherspoon had to hastily close the College as the British were advancing towards Princeton. The British Army occupied the College and used it as its headquarters, and then when George Washington's army made a surprise counter attack in January 3, 1777, they made similar use of Nassau Hall. The depredation and abuse of both armies undid all the work that had gone into building up the library stock. The impoverished state of the Provincial Government and the inability of the Federal Government to command a sufficient authority to gather in taxes for the support of education, left the College bereft of help in the rebuilding of its important resource. In 1784, after the Peace had been agreed, Witherspoon made an appeal for Funds to David Stewart, Earl of Buchan:

> The College of New Jersey being seated in the very centre of the theatre of the late War in America, has suffered greater injury than many other institutions ... . The building was laid waste, the library almost wholly destroyed, the apparatus entirely taken away and the orrery much injured ... .[56]

Also in that year Witherspoon made an ill-advised trip to Britain to try to raise funds for the College. He even considered making a similar trip to France but Benjamin Franklin wrote to him from Passy on April 5, 1784, saying that it would not be worthwhile making a trip to France to attempt to fund raise for the College as this would be seen as the Americans 'being unable to provide for the education of our own children'. Franklin cited the lack of success of Mr Wheeler of the College of Dartmouth, New England who had recently been on a similar mission and had been unsuccessful. Witherspoon's British fund raising tour proved unsuccessful and he returned from it with a net gain of only five pounds and fourteen shillings.[57]

One of Witherspoon's first acts on becoming President was to have the Trustees appoint a librarian. The Trustees' Minutes of August 8, 1768, record:

> Dr. Witherspoon having recommended to the Board, Mr. Hugh Sim [sic], a young man who came over with him to this country, as a person of singular Ingenuity and Merit and well qualified to serve the

Interests of the College, the Trustees thought proper to appoint the said Mr. Sim to the office of Librarian and Inspector of Rooms in this College and resolved that the sum of five pounds procu money p. annum together with his Commons in College be authorized the said Mr. Sim for his services in these departments.[58]

In these early years, following Witherspoon's making of the first appointment of a librarian to the College, the Library was opened twice a week for an hour each time under the supervision of the librarian. The Library Fee was two shillings and sixpence and the fees were to be expended for the use of the Library.

Hugh Simm served less than a year at Princeton, but he used his time well, taking lessons in Divinity from Witherspoon himself and being awarded an honorary B.A. in October 1768. In December that year, in a letter to his brother, who was a weaver in Paisley, he said that at his graduation, he had 'composed and spoke a Latin oration before the Trustees of the College which was very highly received'. Six months later Simm moved on, having been appointed to teach at a Grammar School in Freehold, New Jersey, where he writes again to his brother: 'I teach Latin, Greek and Natural Philosophy ... and I am to receive 50 or 55 pounds of this money a year'. Although his stay at Princeton was brief, Simm must have established the value of the post for a successor, William Houston was appointed in September 1770. By 1775, the Library had grown from 1389 volumes listed in 1760, to approximately 2,000 volumes.[59]

One puzzling thought remains with me regarding the fate of the Library during the war. While Witherspoon saw to the preservation of his own books by taking them with him even amidst the haste of his departure, he did not do anything to protect the Library at the College. Even if, as seems to be the case, it contained up to 2,000 volumes, it would not have taken too much effort to have packed them into a wagon and taken them to a place of safety. One reason why this was not done might have been because Witherspoon thought that the war would be conducted along 'gentlemanly' lines and that respect would be shown for a place of learning. Yet if this was his thinking, it betrays an inconsistency. For once, his Calvinistic belief in the depravity of human nature was not alerting him to the likelihood of the Library's destruction. Even more surprisingly he was decidedly lacking in the use of his so often to the fore common sense, that ought to have told him that any place with which a notoriously vociferous advocate of revolution was associated was likely to become a target for revengeful activity. But it may well have been that again Witherspoon was showing the same naivety as he showed at the battle at

Falkirk in 1746, to which he had gone as a spectator, and then not surprisingly to others, found himself taken as a prisoner of war.

Dix records that, 'by 1788 the library was sufficiently large to warrant the making of a Catalogue'. It is interesting to note that the library laws of that time included a fee of 67 cents to be paid by every student for each session. It opened at noon on one day a week, but unusually for the times, students were able to borrow books.[60] The restoration of the Library continued and in 1794, the French Diarist, Moreau de St. Méry, writes of his visit to New Jersey College that it has, 'a chapel, a refectory, a library of about 2,000 volumes and the justly celebrated planetarium built by Dr. David Rittenhouse'. In this, the last year of Witherspoon's life, the library had been restored to what it had been immediately prior to the war, and equally, as a sign that normality had returned, the Rittenhouse orrery was back in place.[61]

The nature of student life under Witherspoon's reign as President can be only partially ascertained by the physical description of their living conditions and daily routine, the examination of the curriculum in which they were engaged in studying, the statistics of graduations, and the impinging culture and events that provided the context in which they were set. A greater awareness of what it was like to be a student at the College of New Jersey in Witherspoon's time can be gained if the formal information of the kind as outlined above is supplemented by scraps of anecdotal evidence pieced together from the students themselves, and from Witherspoon's letters and notes of the period.

The student's day was, to say the least, designed along Spartan lines. The rising bell was rung at 5 a.m., prayers followed at 5.30 a.m. during which a Senior student read from the Bible and the President offered a commentary. Breakfast was followed by an hour's study and classroom work began with recitations at 9 a.m. and continued until 1 p.m. After Dinner, the hours between 3 and 5 p.m. were again for study, and Vespers were held at 5 p.m. Students were then free until 7 p.m. when Supper was served. The day ended at 9 p.m. when students had to return to their rooms. There was little free time, nor was there any organised sport. The strict timetable with its emphasis on religious offices continued into Sunday when attendance at worship was compulsory in the morning at the Presbyterian Church and in the afternoon at the College Chapel.[62]

It is little wonder that there would be the occasional outburst of student pranks or attempts made to break the rules. The cost of submission to this regime was approximately £25 and 6 shillings per annum. According to Collins this was made up: Tuition £4, Board and Services £15, room rent £1, washing £3, wood and candles £2, Sundries 6 shillings. Upon his arrival, Witherspoon devised a scheme whereby with the part payment in advance of Fees, bulk purchases could be made by the College Steward thereby making savings. The net result of Witherspoon's reform was a saving of approximately £1 and 7 shillings per annum.[63]

Witherspoon's relationship with his students to whom he was *in loco parentis* is occasionally revealed in his letters and in the recollections of students. Not much evidence is available for the early years from 1768 to 1776, perhaps because of the destruction of College papers during the period of the occupation of Nassau Hall by both armies; while the years from the *Declaration of Independence* to the *Peace* in 1783, were a time when Witherspoon was often more concerned with matters of state than with his students. Joseph Clark, a student at the time, records in his journal the day that Witherspoon broke the news to them that because of the advancing enemy forces the college would have to close immediately:

> On the 29th November 1776 New Jersey College long the seat of science and haunt of the Muses was visited with the melancholy tidings of the approach of the enemy … our worthy President deeply affected at this solemn scene entered the Hall where the students were collected, and in a very affecting manner informed us of the improbability of continuing there longer in peace; and after giving us several suitable instructions and much good advice very affectionately bade us farewell.[64]

Cutting through the melodramatic style and ponderous prose Clark, nevertheless conveys a picture of an emotional Witherspoon saying a fearful farewell to the young people for whom he felt responsible, but for whom he could do little but to tell them to go home, knowing that for some of them that would mean a long and hazardous journey. But as a substitute father Witherspoon could also be critical of the lifestyle of a student whom he judged to be indulging in extravagant behaviour. Stephen Van Rensseler, (Class of 1782), was one such student. Richard A. Harrison tells his story:

> In the summer of 1779 President Witherspoon stopped at Kingston, [New York] on his way south, having investigated New Hampshire land grants for the Continental Congress. When he resumed his journey, Witherspoon took Van Rensseler with him to be enrolled in the Grammar School in Princeton, where his father had preceded him some fifteen years before.
>
> Although he was a student in the Grammar School for barely two months, Van Rensseler delivered the English valedictory address at the school's Commencement exercises on September 28, 1779, a

lengthy discourse on the Aristotelian injunction 'know thyself'. The speech was noted for its persistent warnings against the blandishments of wealth and luxury. Along with five other graduates V. R. was admitted into the Freshman Class at the College.

In Princeton he resided with the family of Professor Samuel Stanhope Smith (A.B. 1769). His valedictory sentiments notwithstanding, and within the limits imposed by war and rural location he continued to live according to his ample means, so much so that he must have been one of the students about whose extravagances and ostentation Witherspoon complained in the summer of 1779. That August for example, the young patroon [sic] paid more than £367 for the making of one green suit of clothes from Philadelphia.[65]

Witherspoon's frugal ways were offended by such conduct. His kindness and willingness to oblige the family by conveying the young Van Rensseler from Kingston to Princeton, his granting of the honour of giving the valedictory address, and the ignoring of the no doubt oft repeated encouragements to the avoidance of luxury, indeed the hypocritical indulgence in the very opposite to what had been advocated in the address, must have sorely tried the patience of Witherspoon towards his young charge. It is to be hoped that he did not become aware of the young man's opinion of the President and the College. Harrison Gray Otis, one of Stephen Van Rensseler's contemporaries reports him as expressing the wish 'that time would hasten the desired period when I shall bid adieu to the sophisticated jargon of a superstitious Synod of pensioned Bigots'.[66] These are the only derogatory remarks that I have come across when searching for the comments of the students of Witherspoon, and I am inclined to dismiss them as the rantings of a hugely spoiled and overly indulged young man.

Samuel Stanhope Smith, son-in-law and latterly acting President in Witherspoon's time, a few years after this had similar difficulties with a student, 'Master Peter Desmarie' who was living rather extravagantly. He writes to a Mr Wachmuth of Philadelphia in November 15, 1792, asking for money to cover the expenses of the student:

> He is more extravagant than I would wish in clothes and hiring horses to ride out into the country for his amusement and exercise. It is a delicate thing to controul [sic] with sufficient firmness a young gentleman of his lively and ardent disposition who thinks himself entitled both from habit and fortune to too many indulgences. I wish your advice to co-operate with my remonstrances, which I hope are

beginning to have some effect, in restraining him and inspiring him to *learn* rather than to distinguish himself by show and expense.[67]

Such were some of the problems faced by the College staff in dealing with the sons of rich men.

There is ample evidence that Witherspoon went out of his way to attend to the domestic needs of his College students and Grammar School pupils. Harrison produces details of Witherspoon's attending to the day to day personal needs of students, recording that: 'on July 15, 1775, President John Witherspoon made minor purchases for [Benjamin] Dunlap [of Virginia] at Thomas Patterson's Princeton store' and suggests 'that Witherspoon was administering the benefaction that made Dunlap's studies possible', and noting that this claim is strengthened by the fact that Witherspoon made extensive purchases 'of cloth and apparel' for him [Dunlap] 'in late September 1775'.[68]

On the whole, the domestic arrangements engaged in by Witherspoon seemed to be acceptable to the parents of the young people in his care. Sometimes the parents paid for their children's education in indirect and unusual ways, as a letter of Witherspoon's dated August 3, 1787, addressed to Thomas Fitzsimmons Esq. shows:

> I have just received a letter from Mr. Thos. Godsden of Charleston S. Carolina informing me that he had remitted to you 22 whole and 27 half barrels of rice the proceeds of which to be paid to my order for two young gentlemen, John and William Ferguson. I will be obliged to you to if you will inform me what will be the probable amount when it is turned into money.

A further letter acknowledges receiving a draught for '100 dollars @ 60 days sight, Aug. 28, 1787'.[69] But usually things were paid in a more conventional manner, as is evidenced by Witherspoon's letter to Col. Henry Lee, the father of 'Light Horse Harry', of December 28, 1770, in which he encloses an account 'for the necessities of Henry's chamber'.

Two other letters give a flavour of how Witherspoon gave his personal attention to the domestic matters of his students, and how he endeavoured to keep their parents well informed. On May 12, 1786, he writes to His Excellency Nicholas Van Dyke Esq., Governor of Delaware, with reference to his son Nicholas Van Dyke, who went on to become a U.S. Senator from 1817-1826:

> I have the pleasure to inform you that your son gave complete satisfaction in his examination and is admitted into the Sophomore

Class. I am happy to find that you judge so well as to his education. We are very much distressed with the mistaken parents and their desires to precipitate the education of their children and have been obliged of late to enter into a positive resolution to enter none in college unless in full standing in some one of these classes nor to give them a degree without completing the whole.[70]

The second letter is from St. George Tucker Esq. giving a report on his two sons who had recently been enrolled in the Grammar School, and offering an encouragement to send his eldest son to College. In the letter he emphasises that the Grammar School is under his sole control:

You were right in supposing that the Grammar School is particularly under my Inspection, it being my property in which the Trustees of the College do not intermeddle.

He then expresses his delight in the attitude being taken by Tucker:

It was a pleasure to me to receive your letters because you have precisely the idea which I wish were more general respecting education. We are obliged to contend against the Prejudices of the Times which are much against the ancient languages meaning particularly Latin and Greek. Yet these are plainly the fountains both of Science and History as well as they furnish us with the Standard of Taste ... it is not easy indeed to be a man of sound or general knowledge if he is ignorant of them.

A further letter of July 16, 1787, gives details of the boys' accommodation: 'I have placed your sons to board with a Mr. Tod, a gentleman from Scotland who is married to a niece of mine'. He then indicates that the overall cost for each child is £120 per annum, 'to keep them genteely'.[71]

In his Memorial of the College of New Jersey 1784, Witherspoon writes of his continuing concern 'for the moral government of the scholars'.[72] An incident is recalled by a former student, John Pintard (A.B. 1776) in a letter of January 28, 1817, to his oldest daughter. Referring to a report of recent riotous conduct among students at Princeton, he opines 'that there is something fundamentally wrong in the discipline of the college' and that 'the professors and tutors are too rigid and inexperienced in life and know not how to enforce the laws or to relax with discretion'. He recalled that there had been trouble in his day, but that 'Dr. Witherspoon had understood human nature and we never had such dreadful explosions'. Pintard remembered 'that in his junior year he and Blewer', another student, 'were members of a group of nine students who wasted their winter frolicking, playing all hours and drinking eggnog'. The tutors found out through the students' 'obstreperous mirth at late hours'. Called to account the group agreed that Pintard should 'make our defence, one founded on the principle of sturdy denial and the presumption of no proof against us'. The President opened the hearing by warning the young men that they should not compound their offences 'by telling a lee' and that sufficient proof of their guilt was at hand. When one George Blewer broke down and blurted out the truth he went free of punishment. The other eight got off lightly with a public reprimand 'after prayers in the College'. However, this reflects well on Dr Witherspoon as a mild disciplinarian, who nevertheless upheld the moral value of truthfulness, the end of the story reflects sadly on the rest of the students involved. Pintard recalls rather priggishly, that Blewer:

> lost his character, no one spoke to him or would associate with him after spring vacation, a high spirited youth, he came no more to the College.

Pintard adds a footnote:

> Here we see the generous conduct of Doct. Witherspoon who saved us from ignominy by not suffering us to be entrapped as the Tutors left to themselves wd. [sic] undoubtedly have done.[73]

The nasty taste that this incident leaves in the mouth re-enforces the awareness of just how difficult it must have been for John Witherspoon to maintain an atmosphere conducive to learning among such a community of young men, some of whom were from wealthy families, and with the money to do it, were at the stage of asserting themselves and experimenting with the practices of adulthood. It is little wonder that only a few of the less privileged made it into the College of New Jersey.

The first person from an ethnic minority to matriculate at Princeton was Jacob Wooley, a Delaware Indian, a member of the class of 1762. He was followed by two more tribal Delaware men in the Classes of 1776 and 1789. During John Witherspoon's period as President two Africans, John Quamine and Bristol Yamma, entered the College. They were tutored personally by Witherspoon in preparation for matriculation but the war abruptly ended their education. A source at Princeton Public Library notes:

> that though the records are fragmentary, John Chavis, a free black who became a noted Latinist and tutor to North Carolinians, is

probably the first African American to matriculate at Princeton in the class of 1795.

It is thought that he studied there between 1793 and 1795. This is an area of research that is requiring more work, as the secondary sources that I have read seem at times to be at variance. From the few cases known to me, the main obstacle to entering College, met by the native Americans and the African Americans, was, along with the continuance of slavery, the lack of any formal primary or grammar school education. For whatever reason it was obviously difficult for them to enter Princeton, and it was not until 1945, when Princeton incorporated a Navy ROTC program into its curriculum and accepted the Navy's officer candidates as matriculated students, that African Americans re-entered the Princeton undergraduate body.[74]

I have already touched on the students' involvement in pro-revolutionary activity which at the very least was condoned, but which could be said to have been encouraged by Witherspoon, as in the student demonstrations of the 1770s. No student at The College of New Jersey could have been unaware of Witherspoon's support for the cause of American Independence from Great Britain. From the first overt acknowledgement of the American cause made by Witherspoon in awarding honorary degrees in 1769 to three men prominent in their advocacy of the need for a change in the mode of governing the colonies, through his involvement in the Committee of Correspondence, and eventually in his becoming a member of Congress, to the final signing of the *Declaration of Independence*, he was clearly seen to be committed to the colonies' right to be free and independent of Great Britain.

The students' involvement in revolutionary demonstrations and pronouncements was not an expression of their solidarity with Witherspoon, but rather the other way round, Witherspoon's pro-revolutionary activity was his expression of solidarity with them, and with their fellow countrymen. He knew, and was at pains to declare it, that the revolution was not the product of a few rabble rousers, some clergymen like himself among them, but that it had emerged from a groundswell of the feelings of the great majority of the people.

In the 'Advertisement' of a Glasgow edition of Witherspoon's sermon *The Dominion of Providence*, published in 1777, the editor expressed a typically British view of the American Revolution when he writes that:

the unhappy commotions in our American Colonies have been considerably promoted if not primarily agitated, by clerical influence: and none more of that order have had a greater share of it ascribed to them than Dr Witherspoon.[75]

This sentiment was echoing a commonly held belief in Britain at the time, and was jocularly expressed by Horace Walpole, the son of the British Prime Minister, Sir Robert Walpole in the summer of 1775: 'Cousin America has run off with a Presbyterian Minister'.[76] Although Walpole did not have Witherspoon in mind when he made the remark, but rather the Massachusetts clergy, 'firebrands to a man', the Glasgow editor saw Witherspoon as an example of such men. He hoped that the publication of Witherspoon's sermon would:

> shew what artful means and fallacious arguments have been made use of by ambitious and self-designing men, to stir up the poor infatuated Americans to the present rebellious measures.

What was nearer to the truth, was that Witherspoon was the one who was infatuated with the Americans dream of freedom to organise their lives in ways that were appropriate to them, untrammeled by the interference of a government that was based in another culture on the other side of the world. Witherspoon was as influenced by American opinion as much as he influenced his students. He absorbed as much as he exuded. He was led by the facts to his political opinions much more than he brought his political opinions to the facts. He became a revolutionary more than made revolutionaries. Student life at Princeton was but a microcosm of the ferment that was going on throughout the thirteen colonies and Witherspoon was but one, albeit very active cog, in the vast machine that was inexorably moving towards a new form that would become the United States of America.

CHAPTER 6

Lectures on Divinity

The first lecture is obviously being given within a short time of Witherspoon's arrival in the post as President at New Jersey College. He is very conscious of the change of scene and finds it different from what he has been used to: a very large audience and a pastoral relationship. Now he faces a relatively small number of students who are not under any obligation to be present. He clearly misses the former position of power and authority over a 'numerous, obedient and affectionate people'. But, he tells himself, that it will be 'ample recompense' if he is 'instrumental in sending out faithful labourers into the harvest'. He wants his students to share the same vision in their studies as he has of his teaching:

> to unite together piety and literature - to show their relation to and their influence one upon another and to guard against anything that may tend to separate them and set them in opposition one to another.[1]

Witherspoon continues this theme in his second lecture beginning with a surprisingly blunt refutation of any possibility of knowledge and understanding being imparted by any kind of supernatural revelation. Knowledge, he asserts, can only be acquired by study and application. He further asserts that learning is necessary to keep the sacred truths from contempt and to enable the attacks of adversaries to be repelled. Witherspoon shows an appreciation of the usefulness of all literature, asserting that 'there is no branch of literature without its use'. He reveals another aspect of his understanding when he claims that were it possible for a minister to be acquainted with every branch of science he would be more fit for public usefulness and goes as far as to say that 'a truly good man does grow both in holiness and usefulness by every new discovery that is made to him'. Acknowledging that no man can read all of literature, he cites the areas that are especially relevant for anyone preparing for the ministry: 'Languages: Latin, Greek, Hebrew, French and English; Moral Philosophy; History, both Sacred and Prophane; Eloquence and Belles Lettres'.[2]

In these lectures are the first signs of a new freedom being exercised by Witherspoon now that he has been released from the role of the implacable opponent of the Moderates, and the necessary conformity to what was expected of a parish minister and leader of the Popular party within the Church of Scotland. One such sign is his commendation of Roman Catholic authors that could be read by acquiring an understanding of French. He covers himself by saying:

> But what chiefly disposes me to recommend the French language to divines is on account of the sound Calvinistic reformation divinity. There are many more able and elegant writers in that language than in English.

But then he goes on to say daringly, 'There are also some admirable treatises written by Popish divines in French as well as by the Jansenists of the Roman Catholic communion'.[3] When seen against the Scottish ecclesiastical backdrop these words of Witherspoon are bravely ecumenical, for in those years there was fierce opposition towards any alleviation of the position of Roman Catholics in Scottish society. The British Government's tentative moves towards legislation that would bring about a measure of greater freedom for Roman Catholics to participate in positions of authority were still ten years away, and when the government's proposals were eventually made public there were riots in Edinburgh (1778) and in London (1780). Some of the most vociferous protests came from elements of the Popular party and the evangelical wing of the Church of Scotland.[4]

Lectures III to *VIII* develop the theme of 'The Truth of the Christian Religion'. As part of his preliminary examination of the subject Witherspoon allows that some truths may be found by reason, but that certain truths can only be discovered by revelation. He argues that man's consciousness of guilt is derived by reason and conscience, but that the concepts of repentance and forgiveness 'can never be determined but by an express revelation'. He sees guilt as a 'liableness to just punishment', but then says, 'now whether God will remit a punishment which he may inflict with justice must rest ultimately with himself, and no reasoning can decide upon it'.[5]

I can see a weakness in this argument, as a case can be made for the need for repentance being worked out by our reasoning powers. And by a further projection of thought, reason could lead us through the experience of being on the receiving end of forgiveness, or even in thinking in a pragmatic way to a realisation that the way to reconciliation with those whom we have wronged is to seek their forgiveness. Reason can lead to an appreciation of the need for repentance and the benefits of forgiveness to the forgiver and the forgiven at least in the temporal realm.

Naturally enough in these opening lectures to his divinity students, Witherspoon seeks to impress upon them the importance of learning, but to a certain extent he reduces the force of his later argument that repentance and forgiveness are the fruits of revelation rather than reason, when he says at the beginning of *Lecture II*,

> As to the importance of learning, there being no reason in this age to expect immediate or supernatural revelation, the acquiring a proper measure of knowledge by study and application is absolutely necessary.

Again, in his pressing for diligence in learning, he comes very close to following one of the Maxims for Moderates in his satirical pamphlet *Ecclesiastical Characteristics* when he says, 'A clergyman should be a man of liberal knowledge, and fit for the conversation and society of men of rank and letters'.[6] But in Maxim IV he mockingly gives this advice to the Moderate minister:

> A minister must endeavour to acquire a degree of politeness in his carriage and behaviour and to catch as much of the air and manner of a fine gentleman as he possibly can.

Again, he is nearer than he thinks to the Moderate preacher that he criticises in Maxim IV: 'His authorities must be drawn from heathen writers', when he writes:

> The necessity of revelation was acknowledged by many heathens in their writings. Of these the sayings of Socrates to Alcibiades was a remembered example that it was reasonable to expect God would send one into the world to deliver men from ignorance and error and to bring them to a knowledge of himself.[7]

Witherspoon in *Lecture IV* compares the Christian revelation with 'other heathen revelations' and declares:

> that with respect to purity, consistency, sublimity, dignity and every excellence which a manifestation of the true God must be supposed to have, the Christian religion is superior to every other.

It is significant that Witherspoon sees that the unique feature of the Christian religion is that 'it is the only one that gives a clear and consistent account of human depravity and traces it to its very original source'.[8] Witherspoon might have come to the new world, to a land of opportunity and freedom and the hope of a new beginning, but he came heavily laden with the baggage of the Calvinistic view of the total depravity of man. Others in attempting to single out what makes the Christian religion unique might have fixed on the new understanding of God as given by Jesus Christ; or the primacy of love as embodied in Jesus Christ; or the vision of man as one who will come to know life in all its fullness through following Jesus Christ; but to see the Christian religion's uniqueness in its account of the depravity of man, says more about Witherspoon than the Christian religion. Witherspoon believes that 'the actual state of the world and the present condition of man is very convincing in the way of collateral or presumptive proof' of the doctrine of man's depravity and as far as he is concerned, the fallenness of both the natural world and man within it is proved by the condition of both. In comparing the Christian religion with others, Witherspoon seeks to prove its claim for superiority by means of offering internal proof of its being agreeable to reason, and the external proof of the evidence of miracles and the credibility of witnesses.

Before going on to these proofs, Witherspoon's next lecture deals with the subject of 'The Person of Jesus Christ'. This lecture is remarkable for its brevity and its digression into a discussion of Lord Shaftesbury's views.

In Lecture VI Witherspoon deals with 'The Principal and direct evidence for the Truth of the Christian religion'. He prefaces this lecture with the words:

> A few circumstances of probability do but little, they gradually rise in strength by an addition to their number; but a direct proof, though single, if just, satisfies the mind.

This leads him to conclude that miracles come into the category of direct proof:

> In this view the proof of the truth of the Christian religion is the working of miracles. A supernatural power is the seal or sanction of a supernatural commission.[9]

He sees miracles coming into two categories: the fulfillment of *Old Testament* prophesies and the miracles performed by Christ. But before he deals with these, he tries to tackle Lord Shaftesbury's view of miracles. He quotes Shaftesbury as saying:

> Strange to make the altering of the course of nature a mark of Divinity when this is not so convincing and satisfying a proof of the

being and perfections of God, as the order and regularity of the course of nature.

Witherspoon attempts to counter this by saying that miracle is something that 'further shows the ability and power of God'. He then adds a personal illustration that reveals more about Witherspoon's autocratic nature than it answers Shaftesbury's argument when he says:

> I show my power in my family, by altering, as well as by giving my commands; and my property in my grounds by cutting down a tree when I have use for it in other service, as well as by planting it or pruning it.

He then goes on to make a plea for it being 'highly dangerous, manifestly unjust and inconsistent with the foundation-stone of all revealed religion' to bring our reason to bear upon what is to be judged as revelation, without which he says, we cannot be brought to a knowledge of God and our duty. He again has resort to Socrates's words to Alcibiades, this time quoting him fully: 'It is reasonable that God will come down into the world to teach us his will'.[10]

Witherspoon then goes on to praise the *Old Testament* prophecies: 'Their foreknowledge and foretelling of future events is one of the most satisfying of miracles and least liable to deceit'.[11] In this section of the lectures Witherspoon combines a remarkable naivety with a worldliness that makes me think that he has compartmentalised his knowledge into the world of scripture – which must be taken in a literal way and at face value – and the world of men where nothing is as it seems, and, because of the depravity of humanity, caution has to be exercised in judgement. A modicum of textual criticism, such as is found for example in John Taylor's *The Scripture Doctrine of Original Sin* (London, 1741), (which Witherspoon mentions disparagingly in his commentary on Maxim IV of *Ecclesiastical Characteristics*), might have prevented him from the kind of exegesis that brings such charges to his door.[12]

When Witherspoon turns to the miracles of Jesus he also displays a childlike simplicity when he says, 'his miracles were upon the plainest subjects – the winds, healing the sick, feeding the multitude, raising the dead'.[13] To imply that such miracles were not extravagant examples of power, or that the events described in the accounts of them were not remarkable is to say the least, approaching them in a very idiosyncratic way. He is expecting others to regard the miracles of Jesus, as he seems to do himself, with reason suspended, which of course he has in a previous lecture recommended. He clearly thinks of the miracles referred to above as simple demonstrations of the supernatural, and goes as far as to say that it would have been much easier for Jesus to have 'dazzled their eyes with the appearance of some extraordinary meteor in the airy regions than to have given them the proofs which he actually did'. Witherspoon clearly thinks that Jesus would have been capable of such an act, but that he (Jesus), in the miracles referred to, had already given sufficient proof of his powers.

In *Lecture VII* Witherspoon concerns himself with what he calls 'The consequential proofs of the truth of the Christian religion'. Its truth is proved by: 'Its progress; Its valuable effects; The visible fulfillment of scripture prophesies'. He sees the spread of the *Gospel* message and its progress throughout the world as 'very powerful evidence of its divine original'. He sees the valuable effect of the Christian religion in helping spread knowledge and practice of better conduct by Christians. He has reservations about those 'divines who affirm that all human science is to be found in the *Bible* – natural philosophy, astronomy and chronology' and says that this is going too far. But he reasserts the valuable contribution of the 'sacred penmen' who have written much about the creation of the world and its history and claims that they were prevented from absurdities and contradictions by the direction of an infallible guide. But when he comes to illustrate the truth of the Christian religion by the practice of the Christians he rather facilely resorts to quoting: 'See how these Christians love one another'. He concludes this 'proof' with the claim that the manners of men are greatly improved, even when they are not sanctified. Any astute divinity student might well have thought to counter these claims by citing the internecine warfare engaged in by the leaders and teachers of the Church over the centuries on matters of doctrine or practice or liturgy; or, just as bad, the wars against peoples of other religions perpetrated in the name of the Church and fought by Christians. But such was the magisterial authority of a teacher like Witherspoon, that his argument would remain unchallenged even when it seemed to defy the known facts of history.[14]

When Witherspoon turns to consider the third of what he calls 'The consequential proofs of the truth of the Christian religion: the visible fulfillment of scripture prophesy', he takes up the theme that there are some prophesies which not only had their completion in Christ but continue to be fulfilled in the present state of the world. To support his argument he cites Patrick Delany's *Revelations examined with candour* (1732).[15] Delany features the story of Ishmael, the son of Abraham by his wife's maid Hagar, of whom *Genesis* 16.12 says: 'And he will be a wild man; his hand will be against every man and every man's hand will be against him'. Witherspoon uses Delany's argument that the *Genesis* prophesy is still being fulfilled today, for, 'the posterity of Ishmael, who settled in Arabia, are the wild arabs, a people in a state of opposition to all the neighbouring nations'. What a weak argument, and from a source that was at least over thirty years out of date. Witherspoon goes on to use as an illustration of the fulfillment of the scripture prophesies, 'the history and present state of the Jewish nation'. Referring to the prophesy of the destruction of Jerusalem made by Jesus, he comments that it was 'so distinct and so particular that it is not easy to imagine anything to exceed it … when we compare the event with it'. He claims that what has happened to the Jews in subsequent years is so unique:

> that it appears quite supernatural, as if they were prepared by providence to prove the truth of the Messiah, and to wait till their conversion shall crown the work and be as scripture says 'life from the dead'.

Witherspoon goes to extreme lengths to assert the hand of providence in bringing about the fulfillment of prophesy. He claims that Titus Vespasian, whom he describes as 'one of the mildest men that ever commanded an army', did not intend to destroy the Jewish Temple. Nevertheless, 'the supreme order of Providence seemed to be forcing into its own service every apparent instrument', so that Vespasian's own inclination to preserve the temple was to no purpose, for God had said it should be destroyed. In this instance scholarly *Biblical* and historical interpretation has become subservient to an enthusiasm for the idea of an overarching and manipulative Providence.[16]

When Witherspoon turns to the prophesies in the *New Testament* book of *Revelation* he focuses on the anti-Christ, who oddly enough, is not mentioned by name in a book which is much used to elaborate on the nature of Christ's opponent. It is only in the *Letters of John* (*I John* 2.18,22; 4.3 and *2 John* 2.7) that the term anti-Christ is used. He refuses to speculate on the extravagant imagery of *Revelation,* although he allows for its providing 'accurate parallels and analogies' and distances himself from those Protestants who identify the Pope with the anti-Christ. In this case he displays a much more accurate exegesis and while going along with *2 Thessalonians* 2.4's description of a possible anti-Christ, prefers to define anti-Christ as 'the anti-Christian spirit in every Church'. However, he cannot resist bringing into the argument:

> a late opinion advanced by Messrs. Glas and S - viz that an established Church is Anti-Christ, that whatever has the approbation and authority of the civil government in any state interposed in its belief, not only may but must be contrary to the gospel.

Although he does offer the comment that 'this is carrying matters to excess', Witherspoon is still smarting from the wounds he suffered in the battles he fought within the established Church of Scotland. Yet what is again lacking within this section that purports to deal with the fulfillment of prophesy, is a detailed exegesis of scripture.[17]

Witherspoon concludes this lecture with a brief look at the objections to the Christian Religion. It has to be said that although he sets out some of the objections to the Christian religion, he does not properly deal with them. He says that the objections: 'that reason is a sufficient guide to truth and happiness therefore revelation is unnecessary', and that 'miracles are impossible and incredible', have already been dealt with. But in truth, he dealt with neither of these objections in a thorough way. He then states a third objection: that 'the Christian Religion lacks universality'; and its corollary that:

> if the Christian revelation was necessary, why was it not given earlier, say at the beginning of the world, why was the world left in darkness so long?

But all that Witherspoon offers in response to this objection is this:

> The true and proper answer to every such question is to resolve it into the sovereignty of God. He hath a right to bestow his mercies in the time, manner and measure, that seem good to himself.[18]

To use quite untheological language, what a 'cop-out' to hide behind the concept of the sovereignty of God!

It is clear from such an answer, that Witherspoon has little sympathy for those who experience genuine puzzlement over some doctrines of the Christian Religion. He dismisses without any consideration the genuinely felt objections of those who wonder why God should save some and condemn others. He maintains that it is:

> the great and fundamental doctrine of the gospel that all men are under sin and liable to the divine wrath; and that sending Christ into the world is an act of sovereign grace. If therefore it be really mercy to those that are saved, no objection can be brought against it from the number or circumstances of those that perish.[19]

Witherspoon displays the then considered orthodox Calvinistic doctrine, and in this he is no different from many Christian ministers of the time, particularly within the tradition of the Church of Scotland. But his totally unyielding adherence to this 'orthodoxy' was in no way helpful to young men preparing to enter upon a ministry in a world that was legitimately questioning all matters in the light of the new discoveries that were being made in every realm of human endeavour. His refusal to allow for the discussion of these matters, to take time to tease out the basis of the objector's stance, is a retreat from the reality of the situation into which he was going to send his students upon their graduation. Here again I find evidence of Witherspoon's habit of keeping separate his theology from the real world in which he so ably functioned.

In the final part of this lecture he considers the objection that Christianity 'introduced into the world persecution for conscience sake which was before unknown'. He sees this argument as one that is 'easily refuted', then strangely argues that this charge against the Christian religion was inevitable because Jesus predicted it: 'Think not that I am come to send peace on earth; I came not to send peace, but a sword' (*Matthew* 10. 34ff). He explains these words as a product of Jesus's preternatural knowledge. He blames the Jews and the Gentiles for starting the persecution of the Church and for this has the evidence of the *New Testament*. But he then claims that:

> If the matter will be carefully looked into it will be found that it was the spirit of the world that persecuted the meek in Christ in every age.[20]

He completely ignores the persecution of Christians by Christians, such as in the bitter doctrinal disputes of the fourth and fifth centuries, or by the Roman Catholic Inquisition, or by some of the zealots of the Protestant Reformation. Witherspoon completely fails to look into the accusation for which at least a case can be made, that the Christian Church, if not having been responsible for introducing persecution for conscience sake, has actively engaged over many years in just such a practice. Witherspoon has been dismissive of there being any case to answer, and signally refused to acknowledge the Church's failings.

When Witherspoon turns to consider the Doctrine of the Trinity he is at his most dogmatic and offers little or no teaching that would increase a student's understanding. He begins by lashing about at 'Arians, Pelagians and Socinians', lumping them all together as those who overthrow 'the whole doctrine of redemption'. He has set out to expound two aspects of the Doctrine of the Trinity: the Unity of the Divine Nature and the Trinity of Persons in the Divine Essence. But all of this merges into the doctrine of redemption that is dependent on God. Witherspoon then retreats into the mystery, leaving his students no wiser than before he began. He writes:

The whole economy of our salvation teaches us the necessity of attending to and believing this doctrine; but I see neither necessity nor propriety in endeavouring to dip into the mode of it, and attempting to explain it. If it be a mystery and above our comprehension, every attempt to explain it must be, if not criminal, yet unsuccessful. ... The wisest way for us with regard to all revealed truth, is to receive it as revealed, not presuming to be wise above what is written.[21]

I cannot resist the comment that if Witherspoon had been lecturing to more mature students he would have been in real trouble, for anyone with any experience of life would have demanded more of him than that. Witherspoon claims that 'all objections to doctrine are reducible to one: 'that it is contrary to reason, absurd, inconceivable, or impossible'. The only reasonable argument put forward to counter this objection is when he writes, 'things may be above reason yet not contradictory to it'. But Witherspoon relies too much on the argument: Just because I cannot explain it, there is no reason to doubt it. It is a revelation, therefore accept it. He concludes with this advice: 'Be ready to receive with all humility the revelation of God upon this subject, just as he has been prepared to communicate it'.[22]

Witherspoon next considers the proofs of the Trinity in general. He surprisingly uses the Trinitarian Blessing used in the Service of Baptism as a proof. He also cites *I John* 5.7 'For there are three that bear record in heaven, the Father, the Word and the Holy Ghost and these three are one'.[23] On these two flimsy premises he rests his case as if they are proofs of the truth of the Doctrine of the Trinity. One of them is from the later liturgy of the Church and not from *Scripture*, and the other from one of the latest of the *New Testament* books to be written, which is much influenced by the developments within the Church. Neither of these sources could be said to have anything near to the magisterial authority of any of the *Gospels*, or even any of the *Letters of Paul*, but Witherspoon seems content to offer it as such, thereby calling his judgement in question.

Witherspoon concentrates in the next two lectures on 'The proofs of the proper deity of the Son and the Spirit'. He adopts the 'proof text' method, which tends to ignore the context of the text and the contemporary purpose of the writer as long as the words of the text suit the purpose of the exegete. Quoting *Psalm 110* 'The Lord said unto my Lord. Sit thou at my right hand, until I make thine enemies thy footstool'. Without argument or any reference to the meaning of the text for the time in which and for which it was written, Witherspoon dogmatically asserts 'This must be understood of Christ'. He ignores the local and temporal application of the *Psalm* and uses the text quite without warrant as one of the proofs of the deity of Jesus Christ. He further produces texts to substantiate his claim that Jesus displays the attributes of God in his 'Immutability' (*Hebrews* 1.10); 'Omniscience' (*John* 16.30 *and* 2.17 and oddly *1 Kings* 8.39); 'Omnipresence' (*Matthew* 18.20); 'Omnipotence' (*Colossians 1.17*; *1 John* 1.3; *Hebrews* 1.2).[24]

Witherspoon adopts the same method when he considers the 'Proofs of the divinity of the Holy Spirit'. He tries to establish the personality of the Holy Spirit claiming that he is properly a person or substance and not merely a power. His claim for the personhood of the Holy Spirit relies on three texts: *John* 14.16; 16.13 and *1 Corinthians* 12.4. These texts do not, by any stretch of the imagination, provide any basis for an argument for the personhood of the Holy Spirit, and rather than attempt to develop his case from the texts, Witherspoon shifts to a linguistic argument to substantiate his claim that a person is being referred to. This also fails to impress and the lecture, one of the shortest in the series, closes abruptly.[25]

The opening words of his lecture on 'The Decrees of God' prove to be its keynote. Paraphrasing *Job* 11.7 Witherspoon says, 'Can anyone by searching find out the almighty?' and comments: 'if the nature of God has something in it altogether unsearchable to us, so must also his decrees'. Then follows a passage that clearly outlines Witherspoon's attitude towards what he regards as the decrees of God, and also, equally clearly, the attitude that he expects his students to adopt. He writes:

> Our great wisdom consists in receiving, admitting, remembering and applying whatever is clearly revealed in scripture, with regard both to the nature and government of God; at the same time, *we ought to restrain an impatient curiosity and guard against any unnecessary, inexplicable and hurtful questions on these subjects.* [My emphasis.][26]

Witherspoon is closing the door on theological enquiry. He is asking for acceptance without question, for a quiescent conformity to what is given and a stilling of an entirely natural curiosity to learn more. He continues:

> If it seemed necessary to God to reveal the universality of his providence, and the certainty of his purpose, we ought without doubt to believe and improve it. On the other hand, let us not presume to go any further than he hath pointed out the way. *Whatever he hath covered with a veil, it would be rashness and impiety to attempt to penetrate.* It is therefore my design to state this matter to you in a precise and scriptural a manner as I am able, although I must

necessarily use several of the theological systematical phrases, because without them the various opinions would neither be sifted nor explained. [My emphasis.]

I must confess that I was hugely disappointed when I read these words, for they are in direct contrast to the driving, dynamic, willing to explore new ground and experiences attitude that so characterises Witherspoon in so many of the dramatic episodes of his life outwith the College of New Jersey. Both in Scotland and in America he engages in the kind of activity both physical and intellectual that he seems here to want to deny, both to his students and himself, when working within the theological sphere. It seems that at this stage in his development he would rather have his students become disciples than interpreters, mouthpieces for the words of scripture rather than those who have striven to understand it and expound it from their own experience of it. Taking the attitude that is introduced in this passage, his students could only become indoctrinated followers, as against evaluators and mediators of the Christian message in terms appropriate for a new age. This kind of teaching is another example of a man who at this stage in his life keeps his knowledge in separate compartments. There can be no spilling over of his theology or scriptural understanding into other areas of knowledge, like history, or agriculture, or money, or politics, or education, or even the day to day acquisition of an understanding of human nature as it presents itself through the people that we meet, to all of which he applied his not inconsiderable intellect.

Continuing the subject of the Decrees of God in *Lecture XIII*, Witherspoon very briefly mentions the philosophy of Leibniz by means of a summary, but offers no critique. In *Ecclesiastical Characteristics* Maxim VI, he had mocked the Moderates for their devotion to Leibniz's optimistic theories.[27] Following his excursion into Leibniz, Witherspoon again retreats behind the safety of the doctrine of the Sovereignty of God. On this occasion however he is half apologetic for doing so, and asks his students for their patience, confessing that when he was their age he too found it difficult 'to see the necessity of subjecting ourselves to the divine sovereignty, and making use of it to restrain and repress rash and curious enquiries'. He alludes to John Milton's picture of hell as a place where 'the damned torment themselves with unsearchable questions, fixed fate, foreknowledge absolute ...' and concludes: 'There is a vast number of things in which we must needs resolve the last question, so to speak, into the sovereignty of God'.[28] Again we find Witherspoon avoiding the rigour of full debate, and seeking refuge behind an inscrutable doctrine. Yet there is in his apology to his students, an apparent unease about his advice to them to restrain and repress something as natural as curiosity. Despite his official and overt advice, I suspect that there was the beginning of a disquiet in Witherspoon's mind at the path he was advocating. He was perhaps just becoming aware of the tension between the methodology he adopted in his theological studies and the free spirit of enquiry he adopted when exploring secular subjects. Perhaps too, he was experiencing the tension between what he was expected to believe as one who subscribed to the Westminster *Confession of Faith* and what his reason was suggesting that he might believe if he followed it to its logical conclusion. It is perhaps significant that he refers to the *Confession of Faith* in the final passage of this lecture and that he does so with a peculiar form of words:

> It does *not appear difficult* to me to believe precisely in the form of our *Confession of Faith*; to believe both the certainty of God's purpose, and the free agency of the creature. Nor does my being unable to explain these doctrines form an objection against one or the other. [My emphasis.][29]

It would have sounded more convincing had he said, 'It is not difficult for me to believe'. But by saying it the way he does, his words can be given the meaning: although it does not appear difficult to believe, in reality it is difficult. In addition his second sentence carries the hidden message that he is aware of a weakness in his argument. This statement at the end of his lecture is perhaps indicative that Witherspoon is beginning to waver in his hitherto unequivocally 'orthodox' stance.

However, Witherspoon seems restored to his former certainty in his next lecture entitled 'The Covenant Works and the Fall of Man'. Witherspoon opens by referring to the fall of the angels which he alleges took place before the fall of man. From the use that he makes of the angels' story that many today would see as peripheral, it is clear that Witherspoon takes it in a literal way, and as part of the historical and metaphysical framework within which the fall of man takes place.

The two stories of the angelic rebellion which are found in *Revelation* 12.7-9; and *Jude* 1.6ff. differ from each other considerably. In *Revelation* when the angels are cast out of heaven by God they fall down to earth, but in *Jude*'s version they fall into the torments of hell. The *Revelation* story loses its relevance to the Adam and Eve story because its author seems to intend it to relate to the dragon, that is, the serpent, Satan's attack on Mary the mother of Jesus and therefore has nothing to do with the Genesis story of the fall of man. Witherspoon's use of these stories shows his apparent inability, or his unwillingness, to discern the difference between historical fact, and myth or allegory. He adopts a literalist stance to these *Biblical* texts, indeed in his account of the temptation of Eve this is particularly obvious:

> Eve is said to have been tempted by the serpent, and by many passages of scripture [not listed] it is put beyond doubt that it was the devil, a prince of fallen angels. *It ought not to be understood allegorically.* Probably he made use of this creature as the fittest form in which he could appear. [My emphasis.][30]

At times I find Witherspoon's comments displaying a naivety that seems to be quite out of character. One explanation might be that he has, as it were, bought into a system that outlines a whole scheme of Redemption from Creation to Resurrection, and that he is so convinced by the overall design of the idea that he avoids quibbling over the internal pattern and detail of it. He therefore accepts in a literal way the story of the fall of man as per *Genesis*, and instead of questioning the story to ascertain whether it should be understood as a piece of history that is to be accepted as factual, or an ancient myth or allegory that contains a truth about man, he tries to substantiate it by asserting that its truth is borne out by the state of corruption and wickedness which men are now in. His circular argument is completed when, referring to *Romans* 12.ff which he says explains that the present state of the world 'is the effect and punishment of Adam's first sin'. He then concludes that, 'man now comes into the world in a state of impurity or moral defilement'. As he considers the scriptural proof of original sin, he reveals his dark and negative view of his fellow men: 'The universal and early corruption of men in practice is a standing evidence of the impurity of their original'. His gloomy view of the world persists as he writes: 'What's the history of the world but the history of human guilt?' No one is exempt from the taint of Adam's sin:

> and do not children from the first dawn of reason, shew that they are wise to do evil but to do good they have no knowledge?

Such thoughts lead Witherspoon naturally to Augustine, the great perpetrator of the Doctrine of Original Sin, but instead of raising the issues that arose from Augustine's deliberations, for example, the state of the unbaptised infant, he again dodges the questions of his students and changes the subject, by saying that Augustine said that, 'it was of more consequence to know how we are delivered from sin by Christ than as to how we derive it from Adam'.[31] I get the impression that again Witherspoon has avoided the awkward questions of his students. This feeling is further strengthened by his inclusion at the very end of the lecture of what seems to be an 'off the cuff' remark that introduces, then leaves unanswered, a very odd idea that may hark back to Leibniz's theory of monads. He writes:

> Many have supposed that the souls of all men that ever shall be, were created at the beginning of the world and gradually came to the exercise of their powers as the bodies came into existence to which they belong.[32]

The introduction of such an idea was perhaps a diversionary tactic to dispel thoughts of unanswered questions, after a very unsatisfactory dealing with a subject that had many implications for those who would be entering into the ministry of word and sacrament.

In *Lecture XV* that follows, 'Of Sin in general and its demerit; and Actual sin and its several divisions', Witherspoon gives a hint of a softening of his view on original sin when he writes: 'Some are of the opinion that original sin itself is voluntary, the corrupt bias from the corrupted frame not taking away the liberty necessary to moral action, and sin lying in the solicitation'. But he avoids further discussion of the subject that might have begun to tamper with his hallowed beliefs in Predestination and Election, for if there is liberty for moral action, the way is open to question both these beliefs. Towards the end of the lecture, Witherspoon returns to the subject, but he slams the door on any expectation of human beings being capable of improvement by means of 'the liberty necessary for moral action', when he says:

> Nothing is more plain from Scripture or better supported by daily experience than that man by nature is in fact incapable of recovery without the power of God specifically interposed.

Witherspoon had immediately before this quoted approvingly, from 'a minister of great piety and judgement', who once said to him:

> No man will cordially believe the doctrine of salvation by grace contained in our Catechism and Confession, unless he is born of God. I can shew by reason, that the fall of man, and the corruption of our nature is contained in the Scripture. I can shew that it is entirely correspondent with the course of nature and the system of Providence. But we need hardly expect that it will be received and approved till the pride of the heart is brought down, and the sinner laid at the footstool of divine mercy.[33]

The speaker, as does Witherspoon, makes the assumption that he is 'born of God' or he would not be believing what he does. What moral arrogance. What a lack of humility - to see your mission and method as being to reduce people to an acknowledgement of their sin so that they can then join you on the high moral ground of those who are 'born of God'. The sense of superiority to those who might not be 'born of God', could easily lead to the attitude that minimises explanation and demands acceptance, and could well account for Witherspoon's lack of readiness even to attempt an exploration of what might well be difficult subjects for the unconvinced, far less the unconverted.

This avoidance of dealing with the real questions and issues that concern the minds of thinking people is again in evidence when Witherspoon, who had promised at the beginning of *Lecture XV*, to deal with 'Actual Sin and its Several Divisions', refuses to consider the 'Filthiness of the flesh and the spirit' on the pretext that they are:

> occasional reigning sins. But as they have little difficulty in them, so the explanation of them is no way necessary to the explaining of evangelical truth, for which reason I will not discuss them.[34]

This could be dismissed as rather prudish, but I think that the cause of it is not found in the manners or the customs of the time, but rather more deeply in the personality of Witherspoon, who remains, for all his voluminous writings, a very private person who does not consciously reveal much about himself. We can only begin to build up a partial picture of the man from little unconscious moments like the one above, when the veil slips a little and reveals something of the inner personality. Is he a 'cold' or just a frightened man, afraid of the passions themselves, or afraid of finding out something about himself by discussing them, or even more so, by showing them?

In *Lecture XVI* he considers the 'Covenant of Grace'. He begins with the question, 'Was satisfaction or some atonement necessary?' but instead of attempting an answer, he poses the objection of those who wonder if God could have done otherwise, and again does not answer the question. Instead he accepts as an indisputable fact that God has demanded satisfaction, and then engages in a circular argument that this is so by quoting the very documents that he says have produced the doctrine as evidence of the fact. He does not make any attempt at corroboration, or applying common sense to what some might think of as a grotesque idea of God setting up our humanity with a basic flaw in it and then punishing us for that flaw.[35]

When Witherspoon considers the suffering and death of Christ, he poses the question: 'Can we suppose that such a measure would have been taken if it had not been necessary?' He makes the assumption that it was, and seeks to justify God's sacrifice of Christ because Christ was willing to make the sacrifice. He then moves on to ask: 'Whether it was necessary that the Redeemer or Mediator should be a divine person? Would a perfectly innocent angel not have done as well?' and answers:

> Perhaps this is one of the many questions in theology that are unnecessary or improper. It is sufficient to say that it appears either to have been necessary or best that one truly divine should make the satisfaction for sin, since it has been ordained by God who does nothing unnecessary.[36]

One can almost imagine Witherspoon adding at the conclusion of this argument *quod erat demonstrandum*. This kind of argument and proof is reminiscent of the medieval scholastics with their hypothetical questions and inconsequential answers that added absolutely nothing to the debate.

In *Lecture XVII*, the final lecture in the series being examined, Witherspoon, on the subject of the Covenant, this time calling it the Covenant of Redemption, is explaining that this is a covenant between the father and the son which some call the Covenant of Grace. But clearly this is a limited grace that does not extend to all men and women but only to the Elect. Witherspoon is of the belief that Christ died for the Elect. He writes:

> The Covenant of Grace is said to be more frequently made with men, with the house of Israel, with the chosen of God, with his people. It is a compact or agreement between God and elect sinners, to give freely, and of mere mercy, Christ to die for them, and with him a pardon of sin, and a right to everlasting life, together with the spirit of sanctification to make them meet for it; all of which the believer receives and accepts in the manner in which it is offered and rests his eternal state upon it.[37]

This lecture is more of a pronouncement than any attempt to enlighten and increase the understanding of students. Witherspoon is expounding a system not a faith, incidentally, a word he seldom uses. It is as if he is saying to his students: 'Here is the great scheme of God, do not question it, just accept it'. He seeks to justify what he sees as God's system by reiterating what he says it is about. He writes:

As to the constitution of the covenant, you see the first and leading idea of it is, free and unmerited mercy; that sinners had deserved to perish, that divine justice pronounced their condemnation. This must be at the foundation of the whole. It was for this reason that a Mediator was provided, and the Saviour is offered by God himself as the fruit of his love.

It is ironic that Witherspoon's last word on the subject of the Covenant of Grace should end with the word 'love', a word and a feeling that has been sadly lacking throughout all these 'Lectures on Divinity'. Throughout, he has been a man obsessed by putting across a system of belief, a set of governing ideas for a religion from which all elements of faith and love have been strained away. It is noticeable that Jesus is never mentioned without his title 'Christ'. Jesus does not emerge from these lectures as a person, but only as a figurehead - the Son, or as a functionary - the Mediator or - the Redeemer. As in Witherspoon's Sermons, it is difficult to find any mention of the human aspects of Jesus, so even in Lecture V, which is subtitled 'The Person of Jesus Christ', Witherspoon only deals with what he considers are the divine aspects of Jesus' nature.
It is perhaps significant that Lecture XVII comes to a conclusion with a digression into a discussion of the Moral Law. Witherspoon writes:

> But the moral law, as the unalterable rule of duty to creatures is antecedent to all covenants and cannot be affected by them ... The Moral Law as it requires obedience to the will, and conformity to the nature of God was binding on the angels before the creation of the world and will be the duty of holy angels and redeemed sinners after the resurrection.[38]

He then goes on to assess the Laws established by Moses, and in this he displays a surprisingly liberal view of what he calls the civil laws, observing that 'they are certainly not unalterable because they must be suited to the state of society'; strangely too, he allows for their 'allegorical interpretation'. But he returns to a severity of judgement when he considers the criminal code laid down by Moses. He regrets the departure from this criminal law, as these laws are:

> founded on so much wisdom that it is a question whether the departure from them in punishing crimes has ever been attended with advantage; as for example in regard to violence, the law of retaliation an eye for an eye and a tooth for a tooth; in theft, and fraud, restitution; and the punishment of adultery by death.

Here is Witherspoon 'red in tooth and claw' and such uncompromising morality is in keeping with his uncompromising theology.[39]

The overall impression left with me following this examination of Witherspoon's *Lectures on Divinity* is one of disappointment at what is missing from them. There is no attempt at providing a coherent Christology. There is no approach to understanding Jesus in the context of his humanity and the social and historical context of his time. There is no guidance as to the nature and composition of the *Bible* as a book. There is no relating of the themes that he attempts to explore to the work being done by other scholars and writers in the same field. There is no setting of the theological issues in the context of the time in which he was living. What comes across to me in these lectures is a man who has come to the work of a teacher and finds that he is not prepared for it. He is still acting as if he is a preacher who, enclosed in his elevated pulpit, is protected from the possibility of criticism and can naturally adopt a dogmatic rather than a discursive style. This all reads as very negative comment, but as I hope to show, there will be a development both of the understanding and personality of Witherspoon that will be brought to the surface of his life by the events that lie in his future career.

CHAPTER 7

Lectures on Moral Philosophy

Witherspoon's *Lectures on Moral Philosophy* are divided into three sections: 'Ethics' (I-IX), 'Politics' (X-XIII) and 'Jurisprudence' (XIV-XVI).[1] At the conclusion of *Lecture XVI*, after a 'Recapitulation' he gives a list of books that would seem to be a course of further reading, for although some of the authors or works have been named in the body of the lectures there are many that are being mentioned for the first time. The range of authors and titles reveals the wide reading of Witherspoon and his desire to encourage that same habit in his students. This compensates for Witherspoon's style of lecturing where he often seems only to give a rather cursory acknowledgement of other scholars' views before pressing on with his own argument.

Although the quality of the discourses is vastly superior to his earlier *Lectures in Divinity*, there remains a trace of his reluctance to leave behind the reasoning that was so evident in them. He begins the first lecture by defining the nature of 'Moral Philosophy' and outlining his own approach to it:

> Moral Philosophy is that branch of science which treats of the principles and laws of duty or morals. It is called Philosophy because it is an enquiry into the nature and grounds of moral obligation by reason as distinct from revelation.[2]

Witherspoon then concedes the truth of the observation that 'If scripture is true, the discoveries of reason cannot be contrary to it;' and allows that 'there may be an illustration and confirmation of the inspired writing from reason and observation which will greatly add to their beauty and force'.[3] He acknowledges that just as advances have been made in natural philosophy in the last century, (the seventeenth) the same should be expected of moral philosophy, which he says 'is nothing else but the knowledge of human nature'. But he then goes on to set parameters for that understanding of human nature that is to be pursued by moral philosophy by introducing a concept that comes not from reason but from revelation:

> The principles of duty and obligation must be drawn from the nature of man. That is to say, if we can discover how his Maker formed him, or for what he intended him, that certainly is what he ought to be.[4]

Here, Witherspoon is making the assumption that the moral philosopher has to accept as given: a Maker, and a creature who was made then became deformed, and for whom a purpose had been set. Right at the beginning of this course, Witherspoon is putting a restriction on the exploration of the subject by reason alone. He is not starting his enquiries with a *tabula rasa* but is making the assumption that the starting point in the examination of the nature of man is man in his fallen state. He is making the further assumption that 'human depravity will have caused man to deviate from what his true nature is'. Therefore the moral philosopher is being asked to take into account a view of man that has not been determined by reason, but by what Witherspoon considers as revelation, the very factor, that he had stated at the beginning of his lecture, that is not part of the basis of enquiry of the moral philosopher.

In this opening lecture, although a concession is being made to the place of reason, Witherspoon seems reluctant to allow it free rein, and displays an over-readiness to assert the primacy of revelation. However, one surprising statement is made about the nature of the *Bible* which Witherspoon concedes: 'was never intended to teach us everything', and he further allows for the temporal and temporary nature of some of its teachings when he writes:

> the political law of the Jews contains many noble principles of equity; yet it was so local and peculiar that certainly it was never intended to be immutable and universal.[5]

This admission is one that could hardly have been made in the Scotland he had left behind, where it would certainly have alienated him from some of his contemporaries, but even in his new homeland, some would have taken a more literalist view of the immutability of the *Scriptures*. So in this area of his thinking, Witherspoon has given a greater place to reason than was in evidence in his *Lectures on Divinity*.

In his second lecture, Witherspoon makes the first mention of other scholars, among them, Shaftesbury, (Antony Ashley Cooper, 3rd Earl of Shaftesbury), Francis Hutcheson and Dr Samuel Clarke. Previously dismissive of both Shaftesbury and Hutcheson in *Ecclesiastical Characteristics*, these first mentions, however mildly, are granting the helpfulness of the thinking of these writers on the nature of 'virtue'. Witherspoon's reference to Dr Samuel Clarke is most surprising in that Clarke, late in his career had been accused of Arianism, although he was to perform a Galileo-like recantation when summoned before a Court Convocation in 1714.[6] Clearly, Witherspoon has come to see their views as less challenging to his own, and puts forward a very fair assessment, saying that Shaftsbury and Hutcheson see virtue, 'as being achieved by the control of the affections', whereas Clarke sees it achieved by 'understanding or reason', and allows, 'perhaps neither the one or the other is wholly right. Probably both are necessary'. He is even more forthright in his agreement with Hutcheson's listing of the acts of the will as 'desire, aversion, joy and sorrow', which Hutcheson qualifies by saying that the two last are superfluous. Witherspoon writes of this, 'he seems to be right' and goes on to state his own position that is now identical to Hutcheson's: 'All the acts of the will may be reduced to the two great heads of desire and aversion, or, in other words choosing and refusing'.[7]

Witherspoon's acknowledgement of the value of the contributions of Hutcheson, Shaftesbury and Clarke, is a measure of his broadening outlook and also of his perceptiveness of the writers who have made a significant contribution to the debate on 'virtue'. His good judgement is borne out by no less a person than Adam Smith, who in 1756, when in the process of writing *The Theory of Moral Sentiments*, cited as in some degree original thinkers: 'Mr Hobbes, Mr Lock and Doctor Mandevil, Lord Shaftsbury [*sic*], Dr Butler, Dr Clarke and Mr Hutcheson'.[8] That Witherspoon in his lectures should have approvingly used Hutcheson, Shaftesbury and Clarke as those against whom he should measure his own theories, is a tribute to his awareness of both the earlier and the contemporary work being done in the field of Moral Philosophy. In a later lecture, Witherspoon is found using Adam Smith's argument from justice as corroborative evidence for a belief in an afterlife, giving us yet another sign of his willingness to use the views of some of those whom, at an earlier stage in his life, he had condemned for their Moderate views.[9]

When Witherspoon turns to the subject of the perception of the senses, he relies heavily on Francis Hutcheson's teaching, although he does allow that:

> several distinguished writers have added as an internal sense, that of morality, a sense and a perception of moral excellence and our obligation to conform ourselves to it in conduct.

He asserts that:

> This moral sense is precisely what in Scripture and common language we call conscience. It is the law which our Maker has written upon our hearts and both intimates and enforces duty, previous to all reasoning.

He goes on to attack John Locke as one of 'the opposers of innate ideas and the law of nature' who are 'unwilling to admit the reality of the moral sense', and deems that their objections are 'wholly frivilous'.[10] But in doing this, although agreeing with Hutcheson's concept of an internal sense or a moral sense which has been deduced by reason, Witherspoon again introduces an element into his argument that stems from revelation and what he perceives to be the authority of *Scripture*. However, he seems to recover his initial intent to approach the teaching of Moral Philosophy by means of making it 'an enquiry into the nature and grounds of moral obligation as distinct from revelation' by asserting in the next lecture that reason can reveal God.

In *Lecture IV*, Witherspoon examines Virtue under three headings: 'The Nature of Virtue', 'The Foundation of Virtue' and 'The Obligation of Virtue'.[11] In the first, he sympathetically expounds the various explanations offered by Clarke, Hutcheson, Campbell and Smith, saying: 'there is something true in every one of them', but he is dismissive of Hume who 'annihilates the differences between natural and moral qualities'. It is when he is dealing with 'The Foundation of Virtue' that he makes the claim that:

> From reason, contemplation, sentiment and tradition; the Being and infinite perfection of God may be deduced, and therefore what he is, and commands, is virtue and duty.

Unfortunately, he does not follow up or substantiate this claim. Instead, he engages in a series of aphorisms and a digression that leads him to speculate (perhaps in illustration of the 'infinite perfection of God') on the perfection of the universe as God's creation as a result of Virtue being an act done 'for the good of the whole'. He writes:

> I believe the Universe is faultless and perfect, but I am unwilling to say it is the *best* possible system, because I am not able to understand such an argument, and because it seems to me absurd that infinite perfection should exhaust or limit itself by a created production.[12]

In this seemingly 'off the cuff' statement, he at once dissociates himself from the philosophical view of Leibniz, and re-introduces a theological concept that is derived not from reason but from revelation. Witherspoon is clearly not a utopian in his rejection of this being 'the best of all possible worlds'. Despite his Calvinism and its closed system of predestination, Witherspoon seems to believe in a continuingly creative God for whom the possibilities are infinite. In allowing for this, he seems to have been unaware of the contradiction at the very heart of his thinking. But again, as a moral philosopher, he has departed from a reliance on reason and based his argument on a theological premise. Further, he has still not brought forward evidence of proof that 'from reason, contemplation, sentiment and tradition the Being and infinite perfection of God may be deduced'. As the lecture concludes, Witherspoon again resorts to an argument based on a theological premise when he writes:

> We ought to take the rule of duty from conscience, enlightened by reason, experience, and every way by which we can be supposed to learn the will of our Maker, and his intention in creating us such as we are. And we ought to believe, that it [conscience] is as deeply founded as the nature of God himself, being a transcript of his moral excellence, and that it is productive of the greatest good.[13]

Lecture V that completes Witherspoon's discourse on 'Virtue', concentrates on:

> The Obligation of Virtue, or what is the law that binds us to the performance and from what motive or principles we ought to follow its dictates.[14]

Witherspoon begins by declaring that 'the obligation of virtue may be easily reduced to two general kinds, duty and interest'. He is heavily committed to 'duty' and sees it as far outweighing self-interest as the factor that produces a sense of obligation. However, he is not content to define duty in human terms, either as a duty to our own self to be the best we can be or as a duty to society. He projects these to the ultimate superior. He claims: 'If we attend to the dictates of conscience, we shall find evidently a sense of duty, of self-approbation and remorse, which plainly shows us to be under a law, and that law to have sanctions', concluding, as if it were a proof, 'what else is the meaning of the fear and terror and apprehensions of persons?' In declaring that human beings are 'under a law', he is implying that there is a law-maker, and in the next paragraph he unequivocally declares this law-maker to be a 'Divine Being', belief in whom, 'is certainly either innate and necessary or handed down from the first man, and can now be supported by the clearest reason'. Witherspoon has left the Moral Philosopher behind, forgotten his promise to show how, 'From reason, contemplation, sentiment and tradition the Being and infinite perfection of God may be deduced', and instead has reverted to the role of the Preacher, no doubt assisted by contemplation, sentiment and tradition, but presenting an argument devoid of reason, and in the end, merely declaring what he believes are the irrefutable certainties of the *Gospel*. This lecture is possibly the weakest of the first five lectures as far as Witherspoon's own philosophical arguments are concerned. In fairness, it is also a lecture in which he records the contrasting views of other philosophers, for example, Shaftesbury's abhorrence of the concept that a sanction should be attached to the obligation to virtue and that there should be any association of virtue with rewards and punishments in any afterlife. Witherspoon also makes an oblique reference to Adam Smith's argument that there could be a justification for a belief in an afterlife if only to compensate for the injustices of this life. Witherspoon's departure from addressing the nature of virtue on the basis of reason, is further emphasised by his unsupported assertion that:

> The belief in a Divine Being is certainly innate and necessary, or handed down from the first man, and can now be supported by the closest reason,

Witherspoon is again resorting to preaching, and compounds the error by following those words with the conclusion supplied without any supporting proof:

> and our relation to him not only lays the foundation of many moral sentiments and duties but completes the idea of morality and law, by subjecting us to him, and teaching us to conceive of him, not only as our Maker, Preserver, and Benefactor, but as our righteous Governor and Supreme Judge. As the being and perfections of God are irrefragably established the obligation of duty must ultimately rest here.[15]

I am reminded of an incident in Robert Burns's narrative poem 'Tam o' Shanter', when the hero Tam, carried away in a transport of delight at the exciting scene of witches dancing in Kirk-Alloway, 'tint his reason a' thegither!'[16] At this point in his lecture, Witherspoon 'lost it', and became the preacher enraptured with the fullness of the scene of a world he had conjured up, and whose every activity was within the providential care of God. Reasoning and philosophy had been abandoned, at least momentarily, for belief and theology.

The subject matter of *Lecture VI* may partly explain Witherspoon's lapse into theological mode toward the end of the previous lecture, for it begins with a topic that could just as well be placed in the context of a course in Theology. Witherspoon begins his next set of lectures, which he says are to be on Ethics, with a discussion on 'The State of Man' in relation to God, his fellow-creatures, in solitude or society, in peace or war, and in want or plenty; which he claims, 'lays a foundation for duty'. He also designates other 'States' which he labels 'Adventitious', or brought about by choice and the fruit of industry, viz. marriage, family, master and servant, profession, character and abilities.[17]

In setting out to explore the subject of man's duty to God, Witherspoon declares that: 'the proof of the being of God [is] the great foundation of all natural religion; without which the moral sense would be weak and insufficient'. He then goes on to assert that the proofs are of two kinds: *a priori* and *a posteriori*. The first is a metaphysical argument 'reasoning downward from the first principles of science or truth, and inferring by just consequence the being and perfections of God'. He then cites 'Clark[e]'s Demonstrations' as his source which he claims 'is as complete as anything ever published'.[18] He clearly approves of Clarke's argument in the paragraphs that follow, including what might be argued are the *non sequiturs* of the attributes of God, as 'omnipotent, omniscient, infinitely good, just, true'. He then goes on to describe 'the other medium of proof, commonly called *a posteriori*', which he says:

> begins with contemplating the universe in all its parts; observing that it contains many irresistible proofs, that it could not be eternal, could not be without a cause; that this cause must be intelligent, and from the astonishing greatness, the wonderful adjustment and complication of things, concludes that we can set no bounds to the perfection of the Maker, because we can never exhaust the power, intelligence and benignity that we see in his works.

Again, what might be termed the *non sequiturs,* are not queried, or further explanations offered to justify them; for example why should he or Clarke claim: 'we deduce the moral perfections of the Deity from the faint resemblances we see in ourselves?' Witherspoon seems too easily to accept the force of these arguments as expounded by Clarke, although he is perceptive enough to make the observation on the *a priori* and *a posteriori* arguments as they are used here, that:

> there is, perhaps at bottom, no difference between these ways of reasoning, because they must in some degree rest upon a common principle, viz. That everything that exists must have a cause.[19]

As he continues to discuss the impressions made on the mind by all that is seen, Witherspoon comments:

About this and some other ideas great stir has been made by some infidel writers, particularly David Hume, who seems to have industriously endeavoured to shake the certainty of our belief upon cause and effect, upon personal identity, and the idea of power.

But he offers no counter attack other than to say dismissively, 'It is easy to raise metaphysical subtleties, and confound the understanding on such subjects'.[20] He then tells of 'authors of Scotland' who have successfully answered the metaphysical objects of what he calls the infidel writers. From the context, it seems that Witherspoon might have had in mind Thomas Reid and his *An Inquiry into the Human Mind on the Principles of Common Sense* (1764), and possibly James Beattie whose *Essay on Truth* was published in 1770, and who, along with Reid and George Campbell, had been part of the coterie of philosophers who were members of the Aberdeen Philosophical Society in the years before Reid became Professor of Moral Philosophy in the University of Glasgow. Witherspoon's bias against the metaphysical, and his favouring of the common sense school of thought as exemplified by Reid, shows both in this passage, and in what might be called a recapitulation of his views, in his final lecture (*XVI*) when he writes:

> The evidence which attends moral disquisitions, is of a different kind from that which attends mathematics and natural philosophy; but it remains as a point to be discussed whether it is more uncertain or not. At first sight, it appears that authors differ much more and more essentially, on the principles of moral than natural philosophy. Yet perhaps a time may come, when men, treating moral philosophy as Newton and his successors have done natural, may arrive at greater precision. It is always safer in our reasonings, to trace facts upwards, than to reason downwards upon metaphysical principles.[21]

In closing this section, Witherspoon briefly discusses the idea of the universality of the belief in God as being derived from its being 'a universal dictate of our nature' and instances: 'Dr Wilson of Newcastle' as the advocate of a slant on that idea.

> He [Wilson] says that we receive all our knowledge, as philosophers admit, by sensation and reflection. Now from all that we see, and all the reflection and abstraction upon it we are capable of, he affirms it is impossible we could ever form the idea of a spirit or a future state. They have however been early and universal, and therefore must have been communicated at first [by God], and handed down by

information and instruction from age to age. So that, unless upon the supposition of the existence of God, and his imparting the knowledge of himself to men, it is impossible that any idea of him could ever have entered into the human mind.[22]

Witherspoon comments: 'There is something ingenious, and a good deal of probability, in this way of thinking'. In this remark, Witherspoon displays a willingness to learn from other philosophers as if acknowledging that he himself is not able to confute them.

Having presented the arguments for the existence of God, Witherspoon takes up the theme of the Nature of God, dealing in turn with the unity, spirituality, immensity, wisdom and power as his 'natural perfections'. In passing, he refers his students to 'Baxter's, *Immateriality of the Soul* as 'the best reasoning on the subject' [spirituality]. On 'immensity', he notes the Cartesian and Newtonian difficulties with 'spirituality' in relation to space and therefore the concepts of 'immensity', 'wisdom' and 'power' are dealt with perfunctorily. At this point, the lectures on Moral Philosophy have become a place for the expounding of theological ideas, with no awareness on Witherspoon's part of any sense of their inappropriateness.[23]

The theological as against the philosophical theme continues in the next lecture (*VII*), when Witherspoon goes on to consider 'The Moral Perfections of God', which are listed as 'holiness, justice, truth, goodness and mercy'.[24] His argument seems to proceed on the basis that all these things are found within the nature of men and therefore can be projected in a magnified way and attributed to God. For example, 'Holiness is that character of God to which veneration, or the most profound reverence in us, is the corresponding affection'; and:

> Justice seems to be founded on the strong and unalterable perception we have of right and wrong, good and evil, and particularly that the one deserves reward, and the other punishment. The internal sanction, or the external and providential sanction of natural laws point out the justice of God.

Truth is dealt with briefly as if it hardly needed to be argued that this would be one of the moral perfections of God: 'The truth of God is one of his perfections greatly insisted on by scripture, and an essential part of natural religion'. Witherspoon sees the creation as proof of the goodness of God. But like many who hold up the creation as proof of God's goodness, Witherspoon chooses to ignore the darker side of creation, 'nature red in tooth and claw', much of it part of a food chain in which the stronger eat the weaker.[25]

When Witherspoon comes to consider the mercy of God, he is at his most hesitant, and warns against any complacency, or over-expectancy of God's mercy:

> We must conclude, therefore, that however stable a foundation there is for other attributes of God in nature and reason, the way in which, and the terms on which, he will shew mercy, can be learned from revelation only.[26]

Witherspoon at times is clearly struggling to shake off the influence of long years of acceptance of the closed system of Calvinist belief. Part of him wants to believe in the possibility of mercy being extended by God, at least to the same degree of which most human beings are capable, but he is reluctant to infringe on the over-arching belief in the complete sovereignty of God to do as he sees fit.

This struggle is again seen in the next section of the lectures when he comes to consider 'Man's duty to God'. He begins by asking the prior question as to why should man obey God, and gives as the reasons: 'the divine sovereignty, omnipotence, infinite excellence, and original production and continual preservation of all creatures'. He presents no philosophical argument for these statements, preferring either to let them stand for themselves or with the occasional allusion to scripture or to some unnamed theological writer. He explores the argument from reason, that 'it is the law of reason that the wisest should rule', but objects that this does not seem wholly to satisfy the mind' because although 'one person is wiser than another ... it scarcely seems a sufficient reason that the first should have absolute authority'.[27]

Witherspoon then goes on to examine the duties that are owed immediately to God, which he subdivides into internal and external. The internal duties he lists as love, fear and trust and as to the external duties he then says: 'I shall briefly pass over, being only all proper and natural experiences of the internal sentiments'. He only singles out worship which he sees as a duty of natural religion. He does, however, take account of the objections raised by 'some of the enemies of revealed religion' who oppose worship on the grounds that no good man would either desire to be worshipped or take pleasure in others recording his good qualities. Witherspoon retreats into a defense of the duty of worship by weakly suggesting that we must not compare God with man. However, as an afterthought, he then deals with the duty of prayer, posing the questions:

> Why does God who perfectly knows all our wants, require and expect prayer before he will supply them? and Why should we pray when the whole system of divine providence is fixed and unalterable?

He is dissatisfied with 'Dr Leechman of Glasgow ['s]' response to these questions, and alleges that he (Leechman), makes no other answer than to offer that prayer has an effect on our minds. Witherspoon wants a greater certainty as to the efficacy of prayer, and concludes:

> However unable we may be to explain it notwithstanding the fixed plan of providence there is a real influence of second causes, both natural and moral, and I apprehend the connection between cause and effect is similar in both cases.

Witherspoon has again retreated into the mystery of the being of God and neither offers nor seems to see any reason to offer any explanation. His only attempt at explanation on the basis of reason is to posit an analogy: 'Thus in moral matters, prayer has as real an influence in procuring the blessing, as ploughing and sowing has in procuring a crop'.[28] After this theological digression, Witherspoon returns to a topic which he can be expected to deal with in terms of reason rather than resorting to revelation. *Lectures VIII* and *IX* consider 'Our duty to man' and 'Our duty to ourselves'.[29]

Witherspoon begins by declaring that the principle that governs our duty to men is 'love to others, sincere and active'. He distinguishes between 'particular kind affections, as to family, friends, country,' which 'seem to be implanted by nature'; and 'a calm and deliberate good-will to all', which he suggests is 'a dictate of our conscience of a superior kind' and not as some think just an extension of the 'particular affections'. Revealingly, he warns that 'wherever our attachments to private persons prevent a greater good, they become irregular and excessive'.[30] Is Witherspoon remembering how for a time, a very short time, in 1767, he was so intent on not upsetting his wife by accepting the Trustees' invitation to become President of New Jersey College, that he allowed his 'particular kind affections as to family' to restrain his own desire to take the post, causing him to oppose the pressure of those who wanted him to accept it because of what they deemed to be the 'greater good'? From the other side of that experience, he now suggests that the rule should be to put a restraint on 'particular kind affections' for the greater good of all. He then goes on to discuss the criticism made by 'some unbelievers' that 'the gospel does not recommend private friendships and the love of country'. But he says that the scripture does recommend 'all particular affections', and that it is to its honour that 'it sets the love of mankind above them every one, by insisting on the forgiveness of injuries and the love of enemies'. Witherspoon, although indicating that 'the love of our country ... is a noble and enlarged affection ... yet the love of mankind is still greatly superior', warns that:

> sometimes attachment to country appears in a littleness of mind, thinking all other nations inferior, and foolishly believing that knowledge, virtue, and valour are all confined to themselves.[31]

For all his enthusiasm for the new land of America and its striving after self-government and the building of its own structures and institutions, Witherspoon is aware of the dangers of a narrow nationalism that can blind people to the virtues that are still to be found in people of other nations.

It is at this point in these lectures on Moral Philosophy that the perspicuity of Witherspoon becomes more apparent. Throughout the earlier lectures, sometimes a rigour of thought has been lacking, and too often there has been a readiness to resort to a religious argument to the neglect of pursuing a philosophical one. Here, for the first time, he is adopting a more analytical and philosophical approach. I am well aware that Witherspoon insists that the only satisfactory basis of morality is religion, and that without religion, meaning the Christian religion, there is no prospect of achieving a truly moral stance or standard. But allowing for that, he still in the earlier lectures retreated, and I use the word advisedly, far too readily into a religious argument. Now, in this lecture, the features of his Moral Philosophy for which he has so rightly earned praise, come into view. It is also in this lecture that what were to become the driving forces of his later political activity are clearly revealed.

In dealing with 'rights' Witherspoon puts them into categories: natural and acquired, and perfect and imperfect. Natural rights are defined as 'such as are essential to man and universal'. Acquired rights are defined as those that are 'the fruits of industry, the effects of accident, or conquest'. Immediately he puts forward as an illustration:

> A man has a natural right to act for his own preservation, and to defend himself from injury, but not a natural right to domineer, to riches, (comparatively speaking) or to any particular office in a constituted state.[32]

In one sentence Witherspoon has laid the ground for the establishing of a democratic republic. Here are encapsulated the future reasons for throwing off the shackles of British rule, the rejection of the rights of the rich to patronage, and the denial of Monarchal authority.

Witherspoon then distinguishes between what he calls 'perfect and imperfect rights':

> Those are called perfect rights which can be clearly ascertained in their circumstances, and which we may make use of force to obtain when they are denied us.

Here, long before Witherspoon had fully entered into the struggle for America's independence, he was establishing the understanding that it was legitimate to physically fight for a 'perfect right' that was being denied. On the other hand, 'imperfect rights are such as we may demand, and others ought to give us, yet we have no title to compel them'. He goes on to say that certain 'rights are alienable and [others are] unalienable'. Here we have a use of a concept that found its way into *The Declaration of Independence*, which Witherspoon had a hand in drafting, or at least amending, approving in Congress, and eventually signing it. The second paragraph of the *Declaration* asserts: 'We hold these truths to be self evident, that all men are created equal, that they are endowed by their Creator with certain *unalienable rights*, that among these are Life, Liberty and the pursuit of Happiness'.[33] In the course of explaining the nature of an 'unalienable right', Witherspoon asserts:

> There are several things which he cannot give away, as a right over his own knowledge, thoughts &c. others which he ought not, as a right to judge for himself in all matters of religion, his right of self-preservation, provision &c.

In this assertion of the right of conscience and religious liberty, Witherspoon is again anticipating the spirit that affected the tone of the *Declaration* that mooted a society whose government's powers 'were derived from the consent of the governed'. In this section of the lectures is the observation that later would have significance; 'Some say that liberty is unalienable, and that those who have even given it away may lawfully reclaim it'. Here in this lecture are the seeds of revolution and a justification of its legitimacy.[34]

Witherspoon then turns to expound 'Our duty to others', which he sees as 'comprehended in these two particulars, justice and mercy'. Justice is defined as:

permitting others to enjoy whatever they have a perfect right to, and making such an use of our own rights as not to encroach upon the rights of others.

Mercy, which he says belongs to the category of imperfect rights, 'is generally explained by a readiness to do all the good offices to others that they stand in need of and are in our power'.[35]

He concludes his section on Ethics in *Lecture IX* with a dissertation on 'Our duty to ourselves', which he divides into 'self-government and self-interest'. The key to self-government is moderation in our indulgences. Witherspoon says that we will be required to moderate our self-indulgence if it interferes with our duty to God, to ourselves and to our neighbour. If we achieve this, we will help generate the virtues of humility, contentment and patience. He offers a caution against excessive indulgence of any passion, 'love, hatred, anger, fear'; such indulgence he goes as far as to call 'an evil instead of a blessing'.[36] This is revealing of an aspect of Witherspoon's personality. He seems a man who finds it hard to be loving towards his wife and his children, or at least to express that love in a natural way. I want in a later chapter to look at this more fully, but for the moment three examples of this trait will suffice. In the various references to his wife, she is always 'Mrs. Witherspoon', and in a letter to his son David, he addresses the young man more in the manner of Polonius, more pompous adviser than loving father. It is as if he does not want to 'discompose' himself by indulgence in any display of passion. But even more revealing, is what seems to have been an almost total lack of response to the deaths of his children, the five who died before he left Scotland and James who was killed at the Battle of Germantown. Witherspoon seems to comfort himself for this lack of passionate indulgence by saying that it will bring about the need for 'continence, self denial, fortitude, restraint, and moderation in everything how goodsoever'. As this list is perused, one cannot help but see a life that is being held back from a fuller expression of its humanity.[37]

Self-interest is then examined as a duty to ourselves. It is perhaps significant that Witherspoon sees as important 'our relation to the Divine Being', and of 'attending particular to ... procuring his favour'. He counsels guarding against 'anything that may be harmful to our moral character or religious hopes'. To this end:

we are therefore to take all proper methods to preserve and acquire the goods both of mind and body. To acquire knowledge, to preserve health, reputation, possessions, always however being careful in these acquisitions to guard against 'interfering with the rights of others'. Witherspoon then engages in a long digression into the cardinal virtues, which he lists as, 'justice, temperance, prudence and fortitude'. He concludes this section with a reference to 'the Stoical position, that pain is no evil, nor pleasure any good', which he says arises from:

> comparing external things with the temper of the mind, when it appears without doubt, that the latter is of much more consequence to happiness than the former.

He clearly approves of the Stoics, concluding: 'There was something strained and extravagant in some of their writings, and perhaps ostentatious, yet a great deal of true and just reasoning'.[38] Some of the austerity that Witherspoon seems to advocate may have its roots in this admiration for the Stoics.

This section on Ethics concludes with a consideration of morality as 'conformity to a law which either commands, prohibits or permits an action'. Witherspoon writes:

> Commanded duties oblige absolutely, and as casuists used to say, *semper non vero ad semper*; that is to say, they are obligatory upon all persons at the seasons proper to them, but not upon every person at every time.

However:

> Prohibitions oblige *semper et ad semper*, all persons at all times. We must not lie - This obliges every man at every moment, because no time or circumstances can make it lawful.

When permitted actions are considered, it becomes clear that Witherspoon is impatient with the concept, and will not allow it as a legitimate guidance for action, concluding:

> The truth is, when we consider the morality of action in a strict and proper manner, the whole class of permitted actions vanishes. They become by their intention and application either good or bad.

It is as if Witherspoon has grown tired even of his own argument which has bordered on the casuistical, and comes down hard on himself by saying that

137

actions are either commanded or prohibited, and any attempt at allowing the middle way of permitted action is dismissed.

As Witherspoon winds up this last lecture on Ethics, he deals with what might be seen as afterthoughts, or as tidying up, by mentioning subjects he had meant to include in an earlier lecture. More and more the lecture resembles lecture notes as he perfunctorily deals with such topics as, 'the mistaken conscience that does not wholly absolve from guilt'; or 'the reasons as to why people attend public executions'. He also returns to the subject of 'private affections' saying that:

> sympathy is a particular affection in aid of benevolence, yet like all other private affections, when it is not moderated, it prevents its own effect. One deeply affected with the view of an object of distress, is often thereby incapacitated to assist him.

Perhaps there speaks the Minister, who although feeling great sympathy for the bereaved, has to moderate it, and not be overcome by it, if he wishes to be of help at a funeral service. This lecture ends with Witherspoon returning to an old subject, 'The Stage', and we see that his attitude is unchanged since he wrote his pamphlet of that title in 1757, and joined in the chorus that condemned John Home's play *Douglas*. In his final words of the lecture he expresses his long held opinion that 'the stage [is] the greatest enemy to virtue and good morals'.[39]

Witherspoon then goes on to deal with his next subdivision of Moral Philosophy in four lectures on 'Politics' which he says, 'contain the principles of social union, and the rules of duty in a state of society'. He begins by considering man's state before he formed society, and defines this as his being 'in a state of nature'. He dissociates himself from Thomas Hobbes who had described the state of nature as being a state of war, and equally distances himself from Shaftesbury and Hutcheson, who, he says, plead strongly 'that a state of nature is a state of society'.[40] Witherspoon's view is more aligned to that expressed by John Locke in his *Two Treatises of Civil Government* in which he writes:

> To understand political power aright, and derive it from its original, we must consider what estate all men are naturally in, and that is, a state of perfect freedom to order their actions, and dispose of their possessions and persons as they think fit, within the bounds of the law of Nature, without asking leave or depending upon the will of any other man.
>
> A state also of equality, wherein all the power and jurisdiction is reciprocal, no one having more than another, there being nothing

more evident than that creatures of the same species and rank, promiscuously born to all the same advantages of Nature, and the use of the same faculties, should also be equal one amongst another … [41]

Witherspoon goes on to muse about this freedom and comments: 'Reason teaches natural liberty and common utility recommends it'. But he then reveals how he has not fully entered sympathetically into Locke's thinking when his musing causes him to open up the question of 'Slavery'. As he puts it rather hesitantly, 'Here perhaps we should consider a little the question, Whether it is lawful to make men or to keep them slaves, without their consent?', and the next part of the sentence reveals just how far away from Locke he really is when he writes:

> this will fall afterwards to be considered more fully, in the meantime, observe, that in every state there must be some superior and others inferior, and it is hard to fix the degree of subjection that may fall to the lot of particular persons.

Witherspoon seems to be implying that it is part of the natural state for some to be superior and some inferior, and opens the door for an understanding that slavery might be entered into by consent, when he writes: 'Men may become slaves or their persons and labour be put wholly in the power of others *by consent*' (My italics).[42] To use the phrase 'by consent' to describe the action of man yielding up his freedom to become another man's slave, is to go against all that John Locke has so fervently asserted:

> Freedom, then, is not what Sir Robert Filmer tells us: 'A liberty for everyone to do what he lists, to live as he pleases, and not to be tied by any laws'; but freedom of men under government is to have a standing rule to live by, common to everyone of that society, and made by the legislative power erected in it. A liberty to follow my own will in all things where that rule prescribes not, not to be subject to the inconstant, uncertain, unknown, arbitrary will of another man, as freedom of nature is to be under no other restraint but the law of Nature.
>
> This freedom from absolute, arbitrary power is so necessary to, and closely joined with, a man's preservation, that he cannot part with it but by what forfeits his preservation and life together. For a man, not having the power of his own life, cannot by compact or his own consent enslave himself to any one, nor put himself under the absolute arbitrary power of another to take away his life when he

pleases. Nobody can give more power than he has himself, and he that cannot take away his own life cannot give another power over it.[43]

Witherspoon further reveals how much he is still under the influence of Calvinist thinking on the predetermined state of man, when he writes of 'the degree of subjection that may fall to the lot of particular persons', and how, in continuing to think along these theological lines, he cannot fully enter sympathetically into Locke's ideas of the free and equal status of men.

As Witherspoon proceeds further into his digression into the subject of slavery, even more of his equivocal stance in this matter is disclosed: 'Upon the whole, there are not only many unlawful ways of making slaves, but also some that are lawful'. and then, rather tamely, he adds, 'And the practice seems to be countenanced in the law of Moses'. But the ever-present pragmatism of Witherspoon comes fully to the surface when he says, 'I do not think there lies any necessity on those who found men in a state of slavery to make them free, to their own ruin'.[44] In these words, he offers a sop to those who have purchased or inherited plantations that are dependent on slave labour, and at the same time, a way out for himself. He seems to have used slaves on his own extensive property of Tusculum, there being two slaves listed and valued at $200 in the inventory of his property at his death.[45] Perhaps more to the point, his compromise or equivocation on the issue of slavery might well have been because he was lecturing in a college many of whose students came from the southern states, and whose fathers paid their fees from estates or plantations largely worked by slaves. On this occasion, Witherspoon has sacrificed principle to what he sees as accepted and acceptable practice as well as an established and scripturally authenticated belief. He has abandoned philosophy for a theology that sees it as preordained that some are elected to a superior role while others are allotted to an inferior place according to God's will. Metaphysics which in other parts of these lectures he has decried, is suddenly brought into the argument when his philosophical inadequacies have let him down.

Witherspoon further displays a narrowness of vision when he turns to the issues of 'Property'. In contrast to John Locke, he deals with the concept very largely in material terms: man's rights of property over the animals, and man's rights to private property in terms of goods. Then in a series of very weak arguments he seeks to justify man's right to property:

> Without private property no laws would be sufficient to compel universal industry ... . There is no reason to expect in the present

state of human nature that there would be a just and equal distribution to every one according to his necessity, nor any room for distinction according to merit ... . There would be no place for the exercise of some of the noblest affections of the human mind, as charity, compassion, beneficence &c ... . Little or no incitement to the active virtues, labour, ingenuity, bravery, patience &c.[46]

All of these statements are unsupported by argument of any kind. But strangely, Witherspoon fails to deal with the most important property that is held by man - his life. In this respect Witherspoon has entirely departed from the way in which John Locke approached the subject when he wrote: 'every man has a 'property' in his own 'person'. This nobody has a right to but himself'.[47] In neglecting this aspect of 'property', Witherspoon paradoxically is narrowing down the field of thought for his students by a concentration on the material rather than the metaphysical, a concept he had so recently reintroduced in his immediately previous argument.

The lecture concludes with a brief mention of Sir Thomas Moore's *Utopia* in which he laid down schemes for making property common. Witherspoon dismisses this as 'chimerical and impractical'. He does allow that the Spartan experiment in which goods were held in common 'subsisting for so long, remains a phenomenon for politicians and reasoners yet to account for', suggesting that perhaps it might have worked for a time because of the smallness of the state.[48]

Lectures XI and *XII* are given over to a discussion of social life which Witherspoon puts into the categories of 'Domestic and Civil Society'. He deals with Domestic Society under three headings: Marriage, Parents and Children, and Masters and Servants. Following John Locke, he points out how:

> Human creatures at their birth are in a state weaker and more helpless than any other animals ... and need by far more assistance and cultivation. Therefore a particular union of the parents is absolutely necessary, and that upon such powerful principles as will secure their common care.

He sees marriage as fostering 'the public good' by offering a stable and secure environment for the nurture of children. As he approaches what he would consider as the delicate matter of sex, Witherspoon's discomfort is obvious as he skirts around the subject:

> ... man is manifestly superior in dignity to the other animals; and it was intended that all his enjoyments, and even his indulgence of

instinctive propensities, should be of a more exalted and rational kind than theirs. Therefore the propensity of the sexes to one another, is not only reined in by modesty, but is so ordered as to require that reason and friendship, and some of the noblest affections, should have place.[49]

Once again Witherspoon reveals his uneasy relationship with human passion, as the phrase, 'reined in by modesty' shows. He then goes on to discuss polygamy which he says is 'condemned by nature'. He offers as argument some statistics that show that:

the males born are to females as 13 to 12, or as some say 20 to 19, the overplus being to supply the waste of the male part of the species by war and dangerous occupations, hard labour, and travelling by land and sea.

Here he is anticipating an aspect of the debate that came at the end of the century with the publication of, *An Essay on Population* in 1798, by Thomas Robert Malthus, but Witherspoon's argument is neither developed nor convincing.[50]

Witherspoon, unsurprising, see fidelity and chastity as a 'fundamental and essential' part of the marriage contract, and is at pains to point out that this applies as much to the husband as to the wife. He also suggests that the contract should be for life and that the only allowable reasons for divorce are 'adultery, wilful and obstinate desertion, and incapacity'; and rules out others such as, 'contrariety of temper, incurable diseases, and such as would infect the offspring'. In discussing the relative status of men and women in the marriage contract, he writes:

If superiority and authority be given to the man, it should be used with so much gentleness and love, as to make it a state of as great equality as possible.

He presents the view held by 'Hutchinson [*sic*] and some other writers' that there should be no superiority, but clearly sides with those who think that 'perfect equality of power in two persons is not consistent with order, and the common interest and therefore give authority to the man'. But although Witherspoon sets a limit to male superiority by condemning as 'barbarous and unjust' the 'Heathen writers' who give man the power of life and death over woman, he nevertheless obviously sees the husband as having the right of a superior over the wife.[51]

The authoritarian aspect of Witherspoon's character, which is in evidence in his views on marriage, is again, and perhaps even more clearly seen in his discussion of the 'Relation of Parents and Children'. Witherspoon asserts:

> The rights of the parent may be summed up in these two: 1. Authority, which requires subjection in the children. 2. A right to a grateful return in due time from the children.

The first he describes as a 'perfect right', but allows that even if it is an absolute right, it must also be limited; while the second which he calls an 'imperfect right' is more of a desired ideal. The end to which the authority over children is exercised is that of their 'instruction and protection'. To achieve the education and safety of the child, parental authority must reign supreme. When this is set in the context of Witherspoon's belief in the superiority of the male, it becomes clear that for him parental authority resides primarily in the father of the family. However, he acknowledges that there is a limit to parental authority and disagrees with Hobbes's view of children being 'the goods and absolute property of the parents'. He also grants that 'children are no doubt to judge for themselves in matters of religion when they come to years;' but insists that parents 'are under the strongest obligation to instruct them carefully to the best of their judgement'; and counters the view that says that children should not be taught about religion, claiming that this would only lead to children imbibing prejudices and bad habits from others. As to the 'imperfect right' to a grateful return from their children, Witherspoon approvingly puts forward the practice of some civil authorities to 'oblige children to maintain their aged parents', and offers the comment: 'To the disgrace of human nature, it is often observed, that parental affection is much stronger than filial duty'. He attributes this:

> to the wisdom of Providence in making the instinctive impulse stronger in parents towards their children, than in children towards their parents; because the first is more necessary than the other to the public good.

There is a note of peevishness in this discussion and no hint of unconditional love being the nature of what might be offered by parents. Instead, the relationship between parents and children more resembles that of a contract in which one thing is offered in the expected return for another.[52]

Witherspoon's concept of man in his natural state, is again seen, not as one who is equal and free, but as one who has been born into a world where some are superior to others, and all of this has been predetermined by God. This comes to the fore when he considers the 'Relation between Master and Servant'. In examining the respective duties of master and servant, Witherspoon is very brief and contents himself with observing that the master has the 'right to the labours and ingenuity of the servant for a limited time', but he betrays an understanding of the relationship which makes it more alike to that of a master-slave one, than to that of a master-servant, by adding, 'or at most for life'. The brevity of this passage is tantalizing and prompts the question: did Witherspoon fully appreciate how akin to slavery even 'the duties for life' of a servant are? He makes no attempt at outlining the responsibilities of the master or the privileges to be granted to the servant, other than to say that the master has 'no right to take away life, or to make it unsupportable by excessive labour', and that the servant 'retains all other natural rights'.[53]

It is perhaps an indication of how close in Witherspoon's mind master-servant relationships were to those between a master and a slave, that immediately following this discussion, he launches into a digression about the issue of nations who make slaves of prisoners of war. He allows, 'that those who were the causes of an unjust war deserved to be made slaves', but, like John Locke, believes that those who merely fought on their side should not be enslaved. But the revealing thing in this passage is found in its final sentence on the subject of enslaving conquered nations: 'The practice was also impolitic, as slaves never are so good or faithful servants, as those who become so for a limited time by consent'. The principle of man's right to be free, has been replaced by the rejection of slavery on the basis of the pragmatic practicality of getting a better return from servants who become like slaves 'for a limited time by consent'.[54]

Again Witherspoon is found to be equivocal and ambivalent in his views on slavery. He cannot commit himself to being as forthright as John Locke who wrote as the opening sentence of his *Two Treatises of Civil Government*:

Slavery is so vile and miserable an estate of man, and so directly opposite to the generous temper and courage of our nation, that it is hardly to be conceived that an 'Englishman', much less a gentleman', should plead for it.[55]

Witherspoon might not exactly be pleading for the legitimacy of slavery but he is certainly allowing that a case can be made for it.

LECTURES ON MORAL PHILOSOPHY

As the *Lectures on Moral Philosophy* proceed, it becomes obvious that they are of varying quality, both in the way that subjects are handled and in the depth of perception and breadth of vision of the lecturer. When Witherspoon comes to consider 'Civil Society', it is as if he is dealing with a subject that very much concerns him, and one in which he is widely read. He begins by emphasizing that 'society always supposes an expressed or implied compact or agreement', and spells out what this 'compact' necessarily implies:

> (1) The consent of every individual to live in and be a member of that society. (2) A consent to some particular form of government. (3). A mutual agreement between the subjects and rulers.[56]

Referring to the first, he asserts that notwithstanding this consent, 'they also have the right to remove themselves from this society' at least in time of peace, but he adds the caveat:

> If war or danger to the public should arise, they may be hindered from emigrating at that time, and compelled to contribute their share in what is necessary to the common defence.

Witherspoon acknowledges that whatever form of government is adopted by a society, its members are going to be divided into two classes, the *rulers* and the *ruled.* He then proceeds to lay down the rights of rulers and the ruled, laying greater stress on those of the rulers, and granting that the essential rights are: the right to legislate, to levy taxes, to administer justice, and to act in the name of the people as their representatives in making war or peace. Rulers also have what he calls accidental rights, which he deems less essential rights such as the coining of money, the managing of public buildings and the conferring of honours etc. But when he comes to list the rights of those who are ruled, although the term he uses for them is 'subjects', nevertheless, he sees their rights as summed up by one word 'protection', and asserts that 'those who have surrendered part of their natural rights, expect the strength of the public arm to defend and improve what remains'. Witherspoon in this section is clearly following the thinking of John Locke who in his *Two Treatises of Civil Government* writes: 'The great and chief end, therefore of men uniting into commonwealths, and putting themselves under government, is the preservation of their property' (by this, Locke means: lives, liberty and estates).[57] He again follows Locke when writing of how the government of society is best founded on the consent of the people and acknowledges that, although this might on occasion allow leaders to make laws that will harm the people, ultimately, if the people find them:

> to be pernicious and destructive of the ends of the union, they may certainly break up the society, recall the obligation and resettle the whole upon a better footing.

Again this follows Locke, who writes:

> The legislative being only a fiduciary power to act for certain ends, there remains still in the people a supreme power to remove or alter the legislative, when they find the legislative act contrary to the trust reposed in them.[58]

Witherspoon then considers the different forms of government: Monarchy, Aristocracy, and Democracy. He sees four essentials that must be part of any form of government:

> (1) Wisdom to plan proper measures for the public good. (2) Fidelity to have nothing but the public interest in view. (3) Secrecy, expedition and dispatch in carrying measures into execution. (4) Unity and concord, so that one branch of government may not impede, or be a hindrance to another.[59]

According to Witherspoon, these are principles that must be structured into any form of government if it is to serve the people. It is interesting to look at his own life as a clergyman, college principal, congressman and activist in government, and to see how on so many occasions he exemplified these principles in his own person. It was for 'the public good' not his own, that he followed up his *Dominion of Providence* sermon with political action in Congress, remaining faithful to that concern for his fellow Americans by continuing to proclaim the need for independence when some wavered towards reconciliation with the British and acceptance of their rule. His discretion, speed of response and quick execution of the tasks laid upon him by the young administration during the war, are attested by the numerous pamphlets and the outcomes of his political activity. And as to his endeavours to work for a coherent and united government, his efforts on the issue and the need of Federalism are sufficient evidence.

Witherspoon next attempts to examine the three forms of government, Monarchy, Aristocracy, and Democracy in the light of the four essentials of good government that he has just outlined. He describes in a neutral way the nature of these forms, indicating that there can be combinations of the various forms and observing that 'all of these may be united, as in the British government'. It is when he moves on to evaluate the different forms that his opinions become clear. He sees the advantage that Monarchy has in its ability to govern with unity, secretly and expeditiously. But this advantage is far outweighed by the disadvantages, as it cannot be guaranteed that a monarch will have the wisdom or skill or the ability to meet all the demands of empire, neither is it possible to be assured of his or her goodness. As Witherspoon's assessment of Monarchy develops, he turns away from any possibility of compromise when he says: 'there is no reason to expect an elected monarch will have the public good at heart, he will probably mind only private or family interest', and, I suspect, very much aware of his audience, concludes:

> Monarchy, everyone knows, is but another name for tyranny, where the arbitrary will of one capricious man disposes of the lives and properties of all ranks.[60]

Whereas John Locke painstakingly took apart, utterly demolished, and reduced to absurdity, the arguments for the basis of Monarchy in Sir Robert Fulmer's, *Patriarcha* (1680), Witherspoon contents himself with the given, that apart from the advantage of governing with unity, secrecy and expedition, Monarchy is neither a viable nor desirable form of government.[61]

Witherspoon's latent elitism shows through when he considers Aristocracy as a form of government, making the assumption that it will have the advantage of wisdom because it will be composed of 'a number of persons of the first order'. However, he considers Aristocracy as even worse than Monarchy, observing that:

> the great commonly rule with greater severity than absolute monarchs. A monarch is at such a distance from most of his subjects, that he does them little injury; but the lord of a petty seignory is a vigorous task-master to his unhappy dependents.[62]

Witherspoon is quite critical of Democracy. Having pointed out its greater 'fidelity', as against Monarchy and Aristocracy, he argues that this is because, 'the multitude collectively are true in intention to the interest of the public, because it is their own. They are the public'. Note the pejorative sounding 'multitude', as against the more neutral and natural term, 'people'. Repeating the term, he goes on to warn that: 'the multitude are exceedingly apt to be deceived by demagogues and ambitious persons'. He further shows his reservations by alleging that:

Pure democracy cannot subsist long, nor be carried into the departments of state - it is very subject to caprice and the madness of popular rage. They are also very apt to choose a favourite and vest him with such power as overthrows their liberty, - examples Athens and Rome.[63]

Seeing flaws in all three forms of government, Witherspoon therefore advocates that: 'every good form of government must be complex, so that the one principle may check the other'. He makes various suggestions as to what will assist good government: separation of powers e.g. King and Parliament; vested rulers should be men of 'considerable property, chiefly of lands', which he sees as a 'security for fidelity'; and a sufficient but not overlarge population. He hides behind the opinion of others when he writes: 'It is frequently observed that in every government there is a supreme irresistible power lodged somewhere, in king, senate, or people'. He seems reluctant to come out unequivocally for that power, ideally and of right, to reside in the people. Witherspoon comes across as a reluctant democrat, apparently only allowing for the exercise of the supreme power of the people in the extreme case of where a government exercises its power 'in a manifestly tyrannical manner', then, 'the subjects may certainly, if in their power, resist and overthrow it'. However, there is such caution in his advocacy of this policy that it is almost as if he is reluctant to give this power to the people in case anarchy might ensue. Nevertheless he concedes:

This resistance to the supreme power, however, is subverting the society altogether and is not to be attempted till the government is so corrupt, as that anarchy and the uncertainty of a new settlement is preferable to the continuance as it is.

Witherspoon returns to this theme as he underlines that the right to resist must not be taken up at 'any little mistake of the rulers' to whom we owe submission, but only be engaged in when 'the corruption becomes intolerable'. But however reluctant a revolutionary Witherspoon is, he is drawn by the logic of his own premises to discount the anarchic dangers of resistance by writing:

to refuse this inherent right in every man, is to establish injustice and tyranny, and leave every good subject without help, as a tame prey to the ambition and rapacity of others.

Alexander Carlyle's portrayal of 'Johnny Witherspoon' as a rabble rouser is refuted by the assertion:

> it is not till a whole people rise, that resistance has any effect; and it is not easy to suppose that a whole people would rise against their governors, unless when they have really received very great provocation.[64]

In concluding his survey of the nature of good government, Witherspoon returns to the theme that underlines all his advocacy of the factors necessary for good government to be achieved: 'Dominion, it is plain from all that has been said, can be acquired justly only one way, viz. by consent'. He dismisses as absurd the idea that hereditary power is 'a right from nature independent of the people' and classifies any supposed right acquired by conquest as 'robbery'. As the lecture ends, Witherspoon resumes his attack on Monarchical and Aristocratic forms of government, saying that the first 'has a tendency towards politeness and eloquence of manners, but that it diffuses submission and obsequiousness throughout the whole state', while the second, 'narrows the mind exceedingly'. His praise of Democratic government is tempered with criticism saying that, 'Democracy tends to plainness and freedom of speech, and sometimes to a savage and indecent ferocity'. But then he upholds it with a sentence that must have become fixed in the minds of his hearers and carried by them out of the lecture room and into the street and the very commerce of their political thought and activity: 'Democracy is the nurse of eloquence, because when the multitude have the power, persuasion is the only way to govern them'.[65] Given the context of these lectures such words would be well remembered, and in later years influence the activity of the many, who had been educated at Princeton, and were to play an influential part in a young nation struggling to emerge from under a colonial government to form its own democratic system of government.

Witherspoon's last words in this section on 'Civil Society' are directed to the question: 'What is the value and advantage of civil liberty?' He answers his own question in a manner that lets us see how strongly he sees civil liberty as essential to society, and as the thing that drives it forward in a positive way:

> I suppose it chiefly consists in its tendency to put in motion all the human powers. Therefore it promotes industry, and in this respect happiness, produces every latent quality, and improves the human mind. Liberty is the nurse of riches, literature, and heroism.[66]

Here is the Witherspoon who inspired so many of his students towards public service. For so much of the time, as in these lectures, he is pedestrian, repetitive of long held views, adding little new to the fund of human knowledge, but then suddenly bursting out enthusiastically for the things that really are the greatest concerns of his life, and in so doing, using words that would inspire those who were preparing themselves for life and work in a land full of opportunities and potential.

In *Lecture XIII*, Witherspoon considers the 'Law of Nature and Nations'. He sees a nation as analogous to man: 'If there are natural rights of men there are natural rights of nations'. Bodies politic in this view do not differ in the least from individuals. He goes on to maintain that the perfect rights of man in a state of natural liberty apply also to nations, and referring his students back to *Lecture VIII* in which he had expounded the rights of man, distinguishing between 'perfect rights, which may make use of force to obtain when they are denied us' and 'imperfect rights which are such as we may demand, and others ought to give us, yet we have no title to compel them'. But whereas all the 'perfect rights' that apply to man also apply to nations, Witherspoon observes that there is 'usually less occasion for the imperfect rights', and instances the help offered to Portugal by the other nations of Europe following the earthquake in Lisbon. He also cites the assistance often offered to each other by ships at sea. Witherspoon, having asserted that 'the law of nature and nations has as its chief or only object the manner of making *war* and *peace*', then spends seven pages discussing war, one page on peace and one page on neutrality.[67]
Witherspoon sees war as an entirely legitimate means of seeking redress for:

> the violation of any perfect right - as taking away the property of the other state, or the lives of its subjects, or restraining them in their industry, or hindering them in the use of things common, &c.

He believes that the infringement of a nation's perfect rights provides the just and legitimate causes of making war and is also in favour of preemptive strikes when these are threatened. He offers the analogy:

> it is often easier to prevent and disarm the robber than to suffer him to commit the violence, and then to strip him and rob him of his prey.[68]

In his arguments, Witherspoon seems to be trying to reduce the issues to the barest terms, but in so doing he is in danger of being simplistic. He seems unmindful of the complexity and consequences of the actions of a nation as against an individual and is in danger of pressing too far the analogy of the human to the nation. He again uses the analogy in considering the subject of the duration of a war, when if it were applied, the war should end when the injury had been redressed, but he is obviously aware of the difference between the individual and the nation where when, war is waged between nations, there is even greater danger in a vindictive and revengeful continuance of the state of war that results in it being used for the acquisition of empire and the 'ruin of the offending state altogether'. Yet Witherspoon's tendency towards what today might be called a 'hawkish' attitude, emerges again when he considers the extent to which force or open violence can be used as legitimate means of carrying on a war. He approves the concept of the use of force against 'every member of the hostile state', allowing that:

> This may be hard, that innocent subjects of the state should suffer for the folly and indiscretion of the rulers, or of other members of the same state,

but this, says Witherspoon, is' 'unavoidable'.[69]

He excuses the violence done to innocents on the grounds that 'it would be impossible for an enemy to distinguish the guilty from the innocent'. He rather weakly attempts to justify this, by arguing that, 'when men submit to government, they risk their own possessions on the same bottom of the whole, in return for the benefits of society'. But perhaps having seen the weakness of his own argument, Witherspoon hastily qualifies his 'De'il tak' the hindmaist' attitude, by urging, that:

> all acts of cruelty are to be blamed, and all severity that has not an immediate effect in weakening the national strength of the enemy, is certainly inhumanity.

Further qualifying the legitimacy of using force against 'every member of the hostile state', Witherspoon condemns the killing of prisoners, women and children, and declares as unethical the 'use of poisoned weapons and the poisoning of springs or provisions'. But the half-thought through philosophy continues when he opines:

> To the honour of modern times, and very probably, I think to the honour of Christianity, there is more humanity in the way of carrying on war than formerly.[70]

With this kind of remark, Witherspoon reveals how he has not overcome a tendency to gloss over the shortcomings of the Church, that had not only encouraged its members to participate in such cruel wars as the Crusades, but had blessed the ambitions of various rulers who had espoused it in order to gain respectability and legitimacy to conduct their 'just war'. He chose to ignore the inhumanity of a Church that made war within its own ranks as it purged itself from what it deemed heresy; a Church, that through the religious wars of the Reformation period, and beyond into the bitterly-waged sectarian conflict in the time of the Covenanters (a time that concluded a mere three decades before Witherspoon himself was born), put doctrine or practice before people in its wars fought to preserve what it declared to be the true faith.

Witherspoon goes on to reveal how ill thought out are his views on the conduct of war. Whereas previously he maintained that in war, force could be used against every member of a hostile state, and then had to make some exclusions from that principle, he now begins to quibble about the morality of bringing about the assassination of an opposing leader by bribing his own people. He also doubts the morality of subterfuge and spying. It is hardly the sign of a well thought out philosophy when such things are deemed morally unacceptable after having taken the decision that when war is waged the innocent will suffer. He shows a longing for war to be conducted in a gentlemanly manner, and rather naively cites as 'something very handsome' the Roman general, who refused to avail himself of the treachery of a schoolmaster, as well as considering it 'whimsical' in the way in which he punishes the traitor.[71] Again, his selective memory of the Roman period fails to take account of the ruthlessness with which the Romans pursued their wars. Witherspoon's philosophy relating to war has not been fully thought through, and it certainly left his students with just as many things to sort out for themselves, as giving them guidance on the moral issues surrounding war.

When he turns briefly to the subject 'of making peace', Witherspoon again makes use of the same idea that the same rules as apply to man, should hold in the relationships between nations. He again seems to muddle along in this subject. Having stated the principle, he immediately departs from it, and says that there is an exception, namely that, 'contracts between individuals are (at least by law) always void when they are the effect of constraint upon one side'. He insists that, 'this must not hold in treaties between nations, because it would always furnish a pretext for breaking them'. But he immediately reveals his indecision by saying that, whatever constraints are laid upon one of the parties to a treaty, nevertheless those who agree to a treaty are morally bound to adhere to it. Although he understands that the generations who come after the makers of treaties might not feel themselves 'bound to unjust servitude by the deeds of their fathers'.[72] Witherspoon does not add anything to the understanding of the philosophy that might undergird the work of a peacemaker. At this point, which is very near the end of the lecture, Witherspoon gives the impression that he is either tired of the subject, or that he has not thought it through sufficiently to discourse upon it. He concludes this section with a single page on 'the situation of neutral states'. Other than declaring that, 'Every state has a right, when others are contending, to remain neuter, [neutral] and assist neither party', he merely outlines the consequences that follow from this, and offers no consideration of the moral issues raised by the adoption of a position of neutrality. He allows the subject to wind down to the very weak conclusion:

> On the whole, those things that have been generally received as the law of nature and nations, are founded on principles of equity, and, when well observed, do greatly promote general utility.[73]

Once again, when the lectures have reached a high point of insight, and the audience might have expectation of further stimulation, the following section results in anticlimax. Various commentators have indicated the great impact that these lectures had on those who heard them, and as I have previously commented, this impact must have been considerable. But one thing that the lectures lack is consistency. It is little wonder that Witherspoon himself did not want his lectures published during his lifetime. The reason usually given for this stance is that it was because they were only lecture notes and not intended for publication. It has been suggested that Witherspoon in these lectures may have adopted the Socratic method, and that all that remains of the lectures, in the form that we have them, are the propositions that were set before the students, but not the discussion and the teasing out of the final and more tested and adjusted proposition. This is a possibility, but I think not. There are too many instances of gaps in the subject, or inconsistencies of thought for that to be the reason for Witherspoon's reluctance to publish. The more likely reason is that he knew their shortcomings, and did not want these to be revealed. Having said that, Jeffry H. Morrison in his *John Witherspoon and the Founding of the American Republic* makes two good points in favour of the importance these lectures, and the significance of Witherspoon's role; in summary these are: the lectures were the only ones around at that time, and Witherspoon made no claim to be an original thinker, but was a valuable presenter and synthesiser of other peoples' views. Morrison's book is a hugely well researched survey of Witherspoon's place and role in American history as one of the signatories of the *Declaration of*

Independence, and a significant contributor to the thought process and physical activity that led to the production of the foundation documents of the American form of government and constitution, and to their implementation into the very life of the country. He writes of Witherspoon's contribution to the subject of Moral Philosophy:

> Witherspoon was therefore a bona fide moral philosopher of considerable influence in early American thought. Few intellectual historians, however, have seen him in this light. Many have instead trivialized his contribution and his intellectual abilities because his moral philosophy was unoriginal, eclectic, and occasionally naïve. Compared to several other supposedly more sophisticated founders, Witherspoon is thought to be second rank.[74]

After referring to several other writers who clearly borrowed from other sources and whose role was to bring together and to show, and perhaps to harmonise the various strands of thought in their own work, Morrison continues:

> We should not, therefore, be shocked to find that Witherspoon borrowed heavily from other thinkers. In this respect he was a typical founder. We ought not to think less of him just because he was a philosophical borrower, or, if we do, then for the sake of consistency we ought to think less of the famous founders like Jefferson as well. And in at least one respect, Witherspoon seems to have been more philosophically original, or at least more innovative, than many colonial American thinkers. ... By synthesizing Calvinism and Enlightenment science, he was arguably more original than most orthodox thinkers of his day.

Morrison judges that 'although he may not have been a great moral philosopher in the European mold, still Witherspoon was a legitimate *American* moral philosopher', admitting that this might sound like rather faint praise, considering how few philosophers were around in America at that time, but nevertheless placing Witherspoon above those like Franklin and Jefferson and other founders, 'more renowned for their so-called philosophical abilities'. Witherspoon's achievement in producing a set of lectures on the subject of moral philosophy should be seen as significant, when the subject was hardly being dealt with by anyone else at the time, and when there is no evidence of any of his American contemporaries engaging in 'pure' philosophy.

Regardless of how we might regard his writings today as incomplete, and find it easy to point out the gaps or inconsistencies in his reasoning, nevertheless, for his own time and place, Witherspoon was providing a series of lectures that would stimulate the thinking of his students. He was unable to give his students other contemporary models of American philosophy because they were just not being produced. In this context, what he did produce related well to the European philosophic scene in which he had received his own education. A further examination of his work will, I think, reveal how much America owes to him for the introduction of a type of philosophy to which he was working his way towards giving it expression, one which was to become known as the Scottish Philosophy, or more particularly, the philosophy associated with Thomas Reid, Common Sense Philosophy.[75]

Thomas Reid's, *An Inquiry into the Human Mind on the Principles of Common Sense*, published in 1764, had initially been prompted by the publication in 1739 of David Hume's *Treatise of Human Nature*, and had been developed over the years between by means of papers prepared for and delivered by Reid at the Philosophical Society in Aberdeen. Reid had spent years as a Parish Minister in rural Aberdeenshire, and also as Librarian at King's College in Old Aberdeen, and in the year of the *Inquiry*'s publication, he was appointed as Professor of Moral Philosophy at the University of Glasgow. The tone of the book is set in the first pages of the *Introduction* where Reid writes:

> The man who first discovered that cold freezes water, and that heat turns it into vapour, proceeded on the same general principles, and in the same method by which Newton discovered the law of gravity, and the properties of light. His *regulae philosophandi*, are maxims of common sense, and are practiced every day in common life, and he who philosophises by other rules, either concerning the material system, or concerning the mind, mistakes his aim.[76]

Reid then proceeds to explore the nature of the mind by means of an examination of the senses of smelling, tasting, hearing, touch and seeing. In his concluding chapter, Reid, referring to Hume's system, writes:

> It represents our senses as having no other office but that of furnishing the mind with notions or simple apprehensions of things; and makes our judgement and belief concerning those things to be acquired by comparing our notions together and perceiving their agreements or disagreements. We have shown on the contrary, that every operation of the senses, in its very nature, implies judgement

or belief, as well as simple apprehension. Thus when I feel the pain of the gout in my toe, I have not only a notion of pain but a belief of its existence, and a belief of some disorder in my toe which occasions it; and this belief is not produced by comparing ideas and perceiving their agreements and disagreements; it is included in the very nature of the sensation.[77]

He then goes on to claim, that:

Such original and natural judgements are therefore a part of that furniture which nature hath given to the human understanding … they serve to direct us in the common affairs of life when our reasoning faculty would leave us in the dark. They are part of our constitution and all the discoveries of our reason are grounded upon them. They make up what is called the common sense of mankind; and what is manifestly contrary to any of those first principles, is what we call absurd … when a man suffers himself to be reasoned out of the principles of common sense by a metaphysical lunacy.[78]

Witherspoon warmed to this common sense philosophy and indeed claimed to his students that he had expressed himself in similar terms many years before Reid's publication emerged. An article written by Witherspoon, 'Remarks on an essay on human liberty', that appears in *The Scots Magazine* of April, 1753, confirms this. In it, he demonstrates an appreciation of the concept of the reliability of the senses and the doubtfulness of the Berkelean argument of the secondary qualities, and asserts the reliability of the senses. Witherspoon writes:

I affirm therefore that the ideas we receive by our senses and the persuasions we derive immediately from them, are exactly according to truth, to real truth, which certainly ought to be the same as philosophical truth.

He then goes on to use an argument that is very similar to the one later used by Thomas Reid:

I touch a table and feel it resisting my hand; this I call hardness; I taste honey and because it excites an agreeable sensation I call it sweet. In the same manner arise all the epithets or secondary qualities of objects as hot, cold, hard, soft, dry, moist, sweet, sour &c. Now if the most ignorant person in the world were strictly examined as to what he means by his expressions, would he appear to have been led by his senses into any belief but this, that particular objects have a power of exciting certain sensations in him and others which is manifest they have.[79]

Witherspoon's article clearly puts him in the position of a one who has adopted a basic common sense philosophic stance and who could be expected, as he did, to respond sympathetically to Reid's approach to the subject, and incorporate it into his own exposition of Moral Philosophy.

Returning to the subject matter of the course, Witherspoon then makes a brief foray in *Lecture XIV* into what he calls Jurisprudence, which he defines as: 'the method of enacting and administering civil laws in any constitution'. He proceeds in a way that indicates his awareness of other thinkers on the subject, alluding briefly to Montesquieu when he writes:

> The first preliminary remark is, that a constitution is excellent when the spirit of civil laws is such, as to have a tendency to prevent offences, and make men good, as much as punish them when they do evil.[80]

He reveals what he sees as the purpose of law, namely, 'to make the people of any state virtuous', and immediately puts forward the view that as 'virtue and piety are inseparably connected then to promote true religion is the best and most effectual way of making a virtuous and regular people'. This leads him on to consider how much a part should be played by the 'magistrate (or ruling part of any society) in the promoting and fostering of such laws as will make a virtuous people'. He sees it the role of the ruling body to encourage piety by its own example, and to make it to be seen to be worthy of achieving; to defend the rights of commerce and tolerate the different religious sentiments of a people. He makes room for a toleration of Roman Catholicism which he says is not tolerated in Great Britain, and approvingly cites Holland where it is tolerated 'without danger to liberty'. The Magistrate should also 'enact laws for the punishment of acts of profanity and impiety'. But he stops short of voicing full approval of the views of many who think that 'the Magistrate ought to make public provision for the worship of God', and suggests that the magistrate in this case should more adopt the role of the parent who has 'the right to instruct but not to constrain'. However, in his later practice as a Congressman when he made several calls to the ruling bodies of the United States to encourage special days of prayer, he seems to have favoured a more pro-active role for the magistrate.[81]

In his second preliminary remark, Witherspoon urges that:

Laws should be so framed as to promote such principles in general as are favourable to good government, and particularly that principle, if there be one, that gave rise to the constitution, and is congenial to it.

This seemingly vague remark is however more significant than it first appears. As he elaborates on this, it becomes clear that Witherspoon is thinking about his newly adopted country, which he sees has been peopled in recent times by many men and women who have come to it because they perceived that it promised them freedom, and the chance of a new beginning. Witherspoon had a vision of this land to which he had come as a place in which there was the opportunity and the freedom to assert a new way of living, amid a new structure that would support that way and further enhance it. He sees the magistrate as one who is charged with the responsibility of making and upholding such laws as will embody the very central principle upon which the community is based - in this case, liberty. In support of this primary principle, Witherspoon sees as essential: sobriety, industry and public spirit; these are the principles that will cause a nation to prosper, whereas 'the luxury of a nation always leads to the ruin of that nation'.[82]

Witherspoon's third preliminary remark is that 'laws may be of two kinds, either written, or in the breasts of the magistrates'. It is surprising that he should even countenance the validity of unwritten laws that would be dependent on what was, 'in the breasts of magistrates', as this would cause the laws to vary in relation to the particular magistrate. This loose thinking is more a kind of musing on the pros and cons of a multiplicity of laws whereby everything is as strictly defined as possible, or whether to leave more to the power of the judge, but in the end Witherspoon is in favour of a multiplicity of written laws.[83]

In the fourth and last of his preliminary remarks, Witherspoon makes the important caveat, 'no human constitution can be formed, but that there must be exceptions to every law'. If this is to be the case, then, says Witherspoon, attention must be paid to 'forming the manners of a people'. Here Witherspoon the educationalist is speaking. He wanted his college not just to educate students for the professions, but to prepare them for playing a part in the building of a virtuous society.

Witherspoon then goes on to discourse on the object of civil laws. The first object is 'to ratify the moral laws by the sanction of society'. He wants the already existing moral laws that govern individuals to be applied to society and enforced by the application of sanctions. He sees breaches of the moral law as crimes, and lists profanity, adultery, murder, and calumny as examples. He then cites the need for civil laws to recognise the importance of contracts, and how breaches of contracts should be seen as 'frauds'. To conclude this section, he declares that one of the objects of civil laws is 'to limit and direct persons in the exercise of their own rights, and oblige them to shew respect to the interfering rights of others'. He adds that the transgression of such laws are called 'tresspasses'. Therefore, crimes, frauds and trespasses are to be covered by the civil laws. In other words, there has to be brought into existence by these laws 'the police of the country'.[84]

Witherspoon next spends some time discussing the sanctions that are to be imposed by society when there is a breach of the moral law. He calls attention to the need to define what is a crime, and for a method of ascertaining whether or not a crime has been committed, the number of witnesses required, and the nature of evidence both direct and circumstantial. He then goes on to consider the punishment appropriate to the crime, and declares that punishment must include the elements of reparation to the sufferer, an example to others and where possible 'the reclaim and reform of the offender as in corporal punishment less than death'. The governing factor in determining punishments should be 'Public utility'. However, Witherspoon cautions against great severity in punishments: 'Severe laws, and severe punishments sometimes banish crimes but very often the contrary'. He goes on to make the point that:

> when laws are very sanguinary, it often makes the subjects hate the law more than they fear it; and the transition is very easy from hating the law, to hating those who are entrusted with the execution of it.

And he concludes with words that would be filled with greater significance as these lectures were repeated in the lead up to the outbreak of war with Britain, 'Such a state of things threatens insurrection and convulsions if not the dissolution of government'. He also sagely points out that excessive severity in laws often means that they are not put into execution, because the public are not willing to assist in pursuing offenders to conviction, so that the law loses its authority.[85]

There follows a brief discussion of the *lex talionis* as exemplified in the law of Moses: 'an eye for an eye, a tooth for a tooth &c'. Witherspoon observes that:

> perhaps there are many instances in which it would appear very proper. The equity of the punishment would be quite manifest, and probably it would be as effectual a restraint from the commission of injury as any that could be chosen.

But having said that, Witherspoon seems to revert to a more balanced assessment of the severity of the sanctions of the law when he concludes: 'it is but seldom that very severe and sanguinary laws are of service to the good order of a state'. Yet there remains a hankering after severity in the final words of his lecture: 'Let the laws be just and the magistrate inflexible'.[86]

In expressing his admiration for, and perhaps his half-desire to see the elements of the law of Moses applied as appropriate sanctions, Witherspoon still abides by the position he expressed in his first lecture, when he said that although:

> the political law of the Jews contains many noble principles of equity, yet it was so local and peculiar that certainly it was never intended to be immutable and universal.[87]

However attracted he might have been to the 'quick fix' of the '*lex talionis*', he also acknowledged the danger of an over severity in law. In this respect, he was within the Scottish tradition as exemplified by John Erskine of Carnock, who writes:

> God himself delivered to the Jews a law, distinct from the law of nature, not only in relation to their ritual observances, but with respect to their public polity and private right, the last of which is called the judicial law of Moses. Some have affirmed that this law, being enacted by an infallible lawgiver, ought to be copied, in so far as it goes, by every other state; and it must be admitted that no part of it is contrary to the law of nature; for God, who is the author of both, cannot contradict himself. But no positive law, let it be it ever so agreeable to the law of nature, can oblige those to whom it is not directed. The ordinances of the Jewish law, in as far as they are the necessary result of reason, and so make part of the perceptive law of nature, must without doubt be binding universally; not because God prescribed them as a rule to the Jews, but because natural law had enjoined their observance antecedently to all enactment. But whatever in that law is adapted specially to the Jewish constitution, or framed with a particular view to the genius of that people, may be disregarded by the legislature of other states, without any want of reverence to its great Author. And indeed most of the Jewish laws will be found, on strict examination, to be either wholly or in part of this last kind.[88]

Although Witherspoon does not quote Erskine directly, his manner of dealing with the Law of Moses shows him to be within the mainstream of the current Scottish legal thinking on Jurisprudence. John Erskine (1695-1768) became an advocate in 1737, and was appointed to the Chair of Scots Law at Edinburgh University in 1737, a position he held till 1765. He published his *Principles of the Law of Scotland* in 1754, and his work, *An Institute of the Law of Scotland*, which he had nearly completed by the time of his death, was prepared for publication by his son David, also a lawyer, in 1773. He was in his time regarded as an authority and his work is still in use to this day.

Witherspoon, turning to what he considered as the second object of civil law: 'to regulate the making of contracts', spends the whole of *Lecture XV* indicating the importance of and the nature of contracts. He stresses the importance of the principle of consent in the making of a contract which he says should be: 'free, mutual, possible, careful, with a capable person, and formal'. He considers the question of usury and concludes that it is permissible if money is considered as 'an instrument of commerce'. However, to prevent either 'the necessity of the poor or the covetousness of the rich', the rate of interest should be settled by the state. Witherspoon displays an almost Jesuitical justification of the Law of Moses that had determined that while it is not permissible to charge interest on a loan to an Israelite, it was legally permissible to charge interest to a stranger. He says that the prohibition 'must have been drawn from something in their constitution as a state that rendered it improper', and that the allowing of interest to be charged to someone of another race must have been in order because, 'if it had been in itself immoral, they would not have permitted to take it of strangers'. The naivety that occasionally surfaces in Witherspoon's thinking is again in evidence. In this case, it is possibly born of his great respect for the *Bible* and his conception of its message and laws being God-given, and therefore on matters like this, having to be given the benefit of the doubt on the basis that when the reason for action is not entirely obvious, the fallback position is that God must have a reason.[89]

The uneven nature of these lectures is again seen in the section that follows, where in discussing 'The Marks or Signs of Contracts', Witherspoon pedantically divides signs into: 'natural, instituted and customary'. In attempting to elucidate he obscures, and is led into discussing quite peripheral subjects such as bonfires and drawings and lying, the latter causing him to disagree with Francis Hutcheson's allowing for the need for 'a departure from the truth on occasion for a good end'. This looseness of style continues into the next lecture (*XVI*) on oaths. He declares: 'An oath is an appeal to God, the Searcher of hearts, for the truth of what we say', and sees it as 'an act of worship'. Again, the significance of the subject gets lost in its subdivisions, and the lecturer contributes little to the understanding.[90]

Witherspoon concludes this section on contracts with a consideration of 'The Value of Property'. He contends that:

> Value is in proportion to the plenty of any commodity, and the demand for it ... Hence it follows, that money is of no real value. It is not wealth properly, but the sign of it, and in a fixed state of society, the certain means of procuring it.

He then goes on to argue that any sign of wealth must have 'an intrinsic commercial value', and sees gold and silver as having this intrinsic value, and being durable, desirable, divisible and portable, ideal signs of wealth and wealth in themselves. Witherspoon also believes that it is a responsibility 'of the ruling part of any society to fix the value of gold and silver, as signs of the value of commodities'.[91] In this exploration of economics within the framework of lectures on jurisprudence, Witherspoon is following the same path as Francis Hutcheson and Adam Smith. Both had introduced the subject of economics in the context of jurisprudence. Adam Smith's biographer, Ian Simpson Ross writes:

> It was from Hutcheson's concept of natural jurisprudence that Smith's teaching about economics took its origin. In the *Short Introduction to Moral Philosophy*, and also in the posthumous *System*, Hutcheson introduced chapters on prices, money, and interest as part of a general discussion of contract.

In the same chapter, Ross gives details of the content of Adam Smith's lectures:

> Probably between 1753 and 1755 John Anderson, a former student at Glasgow University who became Smith's colleague as Professor of Oriental Languages (1754-6) and then Natural Philosophy (from 1757), made in his Commonplace Book what seems to be selective extracts from a student's report of the Jurisprudence part of Smith's moral philosophy course ... If reported accurately in the Anderson extracts, Smith's early jurisprudence lectures also dealt with price and money under the heading of contract. The extracts suggest, however, that Smith went considerably beyond Hutcheson through including such matters as bills of exchange, stocks, and paper money. It can be suggested that, in the Anderson extracts we see the birth of Smith's treatment of economics, perhaps resulting from his

awareness that Glasgow had arrived at a relatively advanced stage of commerce, and students there would be naturally curious about a range of topics associated with contract.[92]

Witherspoon is also speaking in a developing society, where the economic factors of a growing colony and the possibility and later the actuality of a separation from Britain would have to be teased out by a generation of his students. Venturing into the area of economics was also for him, as it had been for the likes of Hutcheson and Smith, a natural extension of the subject of jurisprudence. Witherspoon was to develop these tentative explorations of economic theories in various speeches to congress, and in 1786 brought out an *Essay on Money as a Medium of Commerce, with Remarks on the Advantages and Disadvantages of Paper Admitted into General Circulation*. In this paper, which I shall look at in the context of Witherspoon's political life, he seems to hold on to these early reflections on the need for money to have an intrinsic value.[93]

The lecture then returns to a more coherent shape, when in its concluding parts, before he comes to his 'Recapitulation', Witherspoon considers 'The Rights of Necessity and Common Rights'. In this section can be found a basis for Witherspoon's justification of rebellion. He instances a right of necessity:

> Were a man perishing with hunger, and denied food by a person who could easily afford it to him, here the rights of necessity would justify him in taking it by violence.

He follows this with what could later have been read as a sign of his early readiness to engage in the cause of American Independence to the extent of taking up arms, as he writes:

> In our own government, where by the love of liberty general among the people, and the nature of the constitution, as many particulars have been determined by special laws, as in any government in the world; yet instances of the rights of necessity occur every day.

Witherspoon relentlessly pursues this subject almost as if at this early stage in his thinking there was the beginning of a concern, that one day soon, the rights of necessity would require to be asserted in a rejection of British rule and the establishing of American Independence. That future activity might well have been in his mind when he writes:

In rights of necessity, we are to consider, not only the present good or evil, but for all time to come, and particularly the safety or danger of the example.[94]

Lastly Witherspoon considers 'Common Rights', which he says, the public is supposed to have over every member'. Here he lists the rights that a community should have over the individual members of its society: an expectation of a citizen's usefulness; to make laws against suicide; to benefit from their inventions after due compensation; a respect for the dead; and the right to limit the rights of individuals in order to protect their fellow members of society. He then returns to the concept of 'the police of a community', which he had dealt with earlier, and sees this as encompassing roads, building, marketing, organizing assemblies, fostering arts and commerce. He concludes the lecture with the opinion:

A man of real probity and virtue adopts these laws as part of his duty to God, and the society, and is subject, not only for wrath but also for conscience sake.[95]

Having completed his course of lectures, Witherspoon engages in a 'Recapitulation' in which he is apologetic, acknowledging just how incomplete his exploration of the subject of Moral Philosophy has been. But he urges his students to complete the subject for themselves: 'this must be left to every scholar's inclination and opportunities in future life'. In his summing up the importance of Moral Philosophy as a discipline, Witherspoon claims that it 'is related to the whole business of active life'. He defends it against the charge of its lack of certainty and precision when compared with Mathematics and Natural Philosophy, asserting that 'it remains a point to be discussed whether it is more certain or not'. He concedes, however, that advances in precise thinking have been made in Natural Philosophy with Newton, and hopes that the same may happen in the field of Moral Philosophy.[96]

Witherspoon's 'Recapitulation' concludes with an extensive reading list. The list shows his awareness of writers on the subject, and although he has only made overt reference to a few scattered throughout his work, there have been many allusions to the themes covered by many others. The list is a testimony to Witherspoon's willingness to expose his students to a wide range of philosophical discourse, and is an acknowledgement of the debt that he himself owes to the many scholars who have also wrestled with some aspects of Moral Philosophy. It is also a reminder to his students of the need to test his account of the subject against the findings of others; and to reinforce the fact that what they have received from him, in this course of lectures, is but a tiny fragment of a subject whose further reaches might take a lifetime with which to become acquainted.[97]

CHAPTER 8

Lectures on Eloquence

In his opening words to his students Witherspoon rather prosaically describes the nature of his course on 'Eloquence', and suggests that perhaps it ought to be called 'Composition, Taste and Criticism'. But then he goes on to describe it much more dramatically, and one can imagine the theatrical pause as he declares that eloquence deals with 'the power of persuasion'. It is in his *Lectures on Eloquence* that Witherspoon is at his most animated. There is excitement in his delivery, and his language, as if affected by the subject, becomes vivacious. One can almost see him physically reaching out to his students as he enthusiastically sells the subject to them:

> Military skill and political wisdom have their admirers but far inferior in number to those who admire, envy and wish to imitate, him that has the power of persuasion.[1]

Witherspoon's opening gambit is like the baiting of a hook with a very tempting morsel. He is offering his young men the opportunity of acquiring and developing a talent that would cause them to be noticed, envied, admired and attract a following. He even follows this up by recounting that those who have become skilled in eloquence have sometimes been thought to be dangerous, and cites Plato, who in his *Republic* suggests that orators should be banned because their power over the minds of men could lead to abuse. He also cites Sir Thomas Moore, in his *Utopia* as another who shares that sentiment. In these opening passages of his first lecture on Eloquence, Witherspoon is indeed demonstrating the power of persuasion and the skills of an orator. He knew that young men are almost invariably attracted by anything dangerous, and to be told that they were being invited to learn a skill that could be misused to the extent of dangerousness would in itself be an attraction. But then having got his class's attention, Witherspoon, like the good teacher he was, shows his solidarity with his students by disagreeing with Plato and Moore, whom he had cast in the role of those who warned against the dangers of eloquence and oratory, by saying: 'If good men are trained in oratory, they will control its misuse'.[2] He has got their attention. He has introduced them to something potentially dangerous. He has debunked the kill-joys. Now, he implies that they are the 'good men' who are going to be entrusted with and able to control and put to good use this dangerous skill which can give to them 'the power of persuasion'.

Witherspoon himself had been introduced to the subject during his time at the University of Edinburgh. By the time he arrived there in 1736, all Arts students were expected to take Latin, Greek, Mathematics, Logic, Natural Philosophy and Moral Philosophy. The lectures on Logic were given from 1730 until 1777 by John Stevenson, Professor of Logic and Metaphysics, who included rhetoric and literary criticism within his lectures on Logic. Matriculating at the same time as Witherspoon was Hugh Blair, and both attended Stevenson's classes, as did Alexander Carlyle. Thomas P. Miller writes: 'There is considerable evidence that they studied the civic rhetoric of Aristotle, Cicero, and Quintilian in John Stevenson's Logic class'.[3] Stevenson, like Francis Hutcheson, was a moderniser and also lectured in English and French contemporary literary criticism. Three years later when Blair and Witherspoon both graduated on the same day, their theses, delivered before the Professors, showed the influence of Stevenson's teaching in their Ciceronian flavour. But Stevenson's influence was to survive long after Blair's and Witherspoon's graduation. L. Gordon Tait relates that Ashbel Green in his biography of Witherspoon, suggests that 'striking similarities' are to be found between John Witherspoon's *Lectures on Eloquence* and Hugh Blair's *Lectures on Rhetoric and Belles Lettres*.[4]

Before going on to look for any influence of Stevenson on Blair and Witherspoon, it might be useful to look at the development of interest in the subject of rhetoric or eloquence and its fairly natural companion literary criticism. At the University of Edinburgh, Stevenson had been dealing with rhetoric and literary criticism within the context of his class in Rhetoric since 1730. But because of this context, he would not have been able to develop the subject in the fuller way of other expositors, as within that same class he had also to deal with Logic and the History of Philosophy.

When Adam Smith returned to Scotland from his sojourn in England with its unsatisfactory experience of the Universities at Oxford and Cambridge; not at that time having a University appointment, he offered public *Lectures on Rhetoric and Belles Lettres* in the winter of 1748-49. Richard B. Sher sees Smith as responding to the need for such lectures.[5] When Smith moved to Glasgow in October 1751, to become Professor of Logic and Rhetoric, he found his duties added to by having to share some of the work of the Professor of Moral Philosophy, Thomas Craigie, who was ill. It was quite natural for him in that hard pressed situation to use his *Lectures on Rhetoric and Belles Lettres*, previously given in Edinburgh. When Craigie died, Adam Smith was translated to the Chair of Moral Philosophy and continued to give these lectures. J. C. Bryce, Editor of Adam Smith's *Lectures on Rhetoric and Belles Lettres*, notes the important place that Smith gave to these lectures within the curriculum of Moral Philosophy:

> Throughout the eighteenth century the ordinary or 'public' class of Moral Philosophy met at 7.30 a.m. for lectures on ethics, politics, jurisprudence, natural theology, and then at 11 a.m. for an 'examination' hour to ensure that the lecture had been understood. A 'private' class, sometimes called a 'college', attended by those who had already in the previous year taken the public class and were now attending that for the second time - or even third - but not the examination class, met at noon, normally three days a week. Each professor used the private class for a course on a subject of special interest to himself. Hutcheson had lectured on Arrian, Antoninus (Marcus Aurelius), and other Greek philosophers; Thomas Reid on the powers of the mind. Adam Smith chose for his private class the first subject he had ever taught, Rhetoric and Belles Lettres.[6]

Bryce also notes that although Rhetoric was now under the aegis of the Professor of Logic, James Clow, Smith's successor to the post, did not raise any objections to Smith's teaching of *Rhetoric and Belles Lettres*. Whereas at Edinburgh, Stevenson later had protested at the creation of a chair for the subject in 1760, Bryce points out that it was the term *'Belles Lettres'* that made the difference to the courses at Glasgow. This element was strong in Smith's lectures, while in Clow's lectures the emphasis was on 'the rhetorical analysis of passages in keeping with the discipline of logic'. The two courses, one in the department of Logic and the other in Moral Philosophy, complemented each other and were never a source of conflict between the respective Professors.

The subject was clearly held as important and following Smith's departure for Glasgow, Robert Watson continued the series of public lectures on *Rhetoric and Belles Lettres* until 1758, when he was called to St Andrews. In 1759 Hugh Blair offered in private, a set of lectures on the same subject and in the following year, 1760, was appointed Professor of *Rhetoric and Belles Lettres*. In 1762 the Reverend Doctor Hugh Blair, Minister of St Giles Church, Edinburgh, became the first occupant of the Chair of *Rhetoric and Belles Lettres* at the University of Edinburgh.[7]

Edinburgh and Glasgow were not the only University Cities to produce *Lectures in Rhetoric and Belles Lettres*. The University of Aberdeen had long been the seat of scholars of note in the field of Philosophy and in the 1760s these included Thomas Reid who in his *An Inquiry into the Human Mind on the Principles of Common Sense* (1764) made a major contribution to what became known as the common sense school of philosophy, that was in opposition to the ideas of David Hume. Reid was to succeed Adam Smith in the chair of Moral Philosophy at Glasgow in 1764. By that time the Reverend George Campbell, Principal of Marischal College, Aberdeen, had produced his *Dissertation on Miracles* (1762) and was to go on to publish his *Philosophy of Rhetoric* in 1776. A fellow member of The Wise Club at Aberdeen, was the Reverend Alexander Gerard, Professor of Divinity at Kings College, whose *Essay on Taste* (1759) was awarded a prize by the Select Society in Edinburgh. This was followed up by his *Essay on Genius* (1774).[8] Both of these essays must have stimulated Campbell's interest in the subject. These publications are just a further indication of how popular and widespread was the concern to explore the important skills of communication in the period under our consideration. John Witherspoon knew of all of these writers but I shall return to Campbell later to consider what, if any, influence he had upon the lectures at Princeton.

It might now be useful to look at some of the details of the similarities between Witherspoon's *Lectures on Eloquence* and Blair's *Lectures on Rhetoric and Belles Lettres* to see if Ashbel Green's assertion that a common source of influence was that they had both attended the *Lectures on Eloquence* given by John Stevenson in their student days at Edinburgh University.[9]

In *Lecture I* Witherspoon poses the question: 'Whether does art or nature contribute most to the production of the complete orator?' Blair in his first lecture asserts: 'It has long been a contested and remains an undecided point whether nature or art confer most towards excelling in writing and discourse'.[10] Also, in their first lectures they similarly describe the alternative title that might be given to their respective course of lectures. Witherspoon tells his students:

> We are now to enter the study of eloquence, or perhaps it ought to be called from the manner you will find it treated, Composition, Taste and Criticism.

While Blair talks of 'the study of eloquence and composition' as one that 'merits the highest attention' and adds that, 'in the study of composition, we are cultivating reason itself'. When it is remembered that Stevenson's lectures in Rhetoric were given within the context of his class on Logic, the view that he was an influence on Blair is strengthened by this sentence from Blair's opening lecture: 'True rhetoric and logic are very nearly allied'.[11]

Witherspoon was very firmly of the opinion that, 'it is necessary the author or writer should feel what he would communicate'. He claimed in *Lecture VII* that:

> When we see the speaker wholly engaged and possessed by his subject, feeling every passage he wishes to communicate, we give ourselves up to him without reserve.

Blair writes of the orator: 'He must feel what a good man feels if he expects greatly to move, or to interest mankind' (*Lecture I*).[12] He explores the theme that the very discipline of pursuing the subject will be beneficial and improving of the person:

> the study of composition must certainly improve us not a little in the most valuable part of all philosophy, the philosophy of human nature. For such disquisitions are very intimately concerned with the knowledge of ourselves. They necessarily lead us to reflect on the operations of the imagination and the movements of the heart and increase our acquaintance with some of the most refined feelings which belong to our frame.

Witherspoon also touches on the subject in his first lecture, although more briefly: 'Great orators were the consequence of the knowledge of mankind and the study of the human heart'.[13]

In their opening lectures, both Witherspoon and Blair hold up the importance of their subject and the beneficial effect that it is likely to have upon those who study it, by causing them not only to look at the writings and the speeches of great orators, but to perceive the underlying motivation, feelings and understanding of the hearts of those to whom they were appealing. Both men were aware of the artfulness involved in oratory. Witherspoon in his introduction to the subject of Eloquence, which he described as 'a very noble art', had gone on to tantalise his audience by saying that it deals with 'the power of persuasion', while Blair, waits until *Lecture XXV* before writing: 'Eloquence … may be defined as the art of persuasion'. He further emphasises the art involved in Eloquence by adding:

> Conviction affects the understanding only; persuasion, the will and the practice. It is the business of the philosopher to convince me of the truth; it is the business of the orator to persuade me to act agreeably to it.[14]

Both Witherspoon and Blair were aware of the dangers of eloquence. As previously discussed, in Witherspoon's opening lecture, he makes it clear to his students that in the hands of evil men eloquence is a dangerous weapon, but he asserts that there is nothing to be feared when it is used by good men. Blair writes very similarly of the dangers of eloquence:

> Reason, eloquence, and every art which has ever been studied among mankind, may be abused, and may prove dangerous in the hands of bad men, but it were perfectly childish to contend, that upon this account they ought to be abolished. ... the more that eloquence is properly studied, the more shall we be guarded against the abuse which bad men make of it, and enabled the better to distinguish between true eloquence and the tricks of sophistry.[15]

A common source again seems to be indicated when consideration is given to Witherspoon and Blair's discussion of the sublime. Witherspoon finds one source of the sublime in greatness and elevation of thought and includes in a list where such writings may be found: 'in Mr. Addison, the Bible, Alexander the Great, Caesar, Cicero, James III and Homer'. He also asserts that: 'the sublime kind of writing chiefly belongs to the following subjects: epic poetry, tragedy, orations on great subjects and then particularly perorations'. He expresses admiration for, 'the late discovered poems of Ossian', and includes it among the epic poems that reflect life in ancient and primitive societies.[16] Blair, in 'The Sublime in Writing' (*Lecture IV*) opines:

> I am inclined to think that the early ages of the world, and the rude unimproved state of society, are particularly favourable to the strong emotion of sublime.

and adds, 'of all the writings ancient and modern the sacred scriptures afford us the highest instances of the sublime'.

In support of this he quotes *Psalm* 18. 6ff and *Habbakuk* 3.6ff. He also quotes Homer and Ossian, saying of the latter, 'The works of Ossian abound with examples of the sublime'.[17] Now clearly, James MacPherson's, *The Poems of Ossian,* which only began to be published in 1760, cannot be seen as any evidence of the influence of Stevenson, but it is interesting that they should both see in 'Ossian', elements of what they had learned to recognise, through Stevenson, as the sublime. Blair of course had published in 1763, *A Critical Dissertation on the Poems of Ossian, the Son of Fingal*. He makes the assumption, 'that the poems now under consideration are genuine venerable monuments of very remote antiquity' and writes:

> The two great characteristics of Ossian's poetry are, tenderness and sublimity ... He moves perpetually in the high region of the grand and the pathetick [*sic*]. One keynote is struck at the beginning, and supported to the end; nor is any ornament introduced, but what is perfectly concordant with the general tone or melody. The events recorded are all serious and grave, the scenery throughout, wild and romantic. The extended heath by the sea shore; the mountain shaded with mist; the torrent running through a solitary valley; the scattered oaks, and the tombs of warriors overgrown with moss; all produce a solemn attention in the mind and prepare it for great and extraordinary events ... His poetry, more perhaps than that of any other writer, deserves to be stiled, *The Poetry of the Heart*. It is a heart penetrated with noble sentiments, and with sublime and tender passions; a heart that glows and kindles the fancy; a heart that is full and pours itself forth.[18]

I have quoted at some length from Blair's *Critical Dissertation on the Poems of Ossian* in order that the full force of Blair's briefer comments on Ossian in his *Lectures* might be better understood. The above passage illustrates what he means when in *Lecture IV* he writes: 'Conciseness and simplicity are essential to sublime writing. Simplicity I place in opposition to studied and profuse ornament, and conciseness to superfluous expression'. Or again in that same lecture when he concludes: 'the main secret of being sublime is to say great things in fair and plain words'. In both these comments he is aligned with Witherspoon who in trying to describe the nature of the sublime in writing or in oratory stressed the brevity, the drama and the impact of the words in this way:

> An oration or the sublime parts of a poem have been compared to the voice of thunder, or penetration of lightening, to the impetuosity of a torrent; this last is one of the best metaphorical expressions for sublimity in eloquence, because it carries in it, not only the idea of great force but of carrying away everything with it that opposes or lies in its way.

Blair too emphasises the short lived yet powerful nature of the sublime when he writes:

It [the sublime] is an emotion which can never be long protracted. The mind by no force of genius, can be kept for any considerable time, so far raised above its ordinary situation.[19]

There are other illustrations that are common to both sets of lectures. They both make use of William Hogarth's *Analysis of Beauty* (1753). Witherspoon, rather surprisingly, in *Lecture XVI* when he is discoursing on the 'General Principles of Taste', chooses this illustration:

> Mr. Hogarth observes that ringlets of hair waiving in the wind have been an expression of grace and elegance in every age, nation and language.

The quotation is surprisingly sensual for Witherspoon, who is usually so against unnecessary ornamentation in his writing. Blair, working on the same theme in *Lecture V*, 'Beauty and other Pleasures of Taste', writes:

> Mr Hogarth in his analysis of Beauty, has observed that figures bounded by lines are in general more beautiful than those bounded by straight lines and angles.[20]

Witherspoon and Blair seem also to have similarly drawn from Adam Smith's *Considerations on the First Formation of Languages,* which was first published in *The Philological Miscellany*, Vol. 1, (London, 1761) and later included in the Third Edition of Smith's *The Theory of Moral Sentiments* (1767). It continued to be included with the fourth, fifth and sixth editions, and would be known to a wide range of readers.[21] In *Lecture IV*, when considering the origin of alphabet and language, Witherspoon seems to be alluding to Smith's work on languages and writes:

> It seems probable that this, and indeed the radical principles of all great discoveries were brought about by accident, that is to say, by Providence: therefore it is probable that God gave to *our first parents*, who were found in a state of full growth, all the instruction necessary for the purpose of life. It is also probable, from the analogy of Providence, that he left as much to the exercise of human powers as experience and application could conveniently apply.[22]

Blair makes explicit reference to what he calls, 'Dr. Adam Smith's, *Dissertation on the Formation of Languages*'. Blair tries to picture early man when language began to be formed:

We cannot however suppose that a perfect system of it was all at once given to man. It is much more natural to think, that God brought *our first parents* only such language as suited their present occasions; leaving them as he did in other things, to enlarge and improve it as their future necessities should require.[23]

In the second sentence of Smith's *Considerations Concerning the First Formation of Language* he envisions the beginnings of language:

Two savages, who had never been taught to speak, but had been bred up remote from the societies of men, would naturally begin to form that language by which they would endeavour to make their mutual wants intelligible to each other, by uttering certain sounds, whenever they meant to denote certain objects.[24]

The two savages also appear in the third lecture in Smith's *Lectures in Rhetoric and Belles Lettres* where Smith writes:

It seems probable that those words which denote certain substances which exist, and which we call substantives, would be *amongst* the first contrived by persons who were inventing a language. Two Savages who met together and took up their dwelling in the same place would soon endeavour to get signs to denote those objects which most frequently occurred and with which they were most concerned.[25]

In Witherspoon's and Blair's accounts of the formation of language, the 'two savages', become 'our first parents'. It would have gone against the grain of the clergymen to have called Adam and Eve 'savages'. Witherspoon's account seems to be the more naïve of the two, clinging to the *Biblical* story and claiming that the first pair were 'in a full state of growth' but he does seem, as do both Blair and Smith, to allow for language not having been given fully at the first, but having developed as the experience and the activities of early people became more extensive. A possible common source of all three writers, that was perhaps made more use of by Witherspoon and Blair than by Smith, is the Abbé Étienne Bonnet de Condillac's, *Essai sur l'origine des connaissances humaines* (1746), in which it is suggested that Adam and Eve had the gift of speech as part of their God-given perfection.[26]

When a comparison is made of the structures and contents of the lectures of Witherspoon and Blair, the limited nature of Witherspoon's course becomes clear. It is in its brevity that Witherspoon's course of lectures is most likely to resemble the *Lectures in Rhetoric* given by John Stevenson to both Witherspoon and Blair as students at the University of Edinburgh. Stevenson's *Lectures in Rhetoric* were only part of his course on Logic and as such would not likely be very extensive in range because of the pressure of the other subjects in the curriculum. In Witherspoon's case, his *Lectures on Eloquence* were given in the context of a college whose *raison d'etre* had been to train young men to become ministers of religion and this would naturally cause the focus to be upon training them to become competent communicators of the *Gospel* message. During his time at Princeton, Witherspoon broadened out the scope of the college curriculum and the composition of the students so that it became a place where, through its disciplines young men could acquire the skills that would enable them to enter into other professions such as Law or Teaching; and in the emerging Republic to play their part in the business, civic, and political life of their community and the nation at large.

Witherspoon's *Lectures on Eloquence* therefore focus on the vocational and practical aspects of communication. In sixteen lectures he rarely departs from the main purpose he has in mind, which is to equip his students with the understanding of the methods and the means by which they can become able communicators. If on occasion, he seems to be wandering off into the more esoteric illustrations of the art of eloquence, he soon returns to ground his teaching in some practical and relevant way. For example, having praised the great orators, Pericles, Demosthenes and Cicero, it is as if he does not want his students to be over-awed by them, or feel that oratory is too great a task for lesser mortals, and so he offers this encouragement:

> In the middle region of genius there are often to be found those who reap the greatest benefit from education and study. They improve their powers by exercise, and it is surprising to think what advances are to be made by the force of resolution and application, for example, Demosthenes himself is said at first to have laboured under almost insuperable difficulties; it is said he could not even pronounce at first all the letters of the Greek alphabet, particularly the letter R, the first letter of his art ... [Rhetoric].[27]

I think we are witnessing a moment of whimsical humour from the rather forbidding and grave faced Presbyterian minister as he relished the opportunity to roll his Rs in the naturally guttural Scottish manner. But this brief episode of theatricality further emphasises the fact that this subject was not about displaying the oratorical skills of the larger than life characters of the greats like Pericles and Demosthenes and Cicero, but it was about helping students of the College of New Jersey who might euphemistically be thought of as being 'in the middle region of genius' to acquire a practical skill by means of study, application and practice.

In *Lecture II* - 'Some General Rules', Witherspoon begins with the advice:

> Study and imitate the greatest examples. Get the most approved authors for composition, read them often and with care. Imitation is what commonly gives us our first ideas upon any subject. It is by example that ambition is kindled and youth prompted to excel.[28]

Much more than in Blair, the teacher is at work in Witherspoon's lectures. A conscious endeavour to open up the subject in as simple a way as is possible is in evidence from the language and the structure of his lectures. He was also probably speaking to a much less sophisticated audience as this comment indicates, 'It is very proper for young persons to read authors, after they have heard criticisms and remarks made upon them'. Here is Witherspoon encouraging his students to come to their own decisions about the authors their teacher might set before them. The 'young persons' is a giveaway. It is almost Pooh Bah like in its advice, and certainly not the kind of thing that Blair would have dared to say before the more sophisticated and worldly Edinburgh audience.

Witherspoon goes on in this lecture to give a very useful series of thumbnail sketches of famous orators or authors, which would have offered something of interest to any new student, and given any well-read sophisticate in learning something substantial to think about. He lists as his models from the 'Ancients': Cicero, Demosthenes, Livy, Sallust, Tacitus and Xenophon; and Joseph Addison, James Hervey and Dr William Robertson are among his 'Moderns'. His comments are tantalising, inviting the student to further explore the authors to whom he is referring. For example:

> Cicero is flowing, fervant, ornate - somewhat vain and ostentatious, but masterly in his way ... Livy has a bewitching way of telling a story, he is so expressive and descriptive that one cannot help being pleased with it even after several times reading.

In passing, it should be noted that Witherspoon gives high praise to Dr William Robertson, one of the leaders of the Moderate party who had been one of his opponents in the ecclesiastical debates before he left for America, writing: 'in his *History*, [he] has as just a mixture of strength and elegance, as any other author I know in the English language'. Having just commended a Scottish man of letters, Witherspoon cannot resist engaging in a severe criticism of the English, Dr Samuel Johnson, writing:

> I cannot help here cautioning you against one modern author of some eminence, Johnson, the author of the *Rambler*. He is so stiff and abstracted in his manner, and such a lover of hard words, that he is the worst pattern for young persons that can be named.[29]

Interspersed with all the information that he is imparting about the authors, he is scattering advice on how to study to advantage. In this same lecture he repeats himself on the need for students to have: 'a comprehensive knowledge of many authors, or at least a considerable number is certainly preferred to making one your model'. Another teaching point he twice makes in this lecture is on the value of experience:

> There is something to be learned from practice [of oratory] which no instruction can impart ... after you have learned the theory in the most perfect manner there is still a nameless something which nothing but experience can bestow.

He returns to this theme when in his concluding sentence of the lecture he refers to 'the laudable practice of this College of daily orations'.

In Witherspoon's *Address to the Inhabitants of Jamaica and other West-India Islands*, written in March 1772, as a kind of College Prospectus by which it was hoped to encourage young men from those parts to be sent by their parents for education at the College of New Jersey, the importance of the daily oration was outlined. Witherspoon writes:

> During the whole course of their studies, the three younger classes, two every evening formerly, and now three, because of their increased number, pronounce an oration on a stage erected for that purpose in the hall, immediately after prayers, that they may learn, by early habit, presence of mind and proper pronunciation and gesture in public speaking. This excellent practice, which has been kept up almost from the first foundation of the college, has had the most admirable effects. The senior scholars, every five or six weeks, pronounce orations of their own composition, to which all persons of any note in the neighbourhood are invited or admitted.[30]

That was the kind of experience to which Witherspoon was referring and which he thought of as all important in the development of any skill in oratory. He deals very briefly with what he calls, 'the branches that are subordinate to the study of eloquence': grammar, punctuation, syntax, orthography, choice of words, and use of words with precision. He also gives some practical tips on things to be avoided by the speaker. He concludes his 'Preliminary Remarks' that have been spread over the first three lectures with a plea: 'to follow nature'. He is trying to inculcate the principle that whatever they have learned from the models of good practice that he has set before them, they have to learn not to copy them or imitate them, but to draw the lessons from them that will help them to give expression to themselves in the most natural way.[31]

In *Lecture IV*, Witherspoon outlines the rest of the course. There is a very clear delineation of the various sections, and an immediate awareness of their relevance to anyone who is going into any kind of occupation that will involve the composition of an address or the formulation of an argument or the presentation of a case. The headings speak for themselves:

1. To treat of language in general, its qualities and powers [Lecture IV].
2. To consider oratory as divided into three kinds, the sublime, the simple and mixed [Lectures V-X].
3. To consider it as divided into its constituent parts, invention, disposition, style, pronunciation and gesture [Lectures XI-XII].
4. To consider its object is different. Information, demonstration, persuasion, entertainment [Lecture XIII].
5. As its subject is different. The Pulpit, the Bar, and the Senate or any deliberative Assembly [Lecture XIV].
6. To consider structure and parts of a particular discourse, their order, connexion and ends [Lecture XV].
7. Recapitulation, and enquiry into the principles of taste, or beauty and gracefulness as applicable not only to oratory but to all other (commonly called) fine arts [Lecture XVI].[32]

The seven subjects are spread over the remaining thirteen lectures. Scattered throughout the coverage of these subjects are a series of practical interjections; for example in *Lecture VI* Witherspoon writes: 'You ought always to remember that the language ought to be no higher than the subject'. In *Lecture VII* he reveals a flash of the preacher's fire and the pastor's compassion, but there is also something new, perhaps born of his new occupation, as he acknowledges all that he has learned from living in the world as he writes:

To raise the passions with success, much penetration and knowledge of human nature is necessary ... Recluse students and professed scholars will be able to discover truth, and to defend it, or to write moral precepts with clearness and beauty; but they are seldom equal, for the tender and pathetic, to those who have been much in what is called the *world* - by a well-known use of that word, though almost peculiar to the English language. There is perhaps a double reason for persons well versed in the ways of men, having the greatest power upon the passions. They not only know others better, and therefore how to touch them, but their own hearts, it is likely, have been agitated by more passions than those whose lives have been more calm and even.[33]

This is, I think, a passage that reveals that John Witherspoon, even at this early stage of his sojourn in America, has broken away from his tunnel-vision view of the ministry whose only source of inspiration was from *Holy Scripture*. It is an acknowledgement that 'the world' has insights to offer, and can be learned from in positive ways. In this passage he is writing as one who is now much nearer to the culture of the Moderates whom he had previously castigated for being too much of this world.

In *Lecture X*, after making a plea for plainness and simplicity of style, he commends Dr Samuel Clarke, whom he says exemplifies a just style:

> He is one of the few mathematicians who were good writers and while he did not lose the life and fervor of the orator, preserved the precision of the natural philosopher.

Here again is the attitude that surfaces in his *Moral Philosophy Lectures* when he said that he longed for the day when the same precision that had imbued natural philosophy, would begin to be applied in the study of moral philosophy.[34]

In *Lecture XI*, Witherspoon makes an incisive remark that should cause all who write, to hesitate before beginning a new paragraph: 'The beginning of a paragraph should be like the sharp point of a wedge, which gains admittance to the bulky part behind'. So daunting and so true is that remark, that I am having difficulty in following my opening phrase with 'the bulky part behind'. But it is just that kind of 'off the cuff' remark that would have been remembered by his students, and that might well have come to mind as they set out to begin the next paragraph of a discourse in which they were engaged in constructing. It is those kind of teaching points that appear throughout the lectures that emphasise the practical nature of Witherspoon's course, compared with the kinds of courses constructed in more elaborate and erudite ways by such as Adam Smith, George Campbell and Hugh Blair.[35]

In offering a practical tip to a speaker, Witherspoon is surprisingly modern in his attitude when he writes: 'Keep the tone and key of the dialogue or common conversation as much as possible'. This low key approach to speaking is also applied to gesture. He cites the experience of Cicero, of whom it was said that:

> when he first went to the Bar, the violence of his action was such that it endangered his constitution, so that he took a journey for his health, and on his return took a cool and managed way of speaking.[36]

When he deals with controversial writing and satire, he seems to quite naturally turn to his previous experience in Scotland, where his pamphlet, *Ecclesiastical Characteristics* had attacked the Moderates in the Church of Scotland. He offers this rueful account of the motives and the pitfalls of this kind of writing:

> There is nothing they are so fond of as exposing the weakness of their adversaries by strokes of raillery and humour. *This I did on purpose that I may state the matter to you clearly.* Controversy should mean and very generally such writers pretend to mean, weighing the arguments on each side of a contested question, in order to discover the truth. What strong professions of infallibility have we sometimes from the very champions of a party quarrel, yet it is plain that searching after truth is what they never think of, but maintaining by every art, the cause which they have already espoused. I do not deny that there are sometimes good reasons for making use of satire and ridicule, in controversies of the political kind, and sometimes it is necessary in self-defence. If any writer on behalf of a party attempts to expose his adversaries to public scorn, he ought not to be surprised, if the measure he metes out to others is measured out to him again.[37]

Witherspoon leaves his students in no doubt that he is speaking from personal experience as one who had engaged in satirical writing and controversial pamphleteering in ecclesiastical and political matters. Most of his students in the early years at Princeton would know that it had been the outspoken and controversial nature of Witherspoon's ministry that had made its way across the Atlantic, and brought him to the notice of the Trustees, convincing them that he was the man they needed to guide and direct and develop the College of New Jersey. But as he reflects on his own experience, he conveys very clearly that to engage in controversy and to use satire or ridicule cannot be done without the risk, or even the likelihood, of personal hurt. However he rounds off this section with another personal reference to the past experience of a satirist, when he quotes from 'Dr Brown in his essay on the *Characteristics*' one of the responses to his pamphlet: 'ridicule is not the test of truth but it may be very useful to expose and disgrace known falsehood'.[38] It is such episodes as the above, that enlivens Witherspoon's lectures, and distinguishes them from other more polished performances.

In the final section of his lectures (*XIV-XVI*) Witherspoon deals in detail with the practical issues that arise in speaking from the Pulpit, at the Bar and in a Public Assembly. Naturally Witherspoon is strong in his advocacy of the matters needed to acquire the quality of eloquence in the pulpit. These he reduces to two: piety and simplicity. Of the first, the sincerity of the preacher is all important. Witherspoon sees it as an absolute necessity for the preacher: 'To have a firm belief of that gospel he is called to preach and a lively sense of religion upon his own heart'. Throughout his previous ministries at Beith and at Paisley Witherspoon had been at pains to assert the personal nature of the commitment involved in being a Christian. Religion was not just a matter of formally being a member of a denomination, be it Presbyterian or Roman Catholic. 'Real religion', as against a formal attachment to a church, had to do with a personal acknowledgement of God and what he had done in sending Jesus Christ into the world. Therefore to be a minister of the *Gospel* was to have placed upon one a huge, almost unbearable responsibility. A passionate concern for the salvation of the individual soul lies at the heart of Witherspoon's piety, and this passion pours over in the words that he addresses to his students about the need for them to be themselves convinced and committed to the *Gospel* that they are called to preach. As he says:

> Remember then in a single word that there is neither profession nor station, from the king on the throne to the beggar on the dunghill to whom a concern for eternity is not the one thing needful.

Again Witherspoon turns to assert the all important factor of the speaker's own experience. A preacher in the pulpit can have at his fingertips all the refinement of theological belief, all the nuances of faith, all the intricate detail of ecclesiastical procedures and doctrine, but if he does not have the experience of the importance of the truth of the *Gospel* he preaches, then he will never achieve the eloquence that might just bring one of his hearers to an awareness of the eternal issues. Witherspoon, being the teacher who knows the value of reiteration of a truth, repeats in another form what he has been long asserting: 'experiential knowledge is superior to all other, and necessary to the perfection of every other kind'.

Yet with all this emphasis on the necessity of experience, and the acknowledgement that experience alone can teach certain things, Witherspoon does not neglect the importance of learning, and the contribution that it can make to piety. He writes:

> True piety will direct a man in the choice of his studies. The object of human knowledge is so extensive, that nobody can go through the whole, but religion will direct the student to what may be the most profitable to him, and will also serve to turn into its proper channel all the knowledge he may otherwise acquire.[39]

Witherspoon's life to a certain extent can be said to exemplify this theory. His habits of reading had been catholic. His interests ranged widely, as his book and library lists show, from *Biblical* studies through theology to ecclesiastical history, secular history, literature in the ancient languages of Hebrew, Greek and Latin, modern literature in English and French, philosophy, natural philosophy, political theory, mathematics and astronomy. All of which, even by the time he began teaching at Princeton, were proving to be beneficial to him in his new career as an educationalist, and in a future that was still to be disclosed, would serve him well in government. All of that had started and been developed by his interest in religion, a religion that directed his studies in ways that were to continue to benefit him.

Witherspoon then turns to consider the contribution that simplicity makes to eloquence in the pulpit. To achieve eloquence in the pulpit the preacher should strive for simplicity, he says and gives a number of reasons, asserting first of all that simplicity is necessary because many of his audience are 'poor ignorant creatures'. Therefore the preacher should 'keep to what they understand'. In addition, simplicity will help 'preserve the preacher's character for sincerity'. It is a simple message that he has to proclaim, so simplicity in the pulpit 'is suited to the Gospel itself'.

Simplicity will also help the preacher to accurately present the facts of religion and to do so with 'force and vehemence'. He maintains that it is best to adopt a simple style because it will be more easy to stay within 'the constraint of propriety and judgement'.

Despite giving these reasons for simplicity in the pulpit, Witherspoon is not content to leave it at that. He turns again from the method to the man; from the style of the preacher, to the preacher himself and how he can prepare himself for the task. Witherspoon concludes this lecture by reiterating the advice that a minister 'ought to be well furnished with literature of every kind', and that, 'he should acquire not a specialist, but a general knowledge of other subjects'.[40] He seems to want his young men to be well read ministers with a good general knowledge, although the earlier advice that he offers on simplicity in the pulpit would seem to discourage a full sharing of this knowledge, and lead them towards a measured distribution of that knowledge governed by the limited capability of their audience. At the heart of this there seems to be a certain degree of elitism being shown here by Witherspoon.

Witherspoon's advice to would-be preachers falls short of Hugh Blair's words on 'Eloquence in the Pulpit' (*Lecture XXIX*). Blair forthrightly declares: 'The end of all preaching is to persuade men to become good. Every sermon therefore should be a persuasive oration'.[41] Blair does not give a list of ways and means by which eloquence in the pulpit may be achieved, but concentrates on the task of the preacher and what he should be concerned to achieve.

> All the preacher's instructions are to be of the practical kind, and that persuasion must ever be his ultimate object. It is not to illustrate some metaphysical truth or to inform men of something which they never heard before; but it is to make them better men; it is to give them at once clear views and persuasive impressions of religious truth. Whenever you bring forth what a man feels to touch his character, or to suit his own circumstances, you are sure of interesting him. No study is more necessary for this purpose, than the study of human life, and the human heart. To be able to unfold the heart, and discover a man to himself in a light in which he never saw his own character before, produces a wonderful effect.

At this point there is no trace of any theme common to both Blair and Witherspoon based on their experience of John Stevenson's lectures. Indeed there is evidence that although John Witherspoon has moved on since the days when he criticised the Moderates for their interest in learning, yet he is still bearing the traces of the Calvinist strain of theology that gives prominence to the acceptance of a doctrine rather than to a change of heart as a sign of having entered into the Christian life with its prospect of salvation. Witherspoon's advice to his preachers seems to be based on things that will assist them to proclaim the facts of the *Gospel* message; whereas Blair's advice is based on assisting the preacher in the task of helping men to gain a new insight into themselves in the light of the *Gospel* message.

At the end of this lecture Blair is critical of Dr Samuel Clarke whom Witherspoon had praised in *Lecture X*:

as one of the few mathematicians who are good writers and while he did not lose the life and fervour of an orator, preserved that precision of the natural philosopher.

In listing sermon writers, Blair's criticism of Clarke is that:

> He instructs and he convinces; in what then is he deficient? In nothing except in the power of interesting and seizing the heart. He shews you what you ought to do; but he excites not the desire of doing it; he treats man as if he were a being of pure intellect, without imagination or passion.[42]

Witherspoon and Blair's very different opinions of Clarke are indicative that, despite the fact that they had been introduced to the subject of Eloquence by the same Professor, they are quite distinctly different in how they themselves expound the subject.

Witherspoon and Blair started out as students at the same University and underwent the same disciplines in arts and divinity in preparation for entering the ministry of the Church of Scotland, but nurtured by different traditions within that church, they developed in quite different ways. In the advice that they give to those who would be preachers, it is clearly seen that while Blair has developed as one who is clearly influenced by the Scottish Enlightenment's ideas of sensibility, Witherspoon has remained much more firmly attached to the manners and practice of the preachers of the previous century.

Witherspoon deals very briefly with the next subdivision: 'Eloquence at the Bar' (*Lecture XV*), concentrating mainly on the qualities and character necessary for being a lawyer. He begins by emphasizing the importance of a lawyer being well read, of being a man 'of probity and untainted integrity'. A lawyer should have 'address and delicacy in his manners and deportment'; and 'extensive knowledge of the arts and sciences, in history, and in the laws'. He sees 'quietness and vivacity' as absolutely necessary in a lawyer, 'not so in a minister'; and offers the comment: 'wit which is intolerable in the pulpit, is often not barely pardonable in a lawyer, but very useful'.[43] By concentrating on the qualities of character necessary for a lawyer, Witherspoon offers little on how eloquence at the Bar can be achieved.

When he turns to consider 'the Eloquence of Promiscuous Deliberative Assemblies', he is at first almost dismissive. So much so, that I think that this provides evidence for the early date of these lectures, and for me, helps confirm that they stem from the period soon after his arrival in Princeton in 1768, and before he had any involvement in any formal way with political assemblies; which might be said to have happened in 1774 when he became a founding member of the Committee of Correspondence for Somerset County and was appointed to the New Jersey provincial legislature. Perhaps too his elevated view of the matters a minister of religion has to deal with, causes him to look down upon those whose business was with the much more mundane matters of politics, but whatever was dominating his thoughts at that time, he rather deprecatingly writes:

> For though no matters of a merely temporal kind, are of equal moment in themselves, with the things a minister has to treat of, yet men's passions are almost as much, and in many cases more, excited and interested by them.

However, he goes on to list the most important qualities that a person should have if he would succeed in speaking in 'public deliberative assemblies', as: 'dignity of character and disinterestedness, knowledge of men and manners, of history and human nature, and a power over the passions'. He also offers this advice to anyone who would enter into political debate:

> All who intend to be speakers in political assemblies must begin early; if they delay beginning until years shall add maturity to their judgement, and weight to their authority, the consequence will be that years will add so much to their caution and diffidence, that they will never begin at all.[44]

Witherspoon was certainly giving advice that was in keeping with his own experience.

At the time when he was completing his Master of Arts degree at the University of Edinburgh, it had not been customary to defend the final thesis before the Professors and other members of the University community. But Witherspoon along with two others asked for the opportunity to present their theses publicly and this was granted. So on the 23 February, 1739, aged just sixteen, John Witherspoon delivered his thesis, *De Mentis Imortalitate*, before the assembled representatives of the Senate. The oration in Latin, in its printed version, covers ten pages, and is signed 'Joannes Wederspan'. The other two orations given that day were by 'Matthaes Mitchell on *De Origine Mali* [12 pages] and Gulielmus Cleghorn on *Analogia & Philosophia Prima* [13 pages]'.[45] The early start to public speaking encouraged in his students by Witherspoon was something to which he could attest by his own experience. This early assertiveness, that could have been rated as precociousness, was later followed up by his confidently accepting the call to Beith Parish Church in the full knowledge that their previous minister William Leechman, who was an outstanding scholar, was going to the University of Glasgow to take up the Chair of Divinity. Leechman was one who was not afraid of, and well prepared to enter into, controversy as his later career at Glasgow was to witness. Francis Hutcheson had for some time been the friend of Leechman and had skillfully lobbied for him to be presented as a candidate for the Chair of Divinity, but even when he was elected on December 13, 1743, the battle was not over, as Leechman had to deal with obstructive actions in both the Presbyteries of Irvine and Glasgow before an appeal to the Synod, allowed him to begin teaching.[46] Further controversy followed his appointment when an action was raised on an allegation of heresy said to be contained in his book on *Prayer*. This was the stormy background against which Witherspoon had the temerity to accept the call from Beith. Even although he knew that his extremely conservative, and then considered orthodox theology, was greatly different from the moderate and adventurously speculative theology of Leechman, it took a confident man to enter into that situation and take up a ministry in Beith.

He was ordained and inducted into Beith Parish Church on the April 11, 1745, but not before he had to defend his orthodoxy because a challenge had been made to it with reference to his thesis *De Mentis Immortalitate*. These were not only troubled theological times, but they were also times of political turmoil. In July 1745 Charles Edward Stuart, the Young Pretender, had raised his standard at Glenfinnan, in Scotland in an attempt to regain the throne. The following year, the Church of Scotland, in a show of loyalty to the crown, encouraged its ministers to form local militias. Witherspoon responded to this as a callow twenty-three year old, and helped raise and lead fifty men which were intended to engage the rebellious force at Falkirk.[47] Again he displays that 'get up and go' attitude that he was encouraging his students to adopt in their early years. He was to continue to engage in challenges, that, had he waited to reconsider with more mature thoughts, he might never have taken them up at all. Among these one might list: his early engagement of the Moderates in his pamphlet *Ecclesiastical Characteristics*, or his premature and ill-conceived attack upon the *Stage*, following the production and performance of John Home's play *Douglas*. His long battle against the established practice of patronage, entered into when he was still a relatively young minister did not lead to victory, but his contribution to the debate left its imprint on the minds of many, and the issue did not go away, eventually being resolved at a much later date, in a way that would have satisfied Witherspoon. Although not always successful in the resultant performance,

Witherspoon's willingness to take a risk, and state in public what he thought and felt, always made people think. Even although he knew that it could lead to failure, and sometimes even humiliation, he believed that it was essential that his students should exercise and develop their powers of communication at as early an age as possible.

Witherspoon's advice to those who would engage in political discourse is eminently practical. He simply suggests that each address should have, 'a beginning, a middle and an end'. But his advice on the beginning or introduction to a speech is worth repeating:

> The aim of an introduction is: to make the reader attentive to the discourse, favourable to the speaker, and willing to receive instruction on the subject.

He urges: 'In the Middle - keep it orderly - keep it to the point'. As to the End: 'the conclusion or Peroration - it must be by far the warmest and include a summary of the argument'. In general, Witherspoon advises, political discourse should avoid pomposity, being too hackneyed, or too general and should never be forced or unnatural, too fanciful or whimsical, or tedious. Witherspoon does not theorise on the nature of deliberative assemblies, and contents himself with delivering a series of 'does' and 'don'ts' to those who would speak at them.[48]

Witherspoon concludes the course in *Lecture XVI* with a very brief 'enquiry into the general principle of taste and criticism'. He is content to quote and seemingly agree with Francis Hutcheson's view of what he calls 'the reflex senses, finer internal sensations' that play their part in determining taste. He also approvingly quotes Addison's view in *The Pleasures of the Imagination*, of the three great sources of our delight as 'novelty, greatness and beauty'; and William Hogarth's, *Analysis of Beauty*, which he says 'resolves into the following principles: Fitness, Variety and Uniformity, simplicity, intricacy and quantity'. He returns again to Hutcheson's musings on the internal senses and singles out 'harmony' as:

> the most distinct and separate of all the internal senses that have been mentioned; it is concerned only in sound and therefore must be but remotely applicable to the writer and speaker'.[49]

This last lecture is a bit of a hotch-potch of other people's views on taste, and no clear view of Witherspoon's own opinion emerges from it. The weak ending to this lecture perhaps has to do with Witherspoon entering into a discussion of a subject which he judges, is only of peripheral concern to his students. Adam Smith, George Campbell and Hugh Blair all spend a much greater proportion of their lectures on the subjects of Taste and Criticism, but their work is directed to a much more general audience than Witherspoon's.

Although Witherspoon was anxious that his students should write well, the emphasis in his lectures is on the spoken word, whereas Adam Smith in his, *Lectures on Rhetoric and Belles Lettres*, gives much more time to the written word as against the spoken word. Smith's audience was much more broadly based than that of Witherspoon, and to a certain extent, Smith could assume that it was better informed, and likely to be better read. Smith was also working on the basis of thirty lectures as against Witherspoon's sixteen. Smith could therefore engage in lengthy comparisons of the written speeches of Demosthenes and Cicero, and as a preparation for this, could indulge in a description of the Greek and Roman cultures that helped determine the style of the orators and ensure that their audiences would receive their words in quite different ways. Witherspoon at times could only touch on a subject, while Smith could afford to be expansive, for example: Witherspoon in *Lecture II* summarizes Demosthenes in eight words and Cicero in fourteen words, whereas Smith takes forty words to describe Demosthenes and fifty-two words to describe Cicero. In addition to this, in his *Lecture XXX*, Smith devotes a whole ten pages to a further discussion of the pair.[50] Remember too the first audiences for which these lectures were prepared. Witherspoon's lectures were set before young undergraduates of fairly limited experience in the classical language and literature, while Smith's initial lectures were listened to by members of the Philosophical Society of Edinburgh along with University staff and students and the general public. Smith therefore would have been able to assume in his audience, a reasonable familiarity with classical studies, and consequently deals in a more detailed way in his exposition of them. When Smith went to the University of Glasgow in 1751, he utilised these lectures again, and again he was able to assume that he was addressing a fairly cultured audience, even it was a student body. Contrast this with Witherspoon's scenario; newly into his job as an educationist, one entirely different from that of a Parish Minister, he was having to put together a series of *Lectures in Eloquence* along with others in *Moral Philosophy* and *Divinity* and at the same time administer and fund raise for a College. But most important of all, Witherspoon was working in what today would have been called a vocational college. He was initially working towards preparing the young men in his classes to become ministers of religion, and even in later years when it was acknowledged that the College was a place that could help prepare people for other professions, it remained largely a place of training for work. Hence a course such as *Eloquence* focused on the practical aspect of learning how to address an audience. When these factors are taken into account, it is easy to explain why Witherspoon's *Lectures on Eloquence* are so different from those produced by Smith or Campbell or Blair.

In Hugh Blair's *Lectures on Rhetoric and Belles Lettres* which were prepared to be given as a course in themselves on a subject that stood by itself, a very considerable section of the lectures are given to a critical examination of various texts: for example *Lectures XX-XXIII* examine the style of Addison's Essays in the *Spectator* Editions 411-414. *Lecture XXV* deals with the writings of Dean Swift. There are full lectures on Demosthenes, and Cicero; and the final thirteen of the forty-seven lecture course are given over to a critical examination of Historical and Philosophical Writing, Poetry and Drama. The subject came to be treated in a much more thorough and broad way as it grew in popularity. Blair's forty-seven lectures in the 1813 edition are spread over three volumes and total 1224 pages not including Index and Notes.[51]

Although there appears to be no evidence that would indicate that Witherspoon knew of George Campbell's book, *The Philosophy of Rhetoric* (1776), he certainly knew that author's work on *Miracles* (1762). It is included in a list of books compiled by a student, William Beckman Jnr. and said to be 'A List of Books of Character as Collected by Dr. Witherspoon, 1773'. The Reverend George Campbell (1719-1796), was a minister in Aberdeen and Principal of Marischal College, Aberdeen from 1759-1792 and Professor of Divinity there from 1771-1792. Campbell's lectures cover a wider area of concern than those of Witherspoon in a work of two volumes containing 592 pages.[52]

Although there are occasional similarities to the teaching of Witherspoon, for example when Campbell writes on the uses and abuses of eloquence, he adopts a similar stance to Witherspoon: 'arms are not to be laid aside by honest men, because carried by assassins and ruffians, they are to be used the rather for this very reason'.[53] Again, on the subject of a speaker's conviction, Campbell writes in similar vein to Witherspoon:

> The speaker's apparent conviction of the truth of what he advanceth, adds to all his other arguments an evidence, though not precisely the same, yet near a-kin to that of his own testimony. This hath some weight even with the wisest hearers, but it is everything with the vulgar. Whatever therefore lessens sympathy, must also impair belief.[54]

Like Stevenson, Blair and Campbell recognised the relationship between Logic and Grammar, reasoning and eloquence. Campbell writes:

What opposition is he not prepared to conquer, on whose arms reason hath conferred solidity and weight, and passion such a sharpness as enables them, in defiance of every obstruction, to open a speedy passage to the heart? ... Would we not only touch the heart, but win it entirely to co-operate with our views, those affecting lineaments must be so interwoven with our argument, as that from the passion excited, our reasoning may derive importance, and so be fitted for commanding attention, and by the justness of the reasoning, the passion may be more deeply rooted and enforced; and that thus, both may be made to conspire in effectuating that persuasion which is the end proposed.[55]

There are many echoes of the attitude of Witherspoon towards the need for logical, coherent and grammatically balanced sentences in this section of Campbell's writing. He also adopts the same division of the different spheres of eloquence: the pulpit, the bar and the public assembly, as do both Witherspoon and Blair. Again, his course of lectures cover much more ground than Witherspoon, but many of the topics highlighted by Witherspoon are dealt with by Campbell.

This brief excursion into the work of other contemporary writers on the subject of Rhetoric or Eloquence shows that although Witherspoon's treatment of the subject was on a much smaller scale than Smith, Campbell and Blair, nevertheless, when the more limited aims of his work, and the context within which it took place are remembered, it can be claimed that he gave his students a good introduction to the subject, and indicated the ways in which they could take it further.

CHAPTER 9

Politician I: 1768-1776

In his sermon, The *Dominion of Providence over the Passions of Men*, preached at Princeton on May 17, 1776, John Witherspoon claimed that this was the first time ever, that he had introduced politics into the pulpit. I think it would have been more honest of him to have said that it was the first time he had been overtly political from the pulpit, for it would be more true to say that he had for some considerable time been preaching politics for anyone who could read between the lines of his sermons. But certainly it was on that occasion, less than two months before the *Declaration of Independence* was made on July 4, 1776, that he made it entirely plain that he was wholeheartedly in favour of American Independence from Great Britain. Here are his unequivocal words:

> If your cause is just, if your principles are pure, if your conduct is prudent, you need not fear the multitude of opposing hosts. If your cause is just, you may look with confidence to the Lord and entreat him to plead it as his own. You are all my witnesses that this is the first time of my introducing any political subject into the pulpit. At this season however, it is not only lawful but necessary; and I willingly embrace the opportunity of declaring my opinion without any hesitation, that the cause for which America is now in arms is the cause of justice, of liberty and of human nature. So far as we have hitherto proceeded, I am satisfied that the confederacy of the colonies, has not been the effect of pride, resentment or sedition, but of a deep and general conviction that our civil and religious liberties, and consequently in a great measure, the temporal and eternal happiness of us and our posterity depended on the issue. There is not a single instance in history in which civil liberty was lost and religious liberty preserved entire. If therefore we yield up our temporal property, we at the same time deliver the conscience into bondage.[1]

I shall look later at the theology that lies behind this sermon, for the present, I want to present it simply as what Witherspoon thought of as his first venture into politics from the pulpit.

I would contend that Witherspoon was either suffering from a lapse of memory or that he was not willing to bring to the notice of the public a previous occasion when he had been political in the pulpit, perhaps not as overtly, but had there been a British spy present at Princeton in September

1775 on 'the Sabbath preceding the Annual Commencement' then he would have had cause to report the highly political and potentially seditious nature of the sermon preached by John Witherspoon.

The sermon was entitled *Christian Magnanimity* and was based on the text from *I Thessalonians* 11.12: 'That you would walk worthy of God who has called you into his kingdom of glory'. Witherspoon declares that his 'single purpose for these words at this time is to explain and recommend magnanimity as a Christian virtue'. He sets out a summary of what he will deal with in the sermon:

> To magnanimity it belongeth to attempt:
> 1. great and difficult things
> 2. to aspire after great and valuable possessions
> 3. to encounter dangers with resolution
> 4. to struggle against difficulties with perseverance
> 5. to bear sufferings with fortitude and patience.

When this sermon is placed in the context of the times, its words are loaded with significance and it could easily be seen as applying to the situation of conflict in which the Colonists and their British rulers were already engaged. Witherspoon's audience and the occasion are described in the 'Advertisement' that prefaces the sermon:

> It had been the custom in the College of New Jersey from its first establishment that the president should preach a sermon on the Lord's day preceding commencement, for the benefit of young persons in general, and in the end address a particular exhortation to the seniors of that year who were to receive the first degree in arts, and leave the College. ... But in the year 1775 when the war with Britain was actually begun, and everything seemed to breathe the spirit of defence [*sic*], he [Witherspoon] chose 'Christian Magnanimity' as the subject of the discourse, and not knowing what might be the event of the important contest, he thought it advisable, to make a collection or summary of all the advices that had been given to the young gentlemen's further conduct of life, in different years, under different hands.[2]

The roots of the Colonists' struggle against British rule go at least as far back as the end of the Seven Year's War in 1763 when the British Government forbade the subjects of its older colonies to settle in the newly acquired lands in Canada, and reserved these for the French colonists who had just become its subjects. *The Stamp Act* of 1765 caused further discontent, but even after its withdrawal in 1766 further taxes were imposed. The colonists attempted to evade taxation by boycotting British goods and trouble flared with the Customs officials. On March 5, 1770, the first shots, in what was to become a war, were fired, and four Americans were killed in what became known as the 'Boston Massacre'. Compromise was achieved when the British withdrew the new taxes, except that on tea, which continued to be imposed, probably as a point of principle, asserting Britain's right to impose taxation on its colonies. However, in December 1773 a group of colonists boarded the ships of the East India Company in Boston Harbour and threw overboard the tea cargoes. The British Government retaliated in 1774 by imposing a series of acts: *The Boston Port Bill* which closed the port, *The Massachusetts Government Act* which revoked the colony's charter, *The Quartering Act* that allowed the billeting of troops in the colonists' homes and *The Administration of Justice Act* that allowed people to be sent back to Britain for trial for capital offences. Although not imposed as a direct result of the Boston incident, *The Quebec Act* caused resentment among the colonists by its preventing the older colonies to extend into the new lands and giving recognition to the French settlers' language, religion and institutions. A conference of all thirteen colonies met at Philadelphia in September 5, 1774 and protested against these coercive acts and organised a more effective boycott of all British goods.[3]

Early in April 1775 the new Governor of Boston, General Gage, was informed that patriots were arming themselves and had gathered at the village of Concord. On April 18 he dispatched a detachment to seize the armaments and arrest the leaders, Samuel Adams and John Hancock. The forces met at Lexington and although in the first skirmish the colonists lost eight men, the British force was repulsed at Concord and had to return without accomplishing its mission. On its return march to Boston it was further harried by the colonists and lost 247 men out of a complement of 2,500. This was the first serious loss that British troops had suffered since the dispute had begun, and, as Jacques Godechot points out, 'it was the first time in the history of the revolutions of the late eighteenth century that armed revolutionaries compelled troops of the regular army to retreat'.[4] In May 1775, a second Continental Congress was convened, the people called to arms, and on June 15, 1775, General George Washington was appointed to command the Continental Army.[5] It is against this background that Witherspoon's words in his sermon to his students in September 1775 must be measured.

In expounding the first point of his sermon, 'It belongs to magnanimity to attempt great things', Witherspoon engages in a very thinly veiled call to action in the cause of revolution. There could have been nothing more difficult to contemplate at that time, than the overthrow of the British Army and all that lay behind it in sea-power and commercial interest. Witherspoon is clearly making reference to recent events in the conflict when he criticises those who do not tackle the 'great and difficult things', but rather busy themselves with 'things mean and of small consequence when all around them there are momentous events going on'.[6]

In his second point: 'It belongs to magnanimity to aspire after great and valuable possessions', Witherspoon projects an image of what his young men should aspire to:

> such a man will not be easily satisfied or put up with what is either mean or scanty, while he can acquire and possess a better and more extensive portion.

He goes on to claim that this is an act appropriate to the dignity of our human nature:

> The large and increasing desires of the human mind have often been made an argument for the dignity of our human nature and our having been made for something that is great and excellent.

Here Witherspoon is encouraging his students to seize the land that is theirs by right and not to settle for less than is in accordance with their dignity. After all it is only commensurate with their dignity to want something greater and more appropriate to their status. This section of the sermon is a quite blatant encouragement to go out and 'acquire and possess a more extensive portion'.

When the third point is made: 'It belongs to magnanimity to encounter dangers with resolution', Witherspoon adopts a more insidious and sinister tone. He writes:

> Courage is always considered a great quality; it has the admiration or rather adoration of mankind in every age. Many when they speak of magnanimity, mean nothing else but courage, and when they speak of meanness, have little other idea but that of timidity. Neither is there any human weakness, that is more the object of contempt and disdain than cowardice, which, when applied to life in general is commonly called pusillanimity.

I think that Witherspoon is striking dangerously below the belt in this section of his sermon. He is playing on the emotions of his young men, implying by his words that courage is the nature of magnanimity and encouraging them to be courageous so that they might win peoples admiration or even adoration. Further, he rather nastily implies that if they do not act courageously in the present time they will be thought of as cowards. This section of the sermon leaves a bad taste in the mouth and borders on an unhealthy exploitation of the teacher's and preacher's role.

When Witherspoon comes to point four: 'It belongs to greatness to struggle against difficulties with steadiness and perseverance', a significant change in the sermon becomes clear. Witherspoon has substituted the word 'greatness' for his previously stated 'magnanimity' as if it was a synonym. These words are not synonyms. All the graciousness and benevolent spirit associated with 'magnanimity' does not carry over into 'greatness'. A great man is not necessarily magnanimous in victory; a magnanimous man always is. Witherspoon has got carried away, and is in danger of turning a sermon into a rant; turning a Christian proclamation into an opportunity for propaganda. At this point in the sermon he is acting more like a recruiting officer than a pastor or a College President. Point four begins with the now altered text: 'It belongs to greatness to struggle against difficulties with steadiness and perseverance. Perseverance is nothing else but continued and inflexible courage'. Again there is this looseness of language, this lack of precision in the use of words, or is it a deliberate usage of words that are more suited to his purpose? He continues:

> We see some persons who show the greatest activity and boldness for a season, but time and opposition weaken their force and seems, if I may speak so, to exhaust their courage, as if they wasted the power by the exertion. Perseverance is necessary to greatness. Few things are more contrary to this character than fickleness and unsteadiness. We commonly join together the characters of weakness and changeable.

In dropping the word 'magnanimity' and substituting it with 'greatness' Witherspoon has changed the whole tone of this section of the sermon. By a subtle and I suspect quite deliberate sleight of hand he has changed the emphasis from all the graciousness and large-mindedness of the concept of Magnanimity to the raw seeking after greatness of a selfish quest. I find myself made uncomfortable by what I am hearing. He is rabble rousing. He is inciting young men to go out and fight. But he is not going to be at their head, nor intending to go to battle himself. Witherspoon for all his high flown language, is in a quite unprincipled way, beating the war drum. His concluding section again drops the pre-stated title and begins: 'It belongs to greatness to bear sufferings with fortitude and patience'. He does acknowledge the use of the word 'greatness' instead of 'magnanimity', explaining:

> This is a kindred quality to the former and is necessary to complete the character of magnanimity. Such is the state of human things that suffering is one way or another wholly unavoidable. It often happens that difficulties cannot be removed or enemies cannot be conquered, and then it is the last effort of greatness of mind, to bear the weight of the one or the cruelty of the other, with firmness and patience. This virtue has always been of the greatest reputation. It is a well known saying of a heathen philosopher, that a great man, suffering with invincible patience under a weight of misfortune, is a sight which even the Gods must behold with admiration.

Here, Witherspoon is preparing his students for the possibility of defeat. But he still appeals to them that they will achieve greatness and be much admired. Witherspoon is a wily preacher. He may have justified to himself, that he was not overtly political, because he had not specifically named the historical events and the nature of the growing crisis to which it could be said he was alluding, and was not therefore introducing politics into the pulpit. However I think that Witherspoon understood what he was doing. I cannot help but see this sermon as the kind of political comment that it would have been natural for any preacher to make. But much more worrying to me is the insidious nature of his language, and the morally suspect manner of its use in the particular context, which lays Witherspoon open to the charges of exploitation and manipulative use of his position, both as Preacher and President of the College. If Witherspoon had been more honest, he would have named names and events and spoken unequivocally of his views, but instead he left what he said to be interpreted and in doing it that way, I think that he engaged in a quite inappropriate and ultimately dishonest act.

The sermon, which until now has largely been a barely disguised political call to arms, is next given a top coat of religiosity, as Witherspoon takes the five points that he had made about 'magnanimity' (or latterly, 'greatness'), and substitutes the word 'piety' for 'magnanimity'. Witherspoon writes: 'Let me run over and apply to religion, the above mentioned ingredients of magnanimity' and going back over the first point in his sermon, 'to attempt great and difficult things to do', he continues:

> Religion calls us to the greatest most noble attempts, whether in private or in public view. In Private *it calls us to resist* and subdue every corrupt and sinful passion. In Public *every good man is called*

to live and to act for the glory of God. … He is not indeed permitted to glory or to build an altar to his own vanity, but he is both permitted and obliged to exert his talents, to improve his time, to employ his substance and *to hazard his life in his Maker's service, or in his country's cause.* Nor am I able to conceive any character more truly great than that of one, whatever be his station or profession, who is devoted to the public good under the immediate order of Providence. He does not seek the bubble of Reputation in the *deadly breach*, but he complains of no difficulty, and *refuses no service*, if he thinks he carries *the common cause* of the King of Kings.[7]

My italicised words highlight their openness for interpretation, and their possible application to the conflict in which the colonialists were engaged; and sometimes, their even more overtly war-like tone. Witherspoon then goes on to cover points two to five, substituting 'piety' for 'magnanimity' or 'greatness' and continuing to use emotive language that is also subject to another interpretation: 'The truly pious man aspires after the greatest and most valuable possessions'. What greater possession can be had than having the freedom to govern your own country'? Witherspoon follows this up with a religious reason for any of one of his listeners having this desire: 'His heavenly father knoweth that he needeth these things'. In point three, 'True Piety encounters the greatest dangers with resolution', Witherspoon declares:

> *The fear of God is the only effectual mean to deliver us from the fear of man.* Experience hath abundantly shewn that the servants of Christ have adhered to his cause and made profession of his name *in opposition to all the terrors which infernal policy could present to them and all the sufferings with which the most savage inhumanity could afflict them.*

Suspecting the fear which for good reason must have been part of the daily lives of the young men in his care, Witherspoon re-enforces that fear by referring to it, although he offers the comfort of faith in God as a means of dealing with it. But his next comment about 'infernal policy' is so calculated to be understood as a reference to the policy imposed upon the Colonists by the British Government that Witherspoon cannot possibly be absolved of not being political in the pulpit. As he reaches his fourth point he continues in this explicitly political manner:

> True piety preserves with constancy in opposition to continued trial. This is *what distinguishes Christian warfare from any other.* It

continues through life, and the last enemy is death. *In all conflicts between men on earth*, the issue may be speedily expected, and the reward immediately bestowed, but in religion it is only he who shall endure to the end that shall be saved.

Witherspoon so inexorably maintains a continuation of the theme of conflict, that his hearers could only be led to think of the particular current conflict in which their country was involved. Witherspoon concludes with his fifth point:

> In the last place true piety endures suffering with patience and fortitude. Reflect upon the Christian Martyrs, see with what calmness and composure, with what undaunted firmness and sometimes with exultation and triumph they have gone to the scaffold, or been led to a stake.

He draws back a little from his likening of the present to the era of the early Christian martyrs and asserts that his hearers cannot compare themselves with the martyrs of the past. But he has already invited them to do just that by citing the martyrs in the first place. Witherspoon finally reminds his hearers of how they are committed to a belief in Providence, but even in doing so he cannot refrain from using another motif of conflict, 'surrender', as he writes: 'The believer has made an unreserved surrender of himself and his all to the disposal of Providence'.[8]

When this sermon is examined in detail, as I have tried to do, it is revealed as a highly political document. Using emotive language Witherspoon's opinion on the need for involvement in the American cause would have been made entirely clear in the first half of the sermon, while in the second half he makes much the same points over again coating them with a veneer of religious language. There may well have been other sermons in which he was expressing, however veiled, his political opinions but from the single evidence of the sermon preached in September 1775, it is not true to say that Witherspoon's *Dominion of Providence* sermon delivered on May 17, 1776, was the first time that he had introduced politics into the pulpit.

If I refute Witherspoon's claim that his sermon, *The Dominion of Providence* was the first occasion when he had introduced politics into the pulpit, I can praise him for saying at that same time:

> You shall not, my brethren, hear from me in the pulpit what you have never heard from me in conversation. I mean railing the king personally, or even his ministers and the parliament, and people of

Britain as so many barbarous savages. Many of their actions have probably been worse than their intentions. That they should desire unlimited dominion is neither new nor wonderful. I do not refuse submission to their unjust claims because they are corrupt or profligate, although probably many of them are so; but because they are men, and therefore liable to all the selfish bias inseparable from their human nature.[9]

Witherspoon then comments on the impracticality of effectively governing from a great distance and defends the colonists' opposition to the British ministry as one based on 'a concern for the interest of your country and the safety of yourselves and your posterity'. These comments provide a fair summary of the basis of Witherspoon's stance at the time of his preaching on May 17, 1776. Although he had not made his political opinions as explicit from the pulpit until then, undoubtedly, as his remarks about his conversation in the sermon shows, he had been freely expressing his opinion in informal ways for some time, but also more formally in his increasing political involvement. Witherspoon's political views, of which there had been hints from as early as 1769, the year after his arrival from Scotland, were now becoming very well known.

Prior to Witherspoon's presidency, the award of honorary degrees had always been made to members of the clergy. But after just over a year in office, in 1769 honorary degrees were given to three lay men who had all been politically active. They were chosen not because they were of a like mind to John Witherspoon, but because they were participants in the debate about the relationship between the American Colonies and Great Britain. The first of them, was Joseph Galloway, a Tory and the Speaker of the Pennsylvania Assembly, who later was to play an active part on the British side in the period of the war following the *Declaration of Independence*.[10] The second was John Dickenson, the author of *Letters from a Farmer in Pennsylvania* (1768), in which he had described the rights and privileges of the Colonists and whom Witherspoon recognised as one of the defenders of liberty.[11] The third, John Hancock, had also come to prominence in 1768, by refusing to allow his ship the 'Liberty' to be searched by the British Custom's Officials in protest at the restrictions on American trade. Hancock was to become the President of the Continental Congress that took the decision to declare America's independence and the person to whom Witherspoon dedicated his *Dominion of Providence* sermon. Hancock was by far the most revolutionary of the three, being involved at Lexington and Concord. He went on to play a significant role, when as President of the Continental Congress, he was politically active in supporting George Washington and ensuring the continuance of the revolution in the winter of 1776, when things were not going well with the Continental Army.[12] It was Hancock, who at the signing of the parchment copy of the *Declaration*, made the famous remark: 'There must be no pulling different ways. We must all hang together'. According to the early American historian Jared Sparks, Benjamin Franklin replied: 'Yes, we must, indeed, all hang together, or most assuredly we shall all hang seperately'.[13] It says something about Witherspoon's early awareness of the political scene, in that so soon after he had arrived at Princeton, he was to be instrumental in awarding honorary degrees to these three men, who although varying greatly in their politics, had a common concern for the liberty and good governance of their country.

Another indicator of Witherspoon's growing political involvement, is in evidence in the lenient and uncensorious attitude that he took towards his students when they expressed revolutionary tendencies. A newspaper account of an incident at the College is quoted by Varnum Lansing Collins, Witherspoon's biographer:

> This afternoon (July 13, [1770]) the students at Nassau Hall fired with a just indignation on reading the infamous Letter from the Merchants in New York, to the Committee of Merchants in Philadelphia, informing them of their Resolution, to send Home orders for Goods contrary to their Non-Importation Agreement, at the tolling of the College Bell, went in Procession to a Place fronting the College, and burnt the Letter by the Hands of a Hangman, hired for the Purpose, with hearty Wishes, that the Names of all Promoters of such a daring Breach of Faith, may be blasted in the eyes of every Lover of Liberty, and their Names handed down to Posterity, as Betrayers of their Country.[14]

There is no record of Witherspoon taking any action to censor this very overt pro-revolution demonstration. Also that same month it was reported that the senior class at Nassau Hall had agreed to turn up at the Commencement in September dressed in American manufactured cloth as a public demonstration of their solidarity with the boycott of British imports. Involving Witherspoon in an even more personal way was the fact that his son James, who in 1777 died at the battle of Germantown, gave the oration at that Commencement in September 1770, and with the Governor, William Franklin present, included in his speech the sentiment that it was the obligation of subjects to resist a tyrannical king.[15] Again there was no condemnation from Witherspoon senior.

In 1774 Witherspoon made public his concern for Colonial affairs by becoming a founding member of the Committee of Correspondence for

Somerset County and was appointed by them to the New Jersey Provincial Legislature, where he consistently urged compliance with the directives of the Continental Congress.[16] In the summer of 1774 Witherspoon wrote two papers that had the approaching Continental Congress in mind. The first, *Reflections on the Present State of Public Affairs* reveals some of the philosophy that undergirds his resolve to seek a more just settlement from Britain. Witherspoon implies that the present healthy state of the American population is attributable to 'the liberty throughout the land' and reminds his readers that this 'liberty' is without doubt owing to the liberty which pervades the British constitution and came with the colonists to this part of the world. He refers to Montesquieu as one who has:

> shewn that the natural causes of population and depopulation are not half so powerful as the moral causes, by which he means the state of society, the form of government and the manners of the people.

After asserting that the American people are prospering because of the liberty they have, he warns that they are more than able to cope with any ensuing conflict: 'War, famine and pestilence are scarce felt where there is liberty and equal laws'. Having laid the philosophical foundation that gives the Americans the hope of success in any conflict, Witherspoon then goes on to attack the British who although they benefited by their profits from trade with America, to a far greater extent than they had by taxing America, which taxation had been submitted to in the past without complaint. He goes on to declare that:

> This however did not satisfy the king, the ministry and parliament of Great Britain. They formed golden but mistaken and delusive hopes of lightening their own burdens by laying taxes on us.

He then asserts; that even if on occasion the imposition was in itself of little consequence, nevertheless it was an offence in principle, for, 'the laudable and jealous spirit of liberty was alive and awake, and hardly suffered any of them [the taxes] to pass unobserved'. The tone of this whole paper is American and clearly points the finger of blame at king, ministry and parliament.[17]

The second pamphlet, *Thoughts on American Liberty*, was again written in the summer of 1774, after the New Brunswick Conference, but before the proposed Continental Congress. Witherspoon is aware of how significant this Congress could be as he writes:

It is certain that this Congress is different from any regular exertion, in the accustomed forms of a quiet approved settled constitution. It is an interruption or suspension of the usual forms, and an appeal to the great law of reason, the first principles of the social dimension and the multitude collectively, for whose benefit all the particular laws and customs of a constituted state are supposed to have been originally established.[18]

Witherspoon's statesmanlike language is drawing attention to the momentousness of what is happening. The American Colonies, in his opinion, have reached a point of no return in their relationship with Great Britain. They are not being listened to. Their message has not got through to a British Government that seems intent upon the subjugation of the Colonialists, and so in the strongest possible terms Witherspoon opines:

> There is little reason, as yet, to think that either the King, the parliament, or even the people of Great Britain have been able to enter into the great principles of universal liberty, or are willing to hear the discussion of the point of right, without prejudice. They have not only taken no pains to convince us that submission to their claim is consistent with liberty among us and it seems rather they mean to force us to be absolute slaves.

So utterly pro-American has Witherspoon become by the summer of 1774, that he sees the approaching Continental Congress as having to take the final step towards the Colonies becoming self-governing. Although so pro-America, he retains a loyalty to the king, but reluctantly sees that loyalty as conditional on the recognition by the British government, parliament and people, of America's legitimate claim to liberty and self-government. He then proposes:

> that the great object of the approaching Congress should be to unite the colonies, and make them one body in any measure of self-defence, to assure the people of Great Britain that we will not submit voluntarily, and convince them that it would be either impossible or unprofitable for them to compel us by open violence.

With these words Witherspoon shows his total commitment to the American cause, and also his willingness to make the point even at the cost of going to war, a war he implies, which would not be wise for the British to enter into.

Witherspoon then submits eight resolutions for Congress to consider:

(1)To profess our loyalty to the King, our backwardness to break our connection with Great Britain if we are not forced by their unjust impositions. (2) That we esteem the claim of the British Parliament illegal and unconstitutional ... but we are firmly determined never to submit to it and do deliberately prefer war with all its horrors and even extermination itself, to slavery riveted on us and our posterity.

Other resolutions invoke the need for the Colonies to adopt a united front and not to engage in separate negotiations; that a ban on all imports from Britain be imposed immediately; that means be taken to promote American industry; that every legislative body in the Colonies 'put their militia on the best footing'; and that:

all Americans should provide themselves with arms in case of a war with the Indians, French or Roman Catholics, or in case they should be reduced to the necessity of defending themselves from murder and assassination.

Resolution seven is strongly worded as it recommends a committee be set up to draw up an address to the army and navy, 'putting them in mind of their character as Britons'. Lastly, Witherspoon proposes that:

a plan of union be laid down for all the Colonies, so that as formerly they may correspond and ascertain how they shall effectively co-operate in such manners as shall be necessary to their common defence.

These two papers make it entirely clear that Witherspoon was thoroughly committed to the American cause long before the *Declaration of Independence*. Indeed it might be claimed for him that if it had not been for all his earlier comment and prompting that declaration might not have happened as soon as it did.

During his career as a Minister of the Church of Scotland, Witherspoon had always been a diligent participant in the Courts of the Church: Kirk Session, Presbytery, Synod and General Assembly. He continued this diligence after he came to Princeton and gradually as his experience of the American Presbyterian Church grew, he was increasingly involved in its committees and his talents began to be used in preparing its public proclamations. One such document he drafted was: *A Pastoral Letter from the Synod of New York and Philadelphia*, which was designed to be read from all the Presbyterian Church pulpits on the General Fast Day

called for on Thursday June 29, 1775. The document takes the form of an exhortation followed by a few 'advices'.[19]
The Exhortation to the people begins:

> The Synod of New York and Philadelphia being met at this time when public affairs wear so threatening an aspect and when (unless God in his sovereign Providence speedily prevents it) all the horrors of a civil war throughout this great continent are to be apprehended, were of the opinion that they could not discharge their duty to the numerous congregations under their care without addressing them at this important crisis.

Then follows, a call to repentance, a plea for the acknowledgement of sin and a recognition of the holiness of God, and an urging of the people to a consideration of the things that belong to their eternal peace. The Exhortation then declares:

> Hostilities long feared, have now taken place, the sword has been drawn in one province, and the whole continent, with hardly any exception seem determined to defend their rights by force of arms. If at the same time the British ministry shall continue to enforce their claims by violence, a lasting and bloody contest must be expected. Because of this it is right that those who take up arms should be prepared for death.

The Synod then goes on to declare their solidarity with the people:

> As ministers of the gospel of peace ... we have not been instrumental in influencing the minds of the people ... but things have now come to such a state that we do not wish to conceal our opinions as men and citizens, so the relation we stand in to you seemed to make it the present improvement of it to your spiritual benefit and indispensable duty ... suffer us to exhort especially the young and the vigorous by assuring them that there is no soldier so undaunted as the pious man, no army so formidable as those who are superior to the fear of death.

The tone of the Exhortation becomes much more narrowly religious as Witherspoon, getting into his stride, continues:

> There is nothing more awful to think of that those whose trade is war should be despisers of the name of the Lord of Hosts and that they should expose themselves to the imminent danger of being

immediately sent from the cursing and cruelty on earth to the blaspheming rage and despairing horror of the infernal pit.

For a moment it seems that Witherspoon is back in his Calvinist pulpit. Gone is the statesmanlike posturing and returned is the preacher possessed with the consequences that he is convinced will come to those who have not made their peace with God. Having shown the possible combatants the yawning pit that awaits the unrepentant sinner Witherspoon concludes:

> Therefore let anyone who offers himself as a champion of his country's cause be persuaded to reverence the name and walk in the fear of the Prince of the Kings of the Earth and then he may with the most unshaken firmness expect the issue either in victory or death. It may please God for a season, to suffer his people to lie under unmerited oppression, yet in general we may expect that those who fear and serve him in sincerity and truth will be favoured with his countenance and strength.

Witherspoon displays almost a split personality as he switches from role to role. As a politician his words are full of high flown morality and the tone of his address is that of even tempered reasonableness. But occasionally when he adopts the role of the Preacher he is given to these flights of fancy that are based on an understanding of the *Bible* that is as far from morality and reason as it is from common sense or accuracy and honesty in exegesis. Nevertheless, whatever doubtful theological reasons underlie this outburst, within this Exhortation there is an overt identification with the American cause and a realistic view of the possible consequences of a war with Great Britain.

Following the Exhortation there follow a few 'Advices'.[20] The first piece of advice refers to the struggle in which the Colonists are already engaged and ironically draws a parallel to the revolution that had taken place in Britain in 1688:

> In carrying on this important struggle, let every opportunity be taken to express your attachment to our sovereign king George, and to the revolution principles by which his august family was seated on the British throne.

It makes clear its reverence for 'the prince who has probably been misled into the late and present measures by those about him'. It even offers an excuse for the advisers who 'themselves have in a great degree been deceived by false information from interested persons residing in

America', and offers the assurance that 'the present opposition does not in the least arise from disaffection to the king or a desire of separation from the present state'.

The second 'advice' urges the people to respect the members of the Continental Congress, reminds them that they are the delegates 'chosen in the most free and unbiased manner by the body of the people' and to support the decisions taken by Congress so that they might be implemented throughout the land. There is also a plea for religious tolerance, for people:

> to support the common interest, for there is no example in history, in which civil liberty was destroyed and the rights of conscience preserved entire.

It is interesting that when Witherspoon was writing for Congress he listed Roman Catholics as a possible threat to security, but now writing as an ecclesiastical politician he has softened his views or perhaps subsumed his fears and sees what might be achieved if people of all denominations try to keep a common front. The third 'advice' urges civic virtue and warns against luxury and gambling, as had the last Continental Congress, for:

> it is undeniable that universal profligacy makes a nation ripe for divine judgements and is the natural mean of bringing them to ruin, reformation of manners is of the utmost necessity in our present distress.

In the fourth 'advice' there are recommendations to 'keep public order' and 'to pay your debts'. The fifth 'advice' refers specifically to the conduct of the war, and the Synod recommend that those who are called into action should do so 'in a spirit of humanity and mercy', and offers the view: 'That man will fight most bravely, who never fights till it is necessary, and who ceases to fight as soon as the necessity is over'. The *Pastoral Letter* concludes: 'Continue habitually in prayer'. These writings of Witherspoon in the lead up to the *Declaration of Independence*, show how that was only one more, albeit highly significant step along the road upon which he had been traveling almost from the time he first set foot in America.

On April 18, 1776, Witherspoon convened a meeting of Somerset County delegates at New Brunswick to discuss matters that concerned the Province of New Jersey. At this meeting, as reported by Elias Boudinot in his Journal, Witherspoon spoke of the 'absurdity of opposing the extravagant demands of Great Britain while we were professing a perfect allegiance to her Authority and supporting her courts of justice'.[21] Boudinot, a moderate in the New Jersey Provincial Assembly, was alarmed by Witherspoon's speech. Knowing the reputation of the speaker, his great influence in the community, and 'his known attachment to the liberties of the people' and sensing that the audience was in general agreement with the persuasive argument of Witherspoon's 'able and elegant' speech which lasted for about an hour and a half, Boudinot confesses:

> I was at my wit's end to know how to extricate myself from disagreeable a situation especially as the measure was totally ag's [*sic*] my Judgement.

Witherspoon did not however win the majority support of that meeting, much to the relief of Boudinot and the other moderates present. But Boudinot noted in his Journal, that, that day 'Witherspoon made the first attempt to try the pulse of the People of New Jersey on the Subject of Independence'. What this does show is that in April 1776, Witherspoon was further ahead in his thinking than other members of the Provincial Assembly and was already planning for the self-government of the Colonial Assemblies and the denial of the authority of British rule. Two months later, on June, 1776, he as a member of the New Jersey Provincial Assembly had the loyalist governor William Franklin placed under house arrest, with the intention of deporting him from the province. The sequence of events followed the traditional pattern of many of Witherspoon's sermons: following an 'Exposition' of the text, so that it was understood, there came the 'Improvement', which set out the practical course of action that should logically follow. With the help of Witherspoon, in New Jersey the sequence of revolution had moved from the understanding of the text of revolution to the act of revolution.

Between the two events last referred to above, came Witherspoon's first fully overt political statements from the pulpit in the sermon preached at Princeton on May 17, 1776, *The Dominion of Providence*. Before examining the content of that sermon, some light can be shed on one possible source of what inspired it and in particular, the choice of its text. On the Sunday following March 5, 1770, the Reverend John Lathrop A.M., Pastor of the Second Church in Boston, preached a sermon on the subject of the events of that day when what became known as the 'Boston Massacre' occurred.

The frontispiece and title page of this sermon published in 1771 bears the legend:

> *Innocent Blood Crying to God from the streets of Boston.* A sermon occasioned by the horrid murder of Messieurs Samuel Gray, Samuel Maurice, James Caldwell and Crispus Attucks; with Patrick Carr

since dead and Christopher Monk judged irrecoverable and several others badly wounded, by a party of troops under the command of Captain Preston on the 5th March 1770 and preached on the Lord's Day following; by John Lathrop A.M., Pastor of the 2nd Church in Boston.[22]

This is followed by a double text: 'Cursed be their anger, for it was fierce, and their wrath for it was cruel, Genesis XLIX. 7'; and 'The remainder of their wrath thou shalt restrain, Psalm LXXVI. 10'. The second text in its fuller version, is the one chosen by John Witherspoon on May 17, 1776: 'Surely the wrath of man shall praise thee; the remainder of wrath thou shalt restrain'. That Witherspoon was aware of Lathrop's sermon is not in doubt, but what he thought of it is less clear. Collins quotes part of Witherspoon's letter to *The Scots Magazine* in May 1771 as evidence of Witherspoon's knowledge of the sermon, but the letter itself seems to indicate that Witherspoon is sitting on the fence on this one, perhaps aware of the need to keep the British, or more particularly the Scottish public on his side as a temperate advocate of the Colonists' position.[23] A further indication of his knowledge of the sermon is that it is highly unlikely that Witherspoon would have chosen as obscure a text without having previously been appraised of its use in another and related context.

The Boston sermon calls for justice. Having quoted the Cain and Abel story Lathrop declares: 'He who sheddeth man's blood, by man his blood shall be shed'. He then goes on to address the present situation in Boston:

> ... where there is no civil authority; in the case where everyman is in some sense a minister of justice and may execute the law which God has written in his heart ... in self-preservation, therefore obliges us, on failure of other expedience, to cut off such a common and dangerous enemy.

He then comments on the wider issues:

> Yea, if the essential parts of any system of government are found to be inconsistent with the general good, the end of government requires that such bad system shall be demolished, and a new one formed by which the public weal shall be more effectually secured.

The sermon ends strongly, making the point that it is not vengeance but justice that is sought:

if innocent blood is not heard and avenged according to the strict requirements of the law of God and the laws of every good system of civil government, it will continue to cry not only against the murderer, but the government and land, which suffers murderers to go unpunished.[24]

I am sure that the cry of innocent blood that arose from the streets of Boston was heard and the text of the sermon remembered by John Witherspoon when he came to make his own forthright declaration of the just nature of the American cause in his on sermon, *The Dominion of Providence* preached May 17, 1776.

In expounding the text, 'Surely the wrath of man shall praise thee, the remainder of the wrath shalt thou restrain', Witherspoon begins by setting the text in the context of a belief in the providence of God. He sees that providence as having the power to use even the wrath of men to serve its overall purpose. He pleads with his hearers to grasp the importance of a belief in providence:

> There is not a greater evidence either of the reality or the power of religion, than a firm belief of God's universal presence and a constant attention to the influence of his providence.[25]

It is important to remember that the dominant theme of this sermon, which although it contains several political opinions and makes allusions to events in the revolutionary scene in America, is essentially an assertion, as its title suggests, of the *Dominion of Providence over the Passions of Men*. In it Witherspoon is putting forward the view that the events of the war and the fate of the American Colonists are in the safe hands of a God who will grant them victory if their cause is just. He sets out to expound the idea that is asserted by the text that even the wrath of man is under the control of God's providence and seeks to apply this to the revolutionary war in which he and his hearers find themselves caught up.

Following a brief exegesis, in which he suggests that the *Psalm* was written as a celebration of a victory obtained, he indicates that it might have been referring to 'the unsuccessful assault on Jerusalem by the army of Sennacherib, King of Syria, in the days of Hezekiah'. He also acknowledges the weakness of his case for using the text:

> I am sensible my brethren, that the time and occasion of this Psalm may seem to be in one respect ill-suited to the interesting circumstances of this country at present. It was composed *after* the victory was obtained. Whereas we are now but putting on the harness

and entering upon an important contest, the length of which it is impossible to foresee and the issue of which it will perhaps be thought presumptuous to foretell.

He then goes on:

The truth asserted in this text which I propose to illustrate and improve upon is 'That all the disorderly passions of men whether exposing the innocent to private injury or whether they are the arrows of divine judgement in public calamity, shall in the end be to the praise of God'.

Having stated his contention, he proceeds:

to apply it more particularly to the present state of the American colonies, and the plague of war and the ambition of mistaken princes, the cunning and cruelty of oppressive and corrupt ministers, and even the inhumanity of brutal soldiers however dreadful shall finally promote the glory of God and in the meantime, while the storm continues, his mercy and his kindness shall appear in prescribing bounds to their rage and fury.[26]

Witherspoon has now left all prudent silence behind him and unequivocally declared both his political criticism of the British government's conduct and has interwoven with it the belief that the colonists will be protected and saved from further harm by the all-powerful providence of God.

He then turns to expounding the idea that the wrath of man is clear evidence of the corruption of his human nature: 'But where can we have a more affecting view of the corruption of our nature than the wrath of man'. He then introduces a long digression on Thomas Paine's attack on the doctrine of Original Sin, in his book *Common Sense* which had been published in January 1776 and was, even by the time of Witherspoon's sermon, becoming a 'best seller'. Without naming the author, Witherspoon quotes at length from what he calls 'a well-known pamphlet: Common Sense'. This extremely detailed, virulent, bordering on the scurrilous attack on Thomas Paine and his work distorts the structure of the sermon, but it is also revealing of its underlying theology and brings its ultimately religious nature to the fore, as against what the sermon has nearly always been judged to be, a political sermon.[27] I shall later deal with the detail of Witherspoon's criticism of Paine, but following his outburst, he returns to the theme of the wrath of men that praises God. He signals three ways that this happens:

(1) The wrath of man praises God as an example of the divine truth and clearly points out the corruption of our nature, which is the foundation stone of the doctrine of redemption. (2) The wrath of man praises God as it is the instrument of his hand for bringing sinners to repentance and for the correction and improvement of his children. (3) The wrath of man praises God as he sets bounds to it, or restrains it by his providence and sometimes makes it evidently a means of promoting and illustrating his glory.[28]

Witherspoon's subdivisions are clearly meant to be analogous to the then revolutionary situation in the colonies. The first subdivision implies that the conflict is evidence of man's corrupt nature; the second that the events of the conflict are the instruments of correction by which God is chastening his people in order to improve their condition; and the third, like the carrot after the stick, is holding out the promise that his children will be spared further suffering by God holding in check the forces that have previously done them harm. He goes on in Part II of the sermon to 'apply the principles illustrated above to the present situation'.

Witherspoon begins by inviting his audience to consider the state of their own 'soul's salvation' and asserts:

There can be no true religion, til there be a discovery of your lost state by nature and practice, and an unfeigned acceptance of Christ Jesus as he is offered in the gospel.

Again there is this reminder that this sermon is not just being used by Witherspoon as a political opportunity. Indeed at times it almost seems that to him the occasion is even more of an evangelical opportunity than a political one. But soon he is again engaging in politics by citing as evidence of God's providential help: 'the evacuation of Boston, the shameful flight of the army and navy of Britain' which he says 'was wrought without the loss of a man'.[29]

Witherspoon then issues a clarion call to his listeners, and one that would be relayed to the rest of the colonists:

If your cause is just, if your principles are pure, if your conduct is prudent, you need not fear the multitude of opposing hosts. If your cause is just you may look with confidence to the Lord and entreat him to plead it as his own.

It is at this point that he calls his audience to witness; 'that this is therefore the first time of my introducing any political subject into the pulpit'. But he pleads that it is legitimate and necessary to declare his 'opinion without hesitation that the cause in which America is now in arms is the cause of justice, of liberty and human nature'. He goes on to declare:

> I am satisfied that the confederacy of the colonies, has not been the effect of pride, resentment or sedition, but of a deep and general conviction that our civil and religious liberties, and consequently in a great measure, the temporal and eternal happiness of us and our posterity depended upon the issue.

He then makes an unsubstantiated claim that springs perhaps only from his own conviction, that:

> There is not a single instance in history in which civil liberty was lost and religious liberty preserved entire. If therefore we yield up our temporal property, we at the same time deliver the conscience into bondage.[30]

Here Witherspoon is clearly playing to an audience, many of whose forebears had left their European homelands to escape religious persecution and who in America had found it possible to have freedom of conscience to exercise their personal beliefs in a society that had given them their civil liberty. He then goes on to criticise the 'unjust claims' for political dominion made by the British king, parliament and people; dismissing them because they are claims made by men 'liable to all the selfish bias inseparable from human nature'. Again his theology of the corruption of man is the basis of his judgement. It is a judgement based on religion not politics.

This flitting back and forth between religious and political arguments is again in evidence as he cites the 'impracticality of effectively governing from a distance'. But an imbalance appears in his argument when he puts forward the view: 'Whoever is an avowed enemy of God, I scruple not to call him an enemy to his country'. Here Witherspoon is equating infidelity with treason, which is a very dangerous and illogical position to adopt, and one that would later be found to be offensive to many good men who were great servants of their country yet who did not believe in God.

Witherspoon's strange admixture of beliefs and convictions is in evidence again when he almost immediately follows this offensive remark with one that shows a remarkable tolerance, when he says:

> Perhaps there are few surer marks of the reality of religion, than
> when a man feels himself more joined to a holy person of a different
> denomination, than to a irregular liver of his own.

The sermon peters out towards the end as Witherspoon seems to recall a
vaguely connected illustration of his theme: 'We have sometimes taken the
liberty to forebode the downfall of the British empire from the corruption
and degeneracy of the people'.[31] This hugely judgemental attitude towards
the British people in general is in contrast to the generous spirited comment
regarding a holy person of another denomination. This strange mixture of
disparate elements makes for an untidy end to the sermon. He moves
towards its end with a word to the 'non-combatants' urging them that:
'industry is a moral duty of the greatest moment, absolutely necessary to
the national prosperity and the sure way of obtaining the blessing of God'.
This is a rather strange injunction coming from a person whose ministry
was within the tradition of the primacy of faith as against works, but it
shows the politician rather than the preacher coming to the surface as he
urges the non-combatants, in a manner of speaking, 'to keep the home fires
burning 'til the boys come home'. Witherspoon's peroration combines the
pious and the political:

> It is in the man of piety and convinced principle that we may expect
> to find the uncorrupted patriot, the useful citizen and the invincible
> soldier. God grant that in America, true religion and civil liberty may
> be inseparable and that the unjust attempts to destroy the one, may in
> the issue tend to the support and establishment of both.[32]

A second edition of the sermon was printed in Philadelphia and then
reprinted in Glasgow in 1777 with 'Elucidatory Remarks'. The editorial
preface to the Glasgow edition is very Pro-British and Anti-American and
highly critical of Witherspoon, asserting that he has played a large part in
influencing the colonists to rebel. The 'Advertisement' opens with the
words:

> It hath frequently been said by persons of the best intelligence that
> the unhappy commotions in our American Colonies have been
> considerably promoted if not primarily agitated by clerical influence:
> and none of that order have had a greater share of it ascribed to them
> than Dr. Witherspoon.[33]

The 'Advertisement' goes on to detail some of the contents of the
sermon:

In the Sermon the doctor blends the most rebellious sentiments with the most sacred and important truths; and hath the audacity to affirm, that not only the *temporal* but *eternal* happiness of the revolted colonists depend upon persevering in their independency and undauntedly opposing the arms of their lawful sovereign. ... The reader will easily perceive, that the doctor not only exerts his utmost abilities to instigate the deluded colonists to persevere in their rebellious courses, but he labours to influence their minds against the determinations of the British parliament.

The 'Advertisement', signed 'S. R' continues:

To effectuate this, the best of Kings hath the most vile and unjust epithets ascribed to him; the salutary and equitable acts of the British parliament have been pronounced unjust and tyrannical, the most lenitive measures of administration and government are fluted and treated with contempt, the mildest commanders and best disciplined army are painted as barbarous, inhumane and brutal: the most unexamplified instances of pacific and forgiving dispositions towards the most daring and unprovoked rebels, are rejected in the most contemptuous manner. Whilst on the other hand, the most wanton cruelties, shocking barbarities and unheard of instances of rapine, murder and devastation, on the side of the provincial army have a vail [*sic*] drawn over them!

The 'Advertisement' then goes on to allege Witherspoon's involvement with the production of Congress's *Declaration of Independence* and says that these allegations are confirmed by the sentiments of the sermon. It makes it very clear that the sermon is not published with a view to gaining support for the sentiments contained in the sermon, but rather to prove the truth of the allegations and to:

shew what artful means and fallacious arguments have been made use of by ambitious and self-designing men to stir up the poor infatuated Americans to the present rebellious measures; what an active hand even Dr. Witherspoon has had therein; to convince his friends in this country of the truth of his being a chief promoter of the American revolt; and that if he falls into the hands of government, and meets with the demerits of his offence, he hath justly and deservedly procured it to himself.

One footnote tries to counter Witherspoon's remark about 'the ambition of mistaken prices' with a reference to 'the haughty influence of ambitious and aspiring clergymen'. In another footnote which deals with Witherspoon's providing evidence for human nature's corruption: 'I see it everywhere and feel it every day', 'S. R.' rather tartly writes: 'A truth remarkably verified in the Doctor's late and present conduct'. A further footnote commenting on Witherspoon's reference to the evacuation of Boston, accuses Witherspoon as one who 'publicly recruited for the rebel army'. But 'S. R.', if one might say so, shoots himself in the footnote when he fails to see the irony of his comment on Witherspoon's argument about the impracticality of effectively governing from a distance, when he writes: 'if this is so ... then the inhabitants of South America and the East Indies should revolt from their respective sovereigns'.[34]

The sermon undoubtedly re-enforced the impression held by some in Britain that John Witherspoon was a leader of the rebellion in the American colonies, but although it is branded as a political sermon it is at least as much concerned for the state of America's soul as for its independence. One of the clear indications of this is Witherspoon's lengthy digression from what appeared to be the main thrust of the sermon in order to deal with Thomas Paine's refutation of the doctrine of Original Sin. Witherspoon had just offered the view that:

> a cool and candid attention either to past history, or present state of the world, but above all to the ravages of lawless power, ought to humble us to the dust. It should lead us to acknowledge the just view given us in scripture of our lost state,

when he breaks off the theme to mount an attack on Thomas Paine's views. He writes:

> I cannot help embracing this opportunity of making a remark or two upon a virulent reflection thrown out against this doctrine in a well known pamphlet, Common Sense.[35]

He then goes on to quote a lengthy passage from Paine in which the author sees as analogous the concept of a hereditary Monarchy and the passing on of the taint of Adam's sin, and is dismissive of both. Paine writes:

> If the first king of any country was by election, that likewise establishes a precedent for the next; for to say, that the right of all future generations is taken away by the act of the first electors, in their choice not only of a king, but of a family of kings forever, hath

no parallel in or out of scripture, but the doctrine of original sin, which supposes the free will of all men lost in Adam, and from such comparison, it will admit of no other: hereditary succession can derive no glory. For as in Adam all sinned and as in the first electors all men obeyed; as in the one all mankind were subjected to Satan, and in the other to Sovereignty; as our innocence was lost in the first, and our authority in the last; and as both disable us from re-assuming some former state and privilege, it unanswerably follows, that original sin and hereditary succession are parallels. Dishonerable rank! Inglorious connection! Yet the most subtle sophist cannot produce a juster simile.[36]

Witherspoon comments quite unjustly:

> Without a shadow of reasoning he [Paine] is pleased to represent the doctrine of original sin as an object of contempt and abhorrence. I beg leave to demur to the candor, the prudence and the justice of this proceeding.

He then, by means of a series of rhetorical questions of a very sarcastic nature, begins to cast aspersions on Paine's character while ostensibly making a defense of the doctrine of original sin. His opening question sets the tone of all that follows:

> Was it modest or candid for a person without name or character to talk in this supercilious manner of a doctrine that has been espoused by and defended by many of the greatest and best men that the world ever saw, and which makes an essential part of the established Creeds and Confessions of all the Protestant churches without exception?

Witherspoon follows this with the acid comment: 'I thought the grand modern plea had been, freedom of sentiment, and charitable thoughts of one another'. But his next question betrays his own lack of charity and tolerance of another person's right to be allowed to their own beliefs when he writes: 'Are so many of us then beyond the reach of this gentleman's charity?' Scattered throughout the remaining questions are terms that reveal the contempt and self-righteous anger of Witherspoon towards Thomas Paine, whom he does not ever name but refers to him again pejoratively as 'this gentleman', or 'the author'. He twice describes him as ignorant, on one of these occasions accusing Paine of being ignorant of both 'human nature and the Christian faith'.[37]

In all of this bile directed against Thomas Paine, Witherspoon's defense of the doctrine of original sin gets lost. He does not argue from the detail of scriptural texts but rather from the fact that the doctrine is widely held throughout the 'Protestant churches'. Strangely he confines himself to the Protestant churches although it could be argued that the doctrine is even more adhered to and developed by the tradition within the Roman Catholic Church. Again strangely he does not cite the *Confession of Faith* constructed by the Westminster divines and adopted by the Church of Scotland's General Assembly of 1647 which argued for the authority of the doctrine by means of the proof text method. Instead he relies on the argument that:

> such has been the visible state of the world in every age as cannot be accounted for on any other principles than what we learn from the word of God.

He then puts forward a text that in no way substantiates the argument for the doctrine of original sin, viz: 'the imagination of the heart of man is only evil from his youth and that continually. *Genesis* VI. 5 - VIII. 21'.[38]

Witherspoon displays a cavalier attitude towards Paine and does not offer a detailed argument for holding to what he calls a 'New Testament doctrine', but which - although this is another issue - some would contend can hardly be justified as deserving that name, as it certainly does not emanate from any of the four *Gospels*. The idea of original sin is born of one of the creation stories in the *Old Testament* book of *Genesis*.[39] It was fostered by Paul and taken up by the early church fathers, especially Augustine at the beginning of the fifth century. In his *Confessions*, Augustine is clearly obsessed with the idea of the origin of sin and of how and when it entered into man. It led him to such far-fetched ideas as to write: 'Wherein did I sin? Was it when I cried too earnestly that I might suck?' Later in that chapter he uses part of *Psalm* 51 to conclude:

> Now, if I be *conceived in iniquity and my mother nourished me within her womb in sin*, where I beseech thee, O my God, where, O my Lord, was I thy servant, or at what time was I ever innocent?[40]

It was from such agonised self-examination that in time the idea of original sin came to become a doctrine. In the seventeenth century when the reformed church was attempting to regulate its structures and codify its doctrines in accordance with the *Scriptures* as against the traditions of the church, that it drafted its definitive statement on Original Sin within Chapter VI of the *Confession of Faith*. Under the heading: 'Of the Fall of

Man, of Sin and the Punishment thereof', its statements in this section are supported by 53 texts, 19 from the *Old Testament* and 34 from the *New Testament*, only 2 of the latter come from a *Gospel* (*Matthew* 15.19 and 25.41), but neither of them in any way support the doctrine of original sin directly, and at best are extremely weak attempts at corroboration that fail miserably by any rigorous standard of exegesis or *Biblical* interpretation. The *Confession of Faith* must be one of the best examples of the weakness of the proof text method, as the temptation in the use of such a method is to drag into service any words of scripture which it thinks appropriate, regardless of their context.[41] This method of *Biblical* interpretation had already been called in question by John Taylor of Norwich in *The Scripture Doctrine of Original Sin* (London, 1741) and in 1779 a fellow Scot, John Goldie of Kilmarnock built upon Taylor's work with his own, *An Essay upon what is commonly called Original Sin,* in which like Thomas Paine before him, he attacked the doctrine on the basis of a common sense approach to the *Bible*.[42] Witherspoon, alert ecclesiastical politician that he was, would almost certainly be aware of the debate that was going on in Scotland in those years as to the relative authority of the *Scriptures* as against the *Confession of Faith*. Perhaps this caused him to adopt the more general argument of the truth of the doctrine being testified to by the presence throughout history of the evil of which men are capable and its having been clearly demonstrated down to the present time.

When Witherspoon returns to his text after the long digression in which he had dealt with Thomas Paine's views on original sin, he restates what he hopes to achieve by his sermon: 'What I wish to impress upon your minds, is the depravity of our nature'. He then quotes the *New Testament* letter of *James*: 'From whence come wars and fightings among you'. But he has not yet done with Paine and in what is clearly an oblique reference to him he writes:

> Men of lax and corrupt principles take great delight in speaking to the praise of human nature, and extolling its dignity, without distinguishing what it was, at its first creation from what it is in its fallen state.[43]

Once again Witherspoon is revealing that no matter what he engages in, whether it be lecturing on Moral Philosophy or on Eloquence or playing a role as a politician, he never escapes from being a minister of religion. However great a political opportunity was being provided at Princeton on May 17, 1776, it was over-ridden by his commitment to religion. On that day the preacher eclipsed the politician. If Witherspoon had continued to hold to the political mode in the sermon, he might have emphasised the sound common sense and logic of Thomas Paine's political views and the huge impact that his book *Common Sense* had already made on the political scene. The book's massive circulation was an indication of its popularity and its potential influence even a few months after publication was immense.[44] But on the subject of Thomas Paine's contribution to revolutionary thought Witherspoon the politician remains silent, and it is only the carping voice of Witherspoon the preacher that is heard and heard in a way that brings no credit to him whatsoever.

Many of the views of Thomas Paine on the relationship between America and Britain were ones with which Witherspoon was in total agreement. Paine writes, in *Common Sense*:

> I challenge the warmest advocate for reconciliation to shew a single advantage that this continent can reap by being connected to Great Britain ... . 'TIS TIME TO PART. Even the distance at which the Almighty hath placed England and America, is a strong and material proof, that the authority of the one over the other was never the design of Heaven.

Paine continues with what might be called a religious argument that supports America's bid for independence, when he sees the hand of Providence in the timing of the very 'discovery' of America by the Europeans. He writes:

> The time likewise at which the continent was discovered, adds weight to the argument, and the manner in which it was peopled encreases the force of it. The reformation was preceded by the discovery of America, as if the Almighty graciously meant to open a sanctuary to the persecuted in future years, when home should afford neither friendship nor safety.[45]

Witherspoon's total commitment to a belief in Providence should have had him applauding such sentiments as these that supported the cause of American Independence, instead of latching on to Paine's disdain for the doctrine of original sin. He might have also quoted with approval Paine's view that:

> America is only a secondary object in the system of British politics. England consults the good of *this* country no further than it answers *her own* purpose. Wherefore her own interest leads her to suppress the growth of *ours* in every case which doth promote her advantage, or in the least interfere with it!46

Again Witherspoon would have approved of Paine's assertion that: 'nothing but independence, i.e. a continental form of government can keep the peace of the continent and preserve it inviolate from wars'. Many of Paine's arguments some of which I have quoted would have won Witherspoon's approval and would have supported his plea for independence in the sermon *The Dominion of Providence*, but instead he chose to criticise Paine's religious belief, or lack of it, and to malign his character.

In trying to tease out the reasons for this, the following might be considered as contributing factors: Witherspoon's disagreement over the publication of an article that he had submitted to the *Pennsylvania Magazine* of which Paine was editor. The particular article has not been identified, but is likely to have been submitted early in 1775. Paine's biographer, John Keane records that:

> According to [Benjamin] Rush Paine's view of the deteriorating relations between the American Colonies and Britain was fundamentally altered by the Battle of Lexington (April 19, 1775).

He was therefore a more recent promoter of independence than Witherspoon, whose opinions on the need for independence had been formulating almost since he arrived in America in 1768, and as we have seen, began to result in pro-revolutionary activity as early as 1769. This may well have brought about a tension between the two men and lie behind Witherspoon's objection to Paine's striking out some of his submitted work because it was 'too free'. Witherspoon was ahead of Paine in his thinking about the relationship between the Colonies and Britain and at that stage was committing himself to a more radical breach with Britain than was being contemplated by the yet to be converted Paine.

Another possible reason for Witherspoon not using Paine's revolutionary thoughts in *Common Sense* was the reputation that Paine had as a man dissipated by drunkenness. An incident in 1777 recorded by Varnum L. Collins indicates the strength of Witherspoon's adverse opinion of Paine and can legitimately be transferred to the earlier period of the conflict between Paine and Witherspoon. Collins relates that when Paine was nominated by John Adams to be secretary of the newly named Committee for Foreign Affairs which had sprung from the Committee of Secret Correspondence upon which Witherspoon had served, Witherspoon strongly opposed the nomination. Collins writes:

> He gave his reasons: he knew Paine and his writings; when he first came over he was on the other side of the controversy; he had later

been employed [as an executive editor] by Robert Aitken [the Proprietor of the *Pennsylvania Magazine*] and, following the tide of popularity, had turned to the side of the Colonies; he was very intemperate and could not write "until he had quickened his thought with large draughts of rum and water; in short, he was a bad character and not fit to be placed in such a situation."

John Adams, who dates this incident as April 17, 1777, wrote that no one confirmed Witherspoon's criticism at that time but concluded, 'The truth of it has since been sufficiently established'.[47]

Paine may indeed have liked his rum and water but perhaps no more than many a writer who finds his tongue loosened and his mind relaxed by the spirit. Witherspoon may have had other reasons for his dislike of Paine. Paine's religious stance was to say the least, far from orthodox. Brought up by an Anglican mother and a Quaker father he leaned towards Deism, which for all Witherspoon's protestations about the right of the individual to have freedom to practice their own religion, he rated Deism at only one remove from Atheism. It was certainly not in the category he sought to promote, 'real religion', one that expressed a belief in the scheme of salvation wrought by Jesus Christ. Remember too the connection that Witherspoon made between Atheism and patriotism: he held that no man who was an infidel could be a patriot.[48] It followed then for Witherspoon that Thomas Paine could not be a proper ambassador for the Colonies nor a fully to be trusted patriot. But Witherspoon's was the sole dissenting voice and Paine was duly appointed as Secretary to the Committee on Foreign Affairs.

Paine was also in Witherspoon's eyes a 'Johnny-come-lately', having only arrived in the Colonies on November 30, 1774. But the impact of his arrival was very soon felt and his book or as those who liked to disparage it, his pamphlet, *Common Sense* was published in Philadelphia on January 10, 1776. John Keane, Paine's biographer writes:

> During the spring and summer of 1776 copies of Common Sense poured off the presses in a never ending stream. In Philadelphia alone, seven editions were released.[49]

It is little wonder that John Witherspoon's nose was out of joint. He had been toiling for years in the cause of the colonies and here was someone 'just off the boat' who had had an almost instant success. Witherspoon's lack of generosity of praise towards Paine might well be attributed to a fit of pique at someone who had stolen the limelight and further by the underlying suspicion of a man whose activity might have been interpreted as that of an opportunist.

Benjamin Rush commented on the impact of the pamphlet:

> Its effects were sudden and extensive upon the American mind. It was read by public men, repeated in clubs, spouted in Schools, and in one instance, delivered from the pulpit instead of a sermon by a clergyman in Connecticut.[50]

This was the document whose political impact was ignored by John Witherspoon on that momentous occasion at Princeton on May 17, 1776, but even worse, he could only malign its author's religious opinion and cast doubt on his character.

The grudge that Witherspoon held against Thomas Paine resurfaced in December 1780. Paine had either been asked or had volunteered himself to accompany John Laurens who had been appointed by Congress to be their special envoy on a mission to secure a loan of Twenty-five million Livres from Louis XVI. When Paine's proposed involvement in the mission became known to Congress, the opposition to him was led by John Witherspoon and the old charge of Paine's being unfaithful to the Revolution was repeated. Paine was later convinced writes Keane, that Witherspoon 'was a man of sour grapes who would never forgive me for publishing Common Sense and going one step beyond him in literary reputation'.[51] This time around, Witherspoon won, and Paine withdrew from the official position and determined to go to France at his own expense.

This account of John Witherspoon's relationship with Thomas Paine shows another aspect of the clergyman's character, one that has to a certain extent been overlooked perhaps because of the huge achievements of the man. But in a way these achievements might not have been realised had it not been for the albeit unattractive inner belligerence, the fixed opinions and the undeviating concern for what he believed to be the way forward for his adopted nation.

CHAPTER 10

Politician II: 1776-1783

It must surely be some measure of the standing of John Witherspoon relative to other politicians of the time, that he is the only clergyman to sign the *Declaration of Independence*. In the period following May 17, 1776, when he preached his revolutionary beliefs from the pulpit in the sermon *The Dominion of Providence*, he was especially active in putting what he had preached into practice. Jeffry H. Morrison, one time James Madison Visiting Fellow and visiting assistant professor of politics at Princeton University, writes of Witherspoon's status:

> By any fair measure he deserves to be classed among the founders of this republic. By signing the Declaration of Independence and the Articles of Confederation and by ratifying the Constitution, he had a direct hand in passing three of the four Organic Laws of the United States, and the two most celebrated founding documents, the Declaration and Constitution - the 'apple of gold in the frame of silver' as Abraham Lincoln (borrowing from *Proverbs*) called them.[1]

Morrison goes on to point out the important part that Witherspoon played in the final debates on July 1 and 2, 1776, prior to the passing of Richard Henry Lee's *Resolution for Independence* on July 2, 1776. When it was argued by one of the more conservative members that the country was not yet ripe for independence, 'Witherspoon shot back that in his judgement the colonies were not only ripe for independence but also "in danger of becoming rotten for the want of it"'. Morrison concludes:

> By so replying, he helped prod Congress toward passing Richard Henry Lee's Resolution for Independence on July 2, and the Declaration of Independence two days later.

Immediately following the *Declaration* Witherspoon was appointed to a number of committees including two very important standing committees: the Committee on Foreign Affairs and the Board of War.[2] For the next six years he was a diligent attender and worker within the committees to which he was appointed and as often happens when a person is diligent in the performance of committee work, their burden is added too because of that very diligence. This was certainly the case with Witherspoon, and we find evidence of this commitment and of the trust placed in him by his fellow congressmen and government officials by the additional work assigned to him, for example, as a result of his work on the Board of War, he was delegated to arrange an exchange of Prisoners of War.[3] Evidence of Witherspoon's operating at the highest level of government in the period following the *Declaration* is found in a letter from the Committee of Correspondence of January 1, 1777, to Benjamin Franklin informing him of his appointment as Congress's Commissioner to the Court of Spain, with the brief to 'negotiate a treaty of friendship and commerce'. The letter is in Witherspoon's handwriting, and his signature, one of four, is underlined as if to emphasise that he is the writer. The other signatories are Ben[jamin?] Harrison, Richard Henry Lee and Will Hooper.[4] Even after he had left Congress his diligence was remembered when in 1786 Alexander Hamilton asked him to prepare a paper on Money for the guidance of the government.[5]

When Thomas Jefferson's draft of the *Declaration of Independence* was submitted to Congress for its consideration and approval, various changes were made that had the effect of shortening it and making it more succinct, but these changes did not in any way detract from its pungent common sense delineation of what Jefferson himself had said he hoped to achieve: 'an expression of the American mind'.[6] Two changes from Jefferson's original draft are ones in which Witherspoon almost certainly would have a hand. The first is Jefferson's very pointed attack on George III's policy of the slave trade. Jefferson accused 'his present majesty' as one who:

> has waged cruel war against human nature itself, violating its most sacred rights of life and liberty in the persons of a distant people who never offended him, captivating and carrying them into slavery in another hemisphere, or to incur miserable death in their transportation thither. This piratical warfare, the opprobrium of *infidel* powers, is the warfare of the *Christian* king of Great Britain. (Determined to keep open the market where MEN should be bought and sold).[7]

Much as Witherspoon might have shared the theory of the injustice of slavery, although he himself owned at least two slaves who were listed among his goods and chattels at his death, he would not have approved of the sarcastic tone of the '*Christian* king'. In his own criticism of George III he preferred to think of the king as ill-informed and ill-advised rather than willfully bad. The final draft deleted the reference to slavery, probably because many of the Congressmen, like Witherspoon, owned slaves. Also deleted was the sarcastic remark that implied the inappropriateness of someone who professed to being a Christian, promoting the trade in slaves, again, perhaps because such remarks might just as well have been applied to themselves. However, Congress did support Jefferson's basic premise by including the statement that George III was 'A Prince, whose character is thus marked by every act which may define a Tyrant, is unfit to be the ruler of a free People'.[8] Another alteration in which Witherspoon is likely to have contributed is the deletion of Jefferson's reference to 'Scotch and foreign mercenaries'. In a passage that was not only unjust towards the Scottish soldiers in the ranks of the British army, by calling them mercenaries, but that also betrayed a racist attitude to the Scots by implying that they were of a totally different race altogether, thereby forgetting the huge number of Scottish immigrants, who like Witherspoon, shared their political ideas and their vision of independence and who themselves were also colonists. Jefferson's words reveal a strong anti-Scottish bias, perhaps even a prejudice, not uncommon at the time, but that assuredly would have been taken to task by Witherspoon. The full passage directed against the British people that includes the offensive words:

> They are permitting their chief magistrate to send over not only soldiers of our common blood, but Scotch and foreign mercenaries to invade and deluge us in blood.

does not appear in the finally approved draft. Jefferson's inaccurate and intemperate words could only have brought about severe criticism from Witherspoon. Within some months of the *Declaration*, he published, *An Address to the Natives of Scotland, residing in America* (Glasgow and Philadelphia, 1777) and in it offers the Americans an understanding of why some Scottish immigrants had taken the British side in the war. He then goes on to do his best to win over those same Scots to the American side. The pamphlet was appended to the published version of his sermon preached at Princeton on May 17, 1776, *The Dominion of Providence*.[9]

Reading this pamphlet immediately after attempting to assess the sermon, *The Dominion of Providence*, I came to the conclusion that Witherspoon was writing the secular equivalent of the theological plea for the defence of religious and civil liberty made within the sermon. In the pamphlet, Witherspoon is not only addressing the Scots who reside in America, but every American citizen. It is a trumpet call in secular terms for the defence of the religious and civil liberties which he sees as inextricably bound together. It opens with an explanation:

> Countrymen and friends. As soon as I had consented to the publication of the foregoing sermon, I felt an irresistible desire to accompany it with a few words addressed to you in particular.

He confesses his love for Scotland as a 'natural and pardonable prejudice' and that he has 'never seen cause to be ashamed of the place of my birth'. Witherspoon claims that:

> the natives of Scotland have not been inferior to those of any other country, for genius, erudition, prowess or any of those accomplishments which embellish human nature.

He assures his readers of how much he appreciates the friendship and goodwill shown to him from his fellow Scots and how much he reciprocates their feelings. He is writing this as if he is anxious that what he has to say will be properly understood. He then begins: 'It has given me no little uneasiness to hear the word Scotch used as a term of reproach in the American controversy'.[10] He goes on to challenge the assumption made by:

> some newspapers and contemptible anonymous publications that Scots are more universally opposed to the liberties of America than those who are born in South Britain or in Ireland.

He contends that:

> Many [Scots] in this country, whose opposition to the unjust claims of Great Britain has been as early and uniform, founded on rational and liberal principles, and therefore likely to be as lasting as that of any set of men whatever.

He suggests that the reason why in some states Scots support 'the usurpations of the parent state', is the American support for the very anti-Scottish, English politician John Wilkes. Witherspoon maintains that the Americans have mistakenly thought that Wilkes was an ally in their cause of independence, but asserts that Wilkes was merely using the American unrest as a means of berating the ministry in power in the British government. Wilkes, claims Witherspoon, was notorious for his hatred of the Scots, and sought to 'stir up national jealousy between the northern and southern parts of the island'. In consequence:

> Wilkes and some others were burnt in effigy in Scotland, and had the effect of making the Scots more attached to the king and ministry, which feeling has not yet spent its force.

He offers the explanation:

In these circumstances is it to be wondered at that many who left Scotland within the last fifteen years, when they heard of Wilkes and those who adhered to him, extolled and celebrated by the sons of liberty should be apt to consider it as evidence of the same spirit and that they were engaged in the same cause.

Witherspoon is not offering this as an excuse for the conduct of some Scots, but rather suggests that in the peculiar circumstances of the Scottish experience at the hands of Wilkes, it is an understandable reaction, and writes:

I am far from supposing that this was a good reason for any man's being cool to the American cause, which was as different from that of Wilkes as light is from darkness.[11]

Witherspoon suggests that the Scots and 'every lover of justice and mankind should be in support of America'. He points out that the British settlements have been:

improved in a proportion far beyond the settlements of other European nations and claims that this is because of the degree of liberty which they brought from home and which pervades more or less their several constitutions.

He argues against supporting the British: 'for that way lies loss of liberty'. He holds out the hope that because the colonies 'have united for common defence and resolved that they will be both free and independent, because they cannot be the one without the other'. Now that the *Declaration* has been made, he sees it has having been necessary and that it was both honorable and profitable to do so, and that in all probability far from there being injury, it will be to the advantage to Great Britain.[12] The political and secular nature of his argument is emphasised as he quotes David Hume's essay on *The Jealousy of Trade* in support of his assertion that Britain will benefit more from trade with America than by taxing it, and claims that 'the independence of America will be to the real advantage of the island of Great Britain'. He goes on to cite the fall of the Roman Empire and claims that it was by the acquisition of numerous provinces that Rome hastened its ruin. He also alludes to Montesquieu's, *The Spirit of Laws*, which asserts that nothing contributes so much to the prosperity of a people as the state of society among them and the form of government.[13] Note the secular sources and the material nature of the arguments used as Witherspoon tries to persuade the Scots resident in America who had taken the British side, that it would be in their best interests to join the American side. But near the close of the pamphlet, the moderately worded and persuasive arguments come to an end and a threat is made, as Witherspoon suggests that:

> after democratic discussion on board a ship as to which course should be followed and it is determined by the majority and acted upon; If after that anyone who tries to thwart the course should be thrown overboard.[14]

Again the ruthless aspect of Witherspoon's character appears as he virtually delivers the ultimatum: 'Be with us or you will be thrown out'.

Witherspoon cautions against returning to British rule, warns that Cromwell's revolution failed because it did not immediately have a 'regular form of government', and asserts that by contrast the American cause will succeed as it has already established a government: 'settled from its foundation by deliberate counsel and directed immediately to the public good of the present and future generations'. He remembers how the Commonwealth under Cromwell was:

> broken into parties and bewildered in their views and at last tamely submitted, without resistance to that very tyranny against which they had fought with some glory and success.[15]

This comment is meant to be a salutary reminder of the then fragile state of the newly independent colonies and is followed up by a final appeal to the Scots:

> For this reason I think that every candid and liberal mind ought to rejoice in the measures lately taken through the states of America, and particularly the late declaration of independence, as it will not only give union and force to the measures of defence, while they are necessary, but lay a foundation for the birth of millions, and the future improvement of a great part of the globe.[16]

He writes in closing, that he has been personally abused as a result of his supporting the American cause, and admits that this 'was in some degree indeed what moved him to make this address'. He expresses the hope:

> that an honest and faithful support of liberty and equal government in this part of the world will be no just reproach to his character either as a scholar, a minister, or a Christian, and that it is perfectly

consistent with an undiminished regard for the country that gave him birth.[17]

In this pamphlet Witherspoon makes his plea to those Americans who continue to think of the Scots as enemies, or at least as opposed to the cause of independence, to think again, and invites the Scots who have taken the British side, to reconsider and to see that it is in their best interest to join the cause for independence in order to secure the freedom that they had sought when they had first emigrated.

Witherspoon continued the habit begun in Scotland of submitting articles to newspapers and periodicals using various *nommes de plume* such as 'Epaminondas' or 'Aristides' or 'The Druid'.[18] One such article, signed, 'Aristides' appeared in a newspaper in the summer of 1776 (possibly between February and August 1776), a few weeks after the publication of Thomas Paine's, *Common Sense*.[19] Soon after, a pamphlet called *Plain Truth*, appeared, written by James Chalmers, attacking *Common Sense* and defending the British Constitution. 'Aristides' in his article defended *Common Sense* and attacked *Plain Truth*. 'Aristides' was a name chosen carefully by Witherspoon because of its classical association with a person of that name. Aristides had been an Athenian statesman and general, who died about B.C. 468, and was known as 'The Just'. Witherspoon would have been aware of Aristides from his classical studies, or might even have been reminded of him by a mention of him in a poem by a contemporary Scottish poet of his earlier days, James Thomson, with whose poem *Winter*, published in 1726, Witherspoon was familiar:

> Then Aristides lifts his honest front
> Spotless of heart; to whom the unflattering voice
> Of Freedom gave the noblest name of 'Just'.[20]

That Witherspoon's pen-name was carefully chosen is made clear by this reference to Thomson's poem which depicts a character concerned with three of the subjects that Witherspoon held dear: morality, freedom and justice. But Jeffry Morrison adds yet another dimension to Witherspoon's choice of a name for himself. Unearthing a quote from Aristides, he finds that, 'Aristides, called 'the Just' had argued that:

> the Many are not to be contemned [*sic*], and their opinion held of no account; but that in them, too, there is a presentiment, an unerring instinct, which by a kind of divine fatality seizes darkling upon the truth.[21]

The name under which Witherspoon is writing, is that of a person who believes that the common people are quite capable of having an insight into the truth. It is perhaps too much to claim that Witherspoon's readers would pick up on this finer nuance of his use of Aristides's name for an article that offered a commentary on two recent publications, but allowing for Witherspoon's early grounding in the classics, and his awareness of the work of James Thomson who makes reference to Aristides, it is entirely possible that Witherspoon was making claim to the stance of one who believed that the common people of the American colonies had by 'unerring instinct' seized upon the truth of the need for independence from Great Britain.

Witherspoon offers through 'Aristides' comments on both Thomas Paine's *Common Sense* and James Chalmers's *Plain Truth*. 'Aristides' muses on the reasons for *Common Sense* being read by so many people:

> It was however read very generally, which I suppose must have arisen either from the beauty and elegance of the composition, or from the truth and importance of the matter contained in it. That it did *not* arise from the first of these causes, I shall take for granted, until I meet with somebody who is of a different opinion; and when this is added to the circumstance of its being sold in the manner above mentioned, [pretty cheaply] it is plain that the subject matter of *Common Sense* was proposed to the world under every disadvantage, but that of its own manifest importance and apparent truth or probability.[22]

Behind all this verbosity, a 'back-handed compliment' is lurking. But after this almost grudging admission of the good reason for the popularity of Paine's work, Witherspoon's praise for it rings out loud and clear as he writes in schoolmasterly judgement: '*Common Sense* sometimes failed on grammar but never in perspicuity'. Yet although he is acknowledging the clarity of Paine's thought, Witherspoon cannot resist adopting a slightly superior air to Paine as he writes in the first instance of the worthy intention of the author, but then implies that he [Witherspoon], and others, have been saying these same things for some time:

> The Author of *Common Sense* did not write his book to shew that we ought to resist the unconstitutional claims of Great Britain, which we had all determined to do long before; he wrote it to shew that we ought *not* to seek or wait for reconciliation, which in his opinion, is now both impractical and unprofitable, but to establish a fixed regular government and to provide for ourselves.[23]

'Aristides' at this point could have come out more strongly in support of Paine's argument, but instead he takes the easier option that offers no praise to Paine, but merely criticises the argument of Paine's critic, Chalmers. First of all commenting on the style of *Plain Truth*, 'Aristides' writes: 'If *Common Sense* in some places wanted polish, *Plain Truth* was covered all over from head to foot with a detestable and stinking varnish'. Chalmers asserts that 'it will be vain for us to resist at all', to which 'Aristides' rejoins that the inference of this reasoning is that 'we ought immediately to send an embassy with ropes about their necks to make a full and humble surrender'.[24]

Again, as in the sermon at Princeton, Witherspoon's praise of Thomas Paine's highly influential book, *Common Sense* is restrained, and again there seems to be a reluctance to fall into step with Paine as a fellow worker in the Colonial cause. The article ends with 'Aristides' railing against the unfairness and inadequacy of the practice of writing letters to the press as an answer to the argument of a book:

> To answer a whole book by a series of letters in the newspapers is like attacking a man behind his back and speaking to his prejudice before persons who never saw or heard of him nor are ever likely to do.[25]

Again Witherspoon fails to see the irony of his own words, for by his own writing, he could have been accused of doing something similar, answering a book with an article in a newspaper. However, for all that, 'Aristides' clearly favours, agrees with, and commends the political thrust of Thomas Paine's *Common Sense*, and equally clearly distances himself and condemns the views in defence of the British Constitution expressed by James Chalmers in *Plain Truth*. All of this Witherspoon does under the name of one who was known as 'the Just'.

Elected to Congress in June 1776 for one year, Witherspoon through re-elections, served continuously for three and a half years until December 1779. Then on his being released from Congressional responsibilities for one year in order that he might attend to the urgent needs of the College of New Jersey, he returned to Congress to serve throughout 1781 and from May to November, 1782.[26] During this time he fulfilled many assignments for the executive and seems to appear at times of crisis to such an extent that one would think that there were occasions when his fellow congressmen were only prompted to decision by his intervention. His contributions to the debates in Congress, his papers prepared for its consideration, and the committee work to which he was assigned, seem to indicate the respect in which his abilities were held, his own willingness to be used, and the confidence of his fellow members that any work they asked of him would be done efficiently and expeditiously.

Within a few weeks of the *Declaration of Independence*, and following Lord Howe's arrival with a view to negotiating a reconciliation between Britain and the Colonies, Witherspoon spoke in Congress in strong opposition to any negotiations with him. Witherspoon insisted that before any reconciliation could take place, the independence of the Colonies would have to be fully acknowledged and accepted by Great Britain. He urged total rejection of any treating with Lord Howe. Howe had displayed the same British insensitivity to the Colonists that had been shown in the past and that had been one of the underlying causes of their rebellion. Howe had pointedly addressed the American leader as 'Mr. Washington' and had only offered the American colonists the opportunity of meeting him as private gentlemen, thereby making it clear that he still considered them as rebellious subjects. In Witherspoon's speech to Congress he urges that there is no going back upon the fact that Independence has already been declared:

> Hence it appears that entering into any correspondence with him [Howe] in the manner now proposed, is actually giving up, or at least subjecting to a new consideration the independence which we have declared.[27]

Earlier in his speech he had recalled how, in the first instance:

> We [the Colonists] were contending for the restoration of certain privileges under the government of Great Britain and were praying for re-union with her. But in the beginning of July [1776] with the universal approbation of all the states now united, we renounced this connection and declared ourselves free and independent. Shall we bring this into question again? [28]

Congress resoundingly agreed with Witherspoon's sentiments, and refused to meet with Howe. In his argument for maintaining the independence that had been declared, Witherspoon referred to Howe's contention that reconciliation might be achieved because no decisive battle had yet been fought; and cited his own experience that battles do not determine causes:

> we may fight no battle at all for a long time, or we may lose some battles, as was the case with the British themselves in the Scotch rebellion of 1745, and the cause notwithstanding be the same.[29]

Witherspoon, however, maintained, that regardless of the outcome of battles, if the cause was backed by the body of the nation, it would prevail. He had begun his speech by talking about the nature of the quest for independence:

> I found my hope of success in this cause, not in the valour of the Americans; or the cowardice of the Britons, but upon the justice of the cause, and still more upon the nature of things.[30]

In this very spirited defense of the Independence of the United States, Witherspoon goes to the heart of the matter in reminding his hearers of the justice of the cause, and the reality of the nature of things: that Independence has been declared. The speech is at once both patriotic and statesmanlike, and shows Witherspoon as one who wanted to encourage his fellow congressmen to remember the reasons that had led them to their present position, and to hold firm to their resolve to be independent and free. Eventually, on September 11, 1776, a delegation consisting of John Adams, Benjamin Franklin and Edward Rutledge met with Howe, but when it was revealed that he did not have a brief to treat with them as representatives of an independent nation, but rather as rebellious subjects, the meeting ended in stalemate and the war continued.[31]

Within the same month as *The Declaration of Independence* was made, Congress began to explore the need for a continued federation and to structure the nature of the bond that related the states to each other. This was to result in *The Articles of Confederation* agreed on November 15, 1777, by the 'Delegates of the United States in Congress assembled' and ratified at Philadelphia on July 9, 1778.[32]

From the beginning of the discussion of *The Articles of Confederation*, Witherspoon played a considerable part. In a speech to Congress on July 30, 1776, he says that everyone is agreed, 'that there must and shall be a confederacy for the purpose and till the finishing of this war'.[33] But he believes that it will undermine people's commitment to speak of the confederacy as only temporary, i.e. for the duration of the war. He continues:

> For what would it signify to risk our possessions and shed our blood to set ourselves free from the encroachments and oppression of Great Britain - with certainty as soon as peace was settled with them of a more lasting war, a more unnatural, more bloody and much more hopeless war among the colonies themselves?

He and others like him are looking far beyond the present time of conflict:

> Some of us consider ourselves as acting for posterity at present,
> having little expectation of living to see all things fully settled and
> the good consequences of liberty taking effect.

It is therefore necessary to build a confederacy that is meant to last beyond
the present time of crisis, one that will be able to bring the fruits of the
liberty for which they have struggled. There then follows a passage that
shows that Witherspoon had not left behind his theological beliefs when he
donned the garb of a politician. His Calvinistic belief in the depravity of
human nature is still to the fore, but he maintains that that is no reason for
being without hope of a lasting confederacy. He says:

> I am none of those who either deny or conceal the depravity of
> human nature till it is purified by the light of truth, and renewed by
> the Spirit of the living God. Yet I apprehend there is no force in that
> reasoning at all. Shall we establish nothing good, because we know it
> cannot be eternal? Shall we live without government, because every
> constitution has its old age, and its period? Because we know we
> shall die, shall we take no pains to preserve or lengthen our life? Far
> from it, Sir, it only requires the more watchful attention, to settle
> government upon the best principles, and in the wisest manner, that it
> may last as long as the nature of things will admit.[34]

Again that phrase is used, 'the nature of things'. Witherspoon seems to see
the events through which he is passing as being as they should be - 'as the
nature of things'. It is another aspect of his belief in the providence that is
at work in the world. Therefore despite believing in the depravity of human
nature, he is driven to believe that even that is taken into account by the
providence that 'shapes our ends'. He even permits himself to express what
for him is an extraordinary optimism as he momentarily seems to depart
from his strongly held belief in human depravity and ventures to say:

> I beg leave to say something more, though with some risk that it will
> be thought visionary and romantic. I do expect Mr. President, a
> progress as in every other human art, so in the order and perfection
> of human society, greater than we have yet seen; and why should we
> be wanting to ourselves in urging it forward. It is certain I think, that
> human science and religion have kept company together, and greatly
> assisted each other's progress in the world.[35]

But then, perhaps carried away by his own enthusiasm for the American
cause, and supremely hopeful of making a new world entirely different

from the old one and creating new structures of government in the freedom of the opportunity that must be seized, he puts his long held beliefs aside and declares: 'There have been great improvements not only in human knowledge but in human nature'. Then to substantiate this claim he contradicts the view that he has often voiced: that one only needs to look at the history of the world to see evidence of the truth of the doctrine of original sin, by saying:

> The progress of which can be easily traced in history. Everybody is able to look back to the time in Europe, when the liberal sentiments that now prevail upon the rights of conscience, would have been looked upon as absurd.

Here Witherspoon is giving signs of the conflict that raged within him. He was deeply imbued with the belief in the total depravity of man, brought about by man having been tainted and distorted in his nature by the inherited sin of the first man, Adam, who had disobeyed God even while living in the paradise that was the Garden of Eden. Yet while Witherspoon's mind accepted that man was depraved by original sin, his heart responded to the good and generous aspects of humanity, and in the new setting of America, there seemed so much more opportunity of making a new beginning, and of creating a new pattern of living. He was prompted by these things into believing that man could improve himself, and achieve new standards and become morally better than hitherto. In this outburst before Congress, Witherspoon momentarily forgets his Calvinist beliefs and enters enthusiastically into what was later to be called 'the American Dream'. The Determinist had become the Libertarian. The Calvinistic Pessimist had become the Liberal Optimist. But it would be wrong to think that Witherspoon had been totally and permanently changed by his American experience. He did not allow such feelings and opinions to surface for long and retreated within himself to his long held beliefs. It is as if these outbursts are aberrations, momentary lapses of control over the passions that he seemed to want to keep so firmly under control.

A month after the unproductive meeting with Howe, Witherspoon was appointed to his first congressional committee. Its business was to consider plans for supplying wagons for public service. It duly reported and recommended that if horses and wagons were required by the army, they should only be impressed by the quartermasters if absolutely essential, and returned as quickly as possible to the owners upon their being no longer required. The canny self-interest of the farmer of Tusculum is maybe in evidence here! Witherspoon was also added to the standing committee on clothing for the army, and Collins records that Witherspoon was able to put some of the business of providing army clothing to 'James Finley, a Paisley weaver who had emigrated from Scotland and settled at Princeton'.[36] As we shall perhaps see later, Witherspoon often has an eye for the business opportunity. He took a keen interest in the methods of provisioning for the army, and writes on one occasion in the guise of being 'a plain country farmer', about Washington's proposal to open up the supply of the army to private enterprise. The letter begins:

> His excellency, General George Washington and his officers of the American Army, Sir, about ten days ago I was informed that you were consulting with the farmers in the neighbourhood, and laying a plan for holding a market at the camp. This was to me the most pleasing news I had heard for a long time. I supposed that you had now discovered the true and proper way of providing comforts and refreshments to your soldiers, which, pardon me, I think has hitherto, in God's most holy will, has been hid from your eyes.[37]

In this pawky, and almost cheeky letter, Witherspoon reveals some of his economic theories. He is clearly against a fixed price. He wants recognition of the fluctuations of the market, and declares:

> laws and authority compel; but it is reason and interest that must persuade. The fixing of prices by authority is not only impolitic, as I have shown above, but it is in itself unreasonable and absurd.

Again we see Witherspoon attempting to break away from his traditions, where law and authority compel both belief and practice, to a stance where 'reason and interest must persuade'. Here again is evidence of a new pragmatism and a greater worldliness, than what might be expected of him, trying to break through.

Witherspoon's next congressional appointment, on October 11, 1776, was to the Committee on Secret Correspondence, later to be called the Committee on Foreign Affairs.[38] This committee had just appointed Benjamin Franklin to be its emissary to the court of Louis XVI of France to seek further assistance in the prosecution of the war. Unofficially the Americans had already received encouragement and a promise of French support from an unlikely source, the writer of the comic opera *The Barber of Seville* (1775), Pierre-Augustin Caron de Beaumarchais. In the September 1775 he took it upon himself to write to his king to encourage him to give support to the American Revolution:

Sire, the Americans resolved to go to any lengths rather than yield, and filled with the same enthusiasm for liberty which has so often made the little Corsican nation formidable to Genoa, have 38,000 men under the walls of Boston ... all who were engaged in fisheries which the English have destroyed have become soldiers ... all who were concerned with maritime trade which the English have forbidden have joined forces with them ... the workers in the ports and harbours have swelled this angry array ... and I say, Sire, that such a nation must be invincible.[39]

The king was not as enthusiastic as Beaumarchais for the American cause, and took his time to cautiously consider whether or not to give aid to the Americans. Beaumarchais however went ahead with his own scheme, and in 1776, raised a loan of a million livres and formed a company, Rodrigue Hortalez et Cie to give assistance to the Americans in the form of arms and munitions. Silas Deane who had been sent by the Americans to seek such assistance, on approaching the French court, was directed by the French Government to a secret agent, who turned out to be Beaumarchais. It would appear that the private enterprise of the enthusiastic amateur spy had been used, if not taken over, by the French government as part of a covert operation by which they could assist the American cause, a cause that would also be to the detriment of the British, France's long term enemy. Accordingly, in the spring of 1777, guns, ammunition and equipment for 25,000 men was landed on the American coast, and almost certainly assisted the American victory at the battle at Saratoga in October of that year.[40]

But all had not been as it had seemed. Other aspects of the transactions between Beaumarchais and Silas Deane began to emerge when a representative of Rodrigue et Cie journeyed to Philadelphia in December 1777, to present a bill to Congress for 4.5 million livres to be paid to Beaumarchais for the arms, ammunition and equipment supplied. Silas Deane in an accompanying letter confirmed the accuracy of the account. In the ensuing concern at the magnitude of the debt, Deane was summoned to return from France. On April 1, 1778, he accepted transport on a French vessel that was conveying the new French ambassador, Conrad Alexander Gerard. Arriving at Philadelphia in the middle of July, Deane had been expecting an enthusiastic welcome after what he thought had been a successful two years spent in procuring assistance for the American cause, but instead, found himself in the middle of a furious row. Information had come to light that the company set up by Beaumarchais was really a money laundering tool of the French government. As a Monarchy, France could not afford to be seen as giving assistance to a republican government who were in direct opposition to another Monarchy, Britain. The French king had secretly arranged for surplus arms to be taken from the French armoury and given to the company fronted by Beaumarchais; a scheme, it was being alleged, that he and Silas Deane used to their personal advantage. John Keane, in his biography of Thomas Paine gives this account of the scam devised by Beaumarchais and Deane:

> Deane's negotiations with Beaumarchais had an immediate effect. Within weeks, vessels laden with guns, ammunition and other supplies set sail for America. But the glory of the mission served as a mask for the pocket lining intrigues of the two negotiators - or so Paine thought. According to information supplied to him by Arthur Lee, who had first hand knowledge of the operation, the French did not expect the Americans to pay for the supplies. Although Paine and Lee were later proved right, the Americans were charged inflated prices for many materials, at least some of which were gifts from Franco-Spanish sources. The French gentleman of 'wit and genius', as Deane called Beaumarchais, sold the Americans muskets at half their original cost, despite the fact that they had been discarded by the French army and given to him gratis. He sent bills of lading for shipments of materials that were in fact gifts, and marked up gunpowder sold to the Americans by 500 percent.[41]

What has become known as the 'Silas Deane affair' caused deep divisions in a Congress that had already had to deal with a few minor scandals. Fears were expressed that the freedoms of a republic lead too easily to licence, and public service too soon could turn to private gain.[42] The row simmered on for months in Congress. Paine, as Secretary to the Committee on Foreign Affairs, was privy to papers that caused him to become Deane's most severe critic and accuser. Deane meanwhile prevaricated, claiming that he had left his records behind in France, and could not readily give an account of his transactions. Leading the attack on Deane were Samuel Adams and Richard Henry Lee who were in the forefront of the movement for independence, while on Deane's side were the leaders of the merchant faction John Jay and Governeur Morris, both delegates from New York. The matter entered fully into the public domain when Thomas Paine, who had been in the position of seeing documents that confirmed:

> that the stores which Silas Deane and Beaumarchais pretended they had purchased, were a present from the Court of France and came out of the King's arsenals.[43]

238

Paine took the risky step of publishing an open letter to Deane in mid-December 1778, in the *Pennsylvania Packet*, and over the next four weeks contributed another eight articles on the subject. The resulting furore ended in Paine submitting his resignation from the post as Secretary of the Committee on Foreign Affairs in January 1779. But on January 7 when Congress debated whether to disregard the resignation and instead dismiss Paine, which motion was put by Mr John Penn of North Carolina, seconded by Governeur Morris, the motion was lost because Congress was equally divided. When the matter was raised again on January 16, 1779, the vote was again tied and Congress accepted Thomas Paine's resignation.[44] Oddly enough missing from the vote that day were the delegates from New Jersey. No reason is given for John Witherspoon's absence. I suspect that he would have found himself torn between dismissing Paine on the issue of revealing confidential documents, and voting for acceptance of his resignation on the equally valid grounds of recognising the rights of a man who wants to tell the truth, but is being muzzled by the responsibilities of his office.

The forgoing account gives a flavour of the importance of the committee to which John Witherspoon found himself appointed. The consequences of its activities had a huge impact on national and international affairs. In the ensuing period of service in Congress that followed the *Declaration of Independence* he was operating at the very heart of the new republic's government. The winter of 1776 was to be a difficult one for the thirteen United States. There was an urgent need for assistance from Europe, and France, as we have seen, was the most likely country to be able to offer it. But France alone might not be enough, and the sympathetic understanding of Spain was also deemed to be important. To strengthen these links with Europe the Committee of Secret Correspondence wrote on January 1, 1777, to Benjamin Franklin the most senior of the American emissaries in France:

> Congress relying on your wisdom and integrity, and well knowing the great importance of the case, have appointed you their Commissioner to negotiate a treaty of friendship & commerce with the Court of Spain. The Idea of Congress on this subject you will find in the instructions of Congress sent by this opportunity to yourself and the other Commissioners at the Court of France. Your commission for their special service we have now the honour to inclose to you.[45]

The letter is signed by Benj[amin?] Harrison, Richard Henry Lee, Will Hooper and John Witherspoon, in whose hand it has been written, and whose signature has been underlined as if to signify the writer.

Foreign affairs were not Witherspoon's only concerns in that fraught period between the *Declaration* and the following summer. The British advance towards Princeton caused Witherspoon on November 29, 1776, to close the College, send his students home, leave his own home at Tusculum, help his wife into the family buggy, and ride alongside her to seek refuge with his daughter Anne's in-laws, the Smiths, at Pequea in Pennsylvania. At that same time, with the British obviously heading towards Philadelphia, Congress changed its meeting place to Baltimore. Princeton was overrun by the British and Nassau Hall used as the headquarters of the Army.[46]

Witherspoon as a member of the Board of War became involved at that time with some of the details of the conflict. A footnote in Collins records that in January 1777, Witherspoon was allowed expenses for two prisoners of war he had been supporting at Princeton. Collins also states that four other prisoners were given in November 1776, to be taken to Princeton for safe-keeping but that Witherspoon paroled them and put them to work on his farm. However it now looks as if this last event, which took place in 1779, has been wrongly placed by Collins in 1776.[47]

In the John Witherspoon Collection at the Firestone Library of Princeton University, is a document referring to four prisoners of war given into the care of John Witherspoon. Here is the explanation prefixed to the document:

> The first page gives an order in the handwriting of Richard Peters, noted patriot and friend of General George Washington, addressed to Thomas Bradford, noted newspaper publisher, who was serving as Deputy Commissioner of Prisoners.

The letter reads:

> War Office Aug. 25, 1779
>
> Sirs,
> The Board has agreed that Dr Witherspoon shall have the following Prisoners now confined in the State Prison to work under his direction, he is becoming answerable for their Return as far as possible: Robert Burns, Jos. Craig, Joseph McArthur, John Cochrane. They were taken at Stoney Point. You will keep a note of their Regiments.
> Richard Peters, By order.[48]

The second page shows that Witherspoon took the four Scottish prisoners and penned the following receipt: 'Received from Thomas Bradford, D.C.

of Prisoners, four Prisoners of War for which I am accountable. [signed] Jn. Witherspoon August 25, 1779'. The document concludes:

> Thus began the Americanization of a Robert Burns, a Joseph Craig, a Joseph McArthur and a John Cochrane by the Scottish born patriot-educator John Witherspoon.

The fact that the prisoners are listed as having been taken at Stoney Point is likely to be a reference to the opening sequence of the battle of Princeton near Stony Brook on January 3, 1777.[49] Also, it is highly unlikely that Witherspoon would have been assigned Prisoners of War in November, 1776, as Collins claims, in the very month when he had to vacate Princeton because of the advancing British forces. The letters of August 25, 1779, reveal that Witherspoon continues to be involved in the detail of the events and consequences of the war.

Collins however, usefully lists Witherspoon's assignments in connection with the release of loyalist prisoners from January 1777 through to August 1782. Witherspoon was also involved in recruiting for the army following its depletion as a result of the failures in 1776. In 1781, he was even appointed by Congress to head a committee formed to mediate with the mutineers of the Pennsylvania Line-soldiers, who were based near the College campus, but he wisely enlisted the help of the President of Pennsylvania, General Joseph Reed to do the detailed work of the face to face meetings with the soldiers, and acted only in an advisory capacity. His subsequent report to Congress hints that the harshness of the army regime was one of the causes of the discontent, and that never at any time were those who threatened mutiny ever expressing sympathy toward the British.[50]

However much Witherspoon's service as a member of Congress was concerned with the detailed work of its committees, he continued to play a part in the strategic thinking that he was convinced had to be engaged in if the confederation was to survive beyond the war. There are traces of this activity that surface from time to time in his speeches and papers, and in the documents which he had a hand in shaping. The first article of *The Articles of Confederation*, 1777 declares: 'The stile of this confederacy shall be "The United States of America"'.[51] The very nature of the association of the states was that it was a confederacy, and throughout his career as a politician, Witherspoon strove to uphold that status, and to assert the federal nature of the union as against its being a loose association of like-minded states. Witherspoon was equally keen on the independence of the states as individual entities, but he also strove to ensure that the larger states would not have any advantage over the smaller ones, hence his jealous insistence at the opening discussions, of the need to have an equalising device. This was achieved in *Article V*: 'In determining questions in the united states in Congress assembled, each state shall have one vote'. His vision of the confederacy not as something entered into for the duration of the war, but as a binding and permanent arrangement, is embodied in *Article XIII* where it is written:

> Every state shall abide by the determinations of the united states in congress assembled, on all questions which by this confederation are submitted to them. And the Articles of this confederation shall be inviolably observed by every state, and the union shall be perpetual, nor shall any alteration at any time hereafter be made in any of them; unless such alterations be agreed to in a congress of the united states, and be afterwards confirmed by the legislatures of every state.

One of the factors that confirmed Witherspoon's view of the need for a continued federal union of the thirteen states, was the experience he gained from being appointed to a series of committees whose remit was financial or economic. In May 1777, he was appointed along with Robert Morris and one other, to find ways and means by which to defray national expenses. In 1778, he was appointed to a committee whose remit was to reorganise the Board of Treasury, and a further committee whose report, when it was delivered in September, was debated almost daily until the end of the year, and in October 1779, he was appointed to address the States on the subject of Finance. The September report urged the necessity of punctual payment of the state quotas and argued that if this were done it might become possible to lessen the burden of the states by reducing the quotas. But no action resulted, and the states continued to neglect or ignore their financial responsibility towards Congress.

In 1779 also, he had been appointed to a committee to attempt to resolve the problem of the New Hampshire Grants. Both New York and New Hampshire were claiming the Grants for the lands of Vermont where people were acting as a putative independent state. The committee did not ever function properly and the matter was not resolved. It was many years later, after Witherspoon had retired from Congress, that Vermont achieved statehood. But the dispute illustrated Congress's lack of authority backed up by sanctions, and also that the attitude of the states was hardly one that was in keeping with T*he Articles of Confederation*.[52]

In May 1781, Witherspoon was appointed to chair a committee to work out ways and means by which the expenditure of the war could be met and how better control could be exercised over the public finances, and to consider the oversight of the western territories. He duly reported on

May 14, with a number of recommendations, including: repealing the laws that permitted the individual states to recognise any kind of paper money as legal tender, and that the Treasurer of the United States seek to recover the arrears of debts due by several states. But his most controversial proposal was concerning the western lands. Witherspoon wanted to define the western boundaries of the states adjacent to the unsettled land to the west, and for Congress to determine that those western lands should belong to the United States. Existing states whose land bordered on the western lands sometimes sought to claim right to these lands, but Witherspoon saw these western lands as belonging to the United States and as assets that would secure an income for the Confederation. The report was debated in Congress, but was then returned to the committee for further consideration but with one exception: the part that suggested the fixing of the western boundaries of the states.[53] As with his advocacy of the need for complete independence from Britain, Witherspoon was again proved to be ahead of many of his fellow congressmen in his thinking about the western lands. He did not quietly give in to these opinions, and a month later, as chairman of the committee, he returned to the suggestion that Congress should fix a date to consider the western lands question. He further suggested that when this was done, a committee should be appointed:

> to Prepare a plan for dividing the territory out for disposing it so as to discharge the debts of the United States contracted during the war.

Again Congress postponed consideration. The matter of the western lands was not settled during his time as a member of Congress, and it seems to have rankled in his mind. It is interesting that one of the points mentioned by the Reverend Dr John Rodgers in his account of John Witherspoon's life, given at his memorial service on May 6, 1795, shows that he continued to be concerned about this lack of commitment towards the Confederation. Rodgers writes:

> He complained of the jealousy and ambition of the individual states which were not willing to entrust the government with adequate powers for the common interest. But he complained and remonstrated in vain. But was proved right in the end.[54]

Before the matter of the western lands was settled, Witherspoon was involved in a piece of political activity that was to help bring about the international acceptance of the Independence of the United States and achieve a confirmation of its sovereignty. Witherspoon's contribution was the preparation of the *Instructions* of June 1781, that were to be given to the American emissaries who had been entrusted with the task of enlisting the help of France in negotiating a peace with Great Britain. His part in the debate over the *Instructions*, their final drafting and delivery was to become a matter of controversy that still causes divisions of opinion to this present time.

In Jeffry H. Morrison's, *John Witherspoon and The Founding of the American Republic*, he lists a number of reasons why Witherspoon's contribution to the founding of the republic has often been neglected. Among these are: a lack of primary source material (many of his personal papers have been destroyed), unavailability of editions of his works, his inability to be present at the Federal Convention in 1787 because he was previously committed to attending the Annual Synod of New York and Philadelphia that was meeting at the same time, thus preventing him from being at the crucial meeting of State Delegates to revise the federal system of government. But Morrison sees another possible reason for the neglect of acknowledging Witherspoon's contribution to the founding of the American Republic:

> It has to do with his status as a clergyman-turned-politician. Even in his day some Americans were made uneasy by the idea of clergymen as legislators, and present day Americans have become ever more scrupulous about keeping church separate from state. Thus, Witherspoon, a man who, as we shall see, insisted on wearing his clerical garb to the Continental Congress, who composed religious proclamations in the name of Congress, who scoffed at the suggestion that clergy were somehow disqualified from holding high public office, and who had been accused of embracing a general establishment of Protestantism, can be an uncomfortable reminder of a less 'separated' age. Although he actually advocated non-establishment, Witherspoon can thus appear as a sort of political dinosaur, a relic of an American species long extinct, who is not worth the trouble of digging up.[55]

To Morrison's carefully compiled list, and his extremely perceptive speculation upon the clerical factor in the equation, might be added another reason why Witherspoon is not given the credit that might indeed be his due: the part he played in the preparation of the *Instructions* of 1781, and especially in the intrigues and convoluted political debate over their final form.

In the course of the preparation of the *Instructions* there was much political debate and it was only after a very complicated array of motions and amendments that their final form was determined. Even after that, although the 'secret instructions' that would have given almost 'carte blanche' to the French in negotiating the boundaries to the West and North of the thirteen states, were not passed by Congress. There was a suspicion that they were passed on by Witherspoon to La Luzerne, and in turn to his boss De Vergennes, the French Foreign Minister. John Adams whose vigorous defense of the independence and interests of the United States in the French court had earlier in a way triggered the discussion about putting in place *Instructions*, and also the consideration of the possibility of increasing the number of emissaries to France in order to strengthen, or perhaps to curb the enthusiasm of Adams, so that the American views could be put more diplomatically. Adams later wrote in his *Journal* in terms that suggested that Witherspoon was too close to La Luzerne and De Vergennes than was healthy for the cause of United States. Referring to the curbing of his powers by the *Instructions*, Adams writes:

> The Members of Congress who suffered themselves to become the Instruments of the Count [De Vegennes], and His Minister the Chevalier De La Luzerne and his Secretary Mr. Marbois, in this humiliating and pernicious Measure of annihilating the Power of negotiating on Commerce, I am not able to enumerate very exactly. I have heard mentioned Mr. Livingston, Mr. Madison and Dr. Witherspoon. Those who are disposed to investigate this subject are at liberty to do it. If it would diminish the disposition which has long prevailed and still prevails in too many individuals to sacrifice the honor and Interest of their country to their complaisance to France, it would answer a good purpose.[56]

The *Instructions* had been drafted to curb the diplomatic brief of John Adams about whom the French De Vergennes had complained. Although Witherspoon had at first defended Adams, and in his *Memorial of Facts*, reported of letters from De Vergennes:

> upon the subject of Mr. Adams, complaining of him in the strongest terms and expressing fears of the negotiations being marred by his stiffness and tenaciousness of purpose.

But Witherspoon dismissed the complaints on the grounds that: 'a minister of unquestionable integrity could not be condemned just because he had more zeal than good manners'. He also initially opposed the move to send additional representatives to take part in the negotiations, believing as previously, that one strong voice could put the case better than two or three.

But undoubtedly Witherspoon changed his mind and yielded to the pressure of Congress, and probably too, to that of La Luzerne.[57]

When his committee met on June 11, 1781, it was successfully moved, to add Jay, Franklin, Henry Laurens and Jefferson to the negotiating team, alongside Adams. But as if to add strength to the mission and to put forward his own slant on the negotiations, Witherspoon produced for the guidance of all those taking part in the peace talks, his *Memorial and Manifesto of the United States*. Collins calls it Witherspoon's 'apologia for the American Revolution'. In the *Manifesto*, Witherspoon begins by giving a detailed account of the history of the initial settlement of the American continent by Europeans, especially those from Britain, who, 'considered themselves as bringing their liberty with them and as entitled to the rights and privileges of freemen under the British constitution'.[58] He acknowledges the settlers long compliance with British demands because of their attachment to what had been their homeland. But when Britain sought to exact greater taxes through the *Stamp Act*, it caused such a sense of injustice throughout the land that it was repealed. Yet by the *Declaratory Act* that followed it was made very clear that Britain intended to enforce what it thought of as its right to domain over the colonies. This was the final parliamentary act that brought about the response of revolution. He emphasised that the British assertion that the revolution was fomented by just a few seditious persons must be challenged: 'This unjust and indeed absurd accusation may be refuted by a thousand arguments'. Although reconciliation was sought by the Americans, their pleas remained unanswered and they were declared rebels, hence resistance had to be engaged in, and in the end, independence declared. He then went on to acknowledge the importance of the French treaty with the United States and reaffirmed the gratitude for such help as they offered. In concluding, Witherspoon claims that what had happened had been because the American Colonies were 'ripe for a separation from Great Britain', and he ends with a strong plea for the proper recognition by Britain of America's independence:

> since by her own acts of oppression she has alienated the minds of the Americans and compelled them to establish independent governments, which are distinct though confederated, wholly settled upon republican principles, and fit only for agriculture and commerce, cannot be an object of jealousy to other powers, but by free and open intercourse with them are a general benefit to all; it is hoped that the revolution which they have effected will meet with universal approbation.

This *Manifesto* produced at the time for the benefit of all the parties taking part in the negotiations, if it does nothing else, speaks of the understanding that Witherspoon had of himself as a person worthy of his place at the international table as a representative of the American cause. The very fact that he thought to produce such a document, is in itself an indication of how important he thought himself to be in the structure of the American governing hierarchy. It also reflects his status among his peers that this *Manifesto* should be received by them as a contribution to the understanding of their role in the negotiations. For Witherspoon to have the temerity to produce such a document, also shows the confidence that he has in himself that his voice will be listened to by all who were involved in the talks in France.

It is little wonder that John Adams hinted at something sinister in Witherspoon's role in the preparation of the *Instructions*, and that he felt that he was being confined more than he should be in his role within the negotiations. The final form of the *Instructions* was that he should 'be ultimately guided by the opinion and judgement of the Court of France'. Although the *Instructions* seemed to be consigning away America's autonomy, and giving it over to the hands of the French Court, it also contained two unwavering assertions that the negotiators hold absolutely and unwaveringly to the two principles: of American Independence and the integrity of the already existing Treaty with the French.[59]

John Witherspoon's involvement in the compilation and the delivery of the *Instructions* of 1781, and his writing of his *Manifesto,* were almost his last acts as a Member of Congress, but he was called upon by Congress to do one more thing, this time there could be no doubt as to its being appropriately performed by him. In September 15, 1781, he was appointed by Congress to prepare a statement that would proclaim a Day of Thanksgiving. Whether or not Witherspoon had inside information and because of this did not fulfil his commission until December 1781, but Thanksgiving became even more relevant when in the intervening time, the British forces under Cornwallis surrendered at Yorktown on October 19, 1781.[60]

In his address Witherspoon again takes up the theme of the Providence of God who has given them victory over their enemies: 'The influence of Divine Providence may be clearly perceived in many signal instances of which we mention but a few'. He then goes on to give examples of what he perceives to be God's help, in which he shows a detailed understanding of the significant aspects in the conduct of the war:

> In revealing the councils of our enemies ... on the breach of which our enemies placed their greatest dependence ... in increasing the

number and adding to the zeal and attachment of the friends of liberty … in granting remarkable deliverances.

He then openly pays tribute to France's part in the American success, seeing it as a providential act of God, 'in raising up for us a powerful and generous ally, in one of the first European powers'. He urges the people to recognise the 'goodness of God in the year now drawing to a conclusion; in which the Confederation of the United States has been completed'. He praises the armies for their 'prowess and success' and acknowledges that they have been 'powerfully and effectually assisted by our allies'. He even includes a very topical reference to Cornwallis's surrender: 'a General of the first Rank, with his whole army has been captured'. His concluding paragraph begins:

> It is therefore recommended to the several states to set apart the thirteenth day of December next [1781] to be religiously observed as a Day of Thanksgiving and Prayer, that all the people may assemble on that day with grateful hearts, to celebrate the praise of our gracious Benefactor.

In his final sentence, Witherspoon seems to be anticipating leaving the world of politics behind, as he prays:

> for the speedy establishment of a safe, honorable and lasting peace … and *bless all seminaries of learning*; and cause the knowledge of God to cover the earth, as the waters cover the sea. [My emphasis.]

Witherspoon's term of office ended that December, and he returned to Princeton to resume his duties at the College of New Jersey, that was much in need of his restoring hand after the ravages of war.

CHAPTER 11

Personal Qualities

Over the years I have spent in researching the life and work of John Witherspoon my notes bear testimony to the feelings of frustration, exasperation and incredulity that someone as talented and accomplished as he undoubtedly was, should be sometimes so naïve and seemingly simple minded; that someone so desirous of bettering the lives of others should seem occasionally to be petty or lacking in compassion; that someone so ready to challenge authority should sometimes be so meekly submissive to it. Yet despite the feelings that sometimes burst into expletives in my notes, I persisted in my research because I could not ignore the great achievements of the man.

It is in that spirit that I now attempt to comment on John Witherspoon's personal qualities, physical and mental characteristics, family relationships and habits, in sum, the man. Yet having said that, I shall not try to sum up John Witherspoon's character because it is so multi-faceted that if I were to attempt to turn what I thought to be the correct face toward you, I rather suspect that if you turned my image of him around just a little bit, you might find an aspect of him that is nearer to the truth, at least for you. Summing up John Witherspoon is a near to impossible task. All that I can hope to do is to hold up some of the aspects of his character that have been revealed during the course of several years trying to understand the man, his writings and his actions.

I begin with the negative aspects of John Witherspoon's character, probably beginning here because I want to end with the positive things that I have to say about this remarkable man. There are signs that Witherspoon did not allow for the expression of his feelings and emotions. I suspect that he dealt with them by attempting to suppress them. One of the saddest sights for me during my visit to Princeton, was of the memorial to Mrs. Elizabeth Witherspoon. The words that commemorate her life are inscribed on the end of the rectangular stone sarcophagus that marks the grave of John Witherspoon in the 'Presidents' Plot' in Princeton's Cemetery. As you stand to read the effusive outpourings that cover the top of her husband's stone, the words that mark her passing are hidden from view on the vertical surface at its head. In startling contrast to the inscription that commemorates John Witherspoon, Elizabeth is remembered in this simple way:

To the Memory of
Mrs. Elisabeth Witherspoon

PERSONAL QUALITIES

> Consort of the Rev. Dr. John Witherspoon
> Who died October 1st 1789
> Aged 68 years
> Sincerely good
> Fervently pious[1]

No 'beloved', or 'much loved', or even the more homely, 'wife', but without any expression of feeling towards her, the word 'consort' is used. Consort in the Concise Oxford Dictionary is defined: '1. a wife or husband esp. of royalty (prince consort) 2. a companion; an associate. 3. a ship sailing with another'.[2] Now allowing for the possibility that the words in memory of Mrs. Witherspoon might not have been composed until after Witherspoon's own death in 1794, and therefore written by someone other than Witherspoon, the fact that there is no other commemorative stone of her in the graveyard might indicate that Witherspoon did not mark her grave with any memorial. Either way, it does not speak much of a warm, natural relationship between John and Elizabeth Witherspoon and this might have been the case for many years.

At the time when Witherspoon had been approached by the Trustees of the College of New Jersey to take the post as President at Princeton, it is clear that Mrs Witherspoon was very unwilling to venture to the American colony. Although Witherspoon at first deferred to her, and turned down the Trustees' offer, he readily changed his mind and sought to accept it after she had been subjected to a huge amount of pressure, some of it quite harsh and lacking in understanding of her particular circumstances. People like Thomas Randall, a fellow minister, Benjamin Rush then studying medicine at Edinburgh University, and Richard Stockton a lawyer and businessman all attempted to put pressure on her. Their approach to her was nothing short of emotional blackmail and brings no credit to any of them. The self-righteous tone of Thomas Randall's letter of March 4, 1767, is made worse by his downright judgemental attitude, when without knowing anything of her personal circumstances, indeed of anything about her as a person, he writes to John Witherspoon on hearing of his not accepting the invitation to Princeton:

> My intelligence adds that the principle opposition flows from Mrs. Witherspoon … I cannot, you know, be called an acquaintance of Mrs. Witherspoon therefore I am little entitled to write her upon such an occasion; otherwise I would, as I judge it to be critical with regard to herself, on the matter of pleasing or displeasing God - so to her family - & above you all to the Church of God … I must beg you to represent to her how in his view of things it is awful to cross the

voice and will of God speaking plainly in providence ... that self-will is at one unamiable before men and before a Holy God most provoking.[3]

Randall then calls for her submission to what he sees is God's will for her husband, and refers to the story in *Genesis* chapter 12, of how Sarah followed Abraham. He then uses words from *Psalm* 105.13,14 quite out of context, to back up his argument that God would take care of them in America, as he took care of his people, 'when they went from one nation to another, from one kingdom to another people. He suffered no man to do them wrong'.[4]

Benjamin Rush was just as presumptuous, and his letter of April 23, 1767, from Edinburgh displays several examples of his total insensitivity to both Witherspoon and his wife. As he contemplates the effect of Witherspoon's refusal of the post, he postulates:

> And must poor Nassau Hall be ruined? Must that School of the Prophets - that Nursery of Learning ... become a pray to Faction - Bigottry and Party Spirit?

He then rounds on Witherspoon for disappointing the people at Princeton, because, 'They have had their expectations highly raised by letters from Stockton and myself'. Here perhaps we see the main reason for Benjamin Rush's anger and vituperation. His credibility and standing will be called in question for not 'delivering' Witherspoon to Princeton. Whatever Rush was later to become, at this point he was no more than a petty minded young student whose mission had seemingly failed, causing him to fear the consequences for himself. He further steps over the mark when he says that Witherspoon's refusal will cause his name, 'once precious to them' to be remembered only in terms of 'obloquy and censure'. He then remarks rather sarcastically on Witherspoon's lack of prospects if he remains in Scotland:

> should you refuse ... you can have no prospects of rising into a higher sphere in the Church of Scotland as far as I can understand it from the present state of your Ecclesiastical Affairs ... think how dark and gloomy your future prospects must be here in Scotland.

Then twisting the knife even further he paints a picture of Witherspoon:

> Forever buried in an obscure count[r]y village, poss[ess]ed of Talents not employed - censured by every new friend abroad and by

your old friends at home, you will spend your days with little advantage ... [two word indistinct (because of rage?)] unknown, unadmired. And what is worst than all (I must add it), your Conscience will ever reproach you, and hold forth to you the Injury you have done to the College - to learning, and to Religion in America.

Finally, Rush takes a nasty swipe at Mrs. Witherspoon for her part in Witherspoon's refusal, spitefully writing: 'people in America will be little disposed to pardon her'.[5]

Richard Stockton, the Princeton lawyer who was in Scotland on business, travelled to Paisley in February, 1767, after Witherspoon had refused the Trustees' invitation. Apparently his visit went well, and he probably thought that he had been effective in changing Mrs. Witherspoon's mind. Witherspoon wrote from Paisley to Archibald Wallace in Edinburgh, who had been giving him information about life in America, to tell him of the visit:

> My wife recovered spirits a good deal yester night after Mr. Stockton left us and spoke a good deal in favour of him as a Man of excellent sense and fine behaviour, but whether this arose in part from her Expectation that the Affair was wholly over, I can not say.[6]

When Richard Stockton realised that Mrs Witherspoon was adhering to her resolve not to go to America, he wrote to his wife on March 17, 1767, in terms that showed that he was not the person of 'excellent sense and fine behaviour' that Mrs Witherspoon had perceived him to be. Stockton tells of what he has done:

> I have taken most effectual measures to make her refusal very troublesome to her. I have engaged the eminent clergymen in Edinburgh and Glasgow to attack her entrenchments, and they have determined to take her by storm, if nothing else will do.[7]

We do not know if John Witherspoon ever showed her the letters of Randall and Rush, or if she ever heard of Stockton's behind-her-back activity, but the fact that the letters still exist to this day makes that more likely than not that she did see them, and in the small close society of Princeton it is unlikely that she would not in time have heard of Stockton's bully-boy tactics.

Robert Burns (1759-96), the Scottish poet, was but a child when these letters were written, but he later made his judgement upon the type of people who wrote them, and the unkind way in which they judged others. He writes to his friend Alexander Cunningham on September 10, 1792:

> Will you, or can you tell me, my dear Cunningham, why a religioso turn of mind has always a tendency to narrow & illiberalize the heart? They are orderly; they may be just; nay I have known them merciful: but still your children of Sanctity move among their fellow creatures with a nostril snuffing putrescence, & a foot spurning filth, in short, with that conceited dignity which your titled Douglases, Hamiltons, Gordons or any other of your Scots Lordlings of seven centuries standing, display when they accidentally mix among the many aproned Sons of Mechanical Life.[8]

Randall, Rush and Stockton, for all their professed concern for religion, showed no concern for either Witherspoon or his wife as they struggled with the momentous and utterly life-changing decision with which they were being faced. Whether or not Elizabeth ever saw any of the letters, she must have sensed the attitude held by Rush and Stockton when she met them, and even if Witherspoon bore the brunt of their criticism in silence, he could not have been unruffled by it. Witherspoon's letter to Mr Nisbet, minister at Montrose, shows the strain, as he writes to tell him of his turning down the offer from Princeton: 'But with so many difficulties from family and [connections? (indistinct)], particularly my wife's insuperable aversion, that I have been obliged to give it up'.[9] Elizabeth's 'insuperable aversion' was, by one means or another, broken down, the post was accepted, and with their five children: Anne (18), James (16), John (10), Frances (8) and David (7), they arrived in Princeton on August 12, 1768.[10]

If John Witherspoon had had very strong feelings for Elizabeth he would have sharply put down such attempts by Randall, Rush and Stockton to change her mind. He had failed in his own attempts to do that, and he weakly allowed others to take up his case, and to do so in a way that showed no respect for her whatsoever. She yielded to the pressure, and I think possibly lived in quiet resentment for the rest of her life. It is significant that she does not seem to have left any sign of her presence in Princeton society. Whereas other women of Princeton get lengthy mention in William K. Selden's book of that name, whose main purpose is to record the lives of women who had made their mark on Princeton society, the author fails to unearth any anecdote of her life. She is merely noted to have been the wife of the President of the College. Selden writes: 'Consistent with the legal and theological customs of the times, the lives of the wives of the early presidents of the College of New Jersey are not well recorded'.

In the course of the chapter, no details are given of the life of Mrs Elizabeth Montgomery Witherspoon, wife of President John Witherspoon.[11]

Elizabeth does not seem to accompany John to dinner parties, such as the ones recorded by John Adams in his *Diary*, that show that Witherspoon was present, but do not indicate that his wife accompanied him. Other ladies seem to have been present, for example on Saturday, September 3, 1774, Adams records: 'breakfasting with Dr. Shippen and Mrs. Shippen when Dr. Witherspoon was there'. Adams offers an opinion of Mrs. Shippen, with whom he had evidently been in conversation:

> Mrs. Shippen is a religious and a reasoning lady. She said that she had often thought that the people of Boston could not have behaved through their Tryals, with so much Prudence and firmness at the same Time, if they had not been influenced by a Superiour Power.

Adams later that day dines with: 'Mr. Joseph Reed, the Lawyer, with Mrs. Deberdt and Mrs. Reed', indicating that it was quite normal for ladies to be present on these occasions. On February 16, 1777, Adams records another occasion when Dr Witherspoon is present by himself:

> Last evening I supped with my Friends Dr. Rush and Mr. Sergeant at Mrs. Pages over the Bridge, the two Coll. Lees, Dr. Witherspoon, Mr. Adams, Mr. Gerry, Dr. Brownson made up the company.

It is on this occasion that he tells of the custom in connection with the portrait of King George III, and the way in which he tells it confirms the domestic nature of the visit. Adams records in his *Diary*:

> They have a Fashion in this Town of reversing the Picture of King G. 3d, in such Families as have it. One of these Topsy Turvy Kings was hung up in the Room where we supped, and under it were written these lines from Mr. Throop as we were told:

> > Behold the Man who had it in his Power
> > To make a Kingdom tremble and adore
> > Intoxicate with Folly, See his Head
> > Plac'd where the meanest Subjects tread
> > Like Lucifer the giddy Tyrant fell
> > He lifts his Heel to Heaven but points his Head to Hell.[12]

The way in which Adams makes mention of other ladies that he meets and dines with, seems to indicate a society in which women play a natural part and join in the company when visitors arrive at their home, or when they are invited to accompany their husbands to meet in someone else's home. It would appear that Mrs Witherspoon, whether by choice or habit, did not participate in these social gatherings.

An examination of the two *Edinburgh Almanacks*, one for 1763, and the other for 1768, that Witherspoon used as notebooks, reveals very little about Mrs Witherspoon, even although the *Almanacks* contain lists of domestic purchases or things to be attended to in Glasgow, Edinburgh or Philadelphia.

The Almanack for 1763 records: 'two Easter Presents: to my wife £1. to Annie [his daughter] £1.'. Also recorded is the further gift of 'a cloak for Annie £1.2.'. In a list recording his expenses of a trip to London and Holland which costs £96.17.0½, he deducts a sum for 'goods bought and personal £46.11.'. Within this personal expenditure is an item 'To my wife £10.'. Again, Witherspoon does not use the more intimate 'to Elizabeth', but the more formal 'to my wife'.[13]

The Almanack for 1768 covers the last few months of Witherspoon's time in Scotland and the remaining months of the year in America and includes similar domestic information, this time from both sides of the Atlantic. One item again indicates the formal relationship that seems to exist between John and Elizabeth Witherspoon:

Memorandum for Mrs. Witherspoon

White damask gown
Yellow gown 11 pieces to be worked
Watered plain silk
A plaid to be dyed black belonging to Mrs. Bowie
To get Paraphrases for Mrs. Ellis
To buy 6 pair worsted & 2 pair silk stockings

Again these things are to be obtained for 'Mrs. Witherspoon', not 'Elizabeth'. Naturally enough most of the notes in the *Almanack for 1768* refer to his own activities and needs, and I shall return to some these later, but it is noticeable that even in the notes to himself, Witherspoon is formal in his references to his wife. Not once does he refer to her as Elizabeth.[14]

When one considers the experiences through which Elizabeth had passed since her marriage to John in 1748: bearing ten children between the years 1749 and 1763; suffering the deaths of five of them, the last two dying in 1762, and 1763; living the strictly circumscribed life as the wife of the minister in a small town in which her every activity would be observed; withstanding the fraughtness of sharing life with a man who in his ministry was frequently engaged in controversy whether as a battler in Kirk Session, Presbytery, Synod and General Assembly or as a Pamphleteer.[15] It is little wonder that she was less than enthusiastic about the invitation to her husband from the Trustees of the College of New Jersey, to leave Scotland for a new land, a new occupation and to leave behind the five graves of her children, and the wider family to which she was attached.

Witherspoon's relationship with his children is fairly difficult to determine because of the lack of evidence e.g. letters or personal references in his writings. What few details that do exist seem to indicate a fairly formal relationship. Witherspoon writes to his fifteen year old son David who has gone to visit his sister and brother-in-law in May, 6 1776, and from this letter there is some indication of the relationship between father and son. After expressing pleasure at hearing of David's safe arrival at his brother-in-law's house, Witherspoon asks how much the journey cost, and advises David to 'sell the horse and don't buy another unless you can easily maintain him without being burdensome to Mr. Smith' [his host]. Witherspoon resembles Polonius in his manner of addressing his son, as the letter is interspersed with good advice, e.g. 'Take pleasure in doing things with accuracy and perfection', and closes with the exhortation: 'To see you a complete scholar will be the greatest delight you can give to me, except your being a good man'. Other saws follow: 'a character is soon found out and often easily lost'; and, 'I do not know so general or so excellent a Rule for good manners as to think concerning others as every good man ought to think'. There is no domestic news in this letter, no fatherly warmth, only the advice of a pedantic school-master.[16]

When James his eldest, and reckoned to be his favourite son was killed at the battle of Germantown in 1777, Witherspoon is said to have attended Congress shortly afterwards and shown no sign of grief. Witherspoon had earlier given James a present of some land at Ryegate, in Vermont. James had made a start at developing it and had begun to build a house there but as the war had developed he had left the land untended and the house uninhabited. The History of Ryegate records that when Dr Witherspoon visited Ryegate after James's death, he asked to sit on the saddle used by James. That is the only recorded evidence of any show of emotion or gesture of nostalgia indulged in by Witherspoon towards his son James.[17] Witherspoon's eldest daughter Anne, is spoken of as a child of whom he was especially fond, and certainly he seems to have had a good relationship with her after her marriage in 1775, to the Reverend Samuel Stanhope Smith. In 1779, Smith become a lecturer in the College, Witherspoon's deputy in 1786, and succeeded him as President in 1795. It was with his daughter Anne and son-in-law Samuel's parents that

Witherspoon sought refuge when the British forces advanced towards Princeton in 1776.[18]

If Witherspoon practised what he preached, then something of his attitude towards children, perhaps including those of his own family, can be learned from his *Four Letters on Education*.[19]

In *Letter II*, after having laid down some rules that will encourage any household servants to be supportive of the children's education, he writes: 'Servants are reasonable creatures, and are best governed by a mixture of authority and reason'. Then building upon that premise he continues:

> The next thing I shall mention as necessary in order to the education of children, is to establish as soon as possible, an entire and absolute authority over them.

He hints at his method:

> A parent that has once obtained and knows how to preserve authority, will do more by a look of displeasure than another by the most passionate words and blows.

He urges that such authority 'should be established early, at about eight or nine months'. He qualifies this:

> Do not imagine I mean to bid you use the rod at that age, on the contrary, I mean to prevent the use of it in great measure.[20]

Letter III begins where he left off:

> on the subject of establishing parental authority. It must always be remembered that correction is wholly lost which does not produce absolute submission.

At the end of this letter, Witherspoon's underlying belief comes to the surface:

> Whoever believes in a future state - whoever has a just sense of the importance of eternity to himself, cannot fail to have a like concern for his offspring.[21]

The driving force of Witherspoon's insistence on firm discipline is not the natural feeling of affection for the children that he has helped bring into the world, and the equally natural desire that they shall be able to conduct themselves in a sensible way through this world, but that their souls should be prepared for eternity in such a manner that they will escape the torments of hell.

In *Letter IV* Witherspoon stresses the value of a good example being offered to children by their parents. He comes very near to the sentiments of the Moderates with two of his comments in this essay: 'I cannot help thinking that true religion is not only consistent with, but necessary to the perfection of true politeness'. This is quickly followed with another Moderate opinion: 'Religion is the great polisher of the common people'. Witherspoon's superior tone continues as he with an air of male superiority opines: 'it is more difficult for the female sex to acquire "politeness" because they don't get out much and don't mix with the polite set'. As Witherspoon develops this theme, some of his words make me shudder to think of the married life of Elizabeth Witherspoon. He writes:

> True politeness does not consist in dress, or a few motions of the body, but in a habit of sentiment and conversation: the first may be learned from a master, and in a little time; the last only by a long and constant intercourse with those who possess, and are therefore are able to impart it. … They may learn a bit at 'finishing school' but soon relapse at home … there is but one single way of escape, which we have seen some young women of merit and capacity take, which is to contract an intimacy with persons of liberal sentiments and higher breeding, *and be as little among their relations as possible.* [My emphasis.] [22]

From his condescending attitude towards those whom he regards as of the lower class, and his criticism of the 'families in high rank', in another passage, Witherspoon would probably rate himself as 'upper middle class'. Certainly from the above passage, he seems to place himself among those 'persons of liberal sentiments and higher breeding'. Further, one is led to think that if Witherspoon really did apply the sentiments expressed in this letter in his own home, it might provide a clue to what appears to be Mrs Witherspoon's not seeming to participate in Princeton society. Witherspoon had certainly seen to it that she was as far away from her relations as possible.

In spite of the pamphlets title, in *Letter V*, Witherspoon continues the theme of the importance of parental example, declaring the great importance of inculcating an understanding of religion in children:

A parent who wishes that his example should be a speaking lesson to his children should order it so as to convince them that he considers religion as: 1. Necessary. 2. Respectable. 3. Amiable. 4. Profitable. 5. Delightful.

He encourages parents that the time of a child's illness is a good opportunity for them to impress upon them the necessity of religion:

Certainly there is no time in their whole lives when the necessity [of religion] appears more urgent, or the opportunity more favourable, for impressing their minds with a sense of the things that belong to their peace. What shall we say to those parents, who through fear of alarming their minds, and augmenting their disorder, will not suffer mention to be made to them of the approach of death, or the importance of eternity?

Witherspoon holds, that to avoid talking of eternity, is: 'to make a poor dying sinner mistake his or her condition and vainly dream of earthly happiness while hastening to the pit of perdition'.[23] If Witherspoon sought to inculcate these stark beliefs into his children, it must surely have made him seem a remote and austere father, lacking in warmth and natural affection, one who had a desperately serious view of life, with no room for playfulness, or that gentle understanding of a God who was a loving Father, with a special place in his heart for all his children. As for Witherspoon's wife and mother of his children, it seems as if there would be little human comfort and warmth of natural affection coming towards her from one who could adopt such a severe and rigid stance towards their children.

When the *Letters on Education* are studied, a picture emerges of Witherspoon as a domineering father and husband, lacking in any show of emotion, one who could not have been much fun as a father, or for that matter as a husband. In all his writings, there is not to be found one fatherly or husbandly reminiscence of good times shared with his children, or his wife. He comes across as a man who, in his personal relationships with those closely related to him, has subdued all that might be termed normal feelings, for example: a feeling of sadness, or even resentment at a child's death, or disappointment at having to turn down a job that he really wanted to do, or anger at the interference of people like Thomas Randall and Benjamin Rush. If we are to believe his profession of religion, Witherspoon has submitted his life entirely to the over-ruling providence of God, and in so doing has been enabled to put aside the feelings that most others would show in similar circumstances.

Yet although there is evidence of Witherspoon's distrust of emotion and of his unwillingness or inability to show it towards his wife or family, there is evidence of his displaying it to those outwith that circle. In Paisley in 1762, Witherspoon engaged in an intemperate verbal attack upon a young man, James Snodgrass, for his allegedly blasphemous behaviour towards the Sacrament of the Lord's Supper. Without properly checking the facts, Witherspoon, from the pulpit referred to the misconduct of a young man. He then unwisely had the sermon printed, naming Snodgrass. Snodgrass then successfully pursued a libel case against Witherspoon, who was fined £150. Witherspoon's zeal for the Lord, as he would put it, could be seen as a righteous anger at the flouting of something sacred, but his rushing to judgement, does show a capacity for passionate feeling, a trait that never emerges in his personal relationships. Despite being found guilty of libel, Witherspoon retained the sympathy of a number of people in the congregation and community. His *Almanack for 1763*, records a list of names and sums of money donated by at least seventeen people to help pay his fine and expenses. Their contributions ranging from ten shillings to eight pounds and ten shillings, amount to forty pounds, and are described in the narrative as having been, 'Received on Acct. of ye Process carried on against me by Snodgrass & others'.[24]

Signs of John Witherspoon's irascibility were noted early in his life, when they were observed by his fellow student Alexander Carlyle, who, it must be said, seems to have an ill-disguised dislike of him. Carlyle begins writing what he calls his *Anecdotes and Characters of the Times*, on his seventy-eighth birthday, January 26, 1800, so that some of his recollections are of events that happened at least sixty years previously. Although I bring forward Carlyle's reminiscences of Witherspoon, I regard them with a great deal of caution, in that I suspect that the intervening years of John Witherspoon's pro-American activities have hugely coloured Carlyle's attitude towards him. But long before Witherspoon left for America, Carlyle might well have had cause to regard Witherspoon with animosity because of Witherspoon's adoption of an anti-patronage and anti-theatre stance, while Carlyle would have been seen by Witherspoon as the very epitome of a Moderate Minister who was fast becoming part of the establishment. Carlyle must be regarded as a 'hostile witness', and judged accordingly, but nevertheless as his words are listened to, some aspects of John Witherspoon's life seem to attest their truth. While recollecting their student days and his visits to Witherspoon's father's manse, and to the Presbytery at Haddington, he tells of the practice of the Divinity Students to share a dinner following the meeting of the Presbytery, and of how, as Carlyle recalls:

John Witherspoon was of this Party, he who was afterwards a Member of the American Congress, and Adam Dickson, who afterwards wrote so well on Husbandry. They were both Clergymen's Sons, but of very Different Characters: The One Open and Frank and Generous, Pretending only to what he was, and supporting his title with Spirit, the Other Close and Suspicious, and Jealous, and always aspiring at a Superiority that he was not able to maintain.[25]

After writing of John Witherspoon's father, James, in an insulting and dismissive way, Carlyle continues with his description, and of how after the father had retired to bed, he and John:

used to amuse ourselves, with the Daughters of the Family, and their Cousins who Resorted to us from the Village when the Old Man was Gone to Rest.

Then Carlyle inserts a note of sexual innuendo:

This John Lov'd of all things, and this Sort of Company he enjoy'd in greater Perfection, when he Return'd my Visits, when we had still more Young Companions of the Fair Sex and no restraint from an austere Father. So that I always consider'd, the Austerity of Manners and aversion to Social Joy which he affected afterwards, as the Arts of Hypocrisy and Ambition. For he had a strong and Enlighten'd Understanding far above Enthusiasm, and a Temper that Did not seem Liable to it.

Carlyle, not content with what he had already done towards the character assassination of John Witherspoon, then appends to his narrative a note of a scurrilous story that he says circulated in the country, that John Witherspoon had an illegitimate son, 'a Dr. Nisbet, of Montrose'. Carlyle, despite repeating the gossip, tries to distance himself from it by saying that though, 'their Features no Doubt had a Strong Resemblance but their Persons were unlike. Neither were their Tempers at all Similar'. But as if unwilling to depart from the juicy subject he goes on to write:

Whether or not he was his Son, he follow'd his Example, for he became Discontented, and Migrated to America During the Rebellion, where he was Principal of [Carlisle] College for which he was well qualified in point of Learning: But no preferment nor

Climate can Cure a Discont[ent]ed Mind, For he became Miserable because he could not Return.

Alexander Carlyle's vicious and vindictive destruction of John Witherspoon's character is only given space here because it signals the attitude held by some of the establishment figures in the Church of Scotland. Carlyle went to the extremes of criticism, and his words have to be measured in the context of who he was, and what he stood for, a monarchist who had joined the Militia in Edinburgh, (as had his fellow minister Witherspoon at Beith). But while Witherspoon became a republican, Carlyle remained loyal to the British Monarchy. Carlyle, minister of the well-endowed Inveresk Parish Church in Musselburgh, was awarded his Doctor of Divinity in 1760, and with court and aristocratic friends, had been appointed Almoner to the King in 1762. He was part of the Moderate coterie in Edinburgh before Witherspoon left for America in 1768, and thereafter soon rose to a position of influence within the Church of Scotland. In 1769, the General Assembly appointed him as their Commissioner to negotiate with the Government for an exemption of the clergy from the payment of Window Tax, and in the following year he was installed as Moderator of the General Assembly of the Church of Scotland. The Royal and Ecclesiastical accolades were completed when in 1779 he became Dean of the Chapel Royal.[26]

With this background in mind, it is easy to see the reasons for Carlyle's criticism of Witherspoon. In his eyes, Witherspoon was the equivalent of a scruffy mongrel terrier yapping at the heels of the powerful and the mighty; Carlyle, with his acceptance of patronage, as against Witherspoon champion of the people's right to choose their own minister. Carlyle, friend of John Home, the minister who had written the play *Douglas* in 1757, remembering Witherspoon's diatribe against the stage in that same year. Carlyle, with his friends at court and a would be friend of the king, as against Witherspoon who had espoused republicanism. Carlyle, lobbyer of Parliament, and Witherspoon helping to establish a Congress in opposition to it. All of this gives motive for the venom that flows from his pen.

Yet, despite all the nastiness of his writing, and the bad taste that it leaves in the mouth, Carlyle seems to get some things right. There is an element in Witherspoon that could have made people think of him as 'suspicious'. He believed in the total depravity of man, and therefore that man was capable of any evil that was possible. 'Close' is also an accurate description to use of Witherspoon. He did not give away much as to what he thought, and what he felt. He kept a lot to himself. He became someone trusted in government because people had come to regard him as a person who could be trusted. Even the worst innuendo that was made by Carlyle about Witherspoon's love of young women, and possibly his improper relationship with one of them, might be because Carlyle witnessed a maturity in Witherspoon that he himself never achieved. A reading of Carlyle's, *Anecdotes*, shows his own great interest in women and his love of their company. Just one excerpt from his own diary will suffice to show that the very things he accuses Witherspoon of, could be laid at his own door:

> In the 2[n]d week I was in Glasgow, I went to the Dancing Assembly with some of my New Acquaintance, and was there Introduc'd to a Married Lady, who claim'd Kindred with me, her Mother's Name being Carlyle of the Limekiln Family. She carried me home to sup with her that night, with a Brother of hers two Years younger than me, and some other young people. This was the Commencement of an Intimate Friendship, that lasted during the Whole of the Lady's life, which was four or five and Twenty Years. She was Connected with all the Best Families in Glasgow, and the Country Round. Her Husband was a Good Sort of Man and very Opulent, as they had no Children, he took pleasure in her exercising a Genteel Hospitality. By this Lady's Means I became acquainted with all the Best Families in the Town; and by a Letter I had procur'd from my Friend James Edgar, afterwards a Commissioner of the Customs, I soon became well acquainted with all the Young Ladies who liv'd in the College.[27]

The very tone of this passage is probably sufficient for any reader to relegate Carlyle's opinion to a status that does not demand any recognition of its veracity. It is indeed tempting to see Carlyle as nothing more than a malicious gossip, a poison pen writer, and one indeed who might well be accused of the same kind of conduct as he has alleged that Witherspoon engaged in.

It might well be, however, that despite the pejorative slant of Carlyle's prose, he is giving us a clue as to Witherspoon's attitude towards women. The first time that Witherspoon is met in Carlyle's *Anecdotes*, Carlyle gives this brief sketch:

> The Future Life and Publick Character of Dr. Witherspoon is perfectly known; at the time I speak he was a Good Scholar, far advance'd for his Age; very Sensible and Shrewd, But of a Disagreeable Temper, which was Irritated by a Flat Voice, and aukward [sic] Manner, which prevented his making an Impression on

his Companions of Either Sex, That was at all adequate to his ability. This Defect when he was a Lad, stuck to him when he grew to Manhood, and so much rous'd his Envy and Jealousy, and made him take a Road to Distinction, very Different from that of his more Successfull Companions.

Carlyle is certainly a hostile witness. There are compliments paid and an acknowledgement made of Witherspoon's abilities, but in the end these are far outweighed by what Carlyle considers are his damning faults. Within this passage however, mention is again made of Witherspoon's awkwardness in establishing relationships. When this natural awkwardness is combined with what Carlyle alleges is an attitude of superiority, it must have provided a very considerable barrier, one that would have made it extremely difficult for Witherspoon to have any notion of romantic love. I suspect that he had particular difficulties in establishing a natural relationship with women, and this would explain the lack of evidence of any loving relationship with his wife.

Witherspoon addressed the senior class at the College 'on the Lord's Day preceding Commencement, September 23, 1775', and in the course of this address came out with words that might shed light on his relationships with people, especially women: 'To love a person who is not worthy of love, is not a virtue but an error'.[28] This strong opinion betrays the fact that Witherspoon has no understanding of the nature of love. Whether a person is worthy of their love is not an issue to the lover. It is even more likely that the lover will turn the spotlight on their own conscience and deem themselves not worthy of loving. Here is the shrewdness that Carlyle observed in action. Did Witherspoon, before engaging in loving someone, first of all consider whether or not they were worthy of his love? If he meant what he said in his address to his students, it seems likely that he would engage in the exercise I have just described, but if he did, and decided that the object of his attention was worth loving, it is unlikely that the resulting action would be love.

Further evidence of Witherspoon's attitude towards women is seen in *The Letters on Marriage*, which Witherspoon says are offered 'in the way of aphorisms or observations and subjoin to each a few thoughts by way of proof or illustration'.[29] Witherspoon writes in a playful and satirical manner in the style of *Ecclesiastical Characteristics*, and care will have to be taken as to his level of seriousness, but bearing in mind the old adage that truth can still be told with a smile, so even from his toying with the subject of marriage, we might learn something about his own relationship with his wife.

PERSONAL QUALITIES

In *Letter I*, Witherspoon criticises the 'sublime and exalted descriptions [of marriage] as are not realised in one case of a thousand', and chides *The Spectator* for:

> drawing the character of a lady in such terms that they may safely say, not above one that answers the description is to be found in a parish or perhaps in a county.

He goes on to declare:

> There is also a fault I think to be found in almost every writer who speaks in favour of the female sex that they overrate the charms of the outward form.

He criticises the novels or romances:

> a class of writing to which the world is very little indebted: the same thing may be said of plays when the heroine, for certain, and often all the ladies that are introduced are represented as inimitably beautiful.

He asserts that 'there is not a single quality, on which matrimonial happiness depends so little as outward form'.[30]

In his second aphorism of *Letter II*, he states:

> In the married state in general there is not so much happiness as young lovers dream of, nor is there by far so much unhappiness loose authors universally suppose.

He makes much of the fading qualities of beauty and seems to come to his ideal recipe for a marriage: 'Wherever there is a great and confessed superiority of understanding on one side, with some good nature on the other, there is domestic peace'. He then surprisingly adds: 'It is of little consequence whether the superiority be on the side of the man or the woman, provided the ground of it be manifest'. I suspect that Witherspoon has witnessed marriages where the female partner assumes the superiority, but I cannot imagine for one moment that that was the case with his own marriage, and in the next *Letter* Witherspoon strongly asserts the superiority of the husband. *Letter II* begins with an aphorism that sees the ideal in marrying persons 'nearly equal in rank and perhaps in age'. But Witherspoon's belief in male superiority emerges when he continues: 'the risk is greater when a man marries below his status than when a woman descends from hers'.[31] Witherspoon offers no evidence to justify his opinion, and only reveals his belief in 'women's low estate'. He pontificates:

> I can recollect instances in which married persons rose together to an opulent state from almost nothing, and the man improved considerably in politeness, or fitness for public life, but the woman not at all. The old groups and the old conversation continued to the very last. It is not even without example that a plain woman, raised by the success of her husband, becomes impatient of the society forced upon her, takes refuge in the kitchen, and spends most of her agreeable hours with her servants, from whom she differs in nothing but name.[32]

There is an ominous ring to those words, and they make me wonder if they provide an insight into the very infrequent ventures upon the stage of public life entered into by Elizabeth Witherspoon. Did she seek refuge in the kitchen and in her domestic tasks, or among her children or her servants in her home, from the world that she had not wanted to enter in the first place?

Witherspoon returns to the subject of marrying below one's status, arguing that, if men marry below their status it is because they have admired a woman's beauty. He writes:

> Now as beauty is much more fading than life, and fades sooner in a husband's eye than any other, in a little time, nothing will remain but what tends to create uneasiness and disgust.[33]

This cynical tone begins to dominate the *Letters on Marriage*, as he asserts the idea of male superiority. He positively and emphatically lays at the man's door the responsibility for the occurrence of 'the calamities of the married state', by reminding the man that it is his right to choose:

> It is also proper to observe, that if a man finds it difficult to judge of the temper and character of a woman, he has a great advantage on his side, that the right of selection belongs to him.

Then, when discoursing on 'the calamities of the married state', he says that they are:

... generally to be imputed to the persons themselves in the following proportion: Three fourths to the man, for want of care, and judgement, and one fourth to the woman.[34]

Now although these views on marriage are being conveyed by means of an article meant for publication, and therefore some of the remarks might be dismissed as having been made 'tongue in cheek', two phrases near the end of this piece indicate to me that they represent Witherspoon's personal and real life views of marriage. Making an emphatic point Witherspoon prefaces it by saying: 'No man in America, *take it from me* ...' and almost immediately following, as he likens those who are discontented in marriage to the man who buys a farm and then complains about it: '*I can assure you* that frugality, industry and good culture, will make a bad farm very tolerable, and an indifferent one truly good'. It is hardly to be expected that Witherspoon would have added 'love', to 'frugality, industry and good culture', as the factors that will improve a marriage, but the words that he does use are so representative of his attitude that I cannot help but think that he considers himself to have been responsible for making the wrong choice of a partner, and that his own marriage has either gone at worst, from the 'bad' to the 'very tolerable', or at best, from the 'indifferent' to the 'truly good'.[35] Whichever it was, from all that we can glean from his written words, it was hardly a love match. Witherspoon is expressing these opinions after at least twenty years of marriage and I get the distinct impression that he has a rather jaundiced view of the institution. He describes it in terms of a working relationship, or as something necessary but not necessarily enjoyable. Certainly there is no mention of the word love in these *Letters on Marriage* and perhaps that is because love did not enter very much into the thinking of John Witherspoon.

Picking up on another of the highly prejudiced views of Alexander Carlyle, who accuses Witherspoon of 'Envy and Jealousy', the relationship between Witherspoon and Thomas Paine comes to mind. Witherspoon had encountered Paine during the time that Paine was briefly in an editorial position with Bradford's *Pennsylvania Magazine*. It appears that Paine had edited out some words of an article that Witherspoon had submitted because they were too strong and might have caused offence. When Paine later published *Common Sense*, whose sentiments would have been heartily approved by most pro-independence politicians, Witherspoon was cool almost to the point of damning it with faint praise. Later in his sermon *The Dominion of Providence*, he entered into a long digression that attacked Thomas Paine's ridiculing of the doctrine of Original Sin in *Common Sense*, when many of those who were for independence might have thought that he might well have used Paine's political arguments to augment his own.[36] I suspect that the cool reception that Witherspoon gave to Paine's book, and his attack upon a minor theme within it, is evidence of Witherspoon's resentment of Paine's editing of his article. Further evidence of Witherspoon's capacity for holding on to a grievance for a considerable time is found in his opposition to the appointment of Paine to be Secretary of the newly formed Congress Committee on Foreign Affairs. Thomas Paine had been nominated for the post of Secretary by John Adams, despite the fact that Adams had disagreed with aspects of Paine's work in *Common Sense*, and had indeed written 'a small pamphlet to counter the Effect of it'. But perhaps Adam's real reason for writing the pamphlet was that Thomas Paine had stolen his thunder.

Adams accuses Paine of using: 'arguments which had been urged in Congress an hundred times' In other words, using his, Adams's, words. Adams refers to Paine as an opportunist who had,

> In the course of this Winter appeared like a Phenomenon in Philadelphia … I mean Thomas Paine. He came from England and got into such company as would converse with him, and ran about picking up what Information he could concerning our Affairs, and finding that the great Question was concerning Independence, he gleaned from those he saw the common place Arguments concerning Independence.[37]

Adams in his description of *Common Sense*, writes:

> The arguments in favour of Independence I liked very well, but one third of the book was filled with Arguments from the Old Testament to prove the unlawfulness of Monarchy and for the United States, in a Congress.

Adams was critical of Paine's comments on Monarchy and did not like the form of government that Paine proposed. His opposition was based on the offences that his references to Monarchy would cause, and its resultant loss of much needed support of the likes of 'the Allens, Penns and many other Persons of weight in the Community'. Adams saw Thomas Paine as a 'Johnny come lately', but not only that, he looked upon him as someone of a lower class than himself and one whose language was coarse and 'suitable for an Emigrant from New Gate'. Paine was too common for the aristocratic gentleman that Adams perceived himself to be, but nevertheless the scheming politician in him put aside these personal feelings and nominated Paine for the post of Secretary to the Committee on Foreign Affairs.

Witherspoon however, was blinded to any use that Paine might be to the American cause, and opposed Adams's nomination. Adams records Witherspoon's reaction:

> Dr. Witherspoon, the President of the New Jersey Colledge and then a Delegate from that State rose and objected to it with an Earnestness that surprized me. The Dr. said he would give his reasons; he knew the Man and his Communications. When he first came over he was on the other Side and had written pieces against the American Cause: that he had afterwards been employed by his Friend Robert Aitkin, and finding that the Tide of Popularity run (*pretty strong*) rapidly, he had turned about; that he was very intemperate and could not write untill he had quickened his Thoughts with large draughts of Rum and Water: that he was in short a bad Character and not fit to be placed in such a situation.[38]

Adams concludes:

> General Roberdeau spoke in his favour: no one confirmed Witherspoon's Account, though the truth of it has been sufficiently established. Congress appointed him: but he was soon obnoxious in his Manners and dismissed.

Adams's account of this is very one-sided and prejudiced, but at the time, despite an awareness of Thomas Paine's background, Adams still nominated him. Witherspoon on the other hand, still bore a resentment and harboured a prejudicial opinion against Paine. Although this incident does not completely prove the correctness of Carlyle's judgement, it is by itself a substantial example of a trait of meanness and possibly jealousy within Witherspoon's nature. Thomas Paine was convinced that Witherspoon was a man of sour grapes, and later would write of Witherspoon that 'he would never forgive me for publishing *Common Sense*, and going a step beyond him in Literary reputation'.[39]

Turning now to look at the habits and life-style of John Witherspoon, I begin with an attempt to assess his health and physical attributes. The activities that John Witherspoon engages in throughout, what for the age in which he was living, is a long life, indicate that he seems to have enjoyed good general health. Brought up to enjoy the fresh air and healthy atmosphere of East Lothian, a shire in the east of Scotland noted for its dry and temperate climate, would give him a good start in life. Moving to Beith and later on, Paisley, both in the west of Scotland with its heavier rain-fall, does not seem to have done him any harm. As a minister in a rural area, he would have had to make frequent journeys on horseback. As one who was also an assiduous Presbyter, he would have had to make regular journeys to attend Presbytery, Synod and General Assembly each of which were held at venues that were from ten to sixty miles away from his two Parishes. The journey to Edinburgh where the General Assembly was held, involved a two day trip as his diaries show, and sometimes caused him an overnight stay at Whitburn. When he moved to America he frequently made trips by coach or horseback that involved him in being away for over a week at a time. Even getting to Philadelphia or New York, as he did on many occasions, involved him in a considerably taxing journey. As this sort of activity in America was sustained for over twenty years (at least), it is one indicator of good general health. I think that this evidence alone challenges Collins's repetition of the idea that came from Ashbel Green: that Witherspoon had a nervous disorder brought about by his capture and brief imprisonment at Doune Castle after spectating at the battle of Falkirk in 1746. Collins twice refers to Witherspoon suffering from a 'nervous complaint', and writes that this might explain Witherspoon's behaviour in his student days, because 'it compelled him to keep the strictest check upon himself'. Collins alleges that 'the whole experience [of capture and imprisonment] had a most serious effect on his constitution and he never fully recovered from the exposure and nervous strain'.[40] This is a very big claim to make, and is totally contradicted and refuted by Witherspoon's energetic pursuit of his interests and concerns throughout the rest of his life. Collins further alleges that:

> Apparently [Witherspoon] did not care to talk about it; for instance he told Dr. Ashbel Green that he had suffered a shock to his nerves soon after his ordination, but he never related the circumstances. Green only learned about the Doune Castle episode, through an article in the Christian Instructor and claimed that Witherspoon 'for at least three years after the adventure, Mr. Witherspoon had a nervous affection of the most distressing kind, which sometimes took the form of a sudden and overwhelming presentiment in the midst of a service that he would not live to finish his task'.[41]

Green maintained to Collins that Witherspoon had said that it was only by his father's help that he was enabled to continue in his profession. Collins concludes that: 'During the rest of his life, his [Witherspoon's] nerves were easily disturbed'.

I am not at all convinced that there is any reason to trust either Green's or Collins's assessment of the Doune incident's effect on Witherspoon's health. Yes, of course it would be an experience that would have caused after-effects, even in the days when post-traumatic stress syndrome had not been thought of. But to see the experience as having a life-long effect is, I am sure, a gross exaggeration. The life of John Witherspoon, in the years in Scotland and the United States of America, does not give any evidence whatsoever of his being adversely affected by the experience he had in 1746, and therefore I do not offer it as an explanation for any oddness of behaviour on his part. Neither in my perusal of any other accounts of his life, nor in his writings, have I come across any evidence of this alleged disorder or its cause to which these earlier biographers allude. The only reference that I have come across is in a letter from 'Tusculum', dated 'March 20th 1780', to an unknown correspondent whom Witherspoon is thanking for sending him news of Glasgow, and from whom he asks if he would 'take in Paisley also'. Witherspoon refers to his health:

> I have been since you wrote your last, in general in good health, and indeed am at present in better health than I have been since I had the last fit. Excepting these fits and the weakness that followed upon them, my health has been good ever since I came to America; and that weakness has been chiefly a swimming in my head, and fear and uncertainty when I went to make a long discourse in public. It was of the opinion of Dr. Rush that these fits were something of the apoplectic kind. It is remarkable that for these twelve months past, I have had almost constantly a succession of pimples or rather small biles [*sic*. possibly? 'boils'] or blotches about the temples, within the hair and sometimes on the forehead; since which time I have been sensibly better and freer from the other complaint.[42]

The first thing to notice about this letter is that Witherspoon does not make any mention of his Doune experience. He does mention a weakness and swimming in his head which to the modern ear sounds like a blood pressure problem; and 'fear and uncertainty', but that is a common experience of any public speaker who is anxious to get their message across, and especially of the kind of speaker who has taken great care over their preparation just because they want to get it right. This is not to be diagnosed as pathological, but rather as entirely natural behaviour. What Witherspoon is relating is vastly different from the story that emanates from Ashbel Green and is repeated by Collins. The other thing to notice is that Witherspoon sounds 'up-beat'. The things he call 'fits' are described by his doctor as apoplectic, that is, related to getting angry or worked up over something. This is quite different from an anxiety caused by something deeply hidden in the sub-conscious or even stemming from a memory repressed. The pimples or boils or blotches he refers to might well be signs of a nervous eczema. Despite the symptoms that he freely describes to his correspondent, Witherspoon claims to be 'in general good health'.

When I compare the conclusion at which Green and Collins arrive, to Witherspoon's own account of his health, I am inclined to dismiss theirs as ill-founded, and to accept the opinion of Witherspoon himself. I rather see the interpretation of Green and Collins as typical of the respective times in which they were writing: Green on the edge of the age of sentiment, and Collins displaying a hangover from the Victorian era. In both ages there was a peculiar and ill-informed view of the causes of physical and mental distress, and more importantly, of the long term or lasting effects. To be almost facetious for a moment, Witherspoon's fear of dying before he could complete a sermon, is as likely to have come to him from his reading of some of the popular would-be theologians of the time, like James Hervey with his imaginative projection of the nature of the day of judgement and the awaiting hellfire for the damned, as from a bad memory of a few days imprisonment in 1746.[43] But it is the lack of evidence from his writings and the many anecdotes that exist about him, for example in the reminiscences of his students at Princeton, that make me think that both Green and Collins overstate the case for the malignant effect of Witherspoon's experience in 1746.

Attesting to Witherspoon's good general health is the fact that while at Beith and Paisley he engaged in outdoor physical activities. His exploits in the winter sport of curling, I have already described, but he also enjoyed golf and fishing, and of course the riding that he had to do to fulfill his parish duties. Collins does not reveal his sources for his physical description of Witherspoon, but abstracting from that, it would seem that in 1768, as a 45 year old, he was of medium stature, blue eyed, thick eyebrows, brown hair, fair complexion, high cheek bones, 'mobile mouth' and had a large nose and ears.[44] The impression given by any of the engravings I have seen of Witherspoon show him as thick set, corpulent, and with heavy prominent features. The painting of John Witherspoon by Charles Wilson Peale, which hangs in the faculty room of Nassau Hall in Princeton University, is a late portrait, and one in which the strong features, though still prominent, have softened with age and the hair has become wispy and thin. The earlier portrait used by Jeffry Morrison on the cover of his book, *John Witherspoon and the Founding of the American Republic*, shows the same features, but they are in a much more vigorous looking frame. It was said by Ashbel Green that Witherspoon had a personal quality that is best described as 'presence'. Green, who had had the experience of being a student under Witherspoon, writes:

His public appearance was always graceful and venerable: and in promiscuous company he had more of the quality called *presence* - a quality powerfully felt, but not to be described - than any other individual with whom the writer has ever had intercourse.[45]

Whether Witherspoon was merely naturally presenting himself as he was, or whether there was an element of cultivated *gravitas* in his demeanour, it is difficult to tell, but it is interesting that even when attending Congress he always wore his clerical garb. Perhaps in this, there is a hint of Witherspoon attempting to make a calculated impact on his audience by wearing the emblems of his ecclesiastical authority.

Witherspoon's habits can to a certain extent be gleaned from a perusal of his activities and an occasional personal note left by him that offers signs of these activities. He was a man of great routine and regularity. The pattern of College life established by him went on unchanged for many years. He liked to be organised in preparation for his activities as the notes that he made for himself show. A fragment in his handwriting found among his papers at Princeton University, headed 'Things to be done at Glasgow Oct. 5 1763', contains a list of books to be ordered from 'a Mr. Beaton for Jo. Montgomery', and a memo to himself: 'To give my watch to be mended'. The two *Almanacks for 1763* and *1768* that he used as personal notebooks, also give a clue to some of his habits. The *Almanack for 1763* contains various headings such as:

> Various things to do in Edinburgh. To call at R. Fleming, Bookseller Shop, in Edin. and Desire the Loan for John Buchanan Jnr. of the First Number of Cunningham's Digest of the Statute Law of England which shall be immediately paid or returned. To pay an a/c. To visit the Lord Tweedale - To call on Lady Bellingry.
> Memo of things to be done in Glasgow Mar 3 1763. To get the Review for February 1759. Apr.3rd 1763. Expenses at the golf 7d.
> A journey to Edinburgh: Tobacco ½d Poor Man ½d Barber 3d Tobacco ½d Snuff 4/- Barber 1d Tobacco ½d[46]

Witherspoon's expenses on tobacco for his pipe seems to average a halfpenny every other day, but it is interesting to note that he makes a large purchase of snuff which is of course tobacco in another form. While away from home he also seems to indulge in a couple of visits to the barber, indicating some concern for his personal hygiene and appearance. Witherspoon also records a stop at Whitburn for Dinner on both outward and return journeys and on a similar journey to Edinburgh in June 6, 1763 he records a purchase of: 'wine 10/-' and indicating that his means of travel had been on horseback: 'horseshoe 4d'.

Five years later the *Almanack for 1768* contains among his notes, some details of the preparations that he had to make prior to sailing for America. The first entries indicate that he is still working at Paisley as he records eighty-two names which seem to be of those desirous of being added to the Communion Roll of the church. There are also travel arrangement notes, a diary of his appointments in London and of his trip to Holland. Alongside these are notes of bills to be paid, people to be thanked, arrangements for Pulpit Supply at the Laigh Kirk in Paisley for the months before his departure, and as if picking up from where he left off five years ago in the *Almanack for 1763*, the *1768* edition has this note:

> Things to do at Philadelphia: Some large candles for my own study.
> To get a nightgown for Jamie.
> To get Sam Puddiman's Grammar and [indistinct] Exercises.
> To get Ink Stands and Materials for making ink.
> To get a velvet nightcap for myself.
> Works of Psalms and Hymns for Andrew Hodge and James Gardner.
> Clothes for Robert Wilson to [indistinct] for Wm. Blair.
> Tea 1pd Crea. 4 Dr ----Coffee Cake.
> Nightgowns.[47]

This list shows that Witherspoon combined his business trip to Philadelphia with the shopping list for both his family and College and students. It also demonstrates the organisation that he put into the most everyday tasks. It tells us too, that despite the balmier climate of Princeton as against Paisley, he still wanted to wear a velvet nightcap. The *Almanack for 1768* also contains entries that show the practical nature of many of Witherspoon's concerns. He has followed up the earlier note about ink stands and lists the ingredients required for making ink: 'Recipe - Proportions of the materials for making ink: 3 pnts water, 1 oz. hogwart, I do. Green Valencil, 3 do. Salts, 1½ do. Gr ...'. This attention to detail and careful planning is characteristic of Witherspoon, and is one of the important qualities that he brings to his work, whether as a minister, a College administrator or a politician. It is clear from these notes that he smoked tobacco, took snuff, and enjoyed a glass of wine. We do not have any detail of his domestic consumption of wine but we do have a record of the generous supply of drink that he made available for his guests at College and Trustee Dinners. The account for The Trustees of New Jersey College Dinner on September 26, 1770, speaks for itself:

Dinner for 40 Gentleman	@ 2/6	£5
37 bottles of wine	@ 5/- each	9. 5
14 bottles of beer	@ 1/6	1. 1
12 bowls of punch	@ 1/6	18
		£16. 12[48]

This account was not paid for until after a more modest 'Dinner for 9 Gentlemen' was held in April 1771, which only cost £2.3/- and was signed off by John Witherspoon and the total of £18.15/- paid on May 10, 1771. Another large dinner for sixty persons was held on September 30, 1772, and this time, the bill was paid more promptly (the following month) and the fare was different:

60 dinners	@ 2/- each	£6.
12 double bowls of punch	@ 3/-	1. 16.
17 bottles of beer	@ 1/6	1. 5. 6
21 ' ' port wine	@ 5/-	5. 5.
16 ' ' madeira	@ 5/-	4.
6 single bowls of Toddy	@ 1/-	6.
		£18. 12. 6 [49]

As President of the College, Witherspoon certainly was generous in his provision of food, wine and spirits for his colleagues and guests. When you add to this the references in John Adams's diary, it suggests that in his own life, Witherspoon enjoyed the social ambience of company, good food and drink and would seem that Witherspoon was far from being the straight laced, narrow-minded, evangelical Presbyterian so often caricatured. Again such evidence seems to contradict the judgement of Alexander Carlyle, and perhaps suggests a certain mellowing of the character had taken place since those earlier days remembered. Perhaps the process had even begun in a modest way at Beith, when Witherspoon is said to have enjoyed the conviviality of the tavern after a curling match. But it would seem that Carlyle got at least one thing right, Witherspoon continued to disapprove of dancing.

CHAPTER 12

Personal Characteristics

To assist me in trying to present a portrait of the complex character of John Witherspoon, I have gathered the characteristics of him that I have perceived into four clusters. The elements of each cluster are, I believe, interconnected and the names given to them allow for their overlapping. The first cluster that I would see as part of the make-up of his personality or as expressions of it, is that he was an activist, outspoken and rebellious.

The first real evidence of John Witherspoon being an activist is to be seen in his student days at Edinburgh University. In the 1730s, it was not customary that everyone who attended University and met all the conditions of their class work, would then proceed to graduation. But John Witherspoon requested that he present his Master of Arts thesis for examination in public before the University. So on February 23, 1739, along with two other students, Witherspoon delivered and defended his *Disputatio Philosophic - De Mentis Immortalitate.*[1] This willingness to put himself forward, (remember he was only sixteen), in order to promote a practice or a policy in which he believed, emerges regularly throughout his career. He was often to be found in the forefront of movements for change, or agitating because of a perceived injustice, or writing to point out or criticise a perceived wrong. Many instances of this are to be found scattered throughout his life and in selecting just a few instances of them I am aware that many other examples might have been used. The first of these is seen in his response to the Presbytery's call to ministers to encourage the forming of a militia from within their local community to meet the crisis of the 1745 Rebellion. Not only did John Witherspoon make the call to arms and fundraise for the equipment of the men, but he placed himself at the head of the resultant body as its commander, and led them to the muster point. Notwithstanding the senior military's decision not to use his men, Witherspoon, after dismissing them and sending them back home, continued on his way, accompanied by his beadle, to see the outcome of the expected battle at Falkirk. On January 17, 1746, Witherspoon, along with several other 'spectators' of the battle, were taken prisoners of war by the forces of Prince Charles Edward Stuart and led off across the river Forth, to Doune Castle a few miles north of Stirling.[2]

Another instance of his activism was his entering into the controversy over the Reverend John Home's play, *Douglas*, which had opened in Edinburgh on December 14, 1756. By the spring of 1757, Witherspoon had published his *Serious Enquiry into the Nature and Effects of the Stage, Being an Attempt to show that contribution to the Support of a Public Theatre is inconsistent with the Character of a Christian.*[3] The pamphlet bears the signs of his immaturity, but it attests to his willingness to be pro-active and to declare his own stance on controversial matters of the time

Witherspoon's activity in Presbytery, Synod and General Assembly on the issue of Patronage gained him the reputation of being a leading activist in the cause of the Popular party within the Church of Scotland. They disputed the powers claimed by the Patrons, and forcefully asserted the rights of congregations to choose their own minister. Witherspoon fearlessly and consistently challenged the majority and controlling Moderate party by his outspokenness, and his written defiance of their practices. He was active in attempting to expose the injustices of the system being unwisely imposed and enforced by those in power. In the Colonies too, from his earliest days, his activism showed in his support of the ideas that were to lead eventually to American Independence, by having the temerity to grant honorary degrees in 1769, to three men who were known to be advocates of various degrees of change in the existing British colonial government.[4] Later on, Witherspoon was one of the first to assert that the individual states should not be the beneficiaries from the development of the lands to the west of their borders, but that these lands should be for the benefit of all the states within the Federation. From the very beginning of his service as a member of Congress he had been willing to investigate new methods of doing things e.g. putting forward new methods of provisioning the army and contriving new ways of dealing with prisoners of war.[5]

Witherspoon was outspoken even towards those with whom he was in broad sympathy. In June 1781, he petitioned Congress on behalf of the Trustees of the College of New Jersey. He complains about the cost to the College of the:

> Damages done by the Enemy to the Building, and the continual quartering of *our own troops* especially the Militia passing from time to time through the town.

Witherspoon forcefully puts forward the case of the College:

> Your petitioners farther pray that a Penalty may be laid on any Civil or Military Officer who shall here after Quarter or suffer to be quartered any Trooper in the Building and its Appurtenances, or grant your Petitioners such other remedy as in your wisdom, you shall think fit.[6]

PERSONAL CHARACTERISTICS

This same outspokenness had led him into trouble in Paisley in 1762, when he had unwisely named a young man, James Snodgrass who had allegedly been making fun of the Sacrament of the Lord's Supper. On this occasion Witherspoon acted precipitately, and came out of the whole affair very badly, being found guilty of libel and fined.[7] He persisted in his outspoken manner right to the end of his Paisley ministry and both parts of his 'Farewell Discourse', spread over two Sundays, end with warnings: the first, a plea to remember 'the corruption of human nature'; and the concluding part, a cautionary word to the Paisley buddies:

> This place, engaged in commerce and traffick, growing in numbers, and I suppose growing in wealth, is in great danger of a worldly spirit, and of importing, if I may speak so, fashionable vices, instead of real improvements.[8]

Witherspoon's rebellious nature shows in his willingness to espouse seemingly forlorn causes. He engaged in the fierce controversy over the patronage issue, which in the years that he gave to the cause of the people's right to choose their minister, he had no success, and with the Moderates occupying the positions of influence, authority and power in the Church and Universities there was little prospect of succeeding, even for years to come. Indeed there were those who saw Witherspoon's leaving for America as a consequence of his ecclesiastical defeats in Scotland. The rapid assimilation of the actuality of life in the Colonies, and the clear-sightedness as to why the laws created by various British *Acts of Parliament* were not appropriate in the American setting, were an incitement sufficient to stir his rebelliousness. He was more persuaded by the Americans' need for a new structure of government than he was for the retention of the old relationship with Britain, and when that was allied to his innate unwillingness to conform, just because of tradition, then rebellion was the natural route to take.

One influence upon Witherspoon was his early reading of George Buchanan's two works: *Rerum Scoticarum Historia*, 'a comprehensive history of Scotland dedicated to, and for the instruction of James VI', and *De Iure Regni apud Scotos Dialogus*, 'a dialogue on the rights and duties of the prince', which was also intended for the edification of the young king.[9] Through these texts Witherspoon had become aware of the Scottish attitude to Monarchy, that had been enshrined in the *Declaration of Arbroath* in 1320, which had outlined a people's contractual agreement with a king in the pledging their loyalty to Robert Bruce in these terms:

To him we are obliged and resolved to adhere in all things, both upon the account of his right and his own merit, as being the person who hath restored the people's safety in defence of their liberties. But after all, if this prince shall leave these principles he hath so nobly pursued, and consent that we or our kingdom be subjected to the king or people of England, we will immediately endeavour to expel him, as our enemy and as the subverter both of his own and our rights, and we will make another king, who will defend our liberties.

George Buchanan in *De Iure Regni apud Scotos* had adopted that attitude of their being a contractual arrangement between ruler and ruled, and John Witherspoon justified his act of rebellion in the colonies of America in that same spirit. He embodied, in his own writings and activity, the spirit of the most oft quoted passage in the *Declaration of Arbroath*:

For it is not glory, it is not riches, neither is it honours, but it is liberty alone that we fight and contend for, which no honest man will lose but with his life.[10]

In John Witherspoon's defense of 'liberty' through his rebellion, he did not seek to live in the rarified atmosphere of theory, or academic isolation, but engaged in it by the practical everyday methods of a man committed to the working out of an ideal.

The second cluster of characteristics of John Witherspoon will exemplify this 'down-to-earthness' endeavour of the man who pursued the cause of liberty. Witherspoon was frugal, industrious, practical and multi-skilled. Some of the best illustrations of his frugality are gleaned from those notes of recorded expenditure, on which I commented earlier.[11] From these notes of recorded expenditure it is clear that he felt accountable for his expenditure. The line that gives a financial account of a journey to Edinburgh: 'Tobacco ½d, Poor man ½d, Barber 3d, Tobacco ½d Snuff 4/-, Barber 1d, Tobacco ½d', to me speaks volumes. Here is a man accounting (at least to himself) for every item of expenditure down to the last halfpenny. There is something very Calvinistic about this sense of accountability, so that he even keeps a note of his gift of a halfpenny to a poor man. When one projects this attitude into his workaday life, it leaves an impression of frugality engaged in almost to the point of meanness; a self-denial that almost amounts to an unhealthy display of it. But on the other hand, it could be a sign that he really had to 'watch his money', to curtail his expenditure because he perhaps was not very good with money, and had to keep reminding himself what he had spent it on. Yet he was to be entrusted with the care of money both in the administration of the

College and in his business dealings with John Pagan, the land dealer, trader and entrepreneur.

During his time in Congress, Witherspoon made several speeches on financial matters, some of which are recorded in his *Works* or *Essays*. In his *Speech to Congress on a Motion for paying the Interest on Loan-Office Certificates*, he warned against non-payment of loan interest, saying that it might lead people to 'combine to refuse to pay their taxes'.[12] He urged the payment of loan interest saying that it would give confidence to people in their government, and 'It would give the people better thoughts of their rulers, and prevent murmuring at public persons and public measures'. Witherspoon's awareness of the need to be faithful in fulfilling financial obligations, led him in Congress to point out its benefits and consequences to a government struggling to assert its independence from a very powerful former ruler. His plea for financial responsibility ended with the reminder: 'I need not tell this house how much depends on having the esteem and attachment of the people'. In another speech to Congress he returned to the theme, warning that the resolutions before the house on finance 'will give the last stab to public credit'.[13] Urging financial responsibility to the house, he again makes the political link between the conduct of financial policies and the stability of the country when with passion he declaims: 'Would to God, that the independence of America was once established by a treaty of peace in Europe'.

Right from the beginning of the time of his political service Witherspoon saw the need for a careful management of financial resources. In the early days after the formation of the continental army he reveals his 'free market' views in a letter to 'His Excellency General George Washington' in which he expresses his pleasure at learning of the intention to hold a market at the camp.[14] Witherspoon's interest in the best methods of managing the economy and his participation in the various economic debates in Congress, caused him to be invited by some of his admirers, three years after he had left it, to give them his advice on money. In 1786, Witherspoon produced *An Essay on Money as a Medium of Commerce, with Remarks on the Advantages of Paper Admitted into General Circulation*. Jeffry H. Morrison calls it: 'One of the earliest American free-market economic treatises'.[15] Witherspoon expounds his theory of money in very simple terms, even making use of theological terminology that would be recognised and appreciated by anyone from a reformed church background:

a piece [of money] is intended first to be the value of a measure of grain, but at last men came to make their bargain by the number of pieces instead of the number of measures; using *the sign for the thing signified.* [My emphasis.]

This was a phrase commonly used when the subject of the Sacrament of the Lord's Supper was being discussed in connection with its comparison with the Mass.[16] In his treatise Witherspoon clings to the idea that a metal coin should have the same intrinsic value as if it were bullion. While acknowledging that there are other thinkers who disagree with this view, Benjamin Franklin and the Scottish economist Sir James Steuart, he holds to his opinion. He is equally conservative in regard to the issue of paper money:

> What is commonly called paper money, that is bills bearing that the person holding them is entitled to receive a certain sum specified in them is not, properly speaking, money at all.

However, although he sees paper money as facilitating commerce, he points out what he sees as its down side:

> The evil is this. All paper introduced into circulation, and obtaining credit as gold and silver, adds to the quantity of the medium, and thereby, as has been shown above, increases the price of industry and its fruits.

His final judgement on paper money is a very cautious approval. He is in favour of gold based currency notes issued by the banks.[17]

Witherspoon anticipates criticism of his views and the questioning of his authority to write upon the subject and posits the question:

> Why has this gentleman to do with such a subject? ... To them I answer, that I have written not as a merchant, but as a scholar. I profess to derive my opinions from the best civilians of this and the last age, and from the history of all ages, joined with a pretty considerable experience and attention to the effects of political causes within the sphere of my own observation.[18]

The matter of the correctness or otherwise of Witherspoon's economic theories regarding currency is not the issue here. The very fact that he was invited to offer his views on the subject, is an indication of the status that he still enjoyed among those still in political life and office. The frugality, that had him recording the spending of halfpennies, was carried over into his political activity and earned him the respect of those who were charged with managing the affairs of state.

A final comment on Witherspoon's frugality is offered by the record of his estate as given in a document drawn up after his death on November 28, 1794: 'A Final Inventory of all the goods and chattels of the late Rev. John Witherspoon'. The total of his household effects and goods including: 1 Yoke of Brown Oxen, cows, 12 pigs, 13 hogs, and 24 sheep' amounts to $2,495.68 to which is added the net amount due from 'Book Debt' to make a final total of $2,835.68. There are two notes to the figures: 'Library valued at $640', and the last item on the Inventory indicates '2 slaves supposed to be worth $200. They arc 28 years of age'.[19] Although the sum was a considerable amount for the times, the total hardly amounts to the leavings of a rich man. It is probably another indication, that despite John Witherspoon's frugality, he still was not all that good at managing his own finances. For although a 'Book Debt of $7,387.11 is listed, only $2,502.97 of this seems to have been already received and $4,543.94 is listed as 'Doubtful'; probably meaning that his records were such that his executor was not entirely sure what had already been received by Witherspoon. Whichever way the figures are taken, the net result is that John Witherspoon's estate at death only amounted to $2,835.68. A footnote to his frugality is seen in a clause in his will where he wishes 'to be buried in the simplest and cheapest manner'.

Another characteristic that is grouped with his frugality is that John Witherspoon was industrious. Whatever he tackled, he was the type who gets things done. Indeed his 'can do' attitude would now be recognised as archetypal American. In whatever sphere of activity of John Witherspoon that you care to look at, you will find signs of his industry. Throughout his Scottish ministries he works with an above average activity. He seems to have fulfilled all the tasks of his ministry at Beith and at Paisley, while still finding time to engage in writing pamphlets, and to be active in attendance at Presbytery, Synod and General Assembly in a way that does not mean just turning up to listen and to vote. His various speeches in Church Courts, and his involvement in petitioning the ecclesiastical and local authorities, indicate that he was no passive pew filler but an activist to be reckoned with. In America the same pattern continues, but his activities are spread over an even wider set of concerns. He takes on the re-organising of a College, and the re-establishing of a Grammar School. In addition to this he engages in fund raising trips, assumes responsibility for lecturing in Divinity, Moral Philosophy, Rhetoric and History, gives tutorials in French and in Hebrew, establishes himself in a farming estate, and helps rear a family. Notwithstanding all of this, he branches out into a political life as a member of the Committee of Correspondence, is then quickly promoted to represent New Jersey in Congress, and from there goes on to serve on committee after committee until he is within the very highest circle of government. All of this speaks of a tremendous drive and industry which continues right to his last years, when he sees through a major restructuring of the Presbyterian Church in America, which he completes in 1789, aged sixty-six and just five years from his death.[20]

All of this is closely linked to another characteristic, and that was that Witherspoon was very practical, e.g. seeking a recipe for making ink, obtaining information about various land grants, and taking the necessary steps to obtain them, advertising for emigrants and making sure that the proper arrangements were in place when they came over from Scotland. A good example of this practical side of his nature is found in his dealings with James Whitelaw and David Allan, the Commissioners appointed by the Scotch American Company of Farmers. Amidst a very busy life, Witherspoon found the time to be at the place where they could access him and eventually complete a deal.[21] Another aspect of his practicality was his attraction to and adoption of the Common Sense philosophy that emanated from Thomas Reid and some of the Aberdeen school of Scottish philosophers. The tenets of the Common Sense philosophy were more suited to Witherspoon's nature than the metaphysical speculations of other European philosophers.

Completing this cluster of characteristics is that John Witherspoon comes across as a person who is multi-skilled. His very ability to keep in the air at one time the several balls of preacher, lecturer, educationalist, administrator, politician, journalist and occasionally prophet, speaks of this capability. It did not result in his excelling in every one of his roles, but in each of them he showed a considerable degree of competence, and in a few of them he achieved distinction.

The third set of characteristics that I would claim for Witherspoon is that he is principled, determined, loyal, brave and adventurous. Every subject that Witherspoon tackled in his lectures, sees him trying to establish the principles that undergird it: e.g. he sees Moral Philosophy as 'that branch of Science which treats the Principles and Laws of Duty and Morals'.[22] In the opening lecture on 'Divinity', he seeks to establish the principle that underlies all the preparation for those who are intending to go on to enter the Christian ministry: 'Learning is necessary to keep the sacred truths we are obliged to handle from contempt. Learning is also necessary to repel the attacks of adversaries'.[23] In all that he teaches Witherspoon strives to establish the basic principles. In the same way he sought to govern his own life by attempting to adhere to certain principles. Two examples of this will suffice because in each case Witherspoon's principles never altered: firstly, in his opposition to the assertion of the patron's rights as against the rights of a congregation to appoint a minister. For the majority of Witherspoon's years at Beith and Paisley this was a recurring theme, and one that Witherspoon joined the fray over for many years, never wavering in his championing of the rights of the people over the patron. Secondly, once he had time to appraise of the true situation in America, and that took him at the most only a year, Witherspoon became an advocate for American liberation from British rule. Even when others among the colonists were wavering, he remained wholly committed to seeing through the claim for independence. His was the attitude of Cicero, one of his early heroes, who had committed himself to oppose the tyranny of Marc Antony and invited Quintus Cornificius, governor of Afriuca Vetui to join him and other Patriots:

> Therefore, dear Quintus, come aboard with us, even at the helm! There is one boat now for all good citizens, which in truth we take pains to hold on its course. May our voyage prosper! But whatever winds there be, we shall certainly not lack skill. For what else can virtue assure.[24]

Witherspoon adopted the American cause upon the principle that liberty was the right of every man, and once he had joined that cause he knew himself to be in the same boat as other revolutionaries, and ever after urged others to join him in that boat.

Closely linked with his being a man of principle, is Witherspoon's being of a determined disposition. When Witherspoon committed himself to a course of action he was utterly determined to see it through. When he first came to the College of New Jersey he discovered that the favoured philosophy was that of George Berkeley, as taught by Jonathan Edwards, (Senior). Witherspoon set about systematically refuting this philosophy through his own lectures on Moral Philosophy, but also in staff changes that lessened the impact of Berkeleyean thought and introduced a more common sense realism mixed with his own brand of Calvinism.[25] Another example is the very strict control that he exercised over the curriculum and methods to be employed in the Grammar School, which as one of the perquisites of the Presidency he wanted entirely under his direction. In another area of his activity his determination is shown in his eagerness to assert that the American rebellion was not the work of a few, but that it was provoked, stimulated and supported by a groundswell of the people. Even in his more lighthearted satirical writing his dogged pursuit of a theme is seen. In *A Letter to the Printer from Epaminondas* in the *Pennsylvania Magazine* of March 1775, Witherspoon writes about this determination under the pseudonym Epaminondas:

PERSONAL CHARACTERISTICS

What can be more glorious than immovable firmness in a good cause and what can be more detestable than unconquerable obstinacy in a bad one.

He develops the theme as the article continues:

A man that is truly firm in a good cause, in which he is engaged from conviction is not therefore remarkably tenacious in everything, but is generally speaking more open to light, and more easily convinced than those of inferior fortitude. On the other hand a man that is headstrong and obstinate without reason at one time is often irresolute and changeable at another, without visible cause. Perhaps we may go further and say that to be humble, cautious, open to light and desirous of information has a powerful and direct influence in making men firm and determined, after they have fixed their choice, whereas rashness and precipitation makes them wavering and unstable, either from natural weakness or absolute necessity ... firmness brings success - a man without firmness brings nothing to perfection.[26]

The gentle musings of 'Epaminondas' are saying a great deal about the determined streak that is part of the nature of John Witherspoon. It is the resoluteness of a man who is convinced of the rightness of his cause. Whenever Witherspoon is so convinced, he pursues his course with an unstoppable vigour. Here in this article is the gentle advocacy of the American cause by a very determined man.

Another quality that Witherspoon had in great measure was loyalty. In his early life he had shown this aspect of his character to the British government by committing himself to armed service for his country. It was not a loyalty without limits, but rather one that was conditional. He was loyal to King George II because he saw him as the upholder of the Protestant religion in the face of the Roman Catholic threat in the person of Prince Charles Edward Stuart, who had raised a rebellion in 1745. The context in which this was a factor in determining the loyalty of John Witherspoon is that it was only fifty-five years previous to that event, that the Protestant religion had had its safety and freedom to worship according to conscience restored by William III, in 1690. But when George III and his government sought to impose their will on the American Colonies at the cost of the liberty, both religious and civil of the Colonies' inhabitants, then Witherspoon's loyalty to the British Crown and Government ceased, and was transferred to the new republic of the United States. But any examination of John Witherspoon's writings or activities in the years between 1768 and 1776 will reveal a very reluctant rebel. He bent over backwards, right up to 1775, to allow for the king and his ministers to have been misinformed of the situation in the American Colonies, and following that misinformation that they had been ill advised. His switch of loyalty was not some Damascus Road experience, but was brought about slowly, and at first reluctantly, because there seemed to be no real alternative, but once given, he was wholehearted and unwavering in his loyalty to the American cause of independence.

Courage is also a component of John Witherspoon's character. In Scotland he was always brave enough to face his powerful ecclesiastical opponents. His life was never in danger from this opposition, but it was often made miserable by it. Even as he received his first call to Beith he met up with opposition from those who questioned his orthodoxy, possibly because of his M.A. thesis on *The Immortality of the Mind* or perhaps because some members of the Presbytery under whose jurisdiction the charge of Beith fell, were wanting to be doubly sure of the orthodoxy of the candidate, in view of the liberal tendencies of his predecessor the Reverend James Leechman. But the young Witherspoon battled through and was inducted. In the years there, he had to contend with criticism because he had dared to write critically of the ruling Moderate party in *Ecclesiastical Characteristics* (1753). Ten years later he was to admit in his own defence in *A Serious Apology for Ecclesiastical Characteristics*:

> A satire that does not bite is good for nothing. Hence it necessarily follows that it is essential to this manner of writing to provoke and give offence. The greatest satirists, in all ages have made as many enemies to themselves, as they exposed objects of scorn and derision to the public ... I acted very prudently in not setting my name to the work, the event justified this precaution ... the rage and fury of many ministers in Scotland when this pamphlet was first published is known almost to all its readers ... The common cry has been, 'The author must be a man of bad heart. - as no good man could write such a piece'.[27]

Witherspoon was brave enough to set about the task of criticizing his fellow ministers and to withstand the resultant criticism.

In America he had to contend with an even more virulent opposition. He was regarded there by the British forces as an enemy to be hunted down and captured. He was counted by them to a member of the Black Regiment, the name given to all those clergymen who agitated for independence, some of whom had actually enlisted and fought for it. David Hackett Fischer in his book *Washington's Crossing* tells how in January 1777, the

PERSONAL CHARACTERISTICS

Reverend John Rosbrugh, an elderly Scots Presbyterian army chaplain from Northampton County, Pennsylvania, had been resting at Trenton's Blazing Star Tavern when he was caught up in one of the street skirmishes. He rushed outside to discover that someone had taken his horse and was then run down by a party of Hessians who earlier in the day had been ordered not to offer any quarter. The soldiers tormented him, robbed, and eventually, killed him. Fischer writes:

> His naked body was found in an open field with thirteen bayonet wounds and many sabre cuts to the head. British officers who hated the 'black regiment' of the Presbyterian clergy celebrated his death.[28]

Such might have been John Witherspoon's fate had the British forces or their Hessian allies caught up with him.

Witherspoon received a 'back-handed' compliment from the British troops at Long Island who in reaction to his signing of the *Declaration of Independence*, burned his effigy along with those of Washington, Lee and Putnam, portraying Witherspoon as haranguing the three generals.[29] It may have been a light-hearted gesture on the part of the soldiers but it is an indication of their perception of Witherspoon's importance as an influential revolutionary leader. John Witherspoon showed his courage following his signing of the *Declaration of Independence* by continuing to fulfil his duties at College and at Congress, and did not close the College until the time came when it became known that the British forces were heading for Princeton on their way to Philadelphia, the seat of government. Witherspoon closed the College on November 29, 1776 and sent his students home. He then immediately left his own home at Tusculum to seek refuge with his relatives at Pequea in Pennsylvania.[30]

The journey to Pequea is just one of many journeys undertaken by Witherspoon in the course of his life, journeys that reveal an adventurous spirit. During the course of his Scottish ministries, he did not travel much beyond the sixty miles or so between Beith or Paisley to Edinburgh. But at the end of his Paisley ministry he made the hazardous four hundred mile trip to London and then on to Holland by sea to establish contacts that might be beneficial to the College and to begin his preparation for a new career in education. Most adventurous of all was to accept a job in Princeton that would involve him in the hitherto unexplored profession of teaching and administration, in a country three thousand miles away, and that could only be reached after an arduous and dangerous journey. All of this had to be accomplished with a less than willing wife, and five children, not all of whom could have been happy at the thought of leaving behind all that was familiar. When he did begin his work the adventurous journeying continued - physically in coping with trips through totally unknown territories to fund raise and make contacts and advertise the College. Added to this, his later political and entrepreneurial schemes involved him in huge journeys. All of this he seems to have taken in his stride, indicating that he was adventurous by nature.

The last cluster of characteristics gleaned from an examination of his life and work indicate that he was pious, zealous, fatherly and combined paradoxically an acceptance of his lot and a willingness to change. The piety of John Witherspoon is linked to the last quality discussed in previous cluster of characteristics, adventurousness. Witherspoon was always on the move, but it was not because of an innate restlessness, it was the movement of a pilgrim. L. Gordon Tait, in the Introduction to his book, *The Piety of John Witherspoon*, makes the point that Witherspoon was imbued with the concept of himself and all other Christians as those who were Pilgrims on a journey.[31] He also spoke to the students of the senior class in 1775, telling them that as pilgrims they should not only concern themselves with the journeys they make in life but should be more concerned with the 'great removal' from this life 'into an eternal state'. He made light of his journey from Paisley to Princeton, believing it was part of a providential plan:

> I make no merit at all, of having left country and kindred and connections of the dearest kind, in order to serve the interests of the church of Christ in this part of the globe.

The adventure in which he engaged was a natural outcome of his piety. Witherspoon regularly speaks of piety in ways that indicate his understanding of it as something of a very practical nature and is based on the prior premise that a person has acquired an understanding of what he often refers to as 'real religion' or 'true religion'. In his *Address to the students of the senior class*, he says:

> True religion, must arise from a clear and deep conviction of your lost state by nature and practice, and on an unfeigned reliance on the pardoning mercy and sanctifying grace of God.[32]

In his sermon *Christian Magnanimity* he spells out the nature of his piety:

> True piety encounters the greatest dangers with resolution. The fear of God is the only effectual mean to deliver us from the fear of man ... True piety endures suffering with patience and fortitude.[33]

PERSONAL CHARACTERISTICS

It was in this spirit that Witherspoon made his many journeys, believing that because of his commitment to true religion, he would be kept safe by God. His piety led him to 'hazard his life in his Maker's service, or his country's cause'. It led to a willingness to attempt the practical expression of his underlying beliefs.

Witherspoon enters into this pious pilgrimage with a zealousness that seems to exclude some of the considerations that others might feel obliged to take into account, like relationships with a wife or a child or in the development of a personal interest. There is a model of the Christian pilgrim given in *Hebrews* 11.13-16 that seems to have contributed to Witherspoon's vision. The writer of *Hebrews* sees Christians as 'strangers and pilgrims on the earth', but also as those who 'seek a country', and who:

> if they have been mindful of that country from whence they came out, they might have had opportunity to have returned. But now they desire a better country, that is an heavenly: wherefore God is not ashamed to be called their God: for he hath prepared for them a city.[34]

Witherspoon subscribed to those sentiments, but because he believed in the providential nature of his move to America - his vision of a 'better country' was not only of a heavenly one, but America was also that 'better country' to which God had called him and in which he wished both to serve God and his new country. That is the basis of the zeal for both the faith he proclaimed and the better good of the country he had been led to by God. There were times when that zeal reached the point of overstatement when for example near the end of his sermon *The Dominion of Providence* he declares:

> He is the best friend to American liberty who is the most sincere and active in promoting true and undefiled religion and who sets himself with all the greatest firmness to bear down profanity and immorality of every kind. Whoever is an avowed enemy to God I scruple not to call him an enemy to his country.[35]

This equating of infidelity with treason is an example of zeal being carried too far. I dare to think that there might have been quite a few staunch American patriots, who if not enemies of the church, were a bit equivocal towards it, and the God it proclaimed; and to see their lack of zeal for the Christian religion as the equivalent of being an enemy to their country is just nonsense. Such illogicality is one of the products of the polarisation of thought that sometimes takes place when great issues are at stake. Later writings of some of Witherspoon's fellow patriots reveal their distrust of the clergy and as those same clergy were the purveyors of 'real religion' it would appear that they would not always be in agreement as to what they believed. John Adams and Thomas Jefferson are two proven patriots who did not share Witherspoon's beliefs. Jeffry H. Morrison quotes Adams's life-long distrust of the clergy: 'My friend', he wrote to Benjamin Rush in 1809, 'the clergy have been in all ages and countries as dangerous to liberty as the army'. Further evidence of Adams's far from orthodox Christian stance is his assertion: 'Philosophers antient and modern appear to me as Mad as Hindoos, Mahomitans and Christians'.[36] Thomas Jefferson is also one who is critical, writing of 'the irritable tribe of priests and clergy' who were 'a very formidable engine against the civil and religious rights of man'.[37] Neither of these gentlemen's loyalty to their country can be doubted, but they do not fall into the category of those who could be said to have adopted 'real religion' as Witherspoon defines it, and appear to have had scant respect for the practitioners and purveyors of it. Yet despite their reservations, both men worked alongside Witherspoon in Congress and he clearly had a respect for their patriotism.

Thomas Jefferson on another occasion offers a critique of Plato's *Republic,* and in passing, takes a side-swipe at those sects of Christians who 'because in his [Plato's] foggy conceptions they found a basis of impenetrable darkness whereon to rear fabrications as delirious, of their own invention'. In offering this view of Plato even although he took the opportunity to attack offshoots of the Christian Church, Jefferson at least shows a solidarity with Witherspoon, who never holds up Plato or his metaphysics. Witherspoon always leans more towards Aristotle and Cicero, as his personal library attests, for it contains no works of Plato but many by the other two philosophers.

Despite these differences, both Adams and Jefferson continued in respect for Witherspoon. Perhaps this was to a certain extent because of their age differences. Witherspoon was a bit of a father figure to them, being twenty years older than Jefferson and twelve years older than Adams. Jefferson's respect for Witherspoon is signaled by the fact that when the first edition of *Witherspoon's Works* was published in 1800, Jefferson bought two sets of volumes, one for his personal library and the other for a gift.[38] Adams, who became President in 1797, and who was often highly critical and judgemental of former colleagues, nevertheless remembered Witherspoon with affection as 'the old Scotch doctor'. This 'fatherly' aspect of Witherspoon's character seems to have been more in evidence in his role as College President and politician than as husband and father. The reminiscences of some of his students and the evidences of his care for them tell of that, but there is little evidence of him as a beloved husband or an affectionate and caring father.

The last aspect of Witherspoon's characteristics that I want to explore is the paradoxical combination of his acceptance of his lot in life, and his willingness to change. One of the earliest indications of his acceptance of the things that happened to him is his attitude during the period from his first receiving the invitation of the invitation of the Trustees to become President of the College of New Jersey to the time of the confirmation of his appointment.

On April 29, 1767, when he writes to Benjamin Rush to tell him of his 'declining the charge', Witherspoon confesses, 'it has been with the greatest uneasiness and sadness to myself which I believe will soon be over'.[39] Although this letter indicates his personal misgivings about not accepting the invitation of the Trustees, yet he had made up his mind to take this action because of the distress that the prospect of the move had caused to his wife and family. On July 7, 1767, he again writes to Rush after Rush had objected to Witherspoon's suggestion that Mr Nisbet of Montrose might be a suitable candidate for the post, and although in this letter he confesses to having second thoughts, he nevertheless reaffirms his reason for not pursuing them: 'the distress and Confusion that was formerly in my family deterred me from it'. Witherspoon then displays his trust in the providence that he so clearly believes in: 'I hope a gracious God will in due time turn everything to his Glory and the advancement of real religion'.[40] In these words there is an acceptance of his lot combined with the attitude that in the end what God wants to happen will happen, and so be it, even if that includes change. By August 4, 1767, Witherspoon is wavering in his acceptance of his present lot, and writes to Rush to say he is going to 'make trial of proposing the thing to my wife', adding that, 'if it can be made agreeable it will be a great pleasure to me'.[41] But eight days later he still has not plucked up courage to raise the matter, making the excuse that 'she has been mostly ill since I wrote you last'. He promises to 'mention it this evening'.[42] But on September 16, 1767, Witherspoon has to concede: 'My wife continues on the same disposition as before, altogether set against'. Witherspoon again shows a willingness to accept what he perceives to be God's will for him and displays a belief that whatever happens will be determined by God, as he continues: 'I was uneasy to think that I should be precluded from accepting yet know that the way is graced'.[43] I sense that Witherspoon, despite knowing his wife's total opposition to his acceptance, believed that it was pre-determined that he would go to Princeton. His use of the phrase, 'the way is graced', is capable of supporting the view that whichever way Witherspoon goes he will experience the help of God. Equally it supports the view, and I think this is what Witherspoon believes, God has so prepared the way for his going to Princeton that it is now inevitable that he will go there.

From that point onwards the correspondence Witherspoon engages in is more concerned with the obstacles that are in the way to his going to America, and there is an air of acceptance on his part that no matter what these obstacles are - his wife and family or another candidate (and there was one) - they will be overcome by a God who has already determined that John Witherspoon will become President of the College of New Jersey. In a letter to Benjamin Rush on December 21, 1767, Witherspoon writes as if he feels himself to be in the hands of God, almost pawn-like in the moves that are going on around him, all of which are being made by the major players: 'I think it now seems highly probable the Design will take place, but I am by no means affected by it in the same manner as you are'.[44] Witherspoon, however much he occasionally gives the impression that he really wants the job, still maintains an aloofness, and displays an almost fatalistic attitude that nevertheless is not born of fatalism, but comes from an unshakable trust in the providence of God and in the design that he has for his creatures.

Witherspoon's supreme confidence in the providential care of God for his world dominates his understanding in sermons like *The Dominion of Providence* in 1776, or earlier in the *Pastoral Letter from the Synod of New York and Philadelphia*, that was to be read from the pulpits of all the congregations under their care on Thursday June 29, 1775, being the Day of the General Fast. The *Pastoral Letter* begins:

> The Synod of New York and Philadelphia, being met at a time when public affairs wear so threatening an aspect and when (unless God in his sovereign Providence speedily prevent it) all the horrors of a civil war throughout this great continent are to be apprehended, were of opinion that they could not discharge their duty to the numerous congregations under their care without addressing them at this important crisis.[45]

Witherspoon's letter seeks to instil in the members of the Presbyterian congregations an assurance that they are in the hands of a God who will provide for them whether in defeat or victory, but it reassures those who take up arms in the American cause that, 'there is no soldier so undaunted as the pious man, no army so formidable as those who are superior to the fear of death'.

It urges that everyone:

who offers himself as a champion in his country's cause be persuaded to reverence the name and walk in the fear of the Prince of the kings of this earth and then he may with the most unshaken firmness expect the issue either in victory or death.

Witherspoon's God will still be in control whatever the outcome, even if, 'for a season' God allows his people, 'to lie under unmerited oppression'.[46]

The Dominion of Providence sermon's opening passage takes up the theme of the all-powerful providence of God:

There is not a greater evidence either of the reality or the power of religion, than a firm belief of God's universal presence, and a constant attention to the influence and operation of his providence.[47]

For Witherspoon, God's providence is forever in evidence, and is forever capable of working things out for the good of mankind, turning events that seem catastrophes into victories. Witherspoon projects such a firm belief in God's providence that he sees God as having the capability of turning even the wrath of men into a means of him achieving his purpose. This belief is so strong in Witherspoon that he can look at the current situation of conflict in which the wrath of the British is turned on the Colonists and still proclaim with hope: 'The wrath of men praises God as it is his instrument in his hand for bringing sinners to repentance'. Witherspoon does not make his sermon into a full blown Jeremiad, as he does not elaborate on the sins of the Americans, but rather he concentrates on another aspect of this theme: 'The wrath of men praises God as he sets bounds to it or restrains it by his providence'. This is the main thrust of his message, and the part that clings most to the text of the sermon: 'Surely the wrath of men shall praise thee, the remainder of wrath shalt thou restrain' (*Psalm* 76.10). In this sermon Witherspoon sets out to apply this text 'more particularly to the present state of the American Colonies and the plague of war'. He really gets going at this point in the sermon as he builds up the theme by further applying the text to:

The ambition of mistaken princes, the cunning and cruelty of oppressive and corrupt ministers, and even the inhumanity of brutal soldiers, however dreadful, shall finally promote the glory of God, and in the mean - time while the storm continues, his mercy and kindness, shall appear in prescribing bounds to their rage and fury.

John Witherspoon is at his most eloquent when he is expounding this, one of his most deeply held and consistent beliefs - the providence of God. In all his writings there is no evidence of his ever departing from it. Perhaps it is one of the strongest components in the make-up of his character, causing him to pass through the varying vicissitudes of life with what appears to be a genuine ability to take what life brings to him and live with it with an equanimity that is much greater than most people are capable of achieving.

The paradox in Witherspoon's life is that whereas such a strong acceptance of his present lot is his first reaction to the things that happen to him in life, there is an equally strong willingness to change when the opportunity arises. Think in broad terms of this willingness to change: from monarchist to republican; from ecclesiastic to educationalist and politician; from being in opposition to the established government to being a part of the new establishment; from living in a country with a long recorded history to making a new life in a country whose history was still being written; from being one who ridiculed a certain type of minister to becoming one who closely resembled the type of minister that he had previously criticised; from a belief in the total depravity of human nature to a belief that allows for the progress of humanity. All of these changes were undergone in the course of a few years.

It would be too easy to claim that it was by his living in America that these changes were brought about, for if his life in Scotland is closely examined some of the seeds of change were already in evidence. But undoubtedly it was America that was the catalyst, or at the very least the factor that gave impetus to the changes that were experienced by John Witherspoon. In 1773, Witherspoon writes:

> A man will become an American by residing in the country, three months with a prospect of continuing, more easily and certainly than by reading or learning of it for three years amidst the sophistry of dailly dispatches.[48]

Living amidst the daily reality of life in America caused Witherspoon to come to quite different views and conclusions than those at which he might otherwise have arrived.

When Witherspoon lived in Scotland he was an enthusiastic monarchist. His Presbyterian stance made him appreciative of the Protestant regime, which had in 1690 restored the Church of Scotland to its place as the national church it been recognised as in 1560. Witherspoon had been born just thirty-three years after the re-establishment of a King who pledged to uphold and protect the Protestant Church. Scotland had undergone a period of great social unrest following the Cromwellian period of the Commonwealth. The restoration of the Monarchy, and the imposition of Episcopal Church Government in 1660, and the subsequent

Acts of Parliament that shortly followed, severely restricted the people's rights to worship according to their conscience. From 1660 to 1690 the Church had suffered under the repressive regime of the Stuarts, and in the part of Ayrshire in which Witherspoon began his ministry, the memory of those 'killing times' would have been still very much alive. William of Orange was the king who had put an end to the conditions that had created the Presbyterian Covenanter martyrs, and Witherspoon's generation of ministers looked upon his successors as kings to whom they owed allegiance. Hence his readily and enthusiastically establishing and leading the local Militia in 1746.[49]

Even after Witherspoon moved to America he remained loyal to the Monarchy of King George III. In his early writings he made excuses for the king by saying that he was ill-advised by his ministers. Even when he comes to give his *Lectures on Moral Philosophy* he begins the discussion of the three forms of government by dealing with Monarchy in a very fair manner. Without judging it, he merely describes it. When later he goes into the subject of Monarchy in greater detail, he at first acknowledges its good points: 'Monarchy has plainly the advantage in unity, secrecy and expedition', and goes as far as to say, 'if a man could be found wise enough, and just enough for the charge, Monarchy would be the best form of government'.[50] But then Witherspoon begins to be critical when he writes: 'there is no reason to expect that an elected monarch will have the public good at heart; he will probably mind only private or family interest'. (It would seem that the doctrine of the total depravity of man has kicked in). Then, even although he has gone on in his lecture to discuss another form of government, 'Aristocracy', he breaks into his argument to declare:

> Monarchy, everyone knows, is but another name for tyranny, where the arbitrary will of one capricious man disposes of the lives and properties of all ranks.

The change is complete. The American perspective has helped Witherspoon to a quite new view of Monarchy. In fairness to Witherspoon, he sees faults in the other two forms of government: 'Aristocracy always makes vassals of the inferior ranks, who have no hand in government'. He even sees faults in his favoured form of government, democracy:

> Pure democracy cannot subsist long, nor be carried far into the departments of state - it is very subject to caprice and the madness of popular rage.

He also earlier says of democracy:

it has very little advantage for wisdom or union, and none at all for secrecy and expedition. Besides the multitudes are exceedingly apt to be deceived by demagogues and ambitious persons.

(an elitist view is coming through here). He concludes: 'that every good form of government must be complex, so that one principle may check the other'. Witherspoon's allegiance has shifted from monarchy to democracy, and that is what he is trying to establish by means of a republican form of government in America.

The change from ecclesiastic to educationalist and politician is of a different kind. It is more of a shift of emphasis, a different allocation of his time, a move to spending his days on matters of a different nature from those things that had previously occupied his attention. Although the change from ecclesiastic to President of a College and Headmaster of a Grammar School is less than that required in changing from ecclesiastic to politician, nevertheless it requires a different set of skills and results in a different life style. Although as College President, Witherspoon continued to preach, it was largely to a student audience, and although he did not have a congregation of his own, the occasions when he did preach to a congregation out-with the College, it would often be associated with a fund raising trip, or in some celebration of a special event that would almost certainly require an adjustment to his preaching material.

In 1774, when Witherspoon entered the world of politics through becoming a founder member of the Committee of Correspondence of Somerset County, New Jersey, and even more so when he became a Congressman the following year, the politician began to take over from the ecclesiastic.[51] One thing that must have happened to him was the realisation that it was only by means of political action that things got done. No amount of fulminating from the pulpit could change the legislation and structures that determine the lives of the people. Only the active politician can achieve that kind of change. I am sure that that must have been one of the great attractions that politics would have for Witherspoon. It is true that the basic theology and philosophy adhered to by Witherspoon is retained in his new occupations but there were also adaptions made to these foundation beliefs and understandings, and whereas some aspects of them lessened in prominence, others developed. In his political statements his piety became ever more practical. Witherspoon had lived by the precept that: 'all moral action must arise from principle',[52] and he continued to work in the educational and political fields on the same basis that he had worked as a minister, believing that if 'one's principle is true, one's actions will be moral'. In his political statements there is no talk of the scheme of redemption, but instead much reference to God's providential care. L.

PERSONAL CHARACTERISTICS

Gordon Tait who has made a special study of the piety of John Witherspoon, in the book of that name, claims that, 'In America, Witherspoon's doctrine of God expanded to encompass a vital belief in God as Providence as well as Redeemer'.[53] Witherspoon's thoughts on Providence seemed to develop from a former belief in Providence in relation to the *individual* to a concept of Providence having to do with a *whole people*. In *The Dominion of Providence*, he gives a specific illustration of Providence at work in the war against the British:

> The signal advantage we have gained by the evacuation of Boston, the shameful flight of the army and navy of Britain were brought about without the loss of a man.

He goes on to engender hope in the activity of Providence:

> Remember the vicissitude of human things, and the usual course of Providence. How often has a just cause been reduced to its lowest ebb, and yet when firmly adhered to has become finally triumphant? I speak this now when the affairs of the Colonies are in so prosperous a state.[54]

Even in the more enclosed world of the lecture room Witherspoon gives evidence of the change that is taking place in him because of his involvement in Education and also I suspect in Politics. In *Lecture VII* on *Eloquence* Witherspoon shows his move away from the Manse Study to an ante-room to the wider world of University and Political debate, as he writes:

> Recluse students and professed scholars will be able to discover truth, and to defend it, or to write moral precepts with clearness and beauty; but they are seldom equal, for the tender and pathetic, to those who have been much in what is called the *world* by a well known use of that word, though almost peculiar to the English language. There is perhaps a double reason for persons well versed in the ways of men having the greatest power upon the passions. They not only know others better, and therefore how to touch them, but their own hearts, it is likely, have been agitated by more passions than those whose lives have been more calm and even.[55]

This is a passage that shows that Witherspoon has broken away from his tunnel vision view of his ministry. It is acknowledging that 'the world' has insights to offer, and can be learned from in positive ways. His new occupations are causing Witherspoon to explore other areas of thought and meet other 'more worldly' people with a resultant change in his understanding and the expression of it. Such a passage from this *Lecture on Eloquence* can only have been written by one who has become much nearer in sympathy to the culture of the Moderates he so castigated in his earlier years. Witherspoon has clearly changed from the man who preached at the Abbey Church of Paisley on Thursday September 17, 1758, a sermon entitled *The Charge of Sedition and Faction against good men, especially faithful ministers considered and accounted for*. Witherspoon offered this advice:

> Avoid officiously meddling in civil matters. A minister should be separated and set apart for his own work. He should be consecrated to his office. It is little glory to him to be eminently skilled in any other science except as may be handmaid to Theology and are by him habitually turned into a divine channel.[56]

Becoming the President of a College for the training of young men for the Christian ministry might have been seen as acquiring a skill that could be 'turned into divine channels', but becoming a politician would be stretching the concept too far (at least by the standards that Witherspoon applied to himself in 1758). Witherspoon had changed and had no qualms about becoming a politician because he continued to hold on to the same principles that governed his conduct as those that he had applied to himself while being a full time minister of the church. Oddly enough the text for that sermon in Paisley Abbey was from *Acts* 17.6 'They that have turned the world upside down are come hither also'. How truly prophetic those words were, but not in the understanding that their preacher envisaged. Witherspoon himself was to become one, whom many on the British side of the Atlantic thought, had 'turned the world upside down'.

Yet another change that goes counter to those earlier sentiments is signalled in a letter that Witherspoon wrote on March 20, 1780, to the Rev. Samuel Stanhope Smith, his son-in-law:

> You know I was always fond of being a scientific farmer. That disposition has not lost but has gathered strength since my being in America. In this respect I got a dreadful stroke indeed from the English when they were here, they having seized and mostly destroyed my whole stock and committed such ravages that we have not fully recovered from it.[57]

Here is a sign that something that he had perhaps started to do in Scotland, and prior to the war in America, had begun to be developed in a fuller way. Again this practice of scientific farming is in opposition to the views expressed in the sermon in 1758, for by no stretch of the imagination can the study of agricultural methods and their application, be said to be a subject that is a 'handmaid to Theology'.

Witherspoon gives us an insight into how he saw himself as he engaged in this new life in America, and offers a kind of justification for his engaging in a political life while still being a clergyman. In his *Four Letters on Education*, he writes:

> Those who are engaged in public life, or what I may call, political life, have an excellent opportunity of making religion appear truly respectable. What I mean is, by shewing themselves firm and incorruptible, in supporting those measures that appear best calculated for promoting the interests of religion, and the God of mankind. In all these cases I admire the man who has principles; and whose principles are known, and whom everybody despairs of being able to seduce, or bring over to the opposite interest.[58]

Having clearly stated his own position, Witherspoon cannot help taking a swipe at other politicians:

> As for your placebos, your prudent, courtly compliant, gentlemen whose vote in assembly will tell you where they dined the day before, I hold them very cheap indeed, as you well know.

The first part of the quotation gives us a flavour of what I believe to be how Witherspoon both saw himself and his role in being a politician and a clergyman at the same time, and the later words give his view of the less savoury elements of some who also engaged in political life. In a way he is perhaps saying: people like me, people of principle are needed in politics because of people like them.

There are two points worth making in connection with this examination of the changes that occurred in Witherspoon's life, and these become clear if we examine the language used by Witherspoon. It is a language that has been tempered by political experience. By mixing in political circles, his own experience of the variety of views held by people of different religious or non-religious views and of the many different shades of political opinion, was greatly enhanced. Having to address such an audience on a daily basis is a vastly different task to that of addressing congregations, or even classes of young men, most of whom would be sharing the same basic beliefs and understandings as himself. In the new political context Witherspoon's language had to change if he was going to be able to persuade his new audience by his arguments. He had to engage in activity in such a way as to make religion, 'appear truly respectable', something that people could recognise as worthy of consideration; and this could be achieved by pursuing policies that would clearly bring benefit to their lives. The God, who in Witherspoon's case provided him with principles, had to be a God who was spoken of in more general terms, and so the God who previously had been the 'Almighty', or the 'Lord', or 'an offended God', became 'the God of mankind'.

As well as this change in language, there is also a change in theological emphasis. L. Gordon Tait sees this change in Witherspoon's theology:

> Yet his thinking about God and how God acts in history was changing. A more exact way of explaining this metamorphosis is to note that his understanding about the divine presence and activity in the world shifted from an almost exclusive focus on God as Redeemer to the same God as Creator, Sustainer, Governor of all things, events and persons. ... He continued to preach his sermons on sin and salvation, but in his new situation at the unfolding events leading to war with Britain prompted him to stretch his theology to emphasize an understanding of God's oversight and care for all of creation and all of God's peoples.[59]

Witherspoon's God has become the 'God of mankind'.

In America Witherspoon's changes of occupation were allowing and encouraging reason rather than revelation to play a greater part in his thinking. He certainly opens his *Lectures on Moral Philosophy* with a statement that defines the discipline as one that makes use of reason rather than revelation:

> Moral Philosophy is that branch of Science which treats of the principles and laws of Duty or Morals. It is called Philosophy because it is an enquiry into the nature and grounds of moral obligation by reason as distinct from revelation.[60]

I have already pointed out that Witherspoon sometimes did not adhere to that principle in the course of his lectures, but in them the acknowledgement of the primacy of reason had been made. In his lectures and political discourses Witherspoon was forced to make greater use of reason. He could not fall back on the authority of revelation, or hide behind mystery or the sovereignty of God when he was expounding an aspect of education or delivering a speech to Congress. L. Gordon Tait, following a study of Witherspoon's American sermons, sees a change of emphasis in them and concludes that for Witherspoon: 'Reason can be trusted more; it plays a larger role in his thinking and in his analysis of human nature and behavior'.[61] This change of emphasis in Witherspoon's writing can only have come about by means of the new focus on educational and political matters as against theological and ecclesiastical concerns.

What did not change in Witherspoon's new life in America were his principles and his piety, but what did happen was that these two important aspects of his life were applied in different areas, and because of this there came about a different emphasis in their application. In the Preface to his *Works*, Witherspoon asserts: 'All moral action must arise from principle'.[62] Both as an educationalist and as a politician he continued to assert his principles, for example, in College asserting the primacy of mastering the basics of any subject to be tackled, and in politics, maintaining consistency in policy, for example in regard to paying interest on government loan debt. His piety was exercised also in a way that was appropriate to his new professions. Tait makes an acute observation when he writes: 'Witherspoon's counsel and example are telling us that real piety is not of this world but *for* this world'.[63] Witherspoon in his work as an educationalist and as a politician had found a new outlet for the expression of his principles and his piety.

Another change that occurs in Witherspoon's life is that from being in almost constant opposition to those who governed his ecclesiastical life, the ecclesiastical establishment of the Church of Scotland, he found himself in a society in which he had come to occupy a place in its establishment. In Scotland Witherspoon had been the perpetual 'nuisance', the terrier that was always yapping at the heels of the figures of power. Although, ostensibly, as a parish minister, he would be looked upon by most of his parishioners as a person of some higher status, as indeed someone of the establishment, he never was fully quite what they thought him to be. Nor did he see himself as part of the establishment. From his very student days he seems to have been a bit of an 'outsider', not quite able to be at ease in society, or join in freely in its pursuits. His activity in his first parish at Beith shows an earnest young man, but one highly critical of the society in which lived, as is indicated both by his pamphlets on the *Stage* (1753) and on the *Moderates* (1757). Added to these things is his increasingly vocal contribution to the controversy that went on for many years over the congregation's right to choose a minister. So often in opposition, so often on the losing side, there were those who saw his departure to America in

1768 as an indication of his leaving because of his continually being at odds with the world and suffering so many defeats.[64]

Contrast that, with his experience in America: he is lauded upon his arrival, achieves almost immediate success in establishing a new regime at the College and in the re-establishing the Grammar School. He finds new friends by his almost immediate espousal of the American cause, rapidly establishes himself as a person of trust, becomes a member of the Committee of Correspondence and then a Member of Congress. Thereafter his rise is meteoric as he becomes an important figure in the revolutionary government, and is entrusted with great responsibility during the war years. Such is the trust in him, that he has a hand in the preparation and passing of two of the foundation documents of the republican government, the *Declaration of Independence* and *The Articles of Confederation*. That all of this happens to him is one of the signs of his willingness to change, and to adapt to the new situation in which he finds himself in America. The changes that he has willingly made in his life have caused Witherspoon to experience and to enjoy a quite new status. Such changes that brought about a quite new status for Witherspoon must have had an effect upon his attitudes and to his understanding of himself and his fellow men and women.

In *Lecture II* in his series on *Eloquence* Witherspoon remarks:

> There is something to be learned from practice, which no instruction can impart ... after you have learned the theory in the most perfect manner there is still a nameless something, which nothing but experience can bestow.[65]

Witherspoon, the man much read in several disciplines, was to have much about him changed by his new experience of being part of an establishment. I suspect that one of the rub offs of this new experience was the acquiring of the air of a statesman, and the cultivating of a certain '*gravitas*', and I believe that traces of these aspects of his life are to be found in his speeches to Congress, or even in his work near the end of his career in preparing the constitutional documents for the Presbyterian Church in the United States of America.

Another strand of this willingness to change is found in Witherspoon's transition from living in a country with a long recorded history, to making a new life in a country whose history was still being written. Witherspoon was born into a land where long established traditions and practices were upheld. The ones that first impinged upon his life were those associated with what it meant to be a Christian, and even more specifically, a member of the reformed branch of the church in Scotland.

Christianity had come to Scotland 1,400 years before Witherspoon was born, and had had the many centuries between to establish itself into the very fabric of the nation's culture. A further refinement and codifying of the Christian religion had come about in a process of reformation culminating in 1560, with the Church of Scotland establishing itself in a total separation from the Roman Catholic Church. It is now generally recognised that the reformation of the church that took place in Scotland in 1560 was the most thorough in Europe. Its peculiar constitution, whereby it became free of state interference in its government, and yet won recognition from the state as being the body responsible for providing religious ordinances throughout the land, made it unique at the time. It became a self-governing body by means of a system of courts: starting at the local level of the elders of each congregation meeting in Kirk Session; then their representatives meeting in Presbytery; then monitoring bodies of groups of Presbyteries called Synods; and finally its supreme governing body, the General Assembly to which representatives of Presbyteries were appointed to meet once a year. By this Presbyterian and relatively democratic form of government, the Church of Scotland freed itself at one and the same time from the overlordship of both King and Pope. One consequence of the reformation in Scotland was the boost that it gave to the establishment of an educational system that was accessible to all. Desirous that every person in Scotland should be able to read the *Bible* for themselves and so become aware of the truths upon which their reformation of the church was based, the reformers worked at and wrote into their *Book of Discipline*, their aim to establish a church and a school in every parish.[66]

On the secular side, Scotland had seen the establishment of a line of kings that went back to the eleventh century and had joined the even older Anglo Saxon dynasty with the Union of the Crowns of Scotland and England in 1603. It had had more than its fair share of wars, from the defensive wars against the Romans, then the Vikings and other Scandinavian predators, to the Wars of Independence against the ambitions of English kings. It even had time for a civil war under Cromwell's rule, and latterly, within the same century, two rebellions that attempted to reinstate a Stuart Monarchy. As if all this is not enough, Scotland had been forced into a more complete union with England in 1707, whereby it lost its parliament and since then had been dragged into wars that had arisen because of English imperialism[67]. All of these factors, and many more that I have not attempted to list, had helped to create a country with a rich cultural background, and a people who had long memories of their country's past. It is from this culture that John Witherspoon left in 1768 to enter a totally different culture, and one less dominated by its past. America was a land where any traditions that did exist were still in their infancy. It was a country that was ripe for the establishment of new ways of being and doing, some of which in time might well become traditions that would influence a future people.

John Witherspoon had battled hard against some of the long established Scottish traditions, but just as much as this he had upheld many of them as well. The transition must have been difficult for him at first, and probably caused him to re-impose some of the traditional frameworks that he had previously experienced, for example: the teaching methods of Grammar School and College, the pattern of worship, the structure of sermons, the style of letters, and the manner of dress. None of these seem to have changed very much from the way in which he had previously practiced them. But as time passed, John Witherspoon began to take advantage of the new freedom. In America there was greater autonomy for ministers. They had only to satisfy a congregation's and a synod's demands. There was no General Assembly and the Synod did not function in the same scrutineering manner as in Scotland. In one respect, Government in America was more local. Although the British parliament did hold the ultimate power, what happened locally was to a great extent determined locally by the Provincial Governor and Assembly. Westminster, although it could not be ignored, it could be and often would be defied, and it was this situation that eventually resulted in rebellion and ultimately independence.

In the new situation after Independence had been declared, the American former colonists had a *tabula rasa* and a freedom to create the form of government that most suited their needs, and John Witherspoon was one person whose life was going to change because of that. Loosed from the strictures and structures of the old country he relished the idea of being able to start afresh in the organisation of society. He must have had a great sense of freedom in this new land, and that in turn would have given him every encouragement to try new ways of doing this and living in a new manner. The things that had just been ideas in a book could begin to be implemented in real life, for example: much of John Locke's, *Two Treatises of Civil Government* had been admired by Witherspoon, and formed a background to some of his Lectures in College, now in this new land he could have the chance to try out these ideas in practise, and this he did as he played his part in the examination of the draft of *The Declaration of Independence* and later in helping in the drafting of *The Articles of Confederation*. The new freedoms granted him by the new young culture of the United States gave him a freedom to express himself in ways from which he had been banned hitherto by tradition.

Another change in John Witherspoon is seen in that from being one who ridiculed a certain type of minister, he grew to acquire some of the characteristics and to engage in some of the activities he had previously criticised. His *Lectures on Moral Philosophy* and on *Eloquence* bear traces of a change in attitude towards two men whom he would have regarded as Moderates, and therefore have come in for his criticism. Francis Hutcheson and Lord Shaftsbury had both been criticised in *Ecclesiastical Characteristics* but in his *Moral Philosophy Lectures* they are given credit for adding helpfully to the debate on 'Virtue'.[68] A further indication of a change in this area is found in Witherspoon's *Lectures on Eloquence* where he sometimes deals with the same subjects as his one-time fellow student and later the leader of the Moderates in the Church of Scotland, the Rev. Dr. Hugh Blair. He and Witherspoon had been taught at Edinburgh University by the same teacher, John Stevenson and that might account for some of their common ground, but when the two sets of lectures Hugh Blair's, *Lectures on Rhetoric and Belles Lettres* and John Witherspoon's, *Lectures on Eloquence* are compared it would be difficult to recognise Witherspoon clearly as one who in earlier years had been a staunch opponent of all that Blair stood for. Having to deal with the same subject, Witherspoon has moved much nearer to Blair than he had been as the author of *Ecclesiastical Characteristics*.[69]

Another among the coterie of the Moderate leadership was the Rev. William Robertson, whose *History of Scotland* was published in 1759, and of whom Witherspoon was to write in *Lecture II* on *Eloquence*: 'Dr. Robertson in his history has as just a mixture of strength and elegance as any other author in the English language'. Also in *Lecture IX* he praises Robertson for his 'sublime yet simple style'.[70] This was high praise for a leader of the Moderates. It is not known whether Witherspoon would later revise his opinion of Robertson when it became known that Robertson was against the move for American Independence. But the new task of preparing academic lectures on the subject of 'Eloquence' had opened Witherspoon's eyes to some of the good things done by members of the Moderate party. In praising what they had praised, he was gradually becoming more like them. His having to re-evaluate the whole field of literature for these lectures seems to have led him nearer to Moderate values: for example in *Lecture VI* he has to admit that:

> Many a great mind has been in narrow circumstances and many a little rascal has been a king. Yet education and manner have a sensible effect upon men in general.

Compare this with Maxim V of *Ecclesiastical Characteristics*:

A minister must endeavour to acquire as great a degree of politeness in his carriage and behaviour, and to catch as much of the air and manner of a fine gentleman, as he possibly can.[71]

Albeit Witherspoon hopes to achieve an improvement of manners by education, nevertheless he is veering nearer to the position of the Moderates he once criticised.

The last of the changes that I perceive in Witherspoon is that from believing in the total depravity of humanity he turns towards a belief in its progress and improvement. In his *Essay on the Connection between the Doctrine of Justification by the Imputed Righteousness of Christ, and Holiness of Life*, Witherspoon makes a paraphrase of the passage from Paul's *Letter to the Romans* that includes these words, 'all have sinned and come short of the glory of God'. Witherspoon declares in uncompromising terms the conclusion he derives from Paul's words as he sets out his total commitment to his belief in the depravity of humanity:

That every intelligent creature is under an unchangeable and unalienable obligation, perfectly to obey the whole law of God; that all men proceeding from Adam by ordinary generation, *are the children of polluted parents*, alienated in heart from God, transgressors of his holy law, inexcusable in this transgression and therefore exposed to the dreadful consequences of his displeasure.[72]

Other similar expressions of this belief in man's depravity are scattered throughout Witherspoon's theological writings. In Sermon III in *Sermons on Practical Subjects*, Witherspoon asserts:

Here is a truth, which not only the word of God everywhere teaches, but which almost every part of his providence towards us is intended to ratify *that in us dwelleth no good thing.*[73]

In *Sermon II* Witherspoon declares:

None who have any knowledge of the corruption of their own hearts, can reasonably hope to be perfectly free from sin in the present life. Yet a *real* Christian will have it, as the object of his daily study, to cleanse himself from all filthiness of the flesh, and spirit, that he may perfect holiness in the fear of God.

Sermon IV refers to 'the effecting evidence of the strength of the corruption within us'. *Sermon V* sees the result of this utter sinfulness as marking us as those who 'are in exile from our father's house'. *Sermon VII* includes some very strong language as Witherspoon goes off on a flight of fancy, contrasting man's corrupted nature with 'angels and other intelligent beings who have kept their first estate and never were polluted by sin'. In this same sermon he refers to the *Old Testament* story of the flood as if it were a historical fact: 'when God swept away a polluted word by an universal deluge'. In *Sermon VIII* Witherspoon acknowledges 'the degree of corruption that prevails at present in the visible church'. In *Sermon IX*, the 'Farewell Discourse' he makes reference to the scriptures of the *Old and New Testament*, where 'we shall find certain leading truths, which are of so great moment that they ought hardly ever to be out of view'; and the first of these he lists is 'the lost state of man by nature'. In the nine sermons that compose *Sermons on Practical Subjects*, Witherspoon returns to the theme of the depravity of man no fewer than seven times. Here in its uncompromising starkness is Witherspoon's belief in the total depravity of humanity.

In expressing this belief Witherspoon is here following in a thoroughly orthodox way, *The Confession of Faith* compiled at Westminster in 1643. Chapter VI 'Of the Fall of Man, Sin and the Punishment thereof' states:

> I. Our first parents being seduced by the subtilty and temptation of Satan, sinned in eating the forbidden fruit. This their sin God was pleased, according to his wise and holy counsel, to permit, having purposed to order it to his own glory. II. By this sin they fell from their original righteousness, and communion with God, and so became dead in sin, and wholly defiled in all the faculties and parts of soul and body. III. They being the root of all mankind, the guilt of this sin was imputed, and the same death in sin and corrupted nature conveyed to all their posterity, descending from them by ordinary generation. IV. From this original corruption, whereby we are utterly indisposed, disabled, and made opposite to all good, and wholly inclined to all evil, do proceed all actual transgressions ...[74]

Two more clauses underline the totality of humanity's corruption, a corruption so complete, that, even after the regenerative activity of Christ and pardon, man's nature is still sinful. Man is still 'bound over to the wrath of God, and the curse of the law, and so made subject to death'. No fewer than fifty-three 'proof texts' are used in the attempt to substantiate the theological claims made in the six sections of this chapter. Once the false premise of the literal and historical truth of *Scripture* has been accepted, then logic is inexorably followed, common sense denied and 'a terrible beauty is born'.

In the years of his Scottish ministries, Witherspoon seems to have been thoroughly within the theological tradition of *The Confession of Faith*, whose compilers liked to think was drawn from the teachings of John Calvin, the Genevan reformer. But sometimes those in the Calvinist tradition seem to go further than their alleged founder. Sometimes in the teaching of Calvin, as in his work, *The Institutes of the Christian Religion*, a slightly less dogmatic line is perceived. It is in this that there might be found a clue to the development of John Witherspoon's thought, and what it is that seems to allow him to make a subtle but important change of emphasis in his theological understanding.

John Calvin in *The Institutes of the Christian Religion*, (Book II, Chapter II Section I) opens up the subject of the extent of man's subjection to the effect of sin:

> Our proper course will be, first, to show that man has no remaining good in himself, and is beset on every side by the most miserable destitution.[75]

In this opening passage Calvin is indeed providing the basis of *The Confession of Faith*'s statement that man is 'wholly defiled in all the faculties and parts of soul and body'. But then he goes on to be much more positive and to point the way to man being able to do something about this, as he proposes a course of action:

> [to] teach him to aspire to the goodness of which he is devoid, and the liberty of which he has been deprived, thus giving him a stronger stimulus to exertion than he could have if he imagined himself possessed of the highest virtue.

As I have tried to absorb the attitude that lies behind John Witherspoon's statements, I am gradually coming to the conclusion that as his life in America developed, he more and more moved away in spirit from the dogmatism of *The Confession of Faith*, and perhaps, even unconsciously, moved nearer in spirit to the attitude of John Calvin. He did not reject *The Confession of Faith* as can be seen from his almost total adoption of it for his *Book of Church Order* in 1789, but it had become little more than a set of words, to be used as a general guideline for his position than a statement of what he exactly believed.

In his many references to man's fallen state, Witherspoon is pursuing one basic idea: to ask his audience to look at themselves in order to understand themselves in relation to God. He is at one with John Calvin who writes:

> He who is most deeply abased and alarmed by the consciousness of his disgrace, nakedness, want, and misery, has made the greatest progress in the knowledge of himself.[76]

Calvin suggests the way of self-knowledge is by means of the *Scriptures:* 'he may see himself as he really is, by looking into the faithful mirror of Scripture'. Witherspoon worked on that same basis. In parallel with this line of thought, Calvin also indicates that despite the fall, there is still something left in man that can respond to the appeal to aspire to goodness. He illustrates this by reference to those whom he calls 'profane authors'. He writes:

> Therefore in reading profane authors, the admirable light of truth displayed in them should remind us, that the human mind, however much fallen and perverted from its original integrity, is still adorned and invested with admirable gifts from its Creator.[77]

Calvin then cites the truths that have been discovered by ancient lawgivers and philosophers, those skilled in medicine and in understanding human reasoning, and sees them as having been led by 'the Spirit of God' and continues:

> Therefore, since it is manifest that men whom the Scriptures term *carnal*, are so acute and clear sighted in the investigation of inferior things, their example should teach us how many gifts the Lord has left in possession of human nature, notwithstanding of its having been despoiled of the true good.

It is this latter note of Calvin's, of the vestiges of integrity and insight that remain with man in his fallen state, that is missing from *The Confession of Faith*, and it is Calvin's, and not the *Confession*'s, emphasis that comes to be adopted by John Witherspoon.

It is this softened view, but one that is more that of Calvin than Calvinistic, that begins to come across in Witherspoon's writings in America. In *The Dominion of Providence* Witherspoon writes in a different and less personal way about man's corruption:

> The wrath of man praises God as an example of divine truth and clearly points out the corruption of our nature which is the foundation of our redemption.

It is as if he has to point out that the wrath of violent men, as it is now being experienced in the confrontation with Britain, is evidence of man's corruption, but he does not dwell upon it, escaping into the theory that it is an essential part of God's scheme of redemption.[78] In a second reference: 'There can be no true religion, til there be discovery of your lost state by nature and practice', Witherspoon does not elaborate on the connection with Adam's original sin, but links it with the practice of sin, which is a shifting of the understanding of sin from being a state, to being something that is done. But if this sermon had been fully Jeremiad in its structure, the theme of wrath would have been much more prominent, instead there is no great dwelling on the sinfulness of the Colonists and much more attention to the wrath of men being turned to serve God's purpose.

Witherspoon is less adventurous in his *Lectures on Divinity* and still clings to the orthodox position as outlined in *The Confession of Faith*. He at first approaches the subject in a very literal way. Dealing with Eve's temptation he writes:

> Eve is said to have been tempted by the serpent, and by many passages of Scripture it is put beyond a doubt that it was by the devil, a prince of fallen angels.

He then says quite categorically: 'It ought not to be understood allegorically. Probably he [the devil] made use of this creature as the fittest form in which he could appear'. He continues with this literal acceptance of the scriptural account of the fall, then speculates:

> As to the effect of Adam's sin upon his posterity, it seems very plain that the state of corruption and wickedness which men are now in, is stated in Scripture as being the effect and punishment of Adam's first sin ... man now comes into the world in a state of impiety or moral defilement.

Witherspoon in this same lecture goes on to discuss the resultant doctrine of original sin and expresses the opinion:

> The universal and early corruption of man in practice is a standing evidence of the impurity of their original ... what is the history of the world but the history of human guilt, and do not children from the

first dawn of reason, shew that they are wise to do evil but to do good they have no knowledge. [79]

It is odd that Witherspoon does not back up his argument for man being tainted by Adam's original sin by quoting scripture as is the practice of *The Confession of Faith* by its 'proof texts' method. Instead he relies on observations: the behaviour of infants, and the evidence of history. It is not a convincing argument, and I think it betrays a lack of confidence in being able to substantiate the claims that he makes by the conventional method of proof texts. There could be two explanations: firstly that these lectures having to be delivered very shortly after his arrival in Princeton, had been ill prepared; or his heart was not in the in the arguments put forward, I think that the clue is that he is relying on his observations rather than theological conviction and that in these lectures can be seen some of the first signs towards Witherspoon developing a more liberal theological stance.

When Witherspoon's secular writings are examined this more liberal stance becomes clear as he expresses himself in humanist rather than in religious terms. Writing as 'The Druid' in the first in a series of *Essays* published periodically, he describes how he has come to understand humanity: 'I confess that a thorough knowledge of the world and extensive reading in history have often produced mean thoughts of human nature'. His belief in the sinfulness of man is not ascribed to the scriptural account but to his experience of life and the evidence presented by history. *A speech to Congress on Confederation* also gives an indication of his new way of thinking about humanity. He at first states his orthodox belief but then goes on to make a much more hopeful view of man's nature.[80] As one 'acting for posterity', Witherspoon writes:

> There is one thing that has been thrown out, by which some seem to persuade themselves of, and others to be more indifferent about the success of a Confederacy - that from the nature of men, it is to be expected, that a time must come when it will be dissolved and broken in pieces. I am none of those who either deny or conceal the depravity of human nature till it is purified by the light of truth, and renewed by the Spirit of the living God. Yet I apprehend there is no force in the reasoning at all. Shall we establish nothing good, because we know it cannot be eternal? Shall we live without government, because every constitution has its old age, and its period? Because we know that we shall die shall we take no pains to preserve or lengthen life? Far from it, Sir, it only requires the more watchful attention to settle government upon the best principles and

in the wisest manner, that it may last as long as the nature of things will admit.[81]

Here is a very positive statement about man's capabilities despite the handicap inherent in his nature. It indicates that Witherspoon is aligned with the thinking of John Calvin rather than with *The Confession of Faith*. But not only that, as he continues, an optimism as to the future of the United States is combined with a view of the possibility of humanity's improvement, that is an indication of a further development and change in his thinking. Witherspoon continues, first of all by making an apology:

> But I beg leave to say something more, though with some risk that it will be thought visionary and romantic. I do expect Mr. President, a progress as in every other human art, so in the order and perfection of human society greater than we have yet seen; and why should we be wanting to ourselves in urging it forward. It is certain, I think, that human science and religion have kept company together and greatly assisted each other's progress in the world. I do say that intellectual and moral qualities are in the same proportion in particular persons, but they have a great and friendly influence upon one another in societies and larger bodies.
>
> There have been great improvements, *not only in human knowledge but in human nature*. The progress of which can be easily traced in history. Everybody is able to look back to the time in Europe, when the liberal sentiments that now prevail upon the rights of conscience, would have been looked upon as absurd. It is but little above two years since that enlarged system called the balance of power took place.[82]

This statement could almost be seen as being made by one who has a view of humanity that is free of any hereditary baggage of sin. There is an optimism about the country, the people and the individual that does not fit in with the rigid Calvinism of Witherspoon's past. For him to say that there has been a change in human nature is a clear departure from his former belief that from the moment of Adam's disobedience in the Garden of Eden humanity has been tainted by a hereditary sin, one passed on without break from generation to generation. Witherspoon in this political speech is putting forward the view that human nature is changing, and changing without the assistance of God's plan of redemption through Jesus Christ. But if the earlier words of this speech to Congress are examined more closely, it can be seen that even Witherspoon's remarks about his acknowledging his orthodox belief in the depravity of human nature are couched in less than orthodox terms. Witherspoon does not say anything about God redeeming the sinner through the sacrificial death of Christ, that upon the sinner's acceptance, grants an imputed righteousness. But instead, sees the depravity of human nature purified: 'by the light of truth and renewed by the Spirit of the living God'. These are terms that are much broader than those used by what Witherspoon would call 'real', or 'true' Christians. The phrase, 'the light of truth' could be used by a non-believer just as well as by a believer. The term, 'the living God' is not specifically a Christian term and is a much more general term and could mean as little as any God that is alive today, or any God that is alive to you. Although I am sure that Witherspoon would be meaning his words to apply to the God who in Jesus Christ was the Redeemer, he uses language that makes this God more generally acceptable. The terms in which he describes the activity of this God are also more open to a secular interpretation. At the very least Witherspoon is toning down his language for his political audience, and even that is a change in one who is so governed by strict moral and religious principles.

This new note in Witherspoon's theological language is seen as he expresses his approbation of American society even earlier in his American life. In a letter sent to *The Scots Magazine* in 1773, in answer to criticism of his encouragement of emigration to the then American Colonies, Witherspoon gives the reasons for their prosperity:

> America is certainly exhibiting at this time, a scene that is new in the history of mankind. It increases in proportion that no political calculations have yet been able to understand, or lay down rule for. The reason for this I take to be, that when colonies were sent out in ancient times, the people and the soil were somewhat similar, and improved by slow degrees; but in America we see a *wild but a noble soil*, taken possession of by all the power, wealth and learning of Europe, which pushes on its improvement with a rapidity which is inconceivable.[83]

Witherspoon's raw excitement and enthusiasm for America spills out on to the page. The tone of the words is reminiscent of those of Brutus in William Shakespeare's, *Julius Caesar*: 'There is a tide in the affairs of men / Which taken at the flood leads on to fortune'.[84] Oddly enough in checking out the details of this quotation, I was reminded of its fuller context. The words follow on from Brutus musing about his tactics before the battle of Philippi, and he uses a phrase that in different ways occurs in Witherspoon's writings, 'our cause is ripe'. Witherspoon was very much aware of the many opportunities for the betterment of life that were to be found in the America of his time. It was ripe for emigration. It was ripe for the experimentation of new ways of living, of working, and perhaps even of being. Witherspoon himself was being led towards a new way of being. Still very much a follower of John Calvin, and to a lesser extent, the tenets of *The Confession of Faith*, but above all, by what he took to be the message of the *Old and New Testaments*, nevertheless the influence of the still being formed culture of America was slowly beginning a process of change. It is a change that surfaces from time to time in the language he uses to express the things that he still believes. It is a change that brings about a shift in the basis of his belief in human depravity being grounded in scripture, to its being supported by the behaviour of men throughout history. However, now, and significantly, as the above passages show, Witherspoon's thinking is changing. He seems to be hinting that he perceives a tinge of hope that the continued generation of human depravity is lessening, and that it even might cease, as he begins to come round to the idea that the very nature of humanity is improving.

CHAPTER 13

Emigration

As part of the extensive coverage of what it always titled British North America, *The Scots Magazine*, for September 1772, printed an advertisement that had first appeared on September 18 in an Edinburgh newspaper:

> Lands to be settled in North America.
> To all Farmers and others, in Scotland, who are inclined to settle upon easy terms in the province of Nova Scotia in North America.
> The Rev. Dr. John Witherspoon, President of the College of New Jersey, North America with some other gentlemen in that country and Mr. John Pagan, merchant in Glasgow, have obtained an extensive grant of lands, lying in the province of Nova Scotia, North America, and upon the gulf of St. Lawrence, extending about twenty miles of sea coast upon the said gulf, bounded by two rivers on each side that run into it, which are navigable a good way up, and situated only about seventy miles distance from Halifax, the principal city in that province. In order to effectuate the speedy settlement of these lands, the proprietors propose the following ample encouragement for settlers, viz. To the first twenty families who shall agree to go over and settle upon these lands, they hereby promise to grant, in fee simple, to them and their heirs forever, 150 acres of land to man and wife and 50 acres more to every member of the family, child and servant, at the low rate of sixpence Sterling for each acre … .[1]

The advertisement continues with offers at the rates of one shilling and one shilling and sixpence per acre, for the next twenty and the next again twenty families. The lands are to be surveyed at the proprietor's expense and the quantity of land will be lessened or increased in relation to the quality of the soil, 'so that the value may be as nearly as possible equal'. The assurance is given that 'Dr. Witherspoon will take particular care that the strictest justice will be done, and the settlers' different places appointed them with the utmost impartiality'. The advertisement promises that, 'as soon as a sufficient number of settlers can be procured', John Pagan will arrange their transportation to Nova Scotia 'at the easy rate of three pounds five shillings for each full passenger'. The full rate to be paid for any child over eight, two years to eight at half price and under twos will travel free. It is anticipated that the voyage will take about four weeks, but provisions will be laid on board for twelve weeks. The point is made that it is a much shorter journey 'being little more than one half of that to North Carolina'. Passage money is to be paid before the ship leaves Scotland. The advertisement indicates that there are good prospects for the settlers to engage in fishing which has proved a success by other settlers in New England to the West and Newfoundland to the East. In addition 'the soil is very good for raising grain of every kind, flocks of cattle', and there is also a plentiful supply of wood of all kinds. Mention is also made of those to whom application can be made, but at this point a sour note is signalled, as it is pointed out by the *Magazine* that one of these persons, Bailie Alexander Shaw of Inverness:

> gives notice … that Mr. Pagan took the liberty to insert his name without his knowledge or consent, and that he is determined to take no concern in these matters.

It is indicated that there are already about twenty families settled on the lands, and 'make up a school of about thirty children'. Application has been made to the Governor of Nova Scotia for a charter for schools and churches, and an incentive of land is offered to any schoolmaster or minister willing to come.

The sceptical tone of the *Magazine* is indicated by the fact that immediately following the advertisement, it prints a letter that had been sent to the *Edinburgh Advertiser* in which the advertisement had originally appeared. The letter from 'A Well wisher to old Scotland', criticises Witherspoon and Pagan's scheme on various grounds: the price of land is too high, and he accuses them of charging twenty times the value of the land while pretending, 'to be doing a service to such poor creatures, as they mean to entice from their native country'. In fairness to the *Magazine*, in a footnote it points out that the writer has misunderstood the terms of the land transactions, confusing a one off payment for an annual rent:

> the lands are proposed to be granted *in fee simple* at *the rate* (not the *yearly rent*) here mentioned; and the purchase money is to be paid in two years after the purchaser's being settled in the lands; so that this writer's first observation seems to be founded on a mistake.

The letter continues, in a very negative way, to talk of the financial struggle that will face the settlers and alleges that 'this scheme will prove certain ruin to poor people'. It mocks the claim of the advertisers, that there is a good opportunity to develop a livelihood from fishing:

We are told, the coast crouds [*sic*] with fish. So do the coasts of Scotland, from which the Dutch gain several millions yearly; but what benefit are they to the bulk of the inhabitants of Scotland? Far less can these poor people who happen to go to Nova Scotia, without money to purchase, boats, nets, &c.'.

The writer then goes on to point out that Dr Witherspoon lives at least one thousand miles away from the lands advertised, and casts doubt on 'what benefit they may promise themselves from his superintendency'. Then in a passage that sounds entirely false, and one in which I suspect he 'protests too much', he writes:

As I have no acquaintance of Dr. Witherspoon, or his partner Mr. Pagan, they may be assured, I write not from any personal grudge, but merely to inform the ignorant who if they unwarily embrace so foolish a scheme, are likely to repent it when it is too late.

He then concludes with a gloomy picture of the consequences of the failure that lies ahead:

they must either starve there, or subject themselves to the condition of banished felons, by drudging to others in some part of that country for their daily bread.[2]

The November issue of *The Scots Magazine* reprinted a letter that had appeared in the *Caledonian Mercury*, headed, 'Near Rutherglen' (a village just outside Glasgow), and dated November 12, 1772, and signed, 'From a Bystander'. The letter gives support to Witherspoon's and Pagan's scheme and reveals the political undertones of the then current situation in Scotland. The letter begins by signalling that the other correspondent whose letter had appeared in the September issue of *The Scots Magazine* was not alone in expressing misgivings about the advertisement: 'The Advertisement by Mr. Pagan of Glasgow and Dr. Witherspoon New Jersey hath been criticised in most of the Scottish papers'. The November letter, while allowing for the natural hazards of settling in another country, gives a much more optimistic view of the prospects of any would be settlers and rather tartly comments:

One will, however, be apt to presume, that a great part of Nova Scotia cannot be more disagreeable to Scottish, than Canada is to French constitutions: and it is well known, that many people from

France had settled in Canada before the late war, and are still living there, in a very comfortable and elegant manner.

The letter then goes on to assert the integrity of Dr Witherspoon, indicating that as he had the opportunity of assessing the soil and the climate in the part of the province in which he has obtained a grant:

> he is abundantly able to judge what is, or what is not a proper place for settlers; and it would be extremely hard to suspect, that he would entice his countrymen to settle in a land where they must either starve or live in misery. His reputation is at stake, and it is also in his interest that the colony may flourish.

The writer then turns on those who have been criticizing Witherspoon's and Pagan's proposition, making the point that perhaps if they had done something about the conditions under which people in Scotland were living, there would not have been the same urge to emigrate. Also if Nova Scotia was not a good option for settlers, why did 'these gentlemen' not point out another colony in America that was a better one. He then alleges that the only concern of these gentlemen is 'their own interest and not the welfare of the emigrants which they have in view' and asserts:

> it will be believed that they are in some degree of fear, lest they be losers if any considerable number of farmers and mechanics should remove to Nova Scotia.

He points out the bad state of economic affairs of the country, brought about in part by 'an extravagant paper currency', and claims that as a consequence, 'thousands of weavers tanners and other mechanics, have been dismissed from business', and that:

> by the racking of land rents, which is also in a great measure owing to that currency, many of the smaller farmers have been ruined and set adrift.

All of this has brought about a huge surplus of unemployed labour. At this point the letter breaks cover from the even tone, and acidly and bitingly suggests in words in italics:

> If the *wise* and *humane* gentlemen I speak of, are sure that Nova Scotia is an improper place for them, they, from humanity and sound policy, should either direct them to settle in a British colony, where

EMIGRATION

their conditions will be comfortable; or else they should immediately find out employment to all mechanics who want it, and they should also lighten the burden which most part of farmers in this country have borne for twenty years past.

The writer warns that if these issues that are drawing people to seek to emigrate are not attended to, then:

hunger is a powerful enemy to fight against; and though they have been hitherto peaceable, it may push them on to the most unlawful and desperate attempts. There have long ago been Levellers in Scotland and very lately Hearts of Steel in Ireland.

The letter concludes with the plea that:

some of your intelligent correspondents would inquire into the causes of that spirit of emigration which prevails so much in this country and what is the best method to put a stop to it.[3]

The correspondence continued to be featured, with the December issue printing a letter to the *Edinburgh Advertiser* from 'Veritas', who offered the suggestion that one major factor prompting emigration was the break-down of the Clan system. The Clan chieftains, sub-chieftains and tacksmen coming in for the most criticism, the letter is very anti-Highlander, yet despite this Lowlander's prejudice, he decries the exploitation, and there is sympathy for:

these deluded, brave and faithful people, fond of money, ready to work to obtain it … [who] become disgusted at their chieftain, take a dislike to the place of their nativity resolve at once to follow their seducers, let the consequences be what they will, little knowing that they will be carried to market, like a herd of cattle, for the total emolument of their leaders.[4]

The October 1773 issue of *The Scots Magazine* reported:

Our emigrations to America still continue. On the 22nd June, between seven and eight hundred people from the Lewis islands sailed thither from Stornoway.

The correspondent offers an explanation:

EMIGRATION

The extravagant rents extracted by the landlords is the sole cause given for this spirit of emigration which seems to be only in its infancy as several of my acquaintances are determined to embrace the first opportunity of going to America.

A further note in the same section of the *Magazine* records:

Orkney; Oct. 6. Last week sailed from Stromness harbour for New York and other places in America, three vessels with 775 emigrants on board.[5]

It seems that the message was slowly beginning to percolate through to 'the powers that be' in Government, as the December 1773 issue of the *Scots Magazine* records that statistics are being gathered:

of the numbers of persons who have emigrated within these two years, distinguishing their ages, sexes, from these it may be concluded, that the emigrations will come under the consideration of parliament next session.[6]

This observation on the gathering of statistics, and the likelihood of the matter being raised in parliament, is indicative of how much attention was being paid in the press to the issue of emigration.

A letter dated February 18, 1774, and first published in the *Caledonian Mercury*, is included in the *Scots Magazine* of February 1774. Signed by 'Philopatriae', it emphasises the extent of the problem and the need for government action:

The emigrations from the more northern and western parts of this country to America, are now grown alarmingly, and loudly call for the help and assistance of legislature, but the talk of preventing people from flying from a country where they are starved, to one where they have the happy prospect of all the conveniences of life in abundance, for their lawful industry is exceedingly difficult; and, indeed, what I hope, the laws of our free constitution cannot reach to. The proposing to confine a British subject in a corner, where he has the certain prospect of famishing, (for the good of the population), is a detestable idea, and unworthy of a British lawgiver; therefore I hope our illustrious senate will never adopt so harsh a method to defeat emigration.

EMIGRATION

The writer acknowledges that a method has to be devised that will stop the haemorrhaging of the population through emigration. He warns that it is not just the 'wild and remotest' parts of the country that are affected, but the more densely populated parts as well: 'that spirit which at first only infected the poorest husbandman, has now taken possession of our manufacturers'. He signals an interest in the place in which Witherspoon himself lived and worked in, noting that:

> The wealthy and opulent town of Paisley cannot now support those ingenious mechanics who have raised it to its present greatness, but they are forced to abandon their friends and country, and seek that subsistence in a different clime, which they cannot obtain in their own.

The writer betrays his antagonism to the American colonists, when he sees this loss of useful British citizens and their families compounded by the fact that, 'they go and naturalize themselves among *the disobedient children of the mother country* and imbibe their *destructive notions of anarchy*' [my italics]. He sees British emigrants as an encouragement to the colonists who:

> are already too prone to throw of the yoke, which in my opinion hangs gently about their necks, and every shipful of emigrants that reaches their shores will hasten that day when they shall throw off their dependence upon Britain altogether.

'Philopatriae' offers one simplistic idea to reverse the emigration from the highland areas: 'the re-establishing of those ancient though misguided chieftains in their paternal properties'. This he thinks will have an immediate effect: 'It is impossible to conceive with what joyous alacrity their remaining dependents will fly under their protection'. By selling these lands back at a cheap rate will enable the proprietor to let them at a low rent, thus stopping the flow of emigration at least in the northern part of the country. His second proposal is less patronising to the poor highlanders and indeed addresses a problem that has been one of the causes of the loss of employment, when he suggests that there is a need to revise the laws surrounding the manufacture of linen.[7] But nothing was done about either suggestion, and in *The Scots Magazine* of May 1775, there is a little item of news that indicates the thinking of those who governed Scotland. Headed, 'Clamp down on emigration', it then rather pompously continues:

Lord Advocate represented to the Commissioners of the Customs the impropriety of clearing away any vessels from Scotland with emigrants for America. Orders ... grant no clearance to any ship for America which had more than the common complement of hands on board.

The same edition of the *Magazine* contained a report of the 'Lexington and Concord skirmishes', which signalled the onset of armed conflict between the American colonists and Great Britain, and with its continuance, that led to the *Declaration of Independence* on July 4, 1776, the problem of how to stop emigration from Scotland was, for the time being, solved.[8]

As yet, I have not been able to evaluate the success or otherwise of the Nova Scotia project, but there is a well-documented account of another venture in Witherspoon's encouragement of emigration, and his acquisition of land upon which emigrants might settle. This episode in his life is tied in with the formation in Scotland of an organisation called The Scotch American Company of Farmers, formed on February 5, 1773, at Inchinnan, on the south side of the river Clyde, about midway between Glasgow and Greenock.[9] According to James Whitelaw, who eventually was commissioned by the Company to go to America along with David Allan to seek out and purchase land on its behalf, the project of forming a company for the purchase and settling of land in America had been discussed for a number of years in the parishes of Renfrewshire and Lanarkshire. Whitelaw's father writes: 'Several meetings of the associates were held before any plan was decided upon', and that they solicited advice from persons who had travelled to America. On February 1, 1772, the first decisive steps were taken and:

> At successive meetings the articles of association were considered and elaborated till they were reduced to writing, and at a meeting of the Company held at Inchinnan, Feb. 5, 1773 they were approved and adopted.

The rules and regulations fill fifteen closely written foolscap pages in the *Journal of Proceedings of the Scotch American Company of Farmers*. The following is a summary of these rules and describes the purpose and functioning of the Company. It was to be a partnership 'for purchasing land in any of His Majesty's Dominions in America'. Joint Stock consisted of four hundred shares whose value appears to be Two pounds and ten shillings sterling. Each shareholder having one vote, and if the purchaser of Ten pounds sterling in stock, two votes. Two men to be sent to America, called, 'Commissioners', empowered to purchase a suitable tract of land which they were to lay out in lots corresponding to the number of shares held in the company and the smallest sum is to be paid. A map or plan of their lands is to be sent back to the company in Scotland. They were to lay out a portion of the tract as a town, divided into lots of 40 by 100 feet, with sites for storehouses, markets, churches, schoolhouses and other public buildings. All who took lots in the town site were to build houses upon them within ten years. The Commissioners were empowered to clear lands and erect public and private buildings, and provide accommodations for settlers till they were able to build houses for themselves. Settlers were urged to conform to their local government, to the laws and customs of the province where they should settle. It was not to be a religious colony.[10]

The Commissioners selected were James Whitelaw (24) of Whiteinch in the Parish of Govan, and David Allan (34) in the Parish of Inchinnan. Whitelaw was well educated and had a thorough knowledge of surveying. He later became Surveyor General of Vermont. Allan, say the historians of Ryegate, 'appears to have been a man of excellent human judgement, sound sense and considerable experience in the valuation of lands'.[11]

In what follows I am indebted to James Whitelaw's, *Journal* for the account of these men's search for suitable lands. Whitelaw records:

> Friday March 19, [1773]. We went to Greenock. Mar. 25 Sailed on Brigantine Matty, Capt. Thomas Cochrane, Commander. Sat. Mar. 27 to Apr. 18 we had fair weather and a good breeze. The Captain is a sensible and discreet man and the sailors are merry fellows, and a great deal more sober than they are commonly represented. Apr. 18th Lat. 40 and long. About 18° Surveyor at work! Sun 9 May. We spoke a sloop from Virginia bound for Nevis. John Roberts, Master, 15 days out, and in 62° 30′ though by ours only in 61° 48′. We had not seen another vessel since April 10th.[12]

I have included this opening passage of the *Journal* as a sample of Whitelaw's attention to detail, which in itself is corroborative evidence of the likely accuracy of his account of his and his fellow commissioner's search for suitable land.

Whitelaw records their arrival in America:

> Thursday 20 May [1773] about 3 o'clock we had our first sight of America. Anchored 9 pm Delaware Bay waiting for the Pilot. Sunday 23rd Anchor below Philadelphia midnight. Obliged to stay until the health officer came aboard to visit the passengers. Each of

us had to pay him one shilling sterling. Mon. the 24th at 12 o'clock we came to the wharfs, the whole distance we sailed being about 5,000 miles by the log. When we arrived here Alexander Semple was standing on the wharf ready to receive us in order to conduct us to his brother's house, where accidently we met with Dr. Witherspoon, who informed us that he had a township of land called Ryegate, in the province of New York upon the Connecticut River containing 23,000 acres which he was ready to dispose of in order to serve us, in case we thought it would suit our purpose, but in the meantime desired us to make every other trial, and not to be too hasty in making a bargain, and instantly desired us to call for him at Princetown on our way to New York.[13]

The manner of Whitelaw's description of the meeting with Witherspoon is indicative of his being familiar with him. From the writing, it is clear that he is already aware of who Witherspoon is, and offers no explanation in the *Journal* as to this, which undoubtedly he would have done, had this been a recording of a meeting with a total stranger. It could well have been that he was aware of Witherspoon's sojourn in Paisley, which is relatively near Whiteinch. But it is more likely that he knew of Witherspoon as one of the people contacted or referred to at the time when the formation of the Scotch American Company of Farmers was still at its planning stage. Nor is it likely that John Witherspoon just happened to be at Alexander Semple's brother's house by chance. I am sure that the good Doctor was aware of the proposed expedition of Whitelaw and Allan, and took the opportunity to put himself in line for a meeting with them immediately upon their arrival. Whitelaw's *Journal* continues:

We stayed in Philadelphia three days ... We had several offers of lands in this province, but deferred the viewing of them at this time as by our commission we were first to begin at New York, for which place we set out with the stage on Thursday, the 27 [May] at six o'clock in the morning, and arrived at Princeton at 5 o'clock in the afternoon, where we again met with Dr. Witherspoon, Robert and John Hyndman and James Findlay; we stayed here until the next stage day, which time we spent viewing Dr. Witherspoon's plantations, as [*sic*] also receiving particular intelligence about the township of Ryegate from James Findlay and John Hyndman, who had both been lately on the ground.[14]

They arrived at New York on Tuesday 1 June, indicating that they had stayed four nights at Princeton in the company of Dr Witherspoon. Again it is clear that Witherspoon was doing his best to present the Commissioners with as much information as possible about the lands in Ryegate, assembling the Hyndmans and Findlay to augment that information with their own experience of the land. It is also significant that Whitelaw makes no mention of the College, indicating the effort made by Witherspoon to allow the focus of attention to be upon the subject of land; hence his organizing of a visit to 'his plantations'. It is not Witherspoon the College President, but Witherspoon the Land Agent/Proprietor, who is to the fore during the period of the Commissioners' stay at Princeton.

The *Journal* then goes on to provide a very detailed account of the journey made by Whitelaw and Allan as they followed up the various leads that they had been given through the contacts made at New York. After their arrival at New York it records:

> We stayed here eight days, which time we were employed in informing ourselves where lands was to be got from surveyors and others that was acquaint in the country, and several gentlemen in this place have given us letters to their correspondents in the country to show us their lands.

The *Journal* then shows how they tried to follow the leads that they had been given, but it also tells us of their personal diligence, as they record: 'On Saturday the 5th [June] The Matty arrived here from Philadelphia & on the 8th we wrote home'. They were taking the first opportunity of getting in touch with those who had commissioned them, by using the ship upon which they had travelled to America to take back their letters with the news so far.[15]

Whitelaw and Allan then travelled by sloop to Albany where upon their arrival they visited, on a recommendation, lands owned Sir William Johnson and nearby the town that bore his name Johnstown. The *Journal* is so carefully written that one can almost smell the sales pitch attempted by their owner, but it also reveals the astuteness and careful assessment being exercised by the commissioners:

> On Saturday morning [June 19] we set off along with the surveyor to view the above mentioned lands, and having passed over a large patent of very fine land, which he only leases on the following terms, viz.: The first five years free, and ever after at six pounds the hundred acres, York currency, reserving to himself all coals or other minerals which may be found in the ground. We next came upon the lands which he proposed selling to us, which is tolerable good land tho not so good as the last mentioned tract. The situation seemed to

us not very agreeable, being about 12 or 14 miles from the Mohawk river and over a high hill, and some large swamps, also the price we thought high, being a dollar an acre. While we stayed here we bought two horses, viz.: one from Dr. Adams at eight pounds, and the other from Billy Luckey at nine York currency.[16]

Not impressed, they travelled on.

They became aware of the dispute between New Hampshire and New York as to who held jurisdiction over the lands between Lake Camplain and the Connecticut river and noticed the effect that this was alleged to have had on some areas on the boundary where families had moved on because of the unsettling nature of the wrangle in which the Governors were engaged. But undeterred they made their way to see the Ryegate lands. The *Journal* records:

> On the 26th [June] we crossed Connecticut river and came to Charleston in New Hampshire, where Mr. Church lives who is partner with Dr. Witherspoon in Ryegate, and Monday, the 28th we set out along with him to view it and arrived at it on Wednesday, the 30th in the morning.

They were impressed by what they saw:

> large brooks fit for mills, a large tract of good land, well watered with plenty of small brooks in excellent pasture, a very large tract of exceedingly good land all lying towards the south and pretty lived in and may be easily cleared ... the wood, beech and maple and some hemlock, the most inconvenience is its distance from navigation.

An interesting insight is provided by the travellers' stay at Hanover:

> where Mr. Wheelock has his Indian Academy or College ... he said he had as much land as would serve about 30 families which he said he would *give* to settlers if they would but come and live upon it ... he would prefer Scotch people before any other as he thought much of their religion and manner of their Church Government. 80 students - 30 of which were upon Charity.[17]

As they travelled back towards New York they recorded 'poor barren ground until Massachusetts Bay, long settled', and then they come to:

fruit growing county - one farmer can make 100 barrels of cider each barrel containing 8 Scotch gallons. The people here are affable and discreet and of a fair complexion. The women in particular are very handsome and beautiful.

They also comment on the Indians:

> tawny complexion, almost naked excepting a blanket which they wrap about their shoulders and two pieces of skin one which hangs before and another behind to cover their nakedness - fond of jewels.

A closing comment on this part of their journey: 'weather mostly dry and for the most part clear, a good deal warmer than at home'.[18]

Their journey being determined by the following up of the contacts given them as to where land was currently available, they returned to New York. The *Journal* records:

> On the 15th [July] we set off for Philadelphia and came to Princetown [*sic*] on the 16th at night, here we staid till the 19th. Dr. Witherspoon being so good as to find us pasture for our horses which was very rare to be got on account of the great drought the like of which had not been known these many years.[19]

The reason for their return visit to Witherspoon was probably that now having seen the Ryegate lands and having ascertained their suitability to the Company's needs, they would be more able to discuss the details in any negotiations with him. For his part, Witherspoon would have had the opportunity of further thought about what he might be able to offer. The *Journal* continues:

> Dr. Witherspoon has now made his proposals concerning Ryegate and his terms are these, if we take the whole reserving to them 2,000 acres, two shillings ster. p. acre, if three-fourths reserving 1500 acres 3-3 York Currency, and if we take only one half three shillings York money. But he advised us to be at all due pains, and if we should find a better place for our purpose, to take it, as he is very fond that our scheme should succeed.

This time, with the proposal firmed up, and having been well discussed, they had time to consider the aspect of Princeton that concerned John Witherspoon other than 'his plantations', the College. The *Journal* notes:

Princetown is a handsome little town and stands on a pleasant situation, and the College is said to be the best and largest building in America, and at present contains upwards of 100 students besides 80 Latin scholars.

It is noticeable that following this visit, Whitelaw gives Witherspoon the title by which he was known in Princeton, as the *Journal* records: 'on the 19th [July] after dining with the President, we left this place and arrived at Philadelphia on the 20th in the afternoon'.

Whitelaw and Allan stayed at Philadelphia until the 26 July, 'which time we spent informing ourselves about this and the southern provinces'. They travelled on to Fort Augusta: 'by good roads for about 50 miles from Philadelphia', but they found that:

> there was no place large enough for our purpose, but plenty too large for our money as woodland sells here for 20 to 50 shillings per acre.

They rested for ten days at Shippenburgh, 'to refresh our horses (150 miles from Philadelphia)'.[20]

The variety of people whom they met as they passed through Pennsylvania is noted:

> Here the people are kind and discreet, except the Dutch or Germans who inhabit the best lands in the Province, who are a set of people who mind nothing of gayity, but live niggardly and gather together money as fast as they can without having intercourse with anybody but among themselves. Most people in this Province look fresh and healthy, except the women, who have for the most part lost their teeth with eating too many fruits which they have in great plenty.[21]

The land through which they were passing in Pennsylvania was nearly fully settled and they noted that the 'little that is left is going at 20-30 shillings an acre'. They noticed its plentiful products as rye, wheat, barley, corn, oats, buckwheat, flax, peas, beans, melons and 'all the roots and garden stuff of the earth'. As they travelled on through Maryland they remarked: 'very good land and all settled'. As they moved into Carolina and crossed over into Virginia, the *Journal* notes: 'ground sandy and poor and the places that are good are all filled up with tobacco and here is but little wheat or grain'.

Whitelaw's comments on the running of the plantations would have made interesting reading for the abolitionists, especially those who advocated the abolition of slavery on economic grounds, believing that more profit would be gained if slaves were freed and paid wages, instead of being held captive, housed and clothed and fed by their owners. Whitelaw writes:

> The Planters here live well and are all quite idle as none but negroes work here, of which some planters will have several hundreds which at an average are worth 60 or 70 pounds ster. apiece and in these all their riches consists, for there are few of them but are in debt to the storekeepers and it commonly takes all their crops to cloath themselves and their negroes. But those that are industrious and labour themselves, and particularly they who make grain, can make a good deal of money, as grain sells pretty well and does not require half of the labour that tobacco does.[22]

Such comments as the above could only have come from a man who was not only able to see the actuality but also the potential of the lands through which he was passing.

As they travelled on they came to what they judged to be the poor land of Edinton, barren, sand, marshy swamps, and a sickly climate which nevertheless has a 'high price'. Whitelaw offers an observation which clearly he has picked up from one of the local people:

> the culture of indigo is so unhealthy that they reason if a negro lives 10 years and works among it, they have a good bargain of him.[23]

Turning north again on Wednesday 15 [September] the *Journal* notes:

> We travelled about 500 miles-viz. from Halifax in Carolina to Dover which is within 80 miles of Philadelphia without seeing a stone of any kind or any sort of eminence … and in all that 500 miles we was not in 5 houses but some people was sick of the fever and ague or some other disease, but we have reason to bless God that though we have travelled through such a sickly country, we are now arrived in perfect health at a place where such sicknesses seldom or never appear.[24]

Their search for land was over, their minds were made up, and at the beginning of October the *Journal* records:

> After having refreshed ourselves and horses and discussed what business we had to do, we left Philadelphia on the first of October

and came to Princeton that night, and next day we bargained with Dr. Witherspoon for one half of the Township of Ryegate.[25]

They stayed until the 5th of October, when having organised tools and provisions, they sent them ahead and made their way via Hartford and New York to Ryegate.

James Whitelaw's *Journal* records the completion of the task of the Commissioners:

> On the 30th of the month [November1773] Mr. Church came up and we divided the town, the south part wherof has faln [*sic*] to us, which in our opinion and in the opinion of all that knows it, has the advantage of the north in many respects. 1st it is the best land in general. 2nd nearest to provisions which we have in plenty within 3 or 4 miles and likewise within 6 of a grist and 2 miles of a saw miln [*sic*], all of which are great advantages to a new settlement. 3rd we have several brooks with good seats [*sic*] for milns, and likewise Wells River runs through part of our purchase and has water enough for two breast milns at the driest season of the year, of which the north part is almost entirely destitute. 4th there is a fall in the Connecticut river just below our uppermost line which causeth a carrying place for goods going up or down the river. 5th we are within six miles of a good Presbyterian meeting and there is no minister above that place.[26]

Whitelaw's enthusiasm for the site he has purchased at Ryegate is palpable. His judgement of the land had been made by making a thorough comparison of it against the other lands that were on offer. In relation to the money at their disposal he and his fellow Commissioner David Allan seemed to be well pleased with the bargain struck with John Witherspoon after all the hazards of their investigative journey. On November 17, 1773, Whitelaw writes to the Scotch American Company of Farmers to tell his fellow shareholders of the successful purchase:

> Considering the newness of the country, the people are very prosperous, and we think that any who come here, and are steady and industrious, may be in very comfortable circumstances within a few years.[27]

Whitelaw settled in Ryegate. The historian of Ryegate takes up his story:

James Whitelaw became Surveyor General of Vermont in 1784. From the time he left Scotland till his appointment as Surveyor General he was the Manager of the Scotch American Company. He kept its accounts and executed deeds of land on its behalf. For his services in surveying he received a grant of land. His first house built in 1775 stood until 1909. He died in April 29, 1829. A Federalist, a Mason of high degree both in Scotland and America. He was a member of the established Presbyterian Church in Scotland but was never connected with any church in America, yet lived a strict religious life and was a strong and liberal supporter of the Associate Church.[28]

Little is known of David Allan other than that on August 1, 1774, after having completed a map of all the lots of the land, he set off from Ryegate to return to Scotland. At his departure, it is recorded that 'the whole of the Ryegate Colonists attended him', travelling with him to Newbury from which place they took their leave of him.[29]

Some questions remain to be asked about John Witherspoon's precise role and involvement in the Ryegate property transactions. The History of Ryegate gives this account:

> The original deed of the south half of Ryegate was discovered and is given here. It is a transaction between John Church of Charleston in the Province of New Hampshire [Witherspoon's contact for the Ryegate lands] and James Whitelaw of Ryegate in the County of Gloucester and Province of New York. 'For the consideration of £1,186 pounds lawful money of New York, already by him received; hath granted, bargained, and sell aliene release and confirm unto the said Party of the 2nd part (in his actual possession), now being by virtue of an Indenture of Bargain and Sale for a year dated yesterday ... all that Tract or Parcel of land lying in the south part of the town of Ryegate ... bounded as follows: ...'.
> [signed] John Church (seal)
> Made 31st Day of October 1775 dealt with by Jacob Bayley one of the Judges of the Inferior Court of Sc. County at Newbury, November 13th 1775.[30]

Because of the dispute between New York and New Hampshire, people who had previously been granted lands had to re-apply to the Governor of New York for the ratification of their transactions. This probably explains why the *History of Ryegate* relates that 'John Church acquired the title on 30th June 1775 of lands that 18 months before had been conveyed to Dr.

John Witherspoon'. Although this document of October 31, 1775, that was drawn up to satisfy the rights of New York, under whose jurisdiction Ryegate now rested, does not seem to mention the detail of the connection between John Church, John Witherspoon and John Pagan, the earlier document drawn up at the time of the transaction makes their relationship very clear. This document made at Newbury on November 19, 1773, is precise about the fact that John Church is the agent of the proprietors:

> The agreement between John Church Esq. of Charleston, in New Hampshire, and taking burden upon him for John Witherspoon, President of the College of New Jersey, and John Pagan, Merchant in Glasgow and William Pagan, Merchant in New York on one part and David Allan and James Whitelaw Commissioners for the Scotch American Company of Farmers is as follows …[31]

There is then given a description of the acreage and its allocation, but then this significant phrase causes all doubt to be removed as to John Witherspoon's role in the sale:

> it was mutually agreed between the above mentioned parties that the aforesaid David Allan and James Whitelaw in consequence of their agreement with John Witherspoon, President of the College is to have the half south of the centrical line.

There follows the precise geographical delineation of the area.

In the period between the signing of the deal in November 1773 and the formal issue of the Deed of Sale in October 1775, a letter from William Pagan in New York to David Allan and James Whitelaw dated February 23, 1774, shows the businesslike manner in which the sale had been handled. John Church had reported to William Pagan that the purchasers were anxious to have the deeds completed. Pagan writes to Allan and Whitelaw that he and Witherspoon are equally anxious to see the transaction formally completed, but offers this assurance:

> Whatever province Ryegate falls under, we are entirely safe, having a Patent under the one and an Order of Council under the other. You need not be in the least uneasy, but go on with your settlement, as if you had the most firm deed now in your possession.[32]

It is when this kind of detail is seen to have been taken into account, that the fair and thoroughly competent practice of Witherspoon and his associates William and John Pagan come to the fore. Undoubtedly much careful planning and thought went into the acquisition of land, and a sufficient foresight is also in evidence that takes into account the possible legal difficulties that might have to be overcome. When this is combined with the very careful assessment made by the Commissioners, of the lands then available, the whole episode of the sale of the Ryegate lands brings credit to the conduct of the people on both sides of the transaction. Looking particularly at Witherspoon, his care for his potential clients is clear. He, no doubt with his own personal interest also in mind, makes himself available to his potential clients on the very day of their arrival. He meets with them a few days later, during which meeting he tells them what he has for sale. He encourages them to see it for themselves but also to look at other lands and not to be too hasty. He meets with them again after they have seen his lands, but again does not press the matter, and they go off to complete their survey of other available lands, before returning to secure a deal. In all of his activity Witherspoon has been blameless in his conduct, and it is against such conduct that the comments of his critics have to be evaluated.

Some years later an entirely separate deal was done between John Church and John Witherspoon, this time concerning land in the Northern part of Ryegate. The Ryegate historian records that:

On January 20, 1776 Mr. Church sold to the Doctor, 28 lots of land in the North Division, containing 2,760 ¾ acres for £210. New York money; and a little later 5,212 ½ acres in the same section to John Pagan a merchant of Glasgow.

He then adds:

This John Pagan and others of the name held considerable land in America. In 1792 Mr. Pagan then removed to Greenock, was the owner of a tract of 833 acres in Newbury, another 2,000 acres in Cavendish and the above mentioned land in Ryegate, while Dr. Witherspoon was proprietor of 12,057 acres in Nova Scotia, being part of what was called the Philadelphia Grant. In that year, the latter [Dr. Witherspoon] being in London, executed a bond to exchange his land in Nova Scotia for the tracts owned by Pagan in Vermont, transferring the former [Nova Scotia] to Robert Thomas and John Pagan Jun., merchants at Poictou, Nova Scotia. The rate of exchange was two acres of the Nova Scotia land for one in Newbury and Cavendish and four acres for one in Ryegate. But the Pagan land in Newbury lay in the hilly region between Limekiln neighbourhood and the centre, so the difference is easily accounted for. This exchange gave the Doctor 1597 acres in Ryegate and the remainder he purchased outright. In 1774, he had purchased for his son James, a tract of 600 acres in the northwest corner of the town.

According to the Ryegate Land Records, Dr Witherspoon finally disposed of his land in Ryegate, when on the February 16, 1792, he conveyed to Robert Hunter of the City of New York 2,075 ¾ acres; and on 24 December of the next year [1793] to William Neilson, merchant of New York, all his remaining land in Ryegate.[33]

Including such detail in this narrative will perhaps convey the extent to which Witherspoon got involved in the various land grant schemes of the developing provincial and later state governments. One cannot but think that what had perhaps started as an altruistic endeavour for the betterment of the lives of settlers from his native land, had become a bit of a hobby, from which he derived some pleasure from the power achieved by it, and to a certain extent, from the excitement of the monetary wheeling and dealing involved.

That the Ryegate settlement by the Scotch American Company of Farmers proved to be a success, is no doubt largely due to the careful management of the project by its two Commissioners. *The History of Ryegate* records that James Whitelaw and David Allan spent the first winter with John Hyndman, whom they helped to build his house, and in return were invited to stay with him. By February 1774, Whitelaw was writing home:

> We have now built a house and live very comfortably though we are not troubled much with our neighbours, having one family about half a mile from us, another a mile and a half and two about two miles and a half, one above us and one below us.[34]

In May, his Diary reveals:

> On Monday the 23rd of May, arrived here from Scotland, David Ferry, Alexander Sym [Symes] and family, Andrew and Robert Brock, John and Robert Orr, John Wilson, John Gray, John Shaw and Hugh Semple.

Alex. Symes, a gardener; David Ferry, a clothprinter at Dalquern; Robert Brock, Robert Orr and John Wilson, farmers; and Hugh Semple, a resident in Kilbarchan had all been signatories of *the Bond of Association* for the Scotch American Company of Farmers. All were set to work, but as the surveying was not yet finished, it was not until July 1, 1774, that the first forty lots of land were issued to them, David Ferry getting Lot Number 1.[35]

The orderliness and meticulous organisation of the Commissioners that is in evidence was no doubt a huge factor in determining the progress of this settlement as was the financial arrangement negotiated by John Witherspoon that the Commissioners judged to be fair and giving value for money. These first settlers were soon joined by a steady stream of others to take up the four hundred lots into which the southern part of Ryegate had been divided by Whitelaw. Only one difficulty in these early days is recorded in Whitelaw's letter home of October 14, 1774:

> We shall have a flourishing colony here in a short time, but we are at a loss for young women, as we have here about a dozen young fellows and only one girl, and we shall never multiply and replenish this western world as we ought without help-meets for us.[36]

However as Ryegate continued to be settled, and letters sent home from its settlers, it is likely that these contributed to peoples' confidence in the whole concept of emigration to America. *The Scots Magazine* of April 1774, contains a series of reports from different parts of Scotland, where it is said: 'The spirit of emigration still continues, and societies are forming for that purpose'. Then follow details of meetings being held to organise emigration in Stirlingshire, at Cardross, Arnprior and Kippen. Alongside, there are reports of groups of emigrants going from 'Stathspey' and 'Campsey' and 'Stromness' and 'Stranraer'.[37] *The Scots Magazine* of February 1775, contains a report of:

> one of the commissioners from the Perth and Stirling Company of Farmers for purchasing lands in North America having returned to Glasgow having purchased a tract of 10,000 acres at a very trifling cost in the Province of New York.

The article also offers the opinion that:

> the disputes with the mother country excepting about the sea coast towns are little known there, only the English inhabitants, from their national principles, bear the greatest aversion to the Canada Bill.[38]

Witherspoon did eventually reply to the criticisms of the advert for settlers in Nova Scotia, and the allegations of his exploitation of the settlers. In a letter produced for *The Scots Magazine*, he makes an initial rather dismissive response:

EMIGRATION

One or two of these papers have been sent me, and contain so many mistakes in point of fact, as well as betray such ignorance of the subject they attempt to treat, that it would be a disgrace for any man to enter into a formal quarrel with such opponents.

However, he does take up the fight. Beginning with what he sees as the main concern of his opponents, he writes:

The accusation, I think may be reduced to the following argument - Migrations from Britain to America are not only hurtful, but tend to the ruin of that kingdom, therefore John Witherspoon by inviting people to leave Scotland, and settle in America, is an enemy to his country.

He tells of how and why he was invited to participate in the Nova Scotia scheme of settlement:

… my having any concern in such an undertaking was wholly accidental and unexpected. I was invited and pressed into it, from a motive that was not at all concealed, *that I would give the people who intended to come out greater confidence that they should [meet] with fair treatment.* [My emphasis.]

Witherspoon then reveals one of the conditions he imposed upon his partner John Pagan:

one of the express conditions of my joining with the company was, that no land should be sold dearer to any coming from Scotland, than I should direct.

He suggests that the stated prices in the advert should cause anyone to realize that any profit made at that price must be small, and indeed he claims:

The plain fact is, that the sum is not at all equivalent to the trouble and expense of serving out the patent; therefore the profit must be future and must arise wholly from the prosperity of the settlement.

Witherspoon then offers some remarks on the first allegation of the hurtfulness to Britain of emigration. Firstly he alleges there is very little grounds for alarm because: 'the numbers have never been nor will be of any consequence to the population of the country'. Secondly he poses the question:

> Can a man be an enemy [to his country] by pointing out to such of them as are poor or oppressed where they might have a happy and plentiful provision and their posterity be multiplied as the sands of the sea?

He sees himself as 'doing a real service to my country [Britain]' when he helps people 'who find it difficult to subsist on the soil in which they were born, to easily transport themselves'. He adds that:

> There are always strong motives to hinder a man's removal from his own country, and it cannot be supposed that any considerable number will think of such a measure, unless … .

and he implies the real cause of emigration, 'they are really in an oppressed state'. Thirdly, he writes: 'Those who try to stop emigration will only encourage it, such is man's contrary nature'. This intended reply to his critics did not meet with a rejoinder, and how the growing trend of emigration might have continued will never be known, for with the outbreak of hostilities in April 1775, the debate on emigration came to an end.[39]

When John Adams visited Princeton in August 1774, among the things he principally remembered of that visit, and the first thing that he recorded in his diary of the day he first met President Witherspoon, was Witherspoon's advocacy that: 'Congress should raise money and employ a number of Writers in the Newspapers in England, to explain to the Public the American Plea'. The second thing that he records is Witherspoon's opinion that, 'we should recommend it to every Colony to form a Society for the Encouragement of Protestant Emigrants from the 3 Kingdoms'.[40] Witherspoon was clearly undeterred by any adverse opinions in Great Britain, firmly believing that, as ever, on the subject of its American Colonies, the British were at least uninformed, or possibly, misinformed.

That Witherspoon was known at the highest level of government to be an encourager of Emigration to America is evidenced by George Washington's letter to him on March 10, 1784. Writing from his home at Mount Vernon, Washington brought to Witherspoon's attention the opportunities for emigrants in the Ohio Lands. He is wanting whole communities, under their pastors, to take up leases of land in Ohio, and sends Witherspoon what is ostensibly a *Prospectus*. It begins:

> Wanted. Leases about 30,000 acres of land on the Ohio's Great Kanhaw and patents ten or twelve years … it is almost superfluous to add that the whole of it is river low ground and of the first quality - but it is essential to remark that a great deal of it may be converted to the finest in growing grounds imaginable with little or no labour.

Washington wrote this very long letter (five and a half pages) to the man who probably was foremost in the former Colonies in his advocacy of emigration from Britain to America.[41]

One last letter written with the help of an amanuensis, but signed by Witherspoon, on December 8, 1792, shows that interest in emigration continued to be held by him even to the point when he could no longer see to write, and was but two years away from his death. In this letter to William Steuart, North Castle Street, Edinburgh, Witherspoon comments on the state of the country (America):

> First there is no doubt that this country is in a rapid state of growth is a proper theatre of industry is promising success to emigrants of every class, character, or profession. Secondly improved scholars and professional men as Divines, physicians and lawyers if young, have an excellent oppy. [opportunity] of being introduced into business; but such persons, or those so qualified if advanced in years have not so good an oppy. Of being introduced in such business as they from their standing may think themselves entitled to what is due to character, but character is altogether found by a stranger in a new country.[42]

Witherspoon for all that he was going blind was still capable of perspicuity. He knew that there was still a good opportunity to make your way as an emigrant, but that people would have to make adjustments to a different way of life and different values, if they were to succeed. He had been 'a stranger in a new country', but he had had the ability to make the changes that were necessary to adjust to its ways and to take hold of its opportunities, opportunities that to the end of his days, he was eager to offer to any would be emigrant.

CHAPTER 14

Impact on Scotland and America

Part 1: Impact on Scotland

A t first glance John Witherspoon's impact on Scotland is negligible. In the first one hundred and fifty years after his death his existence is hardly mentioned. If his significance was to be measured by the number of entries in the histories of the time it would not amount to much. He might well have been deliberately ignored because in the eyes of many in Britain he was a traitor. He had joined the enemy and therefore was not worthy of notice. As I have tried to make an assessment of his treatment by historians, I am aware that this is a very personal and incomplete survey of the subject. But an examination of the histories with which I am familiar, is revealing of the fact that from being ignored in the mid-twentieth century, he is becoming increasingly featured in works of its last decade, and this trend is continuing into the present century.

One measure of the development in seeing the significance of John Witherspoon is illustrated by this brief survey. The entry against John Witherspoon's name in *The Concise Dictionary of National Biography*, published in 1995, contains no fewer than five factual errors, plus a few minor inaccuracies, within the space of one long paragraph.[1] Several general histories do not mention his name: J. D. Mackie, *A History of Scotland* (1964); T. C. Smout, *A History of the Scottish People 1560-1830* (1969); Michael Lynch, *Scotland A New History* (1991). Even the lengthy work by J. H. S. Burleigh, *A Church History of Scotland* (1960), published to commemorate the four hundredth anniversary of the Reformation in Scotland, makes no mention whatsoever of John Witherspoon. Thinking that perhaps some of the dramatic stories in the life of Witherspoon might lend themselves to being related in the more 'popular histories', I looked in vain for a mention of him in J. M. Reid's *Kirk and Nation, The Story of the Reformed Church of Scotland* (1960). He does not even get a mention in *A History of Scottish Theatre* (1998), edited by Bill Findlay, although it contains an excellent account of the controversy over John Home's play *Douglas* which prompted Witherspoon's treatise: *Serious Enquiry into the Nature and Effects of the Stage* etc.[2]

In more recent years there has been a gradual and significant increase in interest shown in Witherspoon. Leading the field in this respect is Professor T. M. Devine, who in *The Scottish Nation 1700-2000* (1999) gave a one sentence mention:

> John Witherspoon, an evangelical minister and resolute enemy of the
> Moderates, who after emigrating to America, became President of
> Princeton University, a member of the first Congress and the only
> clergyman among the signatories to the Declaration of Independence
> of the United States.

The reference to 'Princeton University' can be forgiven, for in Devine's
Scotland's Empire 1600-1815 (2003), he gives a generous mention of
Witherspoon as 'Presbyterian minister and President of the College of New
Jersey (later Princeton) from 1768 to 1794', concentrating over several
pages, in accordance with the thrust of the book, on Witherspoon's
involvement in the encouragement of emigration to America.[3]

Michael Fry, in *The Scottish Empire* (2002), gives Witherspoon three
mentions, but as if to illustrate my point about the dramatic nature of
Witherspoon's life being attractive material for 'popular histories', Fry's
delightfully titled *'Bold, Independent, Unconquer'd and Free' How the
Scots Made America Safe for Liberty, Democracy and Capitalism* (2003)
gives no fewer than thirteen index references to Witherspoon.[4] Arthur
Herman's equally swashbuckling, *The Scottish Enlightenment: The Scots'
Invention of the Modern World* (2001), has nineteen index references to
Witherspoon. Neil Oliver, archaeologist, perhaps best known as a
television presenter, in his ten-part BBC series, *A History of Scotland*
focused on Witherspoon in one episode in a way that might have stimulated
further interest, and in his popular history of the same title, published in
2009, there are three index references to Witherspoon, totalling six pages.
The Cambridge Companion to the Scottish Enlightenment (2003), edited by
Alexander Broadie gives six index references. The more narrowly focused
and specialised *The History of Scottish Literature Vol. 2 1660-1800*, edited
by Andrew Hook (1982) looks in detail at Witherspoon's contribution to
the debate between the Moderate and Popular parties over the space of six
pages. *The Glasgow Enlightenment* (1995) focussing on a   more local
theme gives three index references.

Naturally when one turns to works written by American historians
writing about Scottish history or the Scottish American connection, their
contribution to the understanding of Witherspoon is huge by comparison to
their Scottish contemporaries. All of the works that I have read in which
Richard B. Sher is either author or editor, such as: *Church and University
in the Scottish Enlightenment The Moderate Literati of Edinburgh* by
Richard B. Sher (1985); or *Scotland and America in the Age of the
Enlightenment*, edited by Richard B. Sher and Jeffrey R. Smitten (1990); or
Sociability and Society in Eighteenth-Century Scotland, edited by John
Dwyer and Richard B. Sher (1993) make a big contribution to

demonstrating the important role of Witherspoon both in Scotland and in America, and anyone wanting an introduction to John Witherspoon would benefit from reading them. From this brief and very personal survey of the literature that I have read in recent years, I think it can be safely assumed that interest in John Witherspoon is growing, and that more people are becoming aware of his importance in the history of Scotland and America.

Looking to the long term impact of Witherspoon on Scotland, his encouragement of emigration to America was one of the factors that caused the steady trickle of emigration to become a flood. The picture that he painted of America in his communications with correspondents and journals in Scotland can only have been encouraging to would-be emigrants. His involvement with the representatives of The Scotch American Farmers Company and the subsequent success of the Ryegate settlement must have had a favourable influence on the general understanding of what might be accomplished by those who emigrated to America.[5] This is a less measurable feature of his impact, but if Witherspoon was not a direct influence on the post-war waves of emigrants, then the good impression he created in the minds of the subscribers to The Scotch American Company of Farmers in Renfrewshire, Lanarkshire and Ayrshire, must have spread throughout the land. Apart from the encouragement of emigrants who envisaged developing their farming skills in America, Witherspoon's appeal for clergymen and schoolmasters can also be included as a factor that might partially account for the increased numbers who emigrated to America to join the ranks of the clerical and teaching professions there.[6]

One factor however that prevented Witherspoon's impact on Scotland from being as great as it might have been, was the antagonism of the loyalists to the British Crown that continued after the peace settlement in 1783. Witherspoon had had to battle with this initially in America during the war as his *Address to the Natives of Scotland residing in America*, that was appended to the publication of his sermon *The Dominion of Providence* shows. In the *Address* Witherspoon writes of his 'uneasiness to hear the word "Scotch" used as a term of reproach in the American controversy'. He makes a plea to the Scots residing in America to support the revolution and argues that they misunderstand the Scots' opposition to John Wilkes, the English politician who Witherspoon claims was not really for American liberty, but was just using their cause in order to defeat a British ministry, and that the Scottish opposition to Wilkes was for his anti-British Government stance not for his pro-American stance. If, as we know, the anti-Scottish feeling in America was alive in 1776, causing Witherspoon to seek amendment in the first draft of the *Declaration of Independence* to delete the reference to 'Scotch' mercenaries; then it is likely that his reputation would suffer, as indeed it did suffer in Scotland, for his anti-British stance.[7]

If in the first instance John Witherspoon's impact on Scotland is very restricted, almost confined to being a significant factor in encouraging emigration. His long term impact did not really come into view until the beginning of the second quarter of the nineteenth century when the ecclesiastical issues of the freedom of the Church again arose and eventually came to a head at the Disruption of 1843 when the Church of Scotland experienced a serious schism that saw the emergence of the Free Church of Scotland.[8]

On June 4, 1832, after two years of political and sometimes violent agitation throughout Scotland, the *Reform Bill* passed into law. When the *Bill* was first presented in March 1831, it was defeated by the Tories. The second presentation, in June 1831, was rejected by the House of Lords. It was only at the third attempt, in December 1831, that it was passed, but then only because of a threat from King William IV to create new peers and thereby achieve a majority in the Lords. The passing of the *Bill* caused great apprehension among the conservative and ruling classes as the franchise had been extended and thereby their power bases threatened. Among those who felt threatened by the *Reform Bill* were the Established Churches in England and Scotland. In Scotland the growth of democracy threatened the power of the Patrons, who were largely of the land-owning class, and who in general were opponents of reform.[9]

A sign of the revival of opposition to patronage was that when the General Assembly of the Church of Scotland met in May 1832, overtures were presented from three synods and eight presbyteries calling attention to the need to do something about the injustices and wrongs of patronage, and for a committee to be set up to look into it and report back to the next Assembly. The snag was that Patronage had been re-established by an *Act of Parliament* in 1712, and could only be got rid of by another *Act*. In 1833, the General Assembly attempted to pass legislation that would have given representative members of congregations the power to veto an unacceptable presentee of the patron, but the motion failed. However, at the General Assembly of 1834, virtually the same motion succeeded, and it was agreed that:

> The General Assembly having maturely considered the overtures do declare that it is a fundamental law of this Church that no pastor shall be intruded on any congregation contrary to the will of the people … if the major part of the male heads of families, members of the vacant congregation and in full communion of the Church shall disapprove of the person in whose favour the call is proposed …

> such disapproval shall be deemed sufficient ground for the Presbytery rejecting such person and he shall be rejected accordingly.

It is clear from the wording that the motion was not attempting to abolish patronage but to prevent its abuse.[10]

Within six months of the *Interim Act* that was intended to become the *Veto Act*, it was challenged. The patron of the Parish of Auchterarder, Lord Kinnoul, presented Robert Young as the proposed minister. The candidate preached on two consecutive Sundays but when the Call was examined, it contained the names of only two of the resident parishioners, and no less than 286 out of the 330 male heads of families expressed their disapproval of the patron's presentee. Robert Young was advised by John Hope, Dean of the Faculty of Advocates, a church elder, to appeal to the Court of Session. After long preparation, the case was submitted in November 1837. In March 1838, by a majority of eight to five the judges of Scotland's supreme court found in Young's favour and declared that:

> in passing the *Veto Act* the Church had acted *ultra vires* and that in operating it had infringed the statutary and civil rights of patrons and presentees.

Meeting in May 1838, the General Assembly appealed to the House of Lords against the Court of Session's decision. In March 1839, before an unsympathetic Englishman, the Lord Chancellor Cottingham, and a Scottish ex-Lord Chancellor Brougham, who had long lived in London, the appeal of the General Assembly was contemptuously dismissed. By the House of Lord's decision the Patron's rights had been declared absolute and unchallengeable other than on the grounds of the presentee's professional qualifications.[11]

After the General Assembly of 1839, Chalmers in a three hour speech belligerently declared the Church could not and should not submit to the jurisdiction of the civil courts on a matter that concerned the spiritual wellbeing of its congregations. The General Assembly agreed not to offer any further resistance to the claim of the patron and presentee at Auchterarder, and to form a committee to consider the relationship between Church and State. In January 1841, the Court of Session intervened in another dispute between a patron and a congregation and a presbytery and ordered the presbytery to uphold the patron's choice and induct the presentee. In defiance of the actions of the Court of Session and the House of Lords the General Assembly of 1842, declared:

that patronage is a grievance, has been attended with much injury to the cause of true religion in this Church and Kingdom, is the main cause of the difficulties in which the Church is presently involved and that it ought to be abolished.

The Assembly then appointed committees to prepare petitions to the two Houses of Parliament and an address to the Queen. It then made what has become known as its 'Claim of Right'. It accuses the Court of Session of having:

> invaded the jurisdiction and encroached upon the spiritual privileges of the Courts of this Church. Therefore the General Assembly, while recognizing the absolute jurisdiction of the Civil Courts in relation to all the temporalities conferred by the State upon the Church, *claim as a right freely to possess and enjoy the liberties and rights and privileges bestowed on the Church according to the law*; declare that they cannot in conscience intrude ministers on reclaiming congregations or carry on government of Christ's Church subject to the coercion attempted by the Court of Session; protest against sentences of the Civil Court *in contravention of the Church's liberties*, which rather than abandon they will relinquish the privileges of establishment; and call all Christian people everywhere to note that it is for loyalty to Christ's Kingdom and Crown that the Church of Scotland is obliged to suffer hardship.[12]

Again the government dismissed the pleas of the Church. One final appeal was made to Parliament by a Scottish member who moved that the House of Commons go into Committee mode to take consideration of the grievances of which the Church of Scotland complained. His action fell by an overwhelming majority. The scene was set for schism.

After the opening service on May 18, 1843, attended by the commissioners to the Assembly, instead of constituting the Court, the retiring Moderator Dr Welsh announced that 'he and others could not regard it as a free assembly and was resolved to leave it'. He then read a protest giving his reasons for leaving and handed it to the Clerk and 'left the Chair and the Church'. He was followed out into the street by 190 ministers and elders. They afterwards met and constituted themselves as the first General Assembly of the Free Church of Scotland. At that Assembly a *Deed of Demission* was drawn up and signed by 451 ministers, by which act they relinquished the emoluments and privileges which they had previously enjoyed from being part of the Established Church. 752

ministers stayed in the Church of Scotland. It is estimated that it lost about one third of its membership to the Free Church of Scotland.[13]

It was not until 1921, when in preparation for a re-union of the two separate Churches that a set of *Articles Declaratory* were drafted within which were enshrined the principle that, by its neglect, had brought about the schism. *Article IV* of the *Articles Declaratory* which were agreed as part of the basis of union, states:

> IV. This Church, as part of the Universal Church wherein the Lord Jesus Christ has appointed a government in the hands of Church office-bearers, receives from Him, its Divine King and Head, and from Him alone, *the right and power subject to no civil authority to legislate, and to adjudicate finally, in all matters of doctrine, worship, government, and discipline in the Church,* including the right to determine all questions concerning membership and office in the Church, the constitution and membership of its Courts, and the mode of election of its office-bearers, and to define the boundaries of the spheres of labour of its ministers and other office-bearers. Recognition by civil authority of the separate and independent government and jurisdiction of this Church in matters spiritual, in whatever manner such recognition be expressed, does not in any way affect the character of this government, and jurisdiction as derived from the Divine Head of the Church alone, or give to the civil authority any right of interference with the proceedings or judgments of the Church within the sphere of its spiritual government and jurisdiction.[14]

These tough, almost pugnacious words unequivocally assert the Church's right to govern itself in all matters 'of doctrine, worship, government and discipline'. It had taken nearly eighty years to get to this stage, and indeed it was not until a further eight years had passed that the union between the two Churches took place in 1929. The language appears to have been hammered out on the hard anvil of experience, an experience that might with hindsight have been avoided if other tactics had been used by the Church, and less ignorance of the Scottish scene, and less belligerence and prejudice shown by the English dominated House of Commons and House of Lords. The principles for which the Church fought so long to establish, were the very principles that had been so fiercely defended by John Witherspoon in the debates in which he engaged throughout his two Scottish ministries. He had fought for the Church's liberty to determine its own structure to manage its own affairs, for its people to make their own choice of a minister, to judge the rectitude of its doctrine, to determine its own form of worship, and within it to foster 'true religion'. The language of these documents from the later debates, show many similarities to the language used by Witherspoon in the earlier debates, words such as: liberty, freedom, true religion and conscience are used in a similar context. It is not that it can be claimed that Witherspoon had a direct influence in producing the document of 1921, and that the legislation that to this day protects the Church of Scotland from any civil or state interference derives from him. But his arguments have been vindicated, and his activities have offered examples and precedents to his successors, that enabled them to formulate a basis for the kind of Church that is the Church of a free people within a State that has had to accept that there are some boundaries beyond which it cannot go.

Witherspoon's contribution to the debate over patronage, peoples' right to choose their own minister, the authority of the Church and its relation to the State is not yet recognised in Scotland. To this day he is still a prophet without honour in his own land.

Part 2: Impact on America

The role that John Witherspoon was allowed to play in America enabled him to make a very positive and long lasting contribution to its constitutional structure and its culture. While researching at the Historical Society of Princeton's headquarters in Bainbridge House, Princeton, I found a copy of a *'Senate Joint Resolution No. 3009 of the State of New Jersey'*. On June 16, 1975, a Senator Martindell introduced the resolution designating 1975 as 'John Witherspoon Year', in recognition of the part John Witherspoon had played in the founding of American society. The first clause of the resolution stated:

> Be it resolved by the Senate and General Assembly of the State of New Jersey:
> 1. In tribute to this man of God, patriot, statesman, educator and signer of the Declaration of Independence, and to encourage a return to God, patriotism, fidelity in government, true education and the 'spirit of 1776' the year 1975 is designated as 'John Witherspoon Year' in this State.

Whatever the motivation of the mover, the very fact that John Witherspoon should be selected as the person who epitomises the 'spirit of 1776' is a huge tribute to the lasting respect that is paid to his life and work in America. The justification for this recognition of John Witherspoon is made in a series of statements within the formal paper of the resolution:

Whereas John Witherspoon a Presbyterian Minister of the Gospel ...
Whereas as a patriot, he more than any other Jerseyman, stirred the State for Liberty and resistance to British Tyranny ...
Whereas as a statesman he was a member of the New Jersey Provincial Congress in 1776 (where he was instrumental in forming the first New Jersey Constitution) ...
Whereas as an educator he wielded great influence in the early life of the Republic, his students including a President, vice president, ten cabinet officers, 21 senators, 39 congressmen and 12 governors as well as other public figures ...
Whereas when the Declaration of Independence was submitted to the Continental Congress, and that body wavered, John Witherspoon, the only clergyman at the Congress, declared, 'To hesitate is to consent to our own slavery. That noble instrument should be subscribed this very morning by every pen in this House. Though these gray hairs must soon descend to the sepulcher, I would infinitely rather they descend thither by the hand of the executioner than desert at this crisis the sacred cause of my country'.

Now therefore be it resolved. ...[15]

Here is indisputable evidence that two hundred years after the events in which he was involved, John Witherspoon's part in them is remembered with appreciation and pride.

It is as if it has taken the passage of time to give perspective to Witherspoon's achievements and their lasting effects. For although in the years that immediately followed the signing, he continued to play a significant part in the government of the newly declared United States of America, when he retired from Congress, and the *Peace of 1783* ensued, his immediate political influence naturally lessened, but that influence continued through those whom he had taught and those with whom he had been associated during the years of his activity in government. During his lifetime Witherspoon worked in close association with four men who became in time the first Presidents of the United States of America: George Washington, John Adams, Thomas Jefferson and James Madison. He also had, albeit a more brief, association with Aaron Burr, who became vice President, teaching him for two years at Princeton.

During the war with Britain, Witherspoon held important posts within the inner circle of the revolutionary government. He was the trusted confidante of George Washington, as their correspondence shows. His occasional participation in government on a consultancy basis continued even after he had retired from political life, as the invitation in 1786 to submit a paper on *Money* attests.[16]

Witherspoon made his contribution to the formulation of two out of the three foundation documents of the American Republic: *The Declaration of Independence* and the *Articles of Confederation*. It is likely that he was only prevented from participating in the Constitutional Convention of 1787, that resulted in the drafting of the third and most important document, *The Constitution of the United States of America*, because of a prior commitment to the Synod of New York and Philadelphia. He was unable to attend the Convention of Delegates, who were meeting to consider constitutional matters, and who ended up preparing a draft *Constitution for the United States*, because he had already been invited to draft the constitutional and confessional documents for the Presbyterian Church in America, and by coincidence the Constitutional Convention and the Synod of New York and Philadelphia were scheduled to meet at the same time in Philadelphia. If it had not been for this clash of dates, almost certainly Witherspoon would have had a hand in the drafting and the discussion of *The Constitution of the United States of America*. But if he was not there in person he had a more than able representative of some of his views in his former student and graduate of the College of New Jersey, James Madison, who is acknowledged to have played the principle part in the drafting of the *Constitution*.[17]

All of the events prior to the *Peace of 1783* were promoted by the revolutionary government in which Witherspoon as a Congressman and a member of two highly influential committees, the Board of War and the Committee of Secret Correspondence that became the Committee for Foreign Affairs, played a very prominent part. This work brought him into regular contact with General George Washington, the Commander in Chief of the American forces.[18] There was a particular bond of mutual respect shared by the two men as their correspondence shows, but the events of the winter of 1776-77 drew them even closer together. Washington's campaign, that centred on New Jersey in that winter, is seen as hugely significant by James M. McPherson in his Editor's Note to David Hackett Fischer's *Washington's Crossing*:

> No single day in history was more decisive for the creation of the United States than Christmas 1776. On that night a ragged army of 2,400 colonials crossed the ice-choked Delaware River from Pennsylvania to New Jersey in the teeth of a nor'easter that lashed their boats and bodies with sleet and snow. After marching all night, they attacked and defeated a garrison of 1,500 Hessian soldiers at Trenton. A week later the Americans withstood a fierce British

counter attack at Trenton and stole away overnight to march fifteen miles by back roads to Princeton where they defeated British reinforcements rushing to Trenton.

These victories saved the American Revolution from collapse. Without them there would have been no United States, at least as we know it. Of all the pivotal events in American history, none was more important than what happened on those nine days from December 25, 1776, through January 3, 1777.[19]

The events referred to above was one factor that was responsible for strengthening the bond between Witherspoon and Washington.

The conduct of the British army and its Hessian mercenaries began to give concern in the period just prior to and immediately after Washington's successes at Trenton and Princeton. In December 1776, General Howe gave orders to his troops in New Jersey to supply themselves with food and fuel. This led to foraging parties of soldiers coming into direct contact with the civilian residents. Foraging for the means of sustaining themselves, led to plunder, and then pillaging and rape. Washington received reports of a large number of rapes by British soldiers in the town of Pennington in New Jersey; and the Continental Congress and set up formal investigations. John Witherspoon was involved in gathering evidence which was included in the *Report of the Committee appointed to inquire into the conduct of the enemy, April 18, 1777*, and published in the *Pennsylvania Evening Post* on April 24, 1777.[20] Fischer makes the observation on Washington's conduct at this period:

> much of his time and energy went into relations with members of Congress and leaders of the states. He was beginning to function not only as a military commander but as a leader of the republic.[21]

As a member of the Board of War, and as one who was regularly assigned to deal with specific problems or concerns that arose in the prosecution of the war, Witherspoon's contact with George Washington and his awareness of what he was attempting to do, caused him to become a trusted colleague to the man who was to become the first President of the United States.

Another event brought Washington and Witherspoon even more closely together. While Witherspoon was attending the Synod, in May 1783, the conduct of some mutinous soldiers so alarmed the members of Congress in Philadelphia that they hastily departed for Princeton, where, when Witherspoon returned, he found them convened in Nassau Hall. In August of that year, with Princeton still being used as the seat of government, Washington, in response to the request of Congress, attended their meeting and was presented with a congratulatory address written by John Witherspoon on behalf of the people of the town and the faculty of the College. In the address Witherspoon refers to the significance of Washington's two victories in the locality:

> As the College of New Jersey devoted to the interests of religion and learning was among the first places in America that suffered by the ravages of the enemy, so happily this place and neighbourhood was the scene of one of the most important and seasonable checks which they received in their progress. The surprise of the Hessians at Trenton and the subsequent victory at Princeton redounded much to the honour of the commander who planned and the handful of troops with him which executed the measures. Yet were they even of greater moment to the cause of America than they were brilliant as particular military exploits.[22]

Witherspoon goes on to declare that Washington's appointment as commander of the army was evidence of 'the wisdom and goodness of divine providence', and that 'God himself has raised you up as a fit and proper instrument for establishing and securing the liberty and happiness of these states'. Washington immediately replied to the congratulations, acknowledging the importance of what happened in the winter of 1776-77:

> The prosperous situation of our public affairs, the flourishing State of this place, and the revival of the Seat of Literature from the ravages of war, encrease to the highest degree, the pleasure I feel in visiting (at the return of Peace) the Scene of our Military transactions, and in recollecting the period when the Tide of adversity began to turn, and better fortune to smile upon me.[23]

Witherspoon must have known huge satisfaction when the Commencement celebrations were held in Princeton that year and were attended by the whole Congress, George Washington and the French Minister, La Luzerne. A British officer attended the Commencement exercises incognito and reported back to the British Prime Minister, Lord North. His opinion indicates how the British perceived Witherspoon's place among the revolutionaries:

> An account of the present pace of things in America would be very defective indeed if no mention was made of this political firebrand, who perhaps had not a less share in the Revolution than Washington himself. He poisons the minds of his young students and through

them the continent. He is the intimate friend of the General; and I see no other arguments to support my ideas of Washington's designs, I think his intimacy with a man so different a character with his own (for Washington's private one was amiable) would justify my suspicions.[24]

The status accorded to Witherspoon, is attested by Washington's immediate response to the congratulatory address. The candid acknowledgement of the importance both of the military events that took place there, and the and the value of the College of New Jersey, indicates Washington's appreciation of Witherspoon's involvement with the conflict in the past, and his continued and present support of the American cause. The British observer also attests the important place held by Witherspoon in the revolutionary government. The venom of his words enhance, rather than reduce Witherspoon's reputation, as a prominent contributor to the achievement of America's independence.

Two letters from George Washington confirm the trust he placed in John Witherspoon, but also indicate his willingness to admit him into the most intimate details of his personal life. The first letter, March 10, 1784, a very lengthy epistle (five and a half pages), seeks to enlist Witherspoon's help for the settlement of thirty thousand acres of land in Ohio. The second letter, March 8, 1785, is one in which he is replying to the idea put forward by Witherspoon, 'to write "the Memoirs of my life"'. Washington almost seems to hint that he could do with Witherspoon's help in sorting out his papers so that they might be in order for the suggested biographer, a Mr. Bowie, whom he had promised would have them in the spring. Little episodes such as these show Witherspoon's continued contact with, and his being used as a point of reference, by those who had been involved in the revolutionary struggle alongside him. They, like Witherspoon, wanted to continue to contribute to the development of the emerging nation, and their dealings with him place him among a significant few who helped to create the new republic.[25]

George Washington, having resigned as Commander-in-Chief in December 1783, was to go on to chair the Constitutional Convention in 1787. After the adoption of the *Constitution* by the individual states, he was elected the first President of the United States in 1789, an office he held until he was succeeded in 1797 by John Adams, another of John Witherspoon's former associates in the revolutionary government.

John Witherspoon's involvement with John Adams was not productive of any lasting influence. They had their differences of opinion but underlying these there are signs that each had a respect for certain aspects of the other's character. Adams was surprised by Witherspoon's opposition to his proposal to appoint Thomas Paine, Secretary to the Committee for Foreign Affairs, but he later came to agree (if not on the same grounds) with Witherspoon as to Paine's unsuitability.[26] Adams was suspicious of Witherspoon's relationship with the Compte De Vergennes, believing that Witherspoon was one of those who 'suffered themselves to become Instruments of the Count'. Adams had become very wary of the Foreign Affairs Committee of which John Witherspoon was a member ever since in July, 1781, they had appointed other commissioners: Jay, Laurens and Jefferson to join him in negotiating the peace at Paris. Adams and Vergennes had reached stalemate in their relations, and Witherspoon was convinced that France had to be entrusted with negotiating on America's behalf. Witherspoon had at first resisted the move within Congress to increase the number of plenipotentiaries, believing that it was better to entrust the matter to one person, and had defended Adams against accusations of being obstructive, but later yielded to pressure from La Luzerne.[27] The details of this controversy are being picked over to this day. Suffice it to say here that this very incident is indicative of the hugely influential position then occupied by John Witherspoon. He clearly played a conspicuous and significant part in forming the team who eventually secured the peace with Britain in 1783. As for John Adams, although he had his reservations about Witherspoon's part in the alteration of his instructions, and in assigning others to help him in the negotiations, he did not fall out with Witherspoon and in a letter to Benjamin Rush on May 1812, remembered Witherspoon as a man who had 'Wutt [wit] and sense and taste', and as 'a wise old Scot'.[28] It would seem that Witherspoon had retained the respect of the man who had at his first meeting with him at the College in 1774, had written afterwards that Witherspoon 'was as high a Son of Liberty as any man in America'.[29] Three years later in February 1777, after hearing Witherspoon preach, he recorded in his Diary:

> Yesterday, heard Dr. Witherspoon upon redeeming Time. An excellent Sermon. I find the Doctor better since I have heard him so much in Conversation and in the Senate.

But Adams has a gentle and affectionate poke at Witherspoon as he continues, 'But I perceive that his Attention to civil Affairs has slackened his Memory. It cost him more Pains than heretofore to recollect his Discourse'.[30] Adams's remarks in 1774, clearly express his appreciation of Witherspoon as an American patriot; his further comments in 1777, indicate both how he rated him a good preacher but also acknowledge the fact that he is spending much time on civil affairs. This respect continues to be shown in his later reminiscences of Witherspoon in his letter to

Benjamin Rush nearly forty years after his first meeting with Witherspoon. Now, whereas there is a certain characteristic tartness in Rush's reference to 'our Old Scotch Sachem'; 'Scotch' has pejorative overtones, and 'sachem' refers to an Indian Chief ; Adams's words sound more genuinely affectionate and respectful to Witherspoon.[31] John Adams who succeeded George Washington to become the second President of the United States of America clearly acknowledges the contribution of Witherspoon to the struggle for and achievement of the independence and the autonomy of the American people.

Thomas Jefferson who succeeded Adams in the Presidency in 1801, was another with whom Witherspoon worked in the period leading up to the *Declaration of Independence*, and beyond that to a lesser extent, to the end of the next decade. Even the most cursory comparison of the lives of the Thomas Jefferson and John Witherspoon will reveal how much they have in common in terms of principles, values, concerns and methods of working. But what is unacknowledged, and for which a claim can be made, is what might be seen as Witherspoon's influence upon Jefferson, and the impact that this had on the United States of America.

In December 1768, four months after Witherspoon took up office at the College of New Jersey, Jefferson stood for election as a delegate from Albemarle County to the Virginian House of Burgesses. On May 8, 1769, qualified two years previously as a lawyer, the twenty-six year old Jefferson took the oath of office and began a political life that was to bring him in time to working alongside John Witherspoon in Congress.[32]

Jefferson had begun to meet with a number of the younger burgesses who had a growing concern about the injustices of the system of government under British rule. In this group, which used to meet in the Raleigh Tavern, were Patrick Henry, Richard Henry Lee, Francis Lightfoot Lee and Dabney Carr. They put forward a series of resolutions to the House of Burgesses in March 1773, the result of which caused the formation of a Committee of Correspondence that would become part of an inter-colonial system of committees of correspondence. Jefferson and five of his colleagues were appointed to the committee which was instructed to make contact with all the other colonies. This structure would provide the means of coordinating the activity of the colonists in their endeavours to achieve their ends. It was in response to this move by Jefferson, that John Witherspoon became a member of the Committee of Correspondence for Somerset County in 1774.[33]

In response to the British army's closing of the Boston harbour following the tea protest, Jefferson and his group of friends drafted a resolution to proclaim June 1, 1774, the day on which the *Boston Port Bill* was to become effective, as a day of fasting and prayer. The resolution stated the purpose of this action was: 'to implore heaven to avert us from the evils of civil war, to inspire us with firmness in support of our rights, and to turn the hearts of the king and parliament to moderation and justice'.[34] In that same summer of 1774, Witherspoon's two papers: *Reflections on the Present State of Public Affairs* and *Thoughts on American Liberty*, reflect the same sentiments.[35] Both Jefferson and Witherspoon expressed the view that their British rulers had misunderstood the strength and breadth of the unrest in the colonies. Jefferson was to write to John Randolph, brother of the Speaker of the House, who was to leave for Britain in 1775, that the British government had been deceived by their officers in America, who 'have consistently represented the American opposition as that of a small faction'.[36] Jefferson and Witherspoon were working in different parts of the country but they were making statements that influenced their immediate constituencies and that were sometimes ahead of the current thinking of some of the constituents. In their own separate ways they were sources of influence, but that influence was to become greater when their commitment as Congressmen brought them together in June and July 1776. When Jefferson and Witherspoon met at the Congress that had to deal with Richard Henry Lees's resolution, and eventually Jefferson's draft of the *Declaration of Independence*, they would have recognised just how much they had in common.

Jefferson had prepared a series of resolutions which were adopted by the freeholders of Albemarle County on July 26, 1774, and were intended to be presented by himself and John Walker at the Virginian Convention in Williamsburg. Among the resolutions was one that asserted that the several states of British America were subject only to the laws adopted by their own legislature, and claimed that 'no other legislature whatever may rightfully exercise authority over them'. Only the more modest resolutions pertaining to non-importation and tobacco exports were adopted, the more controversial one fell. However, it was published later as part of a paper, *A Summary View of the Rights of British America*. The resolution had been too extreme for the climate in the House of Burgesses in 1774, but it reveals the development of Jefferson's thinking as being in line with that of Witherspoon's, as Jefferson expounds his view of the colonists' rights of autonomy as based on an initial freedom which they had in Britain:

> Our ancestors, before their emigration to America, were free inhabitants of the British dominions in Europe, and possessed a right, which nature has given to all men, of departing from the country in which chance, not choice has placed them, of going in quest of new habitations, and there establishing new societies, under such laws and regulations as to them shall seem most likely to promote public

happiness. ... Settlements having been thus effected in the wilds of America, the emigrants thought proper to adopt that system of laws under which they hitherto lived in the mother country, and to continue their union with her by submitting themselves to the same common sovereign, who was thereby made the central link connecting the several parts of the empire thus newly multiplied.[37]

This document proved to be a good preparation for the task of drafting the *Declaration of Independence* assigned to Jefferson in July 1776. It was in the experience of the debate and the amendment of his draft that Jefferson would have encountered John Witherspoon. It is clear from an examination of both these documents that the theories of government expounded had been much influenced by John Locke's *Two Treatises of Civil Government*. His reading of Locke, immediately puts Jefferson in the same political camp as Witherspoon, and would have encouraged a rapport between the two men. Other works known to have been read by both men were the *Essays* of Lord Kames, *The Principles of Political Economy* by Sir James Steuart, Adam Ferguson's *An Essay on the History of Civil Society* and the works of Montesquieu.[38]

This background of shared reading and understanding would have provided a firm basis for the mutual respect that emerges from their dealings with each other. If, as is often assumed, Witherspoon was the one to cause the reference to 'Scotch' mercenaries to be deleted from Jefferson's first draft, it is also likely that he contributed to the firming up in more specifically religious terms the opening passage which in the first draft begins:

> We hold these truths to be sacred and undeniable that all men are created equal and independent, that from that equal creation they derive their rights inherent and inalienable among which are the preservation of life, and liberty; the pursuit of happiness ...

In the final draft this reads:

> We hold these truths to be self evident that all men are created equal, *that they are endowed by their Creator* with certain inalienable rights, that among these are life, liberty and the pursuit of Happiness.

But if Witherspoon was involved in tightening up the language, and making use of more specifically religious terminology, he would also have greatly appreciated the Preface to these statements, which referred to men assuming 'the powers ... to which the laws of nature and nature's God entitle them'. In the final draft, the only alterations to the Preface are in a use of more assertive language: 'it becomes necessary for a people to advance from subordination'; becomes 'it becomes necessary to dissolve the political bands which have connected'. The second change is to make the words more emphatically and explicitly religious by the use of capital letters, as in: 'the Powers ... to which the Laws of Nature and of Nature's God entitle them'.[39]

Jefferson writing to Henry Lee, in May 8, 1825, tells of what he attempted to do in the *Declaration of Independence*, asserting that it was:

> Neither aiming at originality of principle or sentiment, nor yet copied from any particular and previous writing, it was intended to be an expression of the American mind, and to give to that expression the proper tone and spirit called for by the occasion.[40]

John Witherspoon was in tune with that 'American mind', as is attested by John Adams in August through September 1774, when he met up with Witherspoon for the first time, or as Witherspoon himself attests in his letter to T*he Scots Magazine*, where he writes: 'a man will become American by residing in the country three months with a prospect of continuing'.[41] It is not too much to claim that Witherspoon was part of that set of writers, preachers and politicians who contributed to that collective understanding to which Jefferson referred in that same latter of 1825, as:

> the harmonizing sentiments of the day, whether expressed in conversation, in letters, printed essays or in the elementary books of public right, as Aristotle, Cicero, Locke, Sydney &c.

Jefferson and Witherspoon had common views on a great number of issues: the philosophy of a natural law, the right of freedom of religious observance, the separation of Church and State, an appreciation of the value of science, slavery, property, and a distrust of the common people's ability to successfully live under democracy without there being some curb upon them.

In Witherspoon's *Lectures on Moral Philosophy* he gives this view of society:

> Society I would define to be an association or compact of any number of persons, to deliver up or abridge their natural rights in order to have the strength of the united body, to protect the remaining, and to bestow others.

He had earlier defined these natural rights as:

> A right to life. A right to employ his faculties for his own use. A right to the things that are common and necessary as air, water, earth. A right to personal liberty. A power over his own life, not to throw it away unnecessarily, but for good reason. A right of private judgement in matters of opinion. A right to associate, if he so incline, with any person or persons whom he can persuade (not force); under this is contained the right to marriage. A right to character, that is to say innocence, (not fame). It is easy to perceive that all these rights belong to a state of natural liberty.[42]

Jefferson endorsed all of these rights, and embraced them on one occasion in a court case in 1770, when he called upon not case law, but the law of nature, when he argued:

> Under the law of nature, all men are born free, everyone comes into the world with a right to his own person, which includes the liberty of moving and using it at his own will.[43]

Closely related to these natural rights is the right of freedom of religious observance, or for that matter conscience. When Jefferson returned to Virginia following the signing of the *Declaration of Independence* he threw himself into the work of legislative reform. *The Virginia Bill of Rights*, presented on June 12, 1776, which had been drafted by George Mason and to which Jefferson had only contributed amendments, declared that:

> all men are equally entitled to the free exercise of religion, according to the dictates of conscience, and it is the mutual duty of all to practice Christian forbearance, love and charity towards each other.[44]

Now although Jefferson agreed with those sentiments, he also believed that the bill did not go far enough, as he would have liked to have seen a total separation of Church and State, and the disestablishment of the Anglican Church. In Virginia, the Dissenters, who had been growing in number, made their protests and petitioned the House of Burgesses. In October 1776, a committee was formed to deal with these 'grievances', and Jefferson was appointed to serve on it. A significant addition was made to the committee when James Madison was appointed to join it. This was the beginning of a friendship and political partnership that was to last the rest of Jefferson's life.[45]

James Madison had graduated from the College of New Jersey in 1771, and had stayed on through the winter of 1771-72, under the personal tutelage of John Witherspoon.[46] Madison was to become another means by which Witherspoon made his influence felt both by Jefferson, and through him, America. However it was not until January 16, 1786, that the *Virginia Statute of Religious Liberty* was established in the State of Virginia. The principles for which Jefferson had striven are exemplified in *Article I*, where any state support of religion by means of taxation is ruled out by the words: 'to compel a man to furnish contributions of money for the propagation of opinions which he disbelieves, is sinful and tyrannical'. The subscription to a particular creedal stance is made unnecessary, and even unlawful by the reassurance that:

> our civil rights have no dependence on our religious opinions, any more than our opinions in physics or geometry; that therefore the proscribing any citizen as unworthy the public confidence by laying upon him an incapacity of being called to offices of trust and emolument, unless he profess or renounce this or that religious opinion, is depriving him injuriously of those privileges and advantages to which in common with his fellow-citizens he has a natural right, ...[47]

In that same *Article* the civil magistrate is denuded of his ability 'to intrude his powers into the field of opinion'. *Article II* includes the words that:

> no man ... shall otherwise suffer on account of his religion, opinions or belief, but that all men shall be free to profess, and by argument to maintain, their opinion in matters of religion.

Thomas Jefferson assisted by James Madison had placed upon the Statute Book of the State of Virginia, the principles long held and expounded by John Witherspoon, in particular those that pertain to the freedom of conscience, allied to the right to be able to worship according to it, and the separation of Church and State.

The reference to Physics and Geometry in the *Virginia Statute of Religious Liberty* is a little reminder of Jefferson's life-long interest in Science, an interest shared by Witherspoon. It was an interest that caused both of these men to take science into account when dealing with belief systems. Witherspoon saw Science and Religion going hand in hand, complementing and enlightening each other. He admired the precise thinking of the natural philosopher, upholding such as Isaac Newton. He encouraged a scientific understanding of the universe, and to that end equipped the College with an Orrery constructed by David Rittenhouse.[48]

Another area of common interest and to a certain extent shared opinion, was that of Slavery. Jefferson was ahead of his time in wanting the emancipation of those already enslaved and in planning for the time when slavery would be abolished, but he was slow to put forward legislation that would have brought these things about. His biographer, Noble E. Cunningham Jnr., attributes this to Jefferson's belief in the racial differences between white and black people. Jefferson believed that there were radical differences determined by race and that the whites were superior to the black in physical and mental abilities to such an extent that if freedom were to be granted to black people it would be impossible for black and white to live together peaceably in society and that any such experiment would end in conflict. Jefferson's reasoning from a racial understanding went against his philosophy that asserted the moral equality of all men, and therefore that the moral rights of black and white are the same. Cunningham writes:

> In an Appendix to the Notes on Virginia, Jefferson published his draft of a *Constitution for Virginia* containing a provision that all persons born after Dec. 31, 1800 would be free. Prepared in 1783 in expectation of a constitutional convention that was never called, that proposition received no serious consideration.

There is no evidence that Jefferson ever tabled the motion and in his biography, he offers the explanation: 'it was found that the public mind would not yet bear the proposition'.[49]

Witherspoon too, sat uneasily to the subject of slavery. Like Jefferson, he believed in the right of all men to be free, but he tried to justify slavery on the grounds that it was permitted in the time of the *Old Testament* patriarchs. But his arguments are never convincing, and I doubt if he even believed them himself. Like Jefferson, he too was a slave owner, and seems to excuse himself on the grounds of the acceptance of slavery by the slaves themselves, and on the acceptance of the practice as part of the inequalities built into the nature of things. His argument is extremely weak and wavering:

> The practice [of slavery] seems to be countenanced in the law of Moses, where rules are laid down for their treatment ... I do not think there lies any necessity on those who found men in a state of slavery to make them free to their own ruin ... But it is very doubtful whether any original cause of servitude can be defended.[50]

The question of slavery remained unresolved by Witherspoon, and when he died, two slaves were listed as part of his estate.[51] It is perhaps significant that in Witherspoon's *Lectures on Moral Philosophy* he deals with the subject of 'property' immediately after his very unsatisfactory and unconvincing treatment of the subject of 'slavery'.

Witherspoon sees the acquisition of private property as beneficial to society, and as something that is 'essentially necessary and founded upon the reason of things and public utility'. He reasons that without private property 'no laws would be sufficient to compel universal industry', and that it would encourage 'idleness and sloth among many who would live off the labour of others'. He decries the idea of common property as 'Utopian, chimerical and impracticable'.[52] Jefferson also appreciated the place and the value of property in establishing and maintaining a republic. Although he was not present at the first Continental Congress in September 1774, its delegates were aware of his views, as his *A Summary View of the Rights of British America* was circulated among them, and in it he expounded his theory of natural rights.[53] He undoubtedly played a part in influencing that Congress to adopt a declaration of rights among which was the right to 'life, liberty and property'. Later, on June 12, 1776, he successfully presented the *Virginia Bill of Rights* which declared in its first *Article*:

> That all men are by nature equally free and independent, and have certain inherent rights, of which when they enter into a state of society, they cannot by any compact deprive or divest their posterity; namely the enjoyment of life and liberty, *with the means of acquiring and possessing property* and pursuing and obtaining happiness and safety.[54]

Jefferson wanted the extension of the franchise, and as the right to vote was then connected with property, the extension of the property owning base would mean the broadening of the franchise, and the reduction of the power of the land owning aristocracy. To this end Jefferson proposed to the Virginian Constitutional Convention 'that persons not owning fifty acres of land should be granted enough land to raise their holdings to that minimum amount'. His motion failed. Jefferson then set about to abolish the system of entail, which perpetuated the system of the same land being held by generation after generation of the same family. It was to take some ten years before he succeeded with the assistance of James Madison in changing the law, with the repeal of the laws of entail and abolishing the law of primogeniture in 1785.[55]

One very important attitude shared by Jefferson and Witherspoon was a certain reservation about democracy, because of their distrust of the of the common people's ability to adequately fulfil the role that they had to play within it. During the committee work and exchange of views in Congress, Jefferson must have become aware of Witherspoon's attitude as stated in *Lecture XII* of his *Moral Philosophy* course:

> Pure democracy cannot subsist long, nor be carried into departments of state - it is very subject to caprice and the madness of popular race. They are also very apt to chuse a favourite, and vest him with such power as overthrows their own liberty - examples, Athens and Rome.[56]

There is sometimes a glimpse of the elitist in Witherspoon, and when it is combined with his belief in the depravity of human nature, he is predisposed to distrust the common people, or as he on another occasion describes them, 'the multitude', who, he says 'are exceedingly apt to be deceived by demagogues and ambitious persons'. His way of dealing with this factor is by a system of checks and balances: 'every good form of government must be complex, so that one principle may check the other'.[57] Jefferson was born into a well to do family who were well established in Virginian society. His father, a justice of the peace, owning a plantation dependent on slave labour, ensured that his son received as good an education as possible. Encouraged by this, after his father's death, Jefferson went to William and Mary College, and then on to study law for five years with George Wythe, all of which might have led him to settle to a pleasant life as a legal practitioner in the congenial small town atmosphere of Williamsburg. Those early years did not bring him into much contact with the ordinary working man. During the time of the convention on the constitution, Jefferson expressed the view to Edmund Pendleton that reveals his lack of trust in the judgement of ordinary people: 'I have ever generally observed that a choice by the people themselves is not generally distinguished for its wisdom'. Jefferson would have preferred, and did indeed propose, that the senate should be chosen by the lower house, whereas the constitution agreed, provided for the senate being elected by the popular vote of the districts. As Jefferson's biographer says: 'in this instance, the convention rather than Jefferson seemed to be on the side of greater democracy'.[58] I suspect that in Witherspoon, Jefferson found someone who would readily acquiesce in his views on the role of the people in a democracy.

In considering Witherspoon's possible influence on Jefferson, one aspect of their parallel thinking that might have had an influence on the latter is that they were both drafters of documents and hard working committee men, rather than orators and dramatic leaders. Over and over again, as previous chapters have shown, Witherspoon was called upon to produce a document for discussion or presentation. *The Fast Day Proclamation for the Synod of New York and Philadelphia* in 1775, and the paper on *Money* in 1786, are but two examples.[59] As for his public speaking, he himself offered the advice to his students to speak only when they had something to say. His writing too was governed by one of his dictums delivered in *Lecture II* of his course on *Eloquence* when he urged his students: 'to learn to give a naked account of facts with simplicity and precision'.[60] It seems that Jefferson shared much with Witherspoon, as John Adams recollects how Jefferson brought to Congress:

> a reputation for literature, science, and a happy talent for composition. Writings of his were handed about, remarkable for the peculiar felicity of expression.

Adams also remembered how seldom Jefferson actually spoke in Congress: 'During the time I sat with him in Congress, I never heard him utter three sentences together'. Adams however, recalled that Jefferson 'was so prompt, frank, explicit and decisive upon committees and in conversation … that he soon seized upon my heart'.[61] Jefferson's capabilities in drafting were soon recognised by Congress, where in the first six weeks of its meeting in 1775, he had a leading role in drafting two major state papers: *Declaration of the Causes and Necessity for taking up Arms*, which he drafted along with John Dickenson, and the *Reply to Lord North's Proposals*.[62]

It is obvious that, in the day-to-day detail of Jefferson's work in Congress, Witherspoon could not be a direct influence upon Jefferson, but as they worked together and contributed to the debates on specific documents such as *The Declaration of Independence* and the *Articles of Confederation*, some of the shared opinions, attitudes and convictions could only have reinforced Jefferson in his commitment to them. This influence of Witherspoon was to be continued in Jefferson's later work through his close collaboration with, and admiration for, James Madison who had been taught by Witherspoon and who had imbibed many of the College President's views and opinions.

When Thomas Jefferson became President in 1801, his Vice President in his first term from 1801-1805, was Aaron Burr, who as a classmate of James Madison, had been taught by Witherspoon at the College of New Jersey. He was there for only two years before leaving to study law at Lichfield, in Connecticut. Like many young men of the time his studies were interrupted by the war, and 1775 found him in the army of General Benedict Arnold in its expedition into Canada. Burr distinguished himself at the battle of Quebec and was for a brief time appointed to George Washington's staff. He reached the rank of Lieutenant Colonel, and commanded a regiment that suffered heavy casualties at the battle of Monmouth in June 28, 1778. Burr suffered a stroke, and had to retire on health grounds in 1779. Despite all these adventures he was only twenty-three years of age. Returning to study law again, he was admitted to the Bar at Albany in 1782, and after the British left, he began to practice law in New York City. His later life was equally colourful, including a duel which resulted in the death of his opponent, Alexander Hamilton, one of his political rivals. Burr was involved in political intrigue, was indicted for treason and acquitted. He died in 1836, aged ninety. Although his name appears on all the lists of those who had been taught at the College of New Jersey by Witherspoon and later distinguished themselves, it would be wrong to claim that Witherspoon had any effect upon the course of his life other than perhaps to have offered a sympathetic encouragement to him and all the younger students in their revolutionary aspirations, prior to the outbreak of hostilities at Concord and Lexington in 1775.[63]

The name of James Madison comes increasingly into the story of Thomas Jefferson and with it the extension of the influence of John Witherspoon.[64] Madison studied at the College of New Jersey from the year of Witherspoon's arrival in 1768, until he graduated in 1771. He then remained for a further six months or so over the autumn and winter of 1771-72, to study under the personal tutelage of Witherspoon. At this time it is thought that among other things, he was studying Hebrew, while considering entering the ministry of the church, and was being tutored by Witherspoon with that in mind. But whatever his thoughts of a future career, those months under the close supervision of Witherspoon would have given Madison the opportunity of imbibing much more from his master than the subject in which he was being instructed.[65]

After over three years of study at Princeton, Madison would be well aware of the importance of education, and particularly of education in relation to the citizenry of any country that wanted to proceed towards the people having a share in the governing of a democracy. As the spirit of revolution grew in the years immediately following his graduation, it would become clear to Madison just how important an educated citizenry would be to a democratic republic.

When Thomas Jefferson left the Congress in 1776 to return to Virginia, he began to work as head of a committee to revise the laws by which the State of Virginia was governed. In January 1777, the committee had met to apportion the work, and for the next two and a half years

Jefferson worked on the production of Bills that were fed into the Virginia legislature for discussion and decision. Because of the huge amount of work involved it all took time. Nevertheless between 1776 and 1779 Jefferson presented more Bills than any other member of the Virginia Assembly.[66] Such was the extent of the detailed changes involved, it was not until 1786 that some of the Bills were eventually passed. One such Bill, first presented in 1778, and again in 1780, was 'For the more general diffusion of knowledge'. It was this *Bill on Education* that was attempted to be steered through the House by James Madison in 1786, while Jefferson was on government business in France. It was a far reaching *Bill* that sought to provide each county within the state with free schooling for its children. By a system of elementary and grammar schools it was hoped that each grammar school, in alternate years, would be able to send their best scholar to the College of William and Mary for three years at the state's expense. The *Bill* did not pass into statute however and it was not until 1796 that any plan for the establishment of public schools was passed.[67] But the significant fact is that James Madison, as Chairman of the Committee of Revisors submitted it to the House as part of their plan to make the laws of Virginia consistent with republicanism. Taught by Witherspoon, Madison knew that it would be essential for the continuance of republican values to have constituents who could think for themselves, and value the freedoms that the system had won for them. In *Lecture XII* in *Moral Philosophy*, Witherspoon describes democracy as 'the nurse of eloquence because when the multitude have the power, persuasion is the only way to govern them'.[68] Education therefore is the tool that will make democracy work. If people have the power they will need to be educated in order to correctly exercise the power to maintain their liberty.

Another concept that Madison would learn at first hand from Witherspoon was the need to be realistic about the nature of man. Witherspoon's theology of man's depravity is initially derived from his acceptance of the *Genesis* story of Adam's fall from the status of the creature God had made, to the creature he had become, condemned to live in sin and to perpetuate that sin because of his initial disobedience to God. Witherspoon's *Biblical* interpretation was re-enforced by what he asserted was the evidence provided by man's wrongdoing throughout history. Madison applied this understanding of humanity to his plans for government. In the *Federalist Papers* Madison writes: 'What is government itself but the greatest of all reflections on human nature. If men were angels no government would be necessary'.[69] Further, Madison was aware that in legislating for human beings he had to take cognisance of their capacity to do evil and that laws must be made to combat this.

Madison realised with the help of his early teaching from Witherspoon, that:

> every good form of government must be complex, so that one principle may check another ... it is folly to expect that a state should be upheld by integrity in all who have a share in managing it. They must be balanced, that when everyone draws on his own interest or inclination, there may be an over-poise upon the whole.

Witherspoon illustrates this from the British system:

> The King has the power of making war and peace, but the Parliament have the levying and distribution of money, which is a sufficient restraint.[70]

Expressing an opinion which is consonant with this, Madison writes in the spring of 1787 a memorandum on *Vices of the Political System in the United States*, stating his concern about the multiplicity and mutability of the laws in the states and the need for restraining the majority 'from unjust violations of the rights of the minority or of individuals'.[71] Madison was concerned that the unchecked sovereignty of the people was threatening republicanism itself, and demonstrated the need for a stronger central government.

In expressing these fears, Madison is again reflecting Witherspoon's view that acknowledges democracy's shortcomings. In *Moral Philosophy, Lecture XII* Witherspoon betrays a sneaking admiration for Aristocracy as a form of government, declaring that:

> Aristocracy has the advantage of all the others for wisdom in [its] deliberations, that is to say, a number of persons from the first rank must be supposed by their consultations to be able to discover the public interest.

Witherspoon here again displays his elitist tendency, although he quickly goes on to acknowledge the faults of Aristocracy as a form of government, and severely criticises it: 'Aristocracy always makes vassals of the inferior ranks, who have no hand in government'. But although favouring Democracy he is also aware of its weaknesses, seeming to believe that it is lacking in wisdom and limited in its application, and claiming that it 'cannot be carried too far into departments of state'.[72] So although Witherspoon is basically in favour of democracy, there is still a hankering after the secrecy of Monarchy, and what he perceives to be the wisdom of the 'persons of first rank' in an Aristocracy, as against the lack of it in the multitude of a Democracy. Madison in presenting a case for the new *Constitution of the United States* in 1787, in a series of articles that have become known as the *Federalist Papers*, takes his cue from Witherspoon's insistence on being mindful of men's depravity and of the need for checks and balances in any system of government, and therefore of the need to take account of these factors in any legislative programme. He writes:

> In framing a government which is to be administered by men over men, the great difficulty lies in this: you must first enable the government to control the governed; and in the next place oblige it to control itself. A dependence on the people is, no doubt, the primary control on the government; but experience has taught mankind the necessity of auxiliary precautions. This policy of supplying, by opposite and rival interests, the defect of better motives, might be traced through the whole system of human affairs, private as well as public.[73]

The above passage provides clear evidence of the direct influence of Witherspoon's teaching on James Madison, a teaching that so influenced his thinking that it affected the very formulation of the *Constitution of the United States of America.*

One further concept that Madison imbibed from Witherspoon was the need for a separation between Church and State. Madison was made aware of the need for religious liberty through Witherspoon's teachings. Witherspoon went as far as he could in asserting the absolute necessity of having religious liberty, the freedom to worship according to conscience, without fear of interference from the State. In his *Moral Philosophy Lectures* Witherspoon asserted that 'every one should judge for himself in matters of religion'.[74] Yet Witherspoon wanted the protection of the State for this religious freedom and upheld the attitude that; 'The magistrate ought to defend the rights of conscience, and tolerate all in their religious sentiments, that are not injurious to their neighbours'. This toleration of which he spoke was extended to all religious denominations including the Roman Catholic. Witherspoon acknowledges that 'Popery is not tolerated in Great Britain; because they profess entire subjugation to a foreign power, the see of Rome'. But Witherspoon steps back from this position and implies that it does not apply in America, pointing out that Roman Catholicism is tolerated in Holland, and expresses the opinion that 'we ought in general to guard against persecution on a religious account as much as possible, because such as hold absurd tenets are seldom dangerous'. He concludes: 'Papists are tolerated in Holland without danger to liberty and although not properly tolerated, they are connived at in Britain'.[75] However ungenerous his opinion of Roman Catholics is, he admits that toleration is the best policy, because he sees the primacy of religious freedom. He believes firmly in this, and in the sermon *The Dominion of Providence* states the extreme position that, 'There is not a single instance in history in which civil liberty was lost and religious liberty preserved entire'. In his mind, civil and religious liberties are inseparable. For each to exist they need each other. He ends his *Dominion of Providence* sermon with the plea:

> God grant that in America true religion and civil liberty may be inseparable, and that the unjust attempts to destroy the one may in the issue tend to the support and establishment of both.[76]

Witherspoon did not want to see any church given the recognition by the State as the Established Church, nor did he want to seek favour for his own denomination, and in this he was expressing an ecumenical view far ahead of his time.

When Madison returned from the Congress in 1776, he was elected to the provincial convention that met in Williamsburg to discuss George Mason's, *Virginia Bill of Rights*. He successfully moved an amendment that replaced Mason's clause advocating tolerance, with a much more forthright defense of people's right to practice their religion according to their conscience.[77] Mason had proposed a clause that rather weakly asserted: 'that all men shou'd enjoy the fullest Toleration in the Exercise of Religion'; which Madison replaced with the quite unambiguous and much stronger: 'all men are equally entitled to the free exercise of religion'. In its complete form, Article 16 of the *Virginia Bill of Rights* states:

> That religion, or the duty which we owe to our Creator, and the manner of discharging it, can be directed only by reason and conviction, not by force or violence; and therefore all men are equally entitled to the free exercise of religion, according to the dictates of conscience; and that it is the mutual duty of all to practise Christian forbearance, love, and charity towards each other.[78]

That the amendment detailed above was the only amendment submitted by Madison for the alteration of George Mason's proposals anent religious freedom indicates that Madison was in broad agreement with the rest of Article 16. Madison's amendment brought Article 16 into line with Witherspoon's strongly held view of the absolute right to act with freedom of conscience. Witherspoon declares in his *Moral Philosophy, Lecture X*, that 'men are originally and by nature equal and consequently free'. In that same lecture he had expounded the rights that belonged to men in this 'state of natural liberty' and from among the eight were two that form the basis of Madison's clause on religious liberty: '(4) A right to personal liberty' and '(6) A right of private judgement in matters of opinion'. Also in that *Lecture* Witherspoon argues that even although:

> as some observe, that few nations or societies in the world have had their constitutions formed on the principles of liberty ... this is no just argument against natural liberty and the rights of mankind ... Reason teaches natural liberty and common utility recommends it.

In that state of natural liberty, Witherspoon argues in his *Moral Philosophy, Lecture XIV*, that 'everyone should judge for himself in matters of religion'.[79] Madison in supporting *Article 16* in its amended form, is clearly following Witherspoon's line of thinking, that religion 'can be directed only by reason and conviction and not by force', and that it is logical to demand that men have the right to live with the freedom to exercise it according to their conscience. It would be too much to claim that in Madison, Witherspoon was virtually appearing on a wider stage, but undoubtedly many of the lessons taught by the President to the younger man helped him formulate his ideas, and to engage in a nation changing exercise of helping to steer through the *Constitution of the United States*.

Harry M. Ward in *The American Revolution, Nationhood Achieved 1763-1788* asserts the huge contribution that James Madison made to the making of the *Constitution*:

> The prime movers of the Constitutional Convention [of 1787], the men who carried the weight of the discussions were James Madison, Gouverneur Morris and James Wilson for the nationalists, and Roger Sherman, Luther Martin and William Paterson, for the local interests. Madison spoke 161 times, Morris 163, Wilson 168 and Sherman 138. William Pierce of Georgia left an undated memorandum sizing up the characteristic ability of each of his fellow delegates ... James Madison, age 36: 'In the management of every great question he evidently took the lead in the Convention ... He always comes forward the best informed man of any point in debate'.[80]

Such was the contribution of James Madison to the Constitutional Convention according to an eyewitness.

It is not claimed that the final document came from Madison's hand. He himself acknowledges this in a letter to Jared Sparks many years later:

'the finish given to the style and arrangement fairly belongs to the pen of Mr. Morris'.[81] But although the finish was Morris's, Madison's contribution to the philosophy and the politics of the *Constitution* is enormous and in much of his understanding he is never far away from the thinking of his old teacher, John Witherspoon. From the opening words, 'We the people of the United States ...' the *Constitution* embodies many of the principles expounded by John Witherspoon, principles that determined his political activity in the years in which he served as a congressman, and that are reflected in his writings. James Madison is not a spokesman for Witherspoon, but a man who had by dint of continuing his studies and developing his own experience absorbed much of what Witherspoon had taught, and used it as a basis upon which to build and extrapolate from the thinking of his former teacher, theories and systems that were of his own devising. He was of course to go on from seeing the *Constitution* adopted by all the States, to become Secretary of State in Thomas Jefferson's administration from 1801-1809 and then President himself in 1809-1817, thereby becoming the fourth President who, in his earlier career, had worked alongside John Witherspoon.[82] Of the four, Madison is perhaps the one most influenced by Witherspoon, but it can be claimed with some justification that the influence of John Witherspoon's philosophy, and to a certain extent his theology, together with his life and work, was further spread by them and had a long lasting effect on American structures and society.

The focus in the immediately previous section has been on the considerable influence exerted by John Witherspoon as is evidenced by the thrust of the work of James Madison. It is also pertinent to note that Witherspoon signalled his approval to the major work of Madison by signing the ratification of the *Constitution* as a delegate of Somerset County on December 18, 1787. In bringing forward the evidence of this, Jeffry H. Morrison quotes in approval Douglass Adair's conclusion on the relationship between James Madison and John Witherspoon:

> Since James Madison became one of the chief architects of our political democracy ... his sojourn at Nassau Hall under the tutelage of the learned Dr. John Witherspoon was of incalculable importance to the destiny of the United States.[83]

I began this attempt at assessing the impact of John Witherspoon's life and work in the United States, by drawing attention to the impressive list of men educated under him at the College of New Jersey, who had gone on to careers in professional, public and political life. At the top of the list were President James Madison and Vice President Aaron Burr, but many hundreds of his students went on to careers in education, becoming teachers, head masters, and College Lecturers, carrying with them the educational theories and practices advocated by Witherspoon. The Church too, felt his influence through the many ministers who had trained under him and who reflected his theological emphasis. Many of his former students entered politics, attracted as he had been, with the vision of political activity as the best means of getting things done. Throughout these different disciplines his influence was at work by means of the common sense philosophy and pragmatism that was so much a part of his way of being. His life was like a stone thrown into a pond, the ripples on the surface emanating from the centre and reaching out to the far edges, but the effect of his life was not confined to the surface ripples. He stirred the depths by his challenging of the established patterns of life in the Colonies, by his commitment to revolution, and to an emergent new form of government that would better protect the people. John Witherspoon's unwavering support of the American struggle for Independence and his work that helped in time to create a government 'of the people, by the people, and for the people'[84] should cause him to be remembered as a respected Signer of the *Declaration of Independence* and one of the Founding Fathers of the republic that is the United States of America.

***

References and Notes

Chapter 1 *Parish Minister*

1. *Statutary Instruments*, 1993 No 558 (S. 77) Education, Scotland. University of Paisley (Scotland) Order of Council 1993. Made: 8th March 1993. Laid before Parliament: 11th March 1993. Coming into force: 1st April 1993.
2. *Memorial of the College of New Jersey*, John Witherspoon Collection, Princeton University Library, Box 2, Folder 2.
3. Varnum Lansing Collins, *President Witherspoon: A Biography*, 2 vols (Princeton, 1925), I, pp. 24-25.
4. Collins, I, pp. 5-10.
5. Alexander Carlyle, *Anecdotes and Characters of the Times*, Edited and with an Introduction by James Kinsley (London, 1973), pp. 34-35.
6. Carlyle, p. 49.
7. Collins, I, p. 10.
8. Collins, I, p.11.
9. Collins, I, pp. 13-20; Carlyle, 16, 22-25.
10. Thomas P. Miller, 'Witherspoon, Blair and the Rhetoric of Civic Humanism', in *Scotland and America in the Age of Enlightenment*, edited by Richard B. Sher and Jeffrey R. Smitten (Edinburgh, 1990), p.104; and Collins, I, 18.
11. L. Gordon Tait, *The Piety of John Witherspoon: Pew, Pulpit, and Public Forum* (Louisville, Kentucky, 2001), Introduction, pp. 5-6.; and Appendix B, pp. 195-201.
12. Collins, I, p. 18.
13. William Robert Scott, *Francis Hutchison: His Life, Teaching and Position in the History of Philosophy*, first published Cambridge, 1900, Reprinted by Thoemmes Press, (Bristol, 1992), pp. 85-95.
14. Collins, I, p. 21.
15. Scott, quoting from a letter of Francis Hutcheson, August 5, 1743, p. 88.
16. Scott, p. 89; Collins, I, p. 21.
17. Bruce Lenman, *The Jacobite Risings in Britain 1689-1746* (Aberdeen, 1995), pp.245-46.
18. Collins I, pp. 21-22.
19. Bruce Lenman, *The Jacobite Clans of the Great Glen 1650-1784* (Aberdeen, 1995), p. 157.
20. James Fergusson, *John Fergusson: 1727-1750* (London, 1948), pp. 141-44.

21. Collins, I, pp. 22-23; and Richard B. Sher, *Church and University in the Scottish Enlightenment: The Moderate Literati of Edinburgh* (Edinburgh, 1985), p. 42.
22. Collins, I, p. 24.
23. *The Cairn of Lochwinnoch Manuscripts* Vol. XXX, Part ii, p. 92.
24. See Chapter 3.
25. David Daiches, 'Style Périodique and Style Coupé: Hugh Blair and the Scottish Rhetoric of American Independence', in *Scotland and America in the Age of the Enlightenment*, edited by Richard B. Sher and Jeffrey Smitten, pp. 209-26.
26. Blaise Pascal, *Pascal's Pensées*, Translated by W. F. Trotter and Introduction by T. S. Eliot (London, 1956), Introduction p. xiv.
27. François Rabelais, *Gargantua and Pantagruel*, Translated and with an Introduction by J. M. Cohen (Harmondsworth, 1957), p. 20.
28. *1707 Act for the Security of the Church of Scotland*, in Gordon Donaldson's *Scottish Historical Documents* (Edinburgh and London, 1974), p. 276.
29. J. H. S. Burleigh, *A Church History of Scotland* (OUP, 1960), p. 279.
30. *1690 Acts Establishing Presbyterian Government and Transferring Patronage*, in Donaldson, p. 260.
31. *1560-61 First Book of Discipline*, in Donaldson, p. 127.
32. *1578 Second Book of Discipline*, in Donaldson, p. 145.
33. Burleigh, p. 245.
34. *1661 Act Rescissory; Act Restoring Episcopal Government*, in Donaldson, pp. 225-27.
35. See reference 30 above.
36. Burleigh, pp. 279-82 for a fuller account.
37. Richard B. Sher, *Church and University in the Scottish Enlightenment: The Moderate Literati of Edinburgh* (Edinburgh, 1985), p. 51.
38. Carlyle, pp. 124-30: see also Sher, ibid, p.50.
39. Sher, pp. 52-53.
40. Burleigh, p. 284.
41. Sher, pp. 52-53.
42. Sher, p. 54.

Chapter 2 *Ecclesiastical Characteristics*

1. *Ecclesiastical Characteritics or the Arcana of Church Policy, Being an Humble Attempt to open up the Mystery of Moderation wherein is shewn: A Plain and easy way to the Character of a Moderate Man, as at present in repute in the Church of Scotlan*d, The Third Edition,

Corrected and Enlarged, Glasgow, MDCCLIV. The Advertisement tells: it was 1st published October 1753, 2nd edition mid December 1753, and 3rd edition May 1754.

2. Jonathan Swift, *Gulliver's Travels,* (London, 1985); Laurence Sterne, *The Life and Opinions of Tristam Shandy, Gentleman,* (Harmondsworth, 1986).
3. *Ecclesiastical Characteristics,* Advertisement, A2.
4. ibid, p. 15.
5. See Thomas D. Kennedy, 'William Leechman, Pulpit Eloquence and the Glasgow Enlightenment' in *The Glasgow Enlightenment*, Edited by Andrew Hook and Richard B. Sher, (East Linton, 1995), pp.57-58; also William Robert Scott, *Francis Hutcheson: His Life, Teaching and Position in the History of Philosophy* (Bristol, 1992), pp. 92-95.
6. *Ecclesiastical Characteristics*, p.17.
7. 'A Serious Apology for the Ecclesiastical Characteristics' in *Essays on Important Subjects* by John Witherspoon 4 vols (Edinburgh, 1805), vol I, p. 232. Varnum Lansing Collins dates the publication of this pamphlet to 1763; see *President Witherspoon: A Biography* 2vols (Princeton, 1925), I, p. 63.
8. *Ecclesiastical Characteristics*, p. 20.
9. ibid, p. 22.
10. ibid, p. 30.
11. ibid, p. 32.
12. ibid, p. 35-36.
13. Bertrand Russell, *History of Western Philosophy*, (London, 1980), p. 564.
14. *Ecclesiastical characteristics*, p. 36.
15. ibid, p. 37.
16. ibid, p. 39.
17. ibid, p. 40.
18. ibid, p. 41.
19. ibid, p. 42.
20. ibid, p. 44.
21. ibid, p. 44.
22. ibid, p. 44.
23. J. H. S. Burleigh, *A Church History of Scotland*, (OUP, 1960), pp. 283-84.
24. *Ecclesiastical Characteristics*, p. 44.
25. ibid, p. 52.
26. ibid, p. 52.
27. Burleigh, p. 283-84.

28. *Ecclesiastical Characteristics*, p. 55.
29. See *The Works of the Rev. John Witherspoon*, (Philadelphia, 1800), 'Lectures on Eloquence, Lecture VII,' p. 204, where he admits: 'Recluse students and professed scholars will be able to discover truth, and to defend it, or to write moral precepts with clearness and beauty; but they are seldom equal, for the tender and pathetic, to those who have been much in what is called the *world...*'.
30. *Ecclesiastical Characteristics*, p. 57.
31. ibid, p. 60.
32. ibid, p. 60.
33. ibid, Advertisement, In Third Edition, (Glasgow, 1754).
34. 'Speech in the Synod of Glasgow: When I was accused of being the author of Ecclesiastical Characteristics', in *Essays* Vol. III, p. 247.
35. 'A Serious Apology for the Ecclesiastical Characteristics', in *Essays* I, p. 283.

Chapter 3   *The Stage*

1. Adrienne Scullion, 'The Eighteenth Century', in *A History of Scottish Theatre*, edited by Bill Findlay, (Edinburgh University Press, 1998), pp. 98-106.
2. John Witherspoon, *Serious Enquiry into the Nature and Effects of the Stage: Being an attempt to show that contributing to the Support of a Public Theatre is inconsistent with the Character of a Christian* (Glasgow, 1757), Advertisement p. A.
3. See Chapter 1.
4. Varnum Lansing Collins, *President Witherspoon: A Biography,* 2 vols (Princeton, 1925), I, pp. 42-45.
5. ibid, I, pp. 25, 47-48.
6. *Serious Enquiry*, p.5. Note Witherspoon's use of capital letters.
7. ibid, p. 8.
8. Note. *The Interlinear Greek-English New Testament: The Nestle Greek Text with a Literal English Translation* by the Reverend Alfred Marshall, D. Litt. (London, 1958), pp. 755 and 918, offers two translations of the same word. In Galations 5.21 *komoi* is part of a phrase *methai-komoi* which is translated literally as 'drunken revellings'; and in 1 Peter 4.3 *komois* is translated literally as 'carousals'. See also *Analytical Concordance to the Holy Bible* by Robert Young, LL.D., Eighth Edition (London, 1961); under 'Revelling - revelry, wantonness, (from Lat. *Comus*), *komus*. Gal. 5.21 Envyings, murders, drunkenness, revellings; 1 Pe. 4.3 when we walked in...revellings, banquet.', p.814. In neither scripture passage

in the Greek text is there any reference whatsoever to the public theatre, nor is there even any allusion to it by the context of the words.

9. *Serious Enquiry*, pp. 14-17.
10. ibid, p. 19.
11. ibid, p. 72.
12. Adrienne Scullion, pp. 93-95.
13. ibid, p. 94.
14. *Serious Enquiry*, p. 30.
15. ibid, p. 31.
16. ibid, p. 45.
17. ibid, p. 46.
18. ibid, p. 48.
19. ibid, p. 48.
20. ibid, p. 51.
21. ibid, p. 63.
22. ibid, p. 64.
23. ibid, p. 65.
24. ibid, p. 71.

Chapter 4   *Theology*

1. *Sermons on Practical Subjects to which is added A Farewell Discourse delivered at Paisley in April and May 1768 by John Witherspoon D.D.*, Glasgow MDCCLXVIII.
2. Sermon I, p. 5.
3. 'The most beautiful system of the sun, planets and comets, could only proceed from the counsel and dominion of an intelligent and powerful Being'; in Isaac Newton's, *The Principia*, Translated by Andrew Motte, (New York, 1995), p. 440. The very titles of William Derham's two books indicate the theology he expounds within them: *Physico-Theology; or a Demonstration of the Being and the Attributes of God from his Creation* (1713); and *Astro-Theology: or a Demonstration of the Being and Attributes of God from a Survey of the Heavens* (1715). The editions examined by me were the third edition of the former (1758), and the seventh edition of the latter (1757).
4. Sermon I, p. 11.
5. *The Scots Magazine*, June 1768, in Vol. 30, pp. 281-336; p. 300 and p. 307.
6. *Sermon II*, pp. 36-53.
7. *Sermon III*, pp. 54-82.

8. *Sermon III*, p. 66.
9. James Hervey, 'Among the Tombs', in *Meditations and Contemplations* (London, 1855), pp. 61-62.
10. *Essay on the Connection between the Doctrine of Justification by the Imputed Righteousness of Christ, and Holiness of Life; with some reflections upon the Reception which that Doctrine hath generally met with in the World*, Glasgow; Printed by John Bryce and David Paterson MDCCLVI. Referred to in *The Works of John Witherspoon* (Philadelphia, 1800) as *Essay on Regeneration*.
11. *The Confession of Faith*, Chapter VI, Of the Fall of Man, of Sin, and of the Punishment thereof.
12. *Sermon IV*, pp. 83-141.
13. *Sermon V*, pp. 142-68.
14. *Sermon VI*, pp. 169-202.
15. *Sermon VII*, pp. 203-34.
16. *Sermon VIII*, pp. 235-60.
17. *Sermon IX*, pp. 261-323.
18. *The New English Bible*, (OUP, 1970), New Testament, Acts 20. 26-27, p. 176; *Good News Bible*, The Bible Societies, (London, 1976), New Testament, Acts 20. 26-27, p. 178.
19. Compare the slightly earlier work of Thomas Watson, *A Body of Practical Divinity* (1692), that went through many editions down to the twentieth century; or that of John Russel, in his *The Reason of our Lord's Agony in the Garden and the influence of Just Views on them on Universal Holiness* (1787). Russel was a contemporary of Robert Burns (1759-96) who referred to him in his letters and poetry. More details of Thomas Watson and John Russel will be found in J. Walter McGinty's *Robert Burns and Religion*, Ashgate, (Aldershot and Burlington, 2003), pp. 42-45, and 172-78.
20. See Chapters 2 and 3.
21. See Chapter 3.
22. *A Practical Treatise on Regeneration* within a volume: *Treatises on Justification* by J. Witherspoon D.D. With an *Introductory Essay* by William Wilberforce, Esq., Author of *A Practical View of Christianity*, Glasgow, printed for Chalmers and Collins 1824. In this damaged copy in the Mitchell Library the *Essay* starts at p. 92.
23. *Treatise on Regeneration*, p. 191.
24. ibid, p. 299.
25. *Almanack and Memorandum Book of Dr John Witherspoon 1768*, in Princeton University Library.
26. *Essay on the Connection between the Doctrine of Justification by the Imputed Righteousness of Christ, and Holiness of Life*, p. vi.

27. ibid, p. 3; and compare also *Lecture on Divinity VIII*, p. 78, where, when dealing with the Creation, Witherspoon writes: 'The true and proper answer to every such question is to resolve it into the sovereignty of God. He hath the merit to bestow his mercies in the time, manner and measure that seem fit to himself'. See also *Lecture IX*, p. 83, where with reference to God's method of achieving man's salvation Witherspoon writes: 'If it be a mystery and above our comprehension, every attempt to explain it must be, if not criminal, yet unsuccessful'.

28. ibid, pp. 11-12.

29. This Chapter, p. 39.

30. *Essay on Justification*, pp. 50-51.

31. ibid, p. 67.

32. Collins, Vol. II, pp. 160-61.

33. Archive and Manuscript Repository for the Continuing Presbyterian Church, *Preliminary Principles Comparison of 1789 and 1973 versions* pp. 1-4.

34. Collins, Vol. II, p. 162.

35. *The Constitution of the Presbyterian Church in the United States of America containing the Confession of Faith, The Catechisms, The Government and Discipline and Directory for the Worship of God: Ratified and adopted by the Synod of New-York and Philadelphia held at Philadelphia May 16th and 18th 1788 and continued by adjournment until the 28th of the same month.* Printed by Thomas Bradford In Front Street fourth door below Market Street, MDCCLXXXIX, Introduction, p. cxxxiii.

36. ibid, cxxxiv, I.

37. *The Confession of Faith*, William Blackwood &Son Ltd., (Edinburgh, 1959), Chapter XX, p. 31. II.

38. *The Constitution of the Presbyterian Church in the United States*, Introduction, pp. cxxxiv-cxxxvi.

39. D. G. Hart and John Muether in a paper produced for the Orthodox Presbyterian Church, *Turning Points in American Presbyterian History, Part 4: A National Presbyterian Church 1789,* p. 2. (Reprinted from New Horizons, April 2005).

40. *The Confession of Faith*, Chapter XXIII, III, p. 36.

41. ibid, Chapter XXI, II, pp. 45-46.

42. Hart and Muether, p. 4.

43. *The Constitution*, section on the *Form of Church Government, Calling and Election of a Minister*, pp. 154-55.

44. ibid: section on the *Confession of Faith*, Chapter XXII.

45. ibid: section on *The Directory for the Worship of God*, Chapters I-IV, pp. 182ff.
46. ibid section on *Of Public Prayer*, Chapter V.
47. Collins, II, pp. 162-63.
48. Joseph J. Falcone, *New Jersey Books 1698-1800*, The Joseph Falcone Collection, (Princeton / Joseph Falcone Inc., 1992), Section 12, Notes pp. 10 and 12. The Collection is located in the Witherspoon Room in Princeton Public Library.
49. See Chapter 9.

Chapter 5 *President of the College of New Jersey*

1. John Witherspoon, 'Address to the Inhabitants of Jamaica and other West India Islands in behalf of the College of New Jersey', in *Essays on Important Subjects,* 4 vols (Edinburgh, 1805), III, pp. 308-331.
2. ibid, pp. 308-09.
3. ibid, pp. 312-13.
4. ibid, pp. 313, 318-22.
5. Robert Burns, *The Poems and Songs of Robert Burns*, 3 vols (OUP, 1968), I, p. 87.
6. Laurence Sterne, in *The Life and Opinions of Tristram Shandy, Gentleman* (Harmondsworth, 1986), pp. 94-95 seeks to justify his digressions: 'Notwithstanding all this you perceive that the drawing of my uncle Toby's character went on gently all the time; - not the great contours of it, - that was impossible, - but some familiar strokes and faint designations of it, were here and there touched in, as we went along, so that you are much better acquainted with my uncle Toby now than you was before'.
7. *Address*, pp. 313-15.
8. ibid, p. 318.
9. ibid, pp. 314-15.
10. ibid, pp. 321.
11. ibid, pp. 326-27.
12. ibid, pp. 318-19.
13. ibid, p. 320.
14. ibid, pp. 323-24.
15. ibid, p. 328.
16. ibid, p. 329.
17. Varnum Lansing Collins, *President Witherspoon: A Biography*, 2 vols (Princeton, 1925), I, pp. 90-91.
18. Note. *John Witherspoon (1723-1794) Diary and Accounts*, General Manuscripts: Bound, Princeton University Library. Inscription on the

inside of the leather binding: "*Almanack & Memorandum Book of Dr John Witherspoon 1768*. Presented by the Antiquarian Society by Rev. Dr. Wm. B. Spraque, May 26, 1849".

19.   *The Concise Dictionary of National Biography: From earliest times to 1985*, The Softback Preview edition by arrangement with Oxford University Press, 3 vols (Oxford, 1992), I, p. 798; see also *Almanack & Memorandum* for details of Witherspoon's engagements in London with the Dillys and Dr Gibbons.

20.   *Almanack & Memorandum 1768,* [February] 'Mon. 7 At 8 a.m. in the morning visit Mr Whitefield. Go to the house [indistinct] prayer ... Wed. 9 See Mr Whitefield at Monfield'. There are no page numbers in this document. See also *Dictionary of National Biography III*, pp. 3202-203.

21.   *Almanack & Memorandum 1768*, [February] 'Wed. 2 Breakfast with Mr Nisbet; Sat. 5 ... visit Dr Franklin'.

22.   Walter Isaacson, *Benjamin Franklin: An American Life*, (New York, 2004), pp. 244-45.

23.   Collins, I, pp. 90-91 and footnote 24.

24.   *Almanack & Memorandum*.

25.   Collins, I, pp. 106-07, 110-11.

26.   ibid, I, p. 112.

27.   ibid, I, pp. 120-22.

28.   ibid, I, pp. 134-35.

29.   Ashbel Green, *Life of the Revd. John Witherspoon D.D., LL.D.*, Ed. Henry Lyttleton Savage, (Princeton, 1973), p. 132.

30.   Jeffry H. Morrison, *John Witherspoon and the Founding of the American Republic,* University of Notre Dame Press, (Notre Dame, 2005), p. 63.

31.   Walter Isaacson, p. 109.

32.   Walter Rauschenbusch, *A Theology of the Social Gospel*, p. 131; quoted by John Macquarrie in *Twentieth-Century Religious Thought: The Frontiers of Philosophy and Theology, 1900-1960* (London, 1963). p. 164.

33.   Macquarrie, p. 165; see also G. R. Cragg, *The Church in the Age of Reason 1648-1789*, (Harmondsworth, 1960), pp. 179-81; and A. Dakin, *Calvinism*, (London, 1949), pp. 179-80.

34.   John Locke, *An Essay Concerning Human Understanding*, Abridged and edited with an introduction by John W. Yolton, (London, 1988), Epistle to the Reader, p. xlii.

35.   G. J. Warnock, ed. *The Principles of Human Knowledge*, by George Berkeley, (London and Glasgow, 1966), Introduction p. 22.

36.   ibid, Appendix, pp. 264-73.

37. 'Lectures on Moral Philosophy VI', in *Essays* II, p. 47.
38. ibid, *Lecture IV*, p. 37.
39. ibid, *Lecture XVI*, p. 150.
40. Williston Walker, *A History of the Christian Church*, (Edinburgh, 1953), p. 572.
41. ibid, p. 573.
42. John Adams, *Diary and Autobiography*, L. H. Butterfield editor, 4 vols (Cambridge, Mass., 1961), II, p. 112.
43. ibid, II, pp. 113; 120-21.
44. Collins, II, p. 214.
45. Abel Johnson, (Class of 1784), *Notes on the History Lectures of John Witherspoon*. Manuscript pages not numbered, containing six lectures. In the Princeton University Library John Witherspoon Collection, Box 1, Folder 40.
46. Collins, II, p. 212.
47. John Adams, II, p. 212.
48. *Lectures on Moral Philosophy, XVI* pp. 151-52; L. Gordon Tait, *The Piety of John Witherspoon: Pew, Pulpit, and Public Forum*, (Louisville, 2001), Appendix B, pp. 195-201, 126-30.
49. William S. Dix, *The Princeton University Library in the Eighteenth Century*, (Princeton, 1978), quoting the Preface to the first printed catalogue of the College Library, written by Samuel Davies, the fourth President, p. 1.
50. ibid, p. 2.
51. ibid, pp. 2, 4, 12: see also Collins, I, p. 41.
52. Charles E. Peterson, 'Robert Smith, Philadelphia Builder-Architect: From Dalkeith to Princeton', in *Scotland and America in the Age of Enlightenment*, edited by Richard B. Sher and Jeffrey R. Smitten, (Edinburgh University Press, 1990), p. 295.
53. William S. Dix, p. 12.
54. ibid, pp. 21-22.
55. ibid, pp. 27, 36-39.
56. *Memorial of the College of New Jersey 1784*, Princeton University, John Witherspoon Collection, Box 2, Folder 2; see also William S. Dix, pp. 55-56.
57. *Letter from Benjamin Franklin to John Witherspoon, April 15, 1784*, John Witherspoon Collection, Box 2, Folder 2; see also William S. Dix, p. 60.
58. William S. Dix, pp. 66-67.
59. ibid, pp. 50, 53, 68.
60. ibid, pp. 60-61.

61. Quoted by Charles E. Peterson in 'Robert Smith, Philadelphia Builder-Architect', in *Scotland and America in the Age of the Enlightenment*, pp. 295-96.
62. Collins, I, pp. 108-109.
63. ibid, I, p. 111.
64. Joseph Clark, Journal, in *Princetonians 1776-1783: A Biographical Dictionary* by Richard Harrison, Princeton University Press, (Princeton, 1981), p. 317.
65. ibid, pp. 379-80.
66. ibid, p. 381.
67. Princeton University, Samuel Stanhope Smith Collection, File AM 1306.
68. *Princetonians 1776-1783*, p. 224.
69. John Witherspoon Collection, Box 2, Folder 7.
70. ibid, Box 1, Folder 17.
71. ibid, Box 1, Folder 16A.
72. ibid, Box 2, Folder 2.
73. *Princetonians 1776-1788*, p. 152.
74. *Thriving at Princeton 2003-04: A Brief History of Students of Color at Princeton*, Princeton University Paper: http://www.princeton.edu/pr/pub/thriving/03/07, p. 1.
75. Quoted by Stanley Weintraub, in *Iron Tears: Rebellion in America, 1775-1783*, (London, 2005), p. 1.

Chapter 6 *Lectures on Divinity*

1. 'Lectures on Divinity', in *Essays on Important Subjects* 4 vols (Edinburgh, 1805), III, Lecture I, pp. 10-11.
2. *Lecture II,* pp. 20-24.
3. ibid, p. 25.
4. For a further discussion of these issues see the different arguments presented by: John R. McIntosh, in *Church and Theology in Enlightenment Scotland: The Popular Party 1740-1800* (East Linton, 1998), pp. 160-66; and Richard B. Sher, in *Church and University in the Scottish Enlightenment* (Edinburgh, 1985), pp. 277-297.
5. *Lecture III*, p. 31.
6. *Lecture II*, pp. 18, 26; see Chapter 2.
7. *Lecture III*, p. 32.
8. *Lecture IV*, p. 42.
9. *Lecture VI*, p. 55.
10. ibid, pp. 56, 60.
11. ibid, p. 62.

12. See Chapter 2: also *Ecclesiastical Characteristics*, p. 22.
13. *Lecture VI*, p. 62.
14. *Lecture VII*, pp. 63-70.
15. *Lecture VIII*, pp. 70-79. Note in *The Concise Dictionary of National Biography*, 3 vols (Bath, 1995), vol I, p. 770: 'Patrick Delany (1685?-1768): divine, senior fellow and tutor, Trinity College Dublin; an intimate friend of Sheridan and Swift, the latter styling him "the most eminent preacher we have"'. Witherspoon spells his name 'Delaney'.
16. *Lecture VIII*, pp. 72-73.
17. ibid, pp. 74-76.
18. ibid, pp. 77-78.
19. ibid, p. 79.
20. ibid, p. 79.
21. *Lecture IX*, pp. 80-83.
22. ibid, pp. 84-85.
23. ibid, pp. 88-89.
24. *Lecture X*, pp. 90-91.
25. *Lecture XI*, pp. 94-95.
26. *Lecture XII*, pp. 97-98.
27. See Chapter 2.
28. *Lecture XIII*, p. 113.
29. ibid, p. 119.
30. *Lecture XIV*, p. 124.
31. ibid, pp. 126-27.
32. ibid, p. 128. Note. Bertrand Russell summarizes Leibniz's idea of 'monads': 'He believed … in an infinite number of substances, which he called "monads". Each of these would have some of the properties of a physical point, but only when viewed abstractly; in fact, each monad is a soul. This follows naturally from the rejection of extension as an attribute of substance; the only remaining possible essential attribute seemed to be thought. Thus Leibniz was led to deny the reality of matter and to substitute an infinite number of souls'. *History of Western Philosophy* (London, 1980), p. 565.
33. *Lecture XV*, pp. 130-31, 133-34.
34. ibid, p. 134.
35. *Lecture XVI*, p. 135.
36. ibid, pp. 136, 141-42.
37. *Lecture XVII*, pp. 145-46.
38. ibid, p. 156.
39. ibid, p. 157.

REFERENCES AND NOTES

Chapter 7 *Lectures on Moral Philosophy*

1. John Witherspoon, 'Lectures on Moral Philosophy', in *Essays on Important Subjects*, 4 vols (Edinburgh, 1805), II, pp. 1-152.
2. *Lecture I*, p. 9.
3. ibid, I, pp. 9-10.
4. ibid, I, p. 12.
5. ibid, I, pp. 11-12.
6. M. A. Stewart, 'Religion and rational theology', in *The Cambridge Companion to The Scottish Enlightenment*, edited by Alexander Broadie, (Cambridge, 2003), pp. 31-59 and Note 14 on p. 56.
7. *Lecture II*, p. 19; Also see Chapter 2; and Samuel Clarke in *The Concise Dictionary of National Biography: from earliest times to 1985*, 3 vols (Oxford, 1995), I, p. 569.
8. Adam Smith in a letter to Alexander Wedderburn in 1756, quoted by Ian Simpson Ross, in *The Life of Adam Smith*, (Oxford 1995), p. 160.
9. Adam Smith, *The Theory of Moral Sentiments*, edited by D. D. Raphael and A. L. Macfie, (Indianapolis, 1982), III, 2. 34, p.132; and J. Walter McGinty, *Robert Burns and Religion*, Ashgate, (Aldershot, 2003), pp. 74-75; and J. Walter McGinty, unpublished Ph.D. thesis, *Literary, Philosophical and Theological Influences on Robert Burns*, University of Strathclyde, 1995, pp. 56-65.
10. *Lecture III*, p. 25.
11. *Lecture IV*, p. 31.
12. ibid, *IV*, pp. 37-38.
13. ibid, *IV*, p. 38. Note, my emphasis.
14. *Lecture V*, pp. 38-43.
15. ibid, pp. 40-42.
16. Robert Burns, *The Poems and Songs of Robert Burns*, edited by James Kinsley, 3 vols (Oxford, 1968), II, p. 563, line 188.
17. *Lecture VI*, pp. 44-51.
18. ibid, p. 45.
19. ibid, p. 46.
20. ibid, pp. 46-47.
21. ibid, p. 47; and *Lecture XVI*, p. 150.
22. *Lecture VI*, p. 48.
23. ibid, pp. 47-51.
24. *Lecture VII*, pp. 51-60.
25. Alfred Tennyson, *In Memoriam*, Canto 56.
26. *Lecture VII*, p. 53.
27. ibid, p. 54.
28. ibid, pp. 55-60.

29. *Lecture VIII*, pp. 60-66; *Lecture IX*, pp. 66-75.
30. *Lecture VIII*, p. 61.
31. ibid, p. 62.
32. ibid, p. 63.
33. 'The Unanimous Declaration of the Thirteen United States of America 4 July 1776', in *Revolutions 1775-1830*, edited by Merryn Williams, (Harmondsworth, 1971), p. 45. [Note: the text used is the Final draft adopted by Congress. Reprinted in H.S. Commager (ed), *Documents of American History* 1963]. See also *Lecture VIII*, p. 64.
34. *Lecture VIII*, p. 64.
35. ibid, p. 65.
36. *Lecture IX*, pp. 66-67.
37. See Chapter 11, pp. 174-175; also *Lecture IX*, p. 67.
38. *Lecture IX*, pp. 68-70.
39. ibid, pp. 73-75; see Chapter 3 The Stage.
40. *Lecture X*, p. 76.
41. John Locke, *Two Treatises on Civil Government*, Introduction by W. S. Carpenter, (London, 1955), Book II, Chapter II. 4, p. 118.
42. *Lecture X*, pp. 80-81.
43. Locke, Book II, Chapter IV, pp. 127-28.
44. *Lecture X*, pp. 81-82.
45. See Chapter 12, p.197.
46. *Lecture X*, p. 84.
47. Locke, Book II, Chapter V, p. 130.
48. *Lecture X*, p. 84.
49. *Lecture XI*, pp. 86-87.
50. ibid, p. 88; see also Thomas Robert Malthus, *An Essay on Population*, Introduction by W. T. Layton, 2 vols (London, 1951 and 1952). First published 1798. Malthus set out to prove: '1. Population is necessarily limited by the means of subsistence. 2. Population invariably increases where the means of subsistence increase, unless prevented by some powerful and obvious checks. 3. These checks, and the checks which repress the superior power of population, and keep its effects on a level with the means of subsistence, are all resolvable into moral restraint, vice and misery'. I, pp. 18-19.
51. *Lecture XI*, p. 89.
52. ibid, pp. 91-93.
53. ibid, p. 93.
54. ibid, pp. 93-94.
55. Locke, Book I, Chapter I, p. 3.
56. *Lecture XII*, p. 94.
57. Locke, Book II, Chapter IX, p. 180.

58. ibid, Book II, Chapter XIII, p. 192; *Lecture XII*, p. 97.
59. *Lecture XII,* P. 99.
60. ibid, p. 100.
61. Locke, Book I, Introduction, pp. x-xi.
62. *Lecture* XII, p. 100.
63. ibid, pp. 100-101
64. ibid, pp. 101-104; see also Collins Biography II, p. 35.
65. *Lecture* XII, p. 105.
66. ibid, p. 106.
67. *Lecture* XIII, pp. 107-108.
68. ibid, pp. 108-10.
69. ibid, p. 111.
70. ibid, p. 112.
71. ibid, pp. 112-15.
72. ibid, p. 116.
73. ibid, pp. 116-17.
74. Jeffry H. Morrison, *John Witherspoon and The Founding of the American Republic*, University of Notre Dame Press, (Notre Dame, 2005), pp. 64-67.
75. Thomas Reid, *An Inquiry into the Human Mind, On the Principles of Common Sense*, First published in Edinburgh and London in 1764, (Bristol, 1990), Reprint of 1785 edition..
76. ibid, p. 3; also see Paul B. Wood's Introduction pp. v-vi.
77. ibid, pp. 480-81.
78. ibid, p. 482.
79. John Witherspoon, 'Remarks on an essay on human liberty', in *The Scots Magazine April 1753*, in Vol. XV in Bound Edition in Mitchell Library, Glasgow, p. 166.
80. *Lecture XIV*, p. 118.
81. ibid, pp. 118-21.
82. ibid, pp. 121-23.
83. ibid, pp. 123-24.
84. ibid, p. 124.
85. ibid, p. 125.
86. ibid, pp. 125-29.
87. See first page of this chapter.
88. John Erskine, 'Of Laws in General', in *The Scottish Enlightenment, An Anthology*, edited by Alexander Broadie, (Edinburgh, 1997), pp. 609-10; also Alexander Broadie's *Preface* to the excerpt from Erskine's work, pp. 598-99 and *Biographical Sketch*, p. 797.
89. *Lecture XV*, pp. 129-34.
90. ibid, pp. 134-39.

91. *Lecture XVI*, pp. 142-44.
92. Ian Simpson Ross, *The Life of Adam Smith*, (Oxford, 1995), pp. 121-22.
93. In *Essays IV*, pp. 9-65
94. *Lecture XVI*, p. 145.
95. ibid, p. 149.
96. ibid, pp. 149-50.
97. ibid, pp. 151-52.

Chapter 8   *Lectures on Eloquence*

1. John Witherspoon, 'Lectures on Eloquence', in *The Works of John Witherspoon,* 4 vols (Philadelphia, 1800), III, p. 144.
2. ibid, p. 144.
3. Thomas P. Miller, Witherspoon, 'Blair and the Rhetoric of Civic Humanism', in *Scotland and America in the Age of Enlightenment*, edited by Richard B. Sher and Jeffrey R. Smitten, (Edinburgh, 1990), p. 103.
4. L. Gordon Tait, *The Piety of John Witherspoon: Pew, Pulpit, and Public Forum*, (Louisville, 2001), p. 5; and p. 206 note 23.
5. Richard B. Sher, *Church and University in the Scottish Enlightenment: The Moderate Literati of Edinburgh*, (Edinburgh, 1985), p. 108.
6. J. C. Bryce, editor, Adam Smith, *Lectures in Rhetoric and Belles Lettres*, (Indianapolis, 1985), Introduction, pp. 8-9.
7. Richard B. Sher, *Church and University*, p. 109.
8. ibid, p. 164 Table 4.
9. Hugh Blair, *Lectures on Rhetoric and Belles Lettres*, 3 vols (Edinburgh, 1813).
10. *Witherspoon Lecture I*, p.147; *Blair Lecture I*, p. 6.
11. *Witherspoon Lecture I*, p.144; *Blair Lecture I*, p. 7.
12. *Witherspoon Lecture VII*, p. 204; *Blair Lecture I*, p. 15.
13. *Witherspoon Lecture I*, p. 152; *Blair Lecture I*, p. 11.
14. *Witherspoon Lecture I*, p. 144; *Blair Lecture XXV*, pp. 161-62.
15. *Blair Lecture II*, p.163.
16. *Witherspoon Lecture VI*, p. 193; I, p. 151.
17. *Blair Lecture IV*, pp. 69, 74.
18. Hugh Blair, 'A Critical Dissertation on the Poems of Ossian Son of Fingal', in *The Poems of Ossian and Related Works*, edited by Howard Gaskill, with an Introduction by Fiona Stafford, (Edinburgh, 1996), p. 356.
19. *Witherspoon Lecture VI*, p. 197; *Blair Lecture IV*, pp. 75, 87, 86.

20. *Witherspoon Lecture XVI*, p. 295; *Blair Lecture V*, p. 103.
21. Note. Adam Smith's *Considerations Concerning the First Formation of Languages and the Different Genius of original and compounded Languages* was first published in the *Philological Miscellany; Consisting of Select Essays from the Memoirs of the Academy of Belles Lettres at Paris and other Foreign Academies.* Translated into English With Original Pieces by the most Eminent Writers in our own Country Vol. I Printed for the Editor and Sold by T. Beckett and P. A. Dechondt in the Strand 1761. The *Considerations* etc. was reprinted along with Adam Smith's, *The Theory of Moral Sentiments*, third edition, in 1767. See J. C. Bryce, 'Introduction' to Adam Smith's *Lectures on Rhetoric and Belles Lettres*, (Indianapolis, 1985), pp. 27-28.
22. *Witherspoon Lecture IV*, p. 179.
23. *Blair Lecture VI*, p. 115.
24. Adam Smith, *Considerations*, in *Lectures on Rhetoric and Belles Lettres*, p. 203.
25. *Adam Smith Lecture III*, p. 9.
26. J. C. Bryce referring to Smith's 'two savages' writes: 'This fanciful account could have been suggested by the passage in the Abbé Étienne Bonnet de Condillac's *Essaie sur l'origine des connoissances humaines* (1746) referred to in Rousseau's *Discours*. Adam and Eve had the gift of speech as part of their God-given perfection'. Bryce notes that 'Smith had copies of both Condillac's *Essai* (1746) and his *Traité des sensations* (1754)'; Adam Smith's *Lectures on Rhetoric and Belles Lettres*, p. 203, Note 2.
27. *Witherspoon Lecture I*, p. 152.
28. *Witherspoon Lecture II*, p. 154.
29. ibid, pp. 156-57, 159, 160.
30. 'Address to the Inhabitants of Jamaica and other West-India Islands on behalf of the College of New-Jersey' in *Essays on Important Subjects by John Witherspoon* 4 vols (Edinburgh, 1805), p. 309.
31. *Witherspoon Lecture III*, pp. 163-72.
32. *Witherspoon Lecture IV*, pp. 172-77.
33. *Witherspoon Lecture VI*, p. 201; VII, p. 204.
34. *Witherspoon Lecture X*, pp. 231-32; *Moral Philosophy Lecture XVI*, p. 149.
35. *Witherspoon Lecture XI*, p. 244.
36. *Witherspoon Lecture XII*, pp. 250-51.
37. *Witherspoon Lecture XIII*, pp. 256-57.
38. ibid, p. 257.
39. *Witherspoon Lecture XIV*, pp. 261-63.

40. ibid, pp. 264-70.
41. *Blair Lecture XXIX*, p. 281.
42. ibid, p. 303.
43. *Witherspoon Lecture XV*, pp. 272-75.
44. ibid, pp. 277, 279-80.
45. Note. The three theses lodged in Princeton University Library John Witherspoon Collection:
    De Mentis Immortalitate by Joannes Wederspan.
    De Origine Mali by Matthaeus Mitchell.
    De Analogia & Philosophia Prima by Gulielmus Cleghorn.
46. For an account of James Leechman's appointment to the Chair of Divinity see William Robert Scott, *Francis Hutcheson: His Life, Teaching and Position in the History of Philosophy,* (Bristol, 1992), pp. 85-93.
47. Varnum Lansing Collins, *President Witherspoon: A Biography*, 2 vols (Princeton, 1925), I, pp. 21-23; see also Chapter 1 of this work.
48. *Witherspoon Lecture XV*, pp. 281-83.
49. *Witherspoon Lecture XVI*, pp. 288-301.
50. *Witherspoon Lecture II*, p. 156; *Adam Smith Lecture XXX*, pp. 186-95.
51. Hugh Blair, *Lectures on Rhetoric and Belles* letters 3 vols (Edinburgh, 1813), I, Contents Page.
52. George Campbell, *The Philosophy of Rhetoric*, 2 vols (Edinburgh, 1808); see also L. Gordon Tait, *The Piety of John Witherspoon* (Louisville, 2001), Appendix B, p. 197.
53. George Campbell, *The Philosophy of Rhetoric*, I, p. 161.
54. ibid, I, p. 211.
55. ibid, I, pp. 29-31.

Chapter 9   *Politician I: 1768-1776*

1. *The Dominion of Providence over the Passions of Men: A Sermon preached at Princeton on 17th May 1776* Being the General Fast Appointed by the Congress through the United Colonies. To which is added *An Address to the Natives of Scotland, residing in America*, By John Witherspoon D.D., President of the College of New Jersey. The second edition with *Elucidatory REMARKS*. Philadelphia printed Glasgow Reprinted MDCCLXXVII, p. 5.
2. *Christian Magnanimity, A Sermon: Preached at Princeton, September 1775*, The Sabbath preceding the Annual Commencement: and again with Additions, September 23, 1787, to which is added *An Address to the Senior Class* who were to receive

the degree of Bachelor of Arts. By John Witherspoon D.D., LLD. President of the College of New Jersey Princeton. Printed 1787: Paisley MDCCLXXXVIII Reprinted by J. Nelson for R. Reid, pp. A.1; and 6-8.

3. Jacques Godechot, *France and the Atlantic Revolution in the Eighteenth Century, 1770-1779,* (London, 1971), pp. 28-32; see also *The Wordsworth Dictionary of British History*, Editorial Consultant J. P. Kenyon, (Ware, 1994), Intolerable Acts, p. 191.

4. Godechot, p. 32.

5. David Hackett Fischer, *Washington's Crossing,* (OUP, 2004), pp. 16-17.

6. *Christian Magnanimity*, for sermon points 1-4, pp. 6-8.

7. ibid, pp. 10-11, (my italics).

8. ibid, pp. 11-13.

9. *The Dominion of Providence*, p. 29.

10. Fischer, pp. 134-35; 160-61.

11. Jeffry H. Morrison, *John Witherspoon and the Founding of the American Republic*, University of Notre Dame Press, (Indiana, 2005), pp. 71-72; and Varnum Lansing Collins, *President Witherspoon, A Biography* 2 vols (Princeton, 1925), I, p. 125.

12. Fischer, pp. 144-45; and Morrison, p. 71.

13. Walter Isaacson, *Benjamin Franklin: An American Life,* (New York, 2003), p. 313.

14. Collins, I, pp. 132-33.

15. ibid, pp. 133-34; see also Morrison, p. 165, note10.

16. Morrison, p. 73.

17. John Witherspoon, 'Reflections on the Present State of Public Affairs', in *Essays, Vol. IV*, pp. 66-72.

18. John Witherspoon, 'Thoughts on American Liberty', in *Essays, Vol. IV*, pp. 73-77.

19. 'A Pastoral Letter from the Synod of New York and Philadelphia To the Congregations under their care to be read from the Pulpits on Thursday June 29, 1775 being the Day of the general Fast', in *The Works of John Witherspoon, DD, LLD*, 3 vols (Philadelphia, 1800) III, pp. 599-605.

20. ibid, III, pp. 602-605.

21. Morrison, p. 74, quoting from Elias Boudinot's *Journal, or Historical Recollections of American Events during the Revolutionary War* (Philadelphia, 1894), pp. 5-6.

22. *Innocent Blood Crying to God from the streets of Boston. A sermon occasioned by the horrid murder of Messieurs Samuel Gray, Samuel Maverick, James Caldwell and Cripus Attucks, with Patrick Carr*

since dead and Christopher Monk, judged irrecoverable and several others badly wounded, by a party of troops under the command of Captain Preston. On the 5th of March 1770, and Preached on the Lord's Day following: By John Lathrop A.M., Pastor of the 2nd Church in Boston. 'Cursed be their anger for it was fierce and their wrath, for it was cruel'. *Gen.* xlix.7. 'The remainder of their wrath thou shalt restrain'. *Psalm* lxxvi, 10. (London, Printed. Boston: Reprinted MDCCLXXI). In Witherspoon Collection Princeton University, Pamphlets Ref. 763.010.01. (ex) p. 94.

23. Collins, I, pp. 132-33.
24. *Innocent Blood*, pp. 9-17.
25. *The Dominion of Providence* (Glasgow, 1777), p. 7.
26. ibid, pp. 8-9.
27. *The Dominion of Providence in Sermons by the Late John Witherspoon* (Edinburgh, 1798), pp. 153, 159-160.
28. *The Dominion of Providence* (Glasgow, 1777), pp. 10-16.
29. ibid, pp. 21-24.
30. ibid, pp. 26-28.
31. ibid, pp. 30, 33, 35.
32. ibid, pp. 36, 38.
33. ibid, *Advertisement*, p. A2.
34. ibid, Footnotes on pp. 9, 11, 24, 30.
35. *The Dominion of Providence* (Edinburgh, 1798), pp. 158-59.
36. Quoting Thomas Paine's *Common Sense* (Bradford Edition, p.11) in ibid, pp. 159-60.
37. ibid, pp. 160-62.
38. ibid, p. 162; note: word count of the digression on Thomas Paine: 550 words approx.
39. Two creation stories are found in the Old Testament book of *Genesis.* The earlier of the two, (*Genesis* 2. 5-24) contains the story of Adam and Eve and the Garden of Eden, and it is this story that provides the raw material for the doctrine of original sin. The later, more sophisticated creation story (*Genesis* 1.1 - 2.4), does not even mention sin, far less the condition original sin, as having been caused by Man's disobedience to God's command.
40. See Paul's *Letter to the Romans*; and *The Confessions of St. Augustine*, Translated by Sir Tobie Matthew, revised by Dom. Roger Hudleston, (London and Glasgow, 1960), Book I, pp. 38-40.
41. *The Confession of Faith*, Agreed upon by the Assembly of Divines at Westminster: Examined and approved *anno* 1647 by the General Assembly of the Church of Scotland; and ratified by Acts of

Parliament 1649 and 1690. Chap. VI. Of the Fall of Man, of Sin, and of the Punishment thereof. pp. 12-13.

42.   For an outline of the views of Taylor and Goldie, see the author's *Robert Burns and Religion*, Ashgate, (Aldershot, 2003), pp. 31-40.

43.   *The Dominion of Providence* (Edinburgh, 1798), p. 158.

44.   John Keane, in *Tom Paine, A Political Life*, (London, 1996), records that Paine 'In April 1776, reported that he was certain that 120,000 copies had already been published' (p. 111). See also this chapter p. 96.

45.   Thomas Paine, *Common Sense* (London, 2004), pp. 30-31.

46.   John Keane, pp. 101, 103.

47.   Collins II, pp. 25-26; and for a less biased view of Paine than Collins or Jay, see John Adams 's account of Witherspoon's objections to Thomas Paine's appointment in *Diary and Autobiography of John Adams* III, p. 334; and John Keane, p.155 who refutes the charges against Paine.

48.   *The Dominion of Providence* (Edinburgh, 1798), p. 188.

49.   John Keane, p. 109.

50.   ibid, p. 112.

51.   ibid pp. 204-206.

Chapter 10 *Politician II: 1776-1783*

1.   Jeffry H. Morrison, *John Witherspoon and the Founding of the American Republic*, (Notre Dame, Indiana, 2005), pp. 3-4.

2.   ibid, p.140, note 13. Drawing upon Washington D.C. General Service Administration National Archives and Records of Service 1976 pp. 421-22, Morrison records that Witherspoon served on 'probably 125' committees.

3.   *Letter from Richard Peters to Thomas Bradford August 25, 1779*, and John *Witherspoon's letter of acknowledgement of receipt of Prisoners of War* in Princeton University Library, John Witherspoon Collection Box 1 Folder 26. See also Varnum Lansing Collins, *President Witherspoon: A Biography*, 2 vols (Princeton, 1925), II, pp. 26, 32, 37-38 for other committee appointments made in the early years of his service in Congress.

4.   *Letter from Committee of Correspondence to Benjamin Franklin informing him of his appointment* as *Congress's Commissioner to the Court of Spain, January 1777*, photocopy in Princeton University Library, John Witherspoon Collection Box 2 Folder 6.

5.   'An Essay on Money', in *Essays on Important Subjects* by John Witherspoon D.D., 4 vols (Edinburgh, 1805), IV, pp. 9-65.

REFERENCES AND NOTES

6.   Letter from Thomas Jefferson to Henry Lee, May 8, 1825, in
      Revolutions 1775-1830, edited by Merryn Williams,
      (Harmondsworth, 1971), p. 54.
7.   Thomas Jefferson, 'First Draft of the Declaration of Independence',
      in *Revolutions 1775-1830*, pp. 48, 50. Note. The Draft has been
      reprinted from 'A Declaration By the Representatives of the United
      States of America in General Congress Assembled 1776'. Reprinted
      in Carl L. Becker, *The Declaration of Independence*, (1942*)*; and is
      part of a collection of historical documents compiled for a textbook
      for the U. K.'s Open University.
8.   *The Unanimous Declaration of the Thirteen United States of
      America*, Final Draft adopted by Congress, reprinted in H. S.
      Commager, (ed), *Documents of American History*, in *Revolutions
      1775-1830*, p. 51.
9.   John Witherspoon, *An Address to the Natives of Scotland residing in
      America*, published with *The Dominion of Providence over the
      Passions of Men*, (Glasgow, 1777); see also *Sermons by the late
      John Witherspoon: A Supplementary Volume* which includes *An
      Address to the Natives of Scotland residing in America* (pp. 196-
      217), (Edinburgh, 1798) p. 196.
10.   *Address to the Natives of Scotland residing in America*, p. 197.
11.   ibid, pp. 199-201. Note. The Scotophobia of John Wilkes is well
      recognised by historians, starting with David Hume to the present
      day T. M. Devine and Michael Fry. Wilkes had a special dislike of
      the Scottish Lord Bute who had been tutor to the young George III.
      Much of the English Scotophobia at that time was born of a
      suspicion of the Scots' disloyalty, because of their part in the
      rebellions of 1715 and 1745.
12.   ibid, pp. 201-204.
13.   ibid, pp. 207-209.
14.   ibid, p. 215.
15.   ibid, p. 207.
16.   ibid, p. 208.
17.   ibid, pp. 216-17.
18.   'Aristides, Common Sense or Plain Truth', in *Essays* IV, pp. 88-98;
      see also 'The Druid', in *Essays* IV, pp. 224-291; and 'A Letter to the
      printer from Epaminondas', in *The Pennsylvania Magazine or
      American Monthly Museum*, March 1775, pp. 115-119.
19.   'Aristides, Common Sense or Plain Truth', in *Essays*, IV, pp. 88-98.
20.   James Thomson (1700-1748), 'Winter', line 459, in *The Wordsworth
      Dictionary of Phrase and Fable*, (Ware, 2001), p. 61.
21.   Jeffry H. Morrison, op cit, pp. 60-61.

22. *The Works of John Witherspoon*, 4 vols (Philadelphia, 1801), IV, p. 313.
23. ibid, IV, p. 315.
24. ibid, IV, pp. 315-16.
25. ibid, IV, p. 319.
26. Collins, *Biography*, II, p. 3, note 1.
27. John Witherspoon, 'Part of a speech to Congress on the Conference proposed by Lord Howe', in *Essays*, IV, p. 105.
28. ibid, IV, p. 104.
29. ibid, IV, p. 102.
30. ibid, IV, p. 102.
31. Walter Isaacson, *Benjamin Franklin: An American Life*, (New York, 2003), p. 319.
32. 'The Articles of Confederation', in H. S. Commager, ed., *Documents of American History*, 1963, in *Revolutions 1775-1830*, pp. 55-64.
33. John Witherspoon, 'Part of a speech to Congress upon the Confederation', in *Essays*, IV, pp. 135-36; see also Jeffry H. Morrison, pp. 94 and 174 notes 8-9.
34. *Speech to Congress*, IV, p. 139.
35. ibid, IV, p. 140.
36. Collins, *Biography*, II, p. 14.
37. 'On the proposed market in General Washington's camp', in *Essays*, IV, pp. 148-53.
38. Collins, *Biography*, II, p. 14.
39. Beaumarchais to Louis XVI of France, September 1775, in *The Barber of Seville*, Translated and Introduction by John Wood, Introduction, p. 19.
40. ibid, Introduction, pp. 20-21.
41. John Keane, *Tom Paine: A Political Life*, (London, 1996), pp. 172-7
42. ibid, see foot of pp. 173-74 ref. to allegations against Thomas Mifflin, quartermaster general and Dr William Shippen, head of medical department.
43. ibid, p. 175.
44. ibid, pp. 179-80.
45. *Letter from Committee of Secret Correspondence to Benjamin Franklin January 1, 1777*, photocopy in Princeton University Library John Witherspoon Collection, Box 2 Folder 6.
46. David Hackett Fischer, *Washington's Crossing*, Oxford University Press, (New York, 2004), pp. 162-63.
47. Collins, *Biography*, II, p. 16.

48. *Letter from Richard Peters to Thomas Bradford August 25, 1779*;
     and *John Witherspoon's acknowledgement of receipt* of *Prisoners of
     War*, John Witherspoon Collection, Box 1 Folder 26.
49. Fischer, *Washington's Crossing*, pp. 328-40.
50. Collins, *Biography*, II, 16-18.
51. 'The Articles of Confederation', in *Revolutions 1775-1830*, pp. 55-
     64.
52. Collins, *Biography*, II, pp. 6, 43-44.
53. ibid, II, pp. 50-51.
54. 'Some account of the life and character of the Author [John
     Witherspoon]. Extracted from a Sermon on the occasion of his death
     at Princeton 6th May 1795', by John Rodgers D.D., in *Sermons by
     the Late John Witherspoon*, (Edinburgh, 1798), Preface (pp. iii-xx) p.
     xvi.
55. Jeffry H. Morrison, op cit, p. 18. Note. If in an American context
     there has been as Morrison asserts, a lack of appreciation of the
     contribution made by Witherspoon to the founding of the American
     Republic, there has been an equivalent exclusion of him from British
     accounts of the revolutionary period and the establishing of
     American Independence. He is cast as a traitor in contemporary
     accounts such as the Glasgow 1777 edition of the *Dominion of
     Providence* sermon and is mockingly dismissed by Alexander
     Carlyle and Adam Ferguson. He has been largely ignored by Scottish
     historians until more recent times (see Chapter 14). What Morrison
     alleges about American historians, also applies in Scotland: 'on the
     whole, modern writers have been content to toss off a paragraph or
     two - or at best a chapter - on Witherspoon and be done with him'.
     See Jeffry H. Morrison*, John Witherspoon and the Founding of the
     American Republic*, p. 17.
56. John Adams, *The Diary and Autobiography of John Adams*, L. H.
     Butterfield, Editor, 4 vols (Cambridge, Massachusetts, 1961), IV, p.
     253.
57. Collins, *Biography*, II, pp. 61-62.
58. ibid, II, 55-58; see also *Essays*, IV, pp. 154-65.
59. ibid, II, p. 59.
60. 'Thanksgiving Proclamation', in Collins, *Biography*, II, pp. 64-65.

Chapter 11 *Personal Qualities*

1. Note. The incorrect spelling of Elizabeth's name on the gravestone
    with an 's' instead of a 'z', is perhaps a further indication of how
    little was known of her. A pamphlet available at the entrance to The

REFERENCES AND NOTES

Princeton Cemetery describes it as 'The Westminster Abbey of America'. Established in 1757 and owned by Nassau Presbyterian Church, its 'Presidents' Plot' contains eleven out of the fifteen former Presidents of the College of New Jersey. The oldest surviving monument is that of Aaron Burr Sr. His son, Aaron Burr Jr who was taught by Witherspoon, became a Colonel in the Army of the Revolution and Vice President of the United States from 1801-1805. He is buried at the foot of his father's grave, and near that of his grandfather Jonathan Edwards, another former President of the College. A motto heads the leaflet: 'The life of the dead consists in being present in the minds of the living'. The quotation is from Cicero, one of Witherspoon's heroes and with whom he probably shared a reticence on the nature of life after death. The pamphlet was written for The Princeton Cemetery by George H. Brown Jr in 1998.

2. *The Concise Oxford Dictionary*, (Oxford, 1995), p. 285.
3. Thomas Randall to John Witherspoon March 4, 1767, in Princeton University John Witherspoon Collection, Box 1 Folder 19.
4. *The Holy Bible*, King James Version, (Glasgow, 1949), *Genesis* 12. 1-8, pp. 18-19; *Psalm* 105. 13-14, p. 723.
5. *Benjamin Rush to John Witherspoon, from Edinburgh, April 23, 1767*, John Witherspoon Collection Box 2 Folder 25.
6. 'John Witherspoon to Archibald Wallace, February 28, 1767', in L. H. Butterfield, *John Witherspoon Comes to America*, (Princeton, 1953), pp. 27-28.
7. 'Richard Stockton to his wife, March 17, 1767', ibid, p. 33.
8. Robert Burns, *The Letters of Robert Burns*, Edited by J. De Lancey Ferguson, second edition edited by G. Ross Roy, 2 vols (Oxford, 1985), II, p. 147.
9. *John Witherspoon to Rev. Mr. Nisbet, minister, Montrose, May 25, 1767*, in John Witherspoon Collection Box 2 Folder 12.
10. Varnum Lansing Collins, *President Witherspoon: A Biography*, 2 vols (Princeton, 1925), I, pp. 25, 103.
11. William K. Selden, *Women of Princeton 1746-1969*, (Princeton, 2000), Section on the wives of the Presidents of New Jersey College.
12. John Adams, *The Diary and Autobiography of John Adams*, L. H. Butterfield editor, 4 vols (Cambridge, Massachusetts, 1961), II, pp. 120-21, 259.
13. John Witherspoon, *Manuscript Notebook 1763*. This is incorporated in *The Universal Scots Almanack for the Year of our Lord MDCCLXIII* Being the *third year after the leap year*, (Edinburgh), in Princeton University Library, Ref. CO 199 No. 1141.

REFERENCES AND NOTES

14. John Witherspoon (1723-1794*) Diary and Accounts*, General Manuscript Bound. Inscribed inside: '*Almanack and Memorandum Book of Dr. John Witherspoon 1768.* Presented by the Antiquarian Society by Rev. Wm. B. Spraque, May 1849'. In Princeton University Library, Ref. CO 199 No. 1140.

15. Collins, *Biography*, I, 25; see also first page of Chapter 3.

16. *John Witherspoon to David Witherspoon, May 6, 1776*, in John Witherspoon Collection, Box 2 Folder 23.

17. Edward Miller and Frederic P. Wells, *History of Ryegate: From its Settlement by the Scotch- American Company of Farmers to the Present Time*, (St. Johnsbury, 1913), pp. 39-40 and note on p. 40.

18. David Hackett Fischer, *Washington's Crossing*, (Oxford, 2004), pp. 162-63.

19. John Witherspoon, *Four Letters on Education*, (Glasgow, 1799).

20. ibid, *Letter II*, pp. 16-18, 21.

21. ibid, *Letter III*, pp. 23, 26-27.

22. ibid*, Letter IV*, pp. 33, 35, 37-38.

23. ibid, Letter V, pp. 44, 48, 50.

24. Collins, *Biography I*, pp. 59-61 for an account of the Snodgrass case. Note the document referred to by Ashbel Green and said by Collins to have been lost, now seems to have reappeared, as the author referred to it when at Princeton University Library in 2005. The details of the subscriptions raised to offset the cost of the Libel case are listed in John Witherspoon's, *The Universal Scots Almanack for 1763*, see ref. 13 above.

25. Alexander Carlyle, *Anecdotes and Characters of the Times*, edited and with an Introduction by James Kinsley, (Oxford, 1973), pp. 34-35; and note on p. 35.

26. ibid, A Chronology of Alexander Carlyle, pp. xxiii-xxiv.

27. ibid, p. 16.

28. *An Address to the Students of the Senior Class on the Lord's Day preceding Commencement, September 23, 1775*, included in the same volume as *Christian Magnanimity, A Sermon Preached at Princeton September 1775 and again with additions September 23, 1787*, (Princeton, 1787 and Paisley, 1788) p. 33.

29. John Witherspoon, 'Letters on Marriage', in *Essays on Important Subjects*, 4 vols (Edinburgh, 1805), III, p. 215.

30. ibid, III, pp. 217-18.

31. ibid, III, pp. 224-25.

32. ibid, III, p. 231.

33. ibid, III, p. 233.

34. ibid, III, p. 244.

35. ibid, III, p. 245.
36. See Chapter 9, pp.151-153.
37. John Adams, *Diary and Autobiography, III,* pp. 330-33.
38. ibid, III, p. 334.
39. Thomas Paine, October 1783, to a Committee of the Continental Congress in Philadelphia, in John Keane, *Tom Paine: A Political Life,* (London, 1995), pp. 206 and 575, note 86.
40. Collins, *Biography,* I, p. 19.
41. ibid, I, pp. 23-24.
42. John Witherspoon, Letter from 'Tusculum, Near Princeton, March 20th, 1780' in On the Affairs of the United States, in *Essays, IV,* p. 172.
43. See Chapter 4.
44. Collins, *Biography, I,* p. 103.
45. Jeffry H. Morrison, *John Witherspoon and the Founding of the American Republic,* (Notre Dame, Indiana, 2005), Portrait on book cover; quote from Ashbel Green, Life of the Revd. John Witherspoon, p. 10. Note. Collins also uses the word 'presence' in his description of Witherspoon, I, 103.
46. *Almanack for 1763,* in Princeton University Library, Ref. CO 199 No. 1141.
47. *Almanack for 1968,* in Princeton University Library, Ref, CO 199 No. 1140.
48. John Witherspoon Collection, Box 1 Folder 27.
49. John Witherspoon Collection, Box 1 Folder 29.

Chapter 12 *Personal Characteristics*

1. See Chapter 1, pp. 3-4; Chapter 7, p. 75.
2. See Chapter 1, pp. 4-6.
3. See Chapter 3.
4. See Chapter 9, p. 140.
5. 'On the Proposed Market in George Washington's Camp', in *Essays* IV, pp. 148-153: also see Collins, *Biography* II, pp. 10, 16-17.
6. *Petition from the Trustees to Congress, June 1781,* Princeton University Library, John Witherspoon Collection, Box 1 Folder 3.
7. See Chapter 4, p. 40
8. John Witherspoon, *Sermons on Practical Subjects to which is added A Farewell Discourse,* (Glasgow, 1768), pp. 285, 316.
9. Philip J. Ford, *George Buchanan: Prince of Poets,* (Aberdeen, 1982), Introduction, p. 11.

10. 'Letter of the Barons of Scotland to Pope John XXII', otherwise called 'The Declaration of Arbroath', (The Translation is based on one published in 1689), in Gordon Donaldson, *Scottish Historical Documents*, (Edinburgh and London, 1974), p. 57.

11. See Chapter 4, p. 36.

12. John Witherspoon, 'Part of a Speech to Congress on a Motion for paying the Interest of Loan-office Certificates', in *Essays,* IV, pp. 121-22.

13. ibid.

14. See ref.5 above.

15. 'An Essay on Money', in *Essays* IV, pp. 9-65; see also Jeffry H. Morrison, *John Witherspoon and the Founding of the American Republic*, (Notre Dame, Indiana, 2005), p. 8.

16. *An Essay on Money*, p. 14; see also *The Confession of Faith*, Chapter XXVII, Of the Sacraments, II 'There is in every sacrament a spiritual relation, or sacramental union, between the sign and the thing signified; whence it comes to pass, that the names and effects of the one are attributed to the other', *The Confession of Faith*, (Edinburgh, 1959), pp. 40-41.

17. *Essay on Money*, pp. 17, 20, 49, 55.

18. ibid, pp. 64-65.

19. A *Final Inventory of all the Goods and Chattels of the late Rev. John Witherspoon. Taken by Anne Witherspoon, sole executrix to the Last Will and Testament of the Deceased and appraised by Daniel Agnew and Walter ---- [indistinct] Streets and Derrick Longsheath the 28th Day of November 1794.* In the archives of the Historical Society of Princeton, 158 Nassau Street, Princeton; Verticle File 41.

20. See Chapter 4, pp. 46-50.

21. ibid. pp. 139ff.

22. 'Lectures on Moral Philosophy', in *Essays* II, Lecture I, p. 1.

23. 'Lectures on Divinity', in *Essays* III, Lecture I, pp. 18-19.

24. Marcus Tullius Cicero, (106-43 BC), *Letters to His Friends* Book 12, Letter 25, in *Its Greek to Me!* By Michael Macrone, (London, 1992), p. 132.

25. See Chapter 5, pp. 59-62

26. 'A letter to the Printer from Epaminondas', in *The Pennsylvania Magazine or American Monthly Review*, March 1775, pp. (115-19), pp. 116,119.

27. Anon [but soon known to be by John Witherspoon], *Ecclesiastical Characteristics or the Arcana of Church Policy*, (Glasgow, 1754); also John Witherspoon, 'A Serious Apology for Ecclesiastical Characteristics', in *Essays*, I, pp. 230-31.

28. David Hackett Fischer, *Washington's Crossing*, (Oxford, 2004), pp. 150-51, 300; see also Jeffry H. Morrison, p. 148, note 3.
29. Collins, *Biography*, I, p. 222.
30. Fischer, pp. 162-63.
31. L. Gordon Tait, *The Piety of John Witherspoon*, (Louisville, 2001), Introduction, p. 1.
32. *Address to the Students of the Senior Class*, in same volume as *Christian Magnanimity*, (Paisley, 1788), p. 18.
33. *Christian Magnanimity*, pp. 11-12.
34. *The Holy Bible*, King James Version, (Glasgow, 1949), *New Testament, Hebrews* 11.13-16, pp. 282-83.
35. 'The Dominion of Providence', in *Sermons by the Late John Witherspoon*, (Edinburgh, 1798), p. 188.
36. Jeffry H. Morrison, quoting Adams, pp. 10-11.
37. ibid, quoting Jefferson, pp. 11, 116.
38. ibid, p. 12.
39. *John Witherspoon to Benjamin Rush* Esq. *Student of Medicine, Edinburgh, April 29, 1767*, in Princeton University Library John Witherspoon Collection, Box 1 Folder 13.
40. *John Witherspoon to Benjamin Rush July 7, 1767*, ibid.
41. *John Witherspoon to Benjamin Rush August 4, 1767*, ibid.
42. *John Witherspoon to Benjamin Rush August 12, 1767*, ibid.
43. *John Witherspoon to Benjamin Rush September 16, 1767*, ibid.
44. *John Witherspoon to Benjamin Rush December 21, 1767*, ibid.
45. 'A Pastoral Letter from the Synod of New York and Philadelphia to the Congregations under their care to be read from the Pulpits on Thursday, June 29, 1775 being the Day of the general Fast', in *The Works of John Witherspoon*, 3 vols (Philadelphia, 1800), III, p. 599.
46. ibid, III, p. 601.
47. John Witherspoon, *The Dominion of Providence*, (Glasgow, 1777). pp. 7, 9, 14, 16.
48. 'On Conducting the American Controversy', in *Essays* IV, p. 85.
49. See Chapter 1.
50. 'Lectures on Moral Philosophy, XII', in *Essays*, II, pp. 98-101.
51. See Chapter 8.
52. *The Works of John Witherspoon*, (Philadelphia, 1800), Preface p. I, 3
53. L. Gordon Tait, p. 143.
54. *The Dominion of Providence*, (Glasgow, 1777), pp. 24, 31.
55. 'Lectures on Eloquence', VII, in *Works*, III, p. 204.
56. *The Charge of Sedition and Faction against good Men, especially faithful Ministers considered and accounted for. A Sermon preached in the Abbey Church of Paisley on Thursday September 7th 1758 at*

*the ordination of Mr. Archibald Davidson as one of the Ministers of
the Church. To which is subjoined The Charge to the Minister and
the Exhortation to the People by John Witherspoon, A.M. one of the
ministers of Paisley. Published at the desire of those who heard it*
(Glasgow, 1758), p. 34.

57. John Witherspoon to Rev. Samuel Stanhope Smith March 20, 1780,
     in *Essays*, IV, pp. 173-74.

58. John Witherspoon, *Four Letters on Education*, (Glasgow, 1799), p.
     54. Note. This pamphlet has been wrongly titled. There are five not
     four letters within it.

59. L. Gordon Tait, pp. 143-44.

60. 'Lectures on Moral Philosophy', in *Essays* II, Lecture I, p. 1.

61. L. Gordon Tait, p. 174.

62. ibid, see ref. 52.

63. ibid, p. 191.

64. Alexander Carlyle, *Anecdotes and Characters of the Times*, (Oxford,
     1973), p. 35, footnote. Note. The surly and vindictive tone of this
     anecdote about Dr Nisbet betrays Carlyle's opinion of Witherspoon,
     and implies that Witherspoon also 'became Discontent' and moved
     to America. See also the sneering tone of the 'Remarks' appended to
     the publication containing the sermon, *The Dominion of Providence*
     (Glasgow, 1777), Advertisement p. A.2., and p. 11 footnote.

65. 'Lectures on Eloquence', in *Works*, III, Lecture II, p. 159.

66. Gordon Donaldson, *Scottish Historical Documents*, (Edinburgh,
     1974):
     First Book of Discipline, 1560-61, pp. 126-134;
     Second Book of Discipline, 1578, pp. 143-50;
     Act Authorising Vernacular Scriptures, 1543, pp. 109-10
     1560 Acts of 'Reformation Parliament', pp. 124-26.

67. Ibid, *Antecedents of Treaty of Union, 1703-04*, pp. 265-68; *Articles
     of Union 1707*, pp. 268-75; *Acts of Security of Presbyterian Church
     1707*, pp. 275-77.

68. John Witherspoon, *Ecclesiastical Characteristics*, (Glasgow, 1754),
     Maxim VI, p. 32; Lectures on Moral Philosophy in *Essays* II,
     Lecture X, p. 76 and XI, p. 89. Note. In Lecture XVI Witherspoon
     lists among his recommended books: Francis Hutcheson's 'Inquiries
     into the Ideas of Beauty and Virtue, and his System', p. 151.

69. See Chapter 7, *Lectures on Eloquence*.

70. *Lectures on Eloquence* II, IX and VI, pp. 157, 224, 198.

71. *Ecclesiastical Characteristics*, Maxim V, p. 30.

72. *Essay on the Connection between the Doctrine of Justification by the
     Imputed Righteousness of Christ and Holiness of Life; with some*

reflections upon the Reception which that Doctrine hath generally met with in the World, (Glasgow, 1756), p. 11; see also *The New Testament, Romans* 5, *The Holy Bible* (Glasgow, 1949), p. 198.

73. John Witherspoon, *Sermons on Practical Subjects*, (Glasgow, 1768), Sermon III, p. 80; II, pp. 51-52; IV, p. 85; V, p. 163; VII, pp. 203, 224; VIII, p. 235; IX, p. 265.

74. *The Confession of Faith*, (Edinburgh, 1959), Chapter VI, I, p. 12; W. B. Yeats, 'Easter 1916', in *Yeats: Selected Poetry*, ed. A. Norman Jeffares (London, 1979), p. 193.

75. John Calvin, *Institutes of The Christian Religion*: A new Translation by Henry Beveridge Esq., 2 vols (Edinburgh, 1879), I, Book II, Chapter II, Section 1, p. 223.

76. ibid, I, Book II, Chapter II, Section 10, p. 231, and Section 11, p. 233

77. ibid, I, Book II, Chapter II, Section 15, p. 236.

78. John Witherspoon, *The Dominion of Providence*, pp. 10, 22.

79. 'Lectures on Divinity', in *Essays*, III, Lecture XIV, pp. 124-26.

80. 'The Druid', Number I, in *Essays*, III, p. 226.

81. 'A Speech to Congress on Confederation', in *Essays*, IV, p. 139.

82. ibid, IV, p. 140.

83. Letter sent to Scotland for *The Scots Magazine*, in *Essays*, III, p. 298.

84. William Shakespeare, 'Julius Caesar', Act IV, Scene III, in Shakespeare, *The Complete Works*, Collins, (Glasgow, undated), p. 883.

Chapter 13 *Emigration*

1. *The Scots Magazine*, September 1772, in Vol. 34 Bound Edition in the Mitchell Library, Glasgow, pp. 482-83.

2. ibid, pp. 483-84.

3. *The Scots Magazine*, November 1772, in Vol. 34, pp. 587-88.

4. *The Scots Magazine*, December 1772, in Vol. 34, pp. 697-700

5. *The Scots Magazine*, October 1773, in Vol. 35, p. 557.

6. *The Scots Magazine*, December 1773, in Vol. 35, p. 667.

7. *The Scots Magazine*, February 1774, in Vol. 36, p. 64.

8. *The Scots Magazine*, May 1775, in Vol. 37, pp. 523 and 229.

9. A Plan agreed upon by a great many FARMERS and OTHERS, in the shires of Dumbarton, Clydesdale and Renfrew &c. for purchasing and improving lands within his Majesty's Dominions in North America, in such Manner as is, or shall be, conformable to the Laws and Privileges of his Majesty's Subjects in Great Britain. Paisley. Printed in the year MDCCLXII Price Three Pence. In Volume 4 of *Pamphlets* in the Witherspoon Collection, Princeton University.

REFERENCES AND NOTES

10. Edward Miller and Frederick P. Wells, *History of Ryegate Vermont: From its Settlement by the Scotch-American Company of Farmers to Present Time, With Genealogical Records of Many Families,* St. Johnsbury, Vt., The Caledonian Company, 1913, p. 16.
11. *History of Rygate*, p. 18.
12. 'The Journal of James Whitelaw', in *History of Ryegate*, p. 20.
13. Journal, p. 21.
14. ibid, pp. 21-22.
15. ibid, p. 22.
16. ibid, p. 23.
17. ibid, pp. 24-25.
18. ibid, pp. 26-27.
19. ibid, p. 27.
20. ibid, p. 28.
21. ibid, p. 30.
22. ibid, p. 31.
23. ibid, p. 33.
24. ibid, p. 34.
25. ibid, p. 34.
26. ibid, p. 35.
27. ibid, p. 37.
28. *History of Ryegate*, p. 570.
29. ibid, p. 42.
30. ibid, pp. 44-45
31. ibid, p. 37
32. ibid, p. 38.
33. ibid, pp. 11-12.
34. ibid, p. 41.
35. ibid, pp. 42 and 18.
36. ibid, p. 43.
37. *The Scots Magazine*, April 1774, in Vol. 36, pp. 221-22.
38. *The Scots Magazine*, February 1775, Vol. 37, p. 106.
39. John Witherspoon, *Works* (Philadelphia, 1801), Vol. IV, pp. 287-91.
40. *The Diary and Autobiography of John Adams*, L. H. Butterfield, Editor, 4 vols The Belknap Press of Harvard University Press, (Cambridge, Massachusetts, 1961), Vol. II, p. 112.
41. *Letter from George Washington to John Witherspoon, March 10, 1784.* In Witherspoon Collection, Box 2, Folder 28, Princeton University Library.
42. *Letter from John Witherspoon to William Steuart, December 8, 1792.* In Witherspoon Collection, Box 2, Folder 28, Princeton University Library. This letter was written by an amanuensis because of

Witherspoon's failing sight. A Library note comments: 'Had he [Witherspoon] seen the poor punctuation in the letter he might have asked it to be re-written'.

Chapter 14 *The Impact of John Witherspoon on Scotland and America*

1. *The Concise Dictionary of National Biography: From Earliest Times to 1985*, 3 vols Published by The Softback Preview by arrangement with Oxford University Press (Bath, 1995), Vol. III, p. 3268.
2. See Chapter 3.
3. T. M. Devine, *The Scottish Nation 1700-2000* (Harmondsworth, 2000), p. 80;
    T. M. Devine, *Scotland's Empire 1600-1815* (Harmondsworth, 2004), pp. 110, 112, 117, 168, 172-73, 180-81, 183.
4. Michael Fry, *The Scottish Empire*, (East Linton and Edinburgh, 2002); and *'Bold, Independent, Unconquer'd and Free': How the Scots Made America Safe for Liberty, Democracy and Capitalism* (Ayr, 2003). Arthur Herman, *The Scottish Enlightenment: The Scots' Invention of the Modern World* (London, 2001); Neil Oliver, *A History of Scotland,* Phoenix (London, 2010), first published Weidenfield & Nicolson (London, 2009); *The Cambridge Companion to the Scottish Enlightenment*, edited by Alexander Broadie (Cambridge University Press, 2003); *The History of Scottish Literature Vol.2 1660-1800*, edited by Andrew Hook (Aberdeen University Press, 1989); *The Glasgow Enlightenment*, edited by Andrew Hook and Richard B. Sher (East Linton, 1995); Richard B. Sher, *Church and University in the Scottish Enlightenment: The Moderate Literati of Edinburgh* (Edinburgh University Press, 1985); *Scotland and America in the Age of Enlightenment*, edited by Richard B. Sher and Jeffrey R. Smitten (Edinburgh University Press, 1990); and *Sociability and Society in Eighteenth-Century Scotland*, edited by John Dwyer and Richard B. Sher (Edinburgh, 1993).
5. See Chapter 13.
6. See T. M. Devine, *Scotland's Empire 1600-1815*, Chapter 5 and Chapter 8 pp.164-69.
7. See the Glasgow publication of the *Sermon* and the *Address* for an illustration of the British reaction : *The Dominion of Providence over the passions of Men: A Sermon preached at Princeton on 17th May 1776 Being the General Fast appointed by the Congress through the United Colonies. To which is added An Address to the Natives of Scotland, residing in America. By John Witherspoon D.D. President of the College of New Jersey, Second Edition with Elucidating*

REMARKS. Philadelphia Printed: Glasgow Re-printed. Sold by Booksellers in Town and County MDCCLXXVII Price Six-Pence.

8. For a fuller account of the Disruption see J. H. S. Burleigh, *A Church History of Scotland* (OUP, 1960), Chapters IV and V.

9. *The Wordsworth Dictionary of British History*, Editorial Consultant J. P. Kenyon (Ware, 1981), pp. 297-98; and Burleigh, p. 335.

10. Burleigh, pp. 336-38.

11. ibid, pp. 340-43.

12. ibid, pp. 344-49.

13. J. R. Fleming, D.D., *The Church in Scotland 1843-1874*, 2 vols (Edinburgh, 1927), p. 22 and Appendix A, p. 265; see also Burleigh, p. 351.

14. 'Articles Declaratory of the Constitution of the Church of Scotland in Matters Spiritual, Approved by Parliament 1921, enacted by General Assembly, 1926': Reproduced in *Kirk and Nation: The Story of the Reformed Church of Scotland*, by J. M. Reid (London, 1960), Appendix C, pp. 195-97.

15. *Senate Joint Resolution No. 3009 of the State of New Jersey*, in the Archives of the Historical Society of Princeton, Bainbridge House, Nassau Street, Princeton.

16. See Chapter 10, p. 156.

17. See this Chapter, pp. 255-256.

18. See Chapter 9.

19. James M. McPherson, in an Editorial Note to David Hackett Fischer's *Washington's Crossing* (OUP, 2004), p. ix.

20. *Washington's Crossing*, pp. 173-79; and note 58 p. 510.

21. ibid, p. 353.

22. Collins, II, p. 131.

23. ibid, p. 132.

24. ibid, p. 133.

25 Witherspoon Collection, Box 2, Folder 28, Princeton University.

26. *The Diary and Autobiography of John Adams*, L. H. Butterfield editor, 4 vols Harvard University Press, (Cambridge Massachusetts, 1961) Vol. III, p. 334.

27. ibid, Vol. IV, p. 253; and Collins, Vol. II, pp. 59-62.

28. Quoted by Jeffry H. Morrison, in *John Witherspoon and the Founding of the American Republic*, University of Notre Dame (Indiana, 2005), p. 1.

29. *The Diary and Autobiography of John Adams*, Vol. II, p. 112.

30. ibid, Vol. II, p. 259.

31. Quoted by Jeffrey H. Morrison, in *John Witherspoon and the Founding of the American Republic*, p. 1.

32. Noble E. Cunningham, Jr, *In Pursuit of Reason: The Life of Thomas Jefferson*, Louisiana State University Press, 1987, p. 14.
33. ibid, p. 23; see also Chapter 7, p. 83.
34. ibid, p. 25.
35. ibid, pp. 83-84.
36. ibid, pp. 39 and 86.
37. ibid, p. 27; and *A Summary View* quoted on p. 28. Compare Witherspoon's 'Manifesto', in *Essays* Vol. IV, p. 155.
38. Cunningham, p. 16.
39. 'The Unanimous Declaration of the Thirteen United States of America 4 July 1776' in *Revolutions 1775-1830*, edited by Merryn Williams, Penguin Books Ltd. (Harmondsworth, 1971), pp. 44-52. Note: this book prints the Final Draft and on the facing pages the First Draft. See also Chapter 13, p. 207.
40. Thomas Jefferson's letter to Henry Lee, May 8, 1825 reprinted in Philip S. Foner, ed., *Basic Writings of Thomas Jefferson* (1944) reproduced in *Revolutions 1775-1830*, p. 54.
41. *Diary and Autobiography of John Adams*, Vol. II, pp. 112 and 121; see also Witherspoon, 'On Conducting the American Controversy', in *Essays* Vol. IV, p. 85.
42. 'Moral Philosophy Lecture X', in *Essays* Vol. II, pp. 77-78.
43. Cunningham, p. 13.
44. Article 16, 'Virginia Bill of Rights' in *Revolutions 1775-1830*, p. 173.
45. Cunningham, p. 55.
46. Jeffry H. Morrison, p. 4.
47. 'Virginia Statute of Religious Liberty 16 January 1786' reproduced in *Revolutions 1775-1830*, p. 169.
48. *Moral Philosophy Lecture XVI*, p. 150.
49. Cunningham, pp. 61 and 94.
50. *Moral Philosophy Lecture X*, p. 82.
51. *A Final Inventory of all the Goods and Chattels of the late Rev. John Witherspoon, 28th Day of November 1794.* Taken by Anne Witherspoon, sole executrix to the Last Will and Testament of the Deceased. In the Historical Society of Princeton, 158 Nassau Street, Princeton, archive, Vertical File 41.
52. *Moral Philosophy Lecture XII*, pp. 82 and 84.
53. Cunningham, p. 31.
54. 'Virginia Bill of Rights 12 June 1776', in *Revolutions 1775-1830*, p. 171.
55. Cunningham, pp. 55-58.
56. *Moral Philosophy Lecture XII*, p. 101.

REFERENCES AND NOTES

57. ibid, pp. 100-101
58. Cunningham, pp. 44-45.
59. See Chapter 9, p.143 and Chapter 10, p.156.
60. 'Lecture on Eloquence II', in *Works of the Rev. John Witherspoon* (Philadelphia, 1800), Vol. III, p. 160.
61. Quoted in Cunningham, pp. 36-37.
62. Cunningham, p. 38.
63. This brief summary of biographical details of Aaron Burr has been assisted by a reading of Nancy Isenberg's *Fallen Founder, The Life of Aaron Burr*, (London, 2007).
64. Cunningham, p. 55.
65. Collins, Vol. I, pp. 125-27
66. Cunningham, pp. 56-57.
67. ibid, pp. 58-60.
68. *Moral Philosophy Lecture XII*, p. 105.
69. James Madison, 'Federalist Paper 51', quoted in Harry M. Ward's *The American Revolution Nationhood Achieved, 1763-1788*, St. Martin's Press, (New York, 1995), p. 351.
70. *Moral Philosophy Lecture XII*, pp. 101-102.
71. James Madison, quoted in Harry M. Ward, p. 286.
72. *Moral Philosophy Lecture XII*, pp. 100-101.
73. James Madison, 'Federalist Paper 51', quoted in Jeffry Morrison's, *John Witherspoon and the Founding of the American Republic*, p. 40.
74. *Moral Philosophy Lecture XIV*, p. 119.
75. ibid, p. 120.
76. *The Dominion of Providence* (Glasgow, 1777), pp. 27-28 and p. 38.
77. Jeffry H. Morrison, p. 38.
78. 'Virginia Bill of Rights 12 June 1776, Article 16', Reprinted in H.S. Commager (ed) *Documents of American History* (1963), in *Revolutions 1775-1830*, p. 173.
79. *Moral Philosophy Lecture X*, pp. 77-79, 80; and *Lecture XIV*, p. 119.
80. Harry M. Ward, p. 339.
81. James Madison to Jared Sparks on April 8, 1831, ibid, p. 346.
82. *U.S. Presidents and Vice Presidents List* at www.presidentusa.net/presvplist. html, (2006), p. 1.
83. Douglass Adair, *Fame and the Founding Fathers*, p. 124, quoted by Jeffry H. Morrison, p. 99.
84. Abraham Lincoln (1809-65), from his address at the dedication of the National Cemetery at Gettysburg, November 19, 1863. The fuller context of the quote is: 'We here highly resolve that the dead shall not have died in vain, that this nation, under God, shall have a new

birth of freedom; and that government of the people, by the people, and for the people, shall not perish from the earth'.
Oxford Concise Dictionary of Quotations, 4th Edition, Edited by Elizabeth Knowles, (OUP, 2001).

***

Bibliography

Adams, John,   *The Diary and Autobiography of John Adams*, edited by L. H. Butterfield, 4 vols The Belknap Press of Harvard University Press (Cambridge, Massachusetts, 1961).

Baine, James,   'A Sermon Preached at the Translation of the Rev. Mr Witherspoon from Beith to the Laigh Kirk of Paisley' in *Paisley Pamphlets Vol I: 1739-77* in Paisley Central Library

Beaumarchais,   *The Barber of Seville* and *The Marriage of Figaro*, Translated with Introduction by John Wood, Penguin Books (Harmondsworth, 1964).

Berkeley, George, *The Principles of Human Knowledge and Three Dialogues Between Hylas and Philonous*, edited and with an Introduction by G. J. Warnock, Collins (London and Glasgow, 1966).

Berlin, Isaiah,   *The Age of Enlightenment*, The New American Library (New York, 1961).

Blair, Hugh,   *Lectures on Rhetoric and Belles Lettres*, 3 vols (Edinburgh, 1813).

'A Critical Dissertation on the Poems of Ossian, The Son of Fingal', in *The Poems of Ossian and Related Works*, edited by Howard Gaskell with an Introduction by Fiona Stafford, Edinburgh University Press (Edinburgh, 1996).

Branch, Lori,   'Plain Style, or the High Fashion of Empire: Colonialism, Resistance and Assimilation in Adam Smith's Lectures on Rhetoric and Belles Lettres', in *Studies in Scottish Literature* XXXIII, XXXIV, pp. 435-53.

Broadie, Alexander, ed., *The Scottish Enlightenment: An Anthology,* Canongate (Edinburgh, 1997).

ed. *The Cambridge Companion to The Scottish Enlightenment*, Cambridge University Press (Cambridge, 2003).

Burleigh, J. H. S., *A Church History of Scotland*, OUP (London, 1960).

Burns, Robert,   *The Poems and Songs of Robert Burns*, ed. James Kinsley, 3 vols (Oxford, 1968).

The Letters of Robert Burns, J. De Lancey Ferguson second edition edited by G. Ross Roy 2 vols (Oxford, 1985).

Butterfield, L. H., *John Witherspoon Comes to America: A Documentary Account Based Largely on New Materials*, Princeton University Library (Princeton, 1953).

Calvin, John,   *Institutes of the Christian Religion*, A New Translation By Henry Beveridge Esq., 2 vols T. & T. Clark (Edinburgh, 1879).

Campbell, George, *The Philosophy of Rhetoric*, 2 vols Printed by George Ramsay & Co for Willam Creech, Edinburgh; and T. Cadell and W. Davies, London (Edinburgh, 1808).
A Dissertation on Miracles, Alex.Gardner, (Paisley, 1834).

Carlyle, Alexander, *Anecdotes and Characters of the Times*, Edited with an Introduction by James Kinsley, OUP (London, 1973).

Collins, Varnum Lansing, *President Witherspoon: A Biography*, 2 vols Princeton University Press (OUP, 1925)

Cragg, Gerald R., *The Church and the Age of Reason (1648-1789),* Pelican Books (Harmondsworth, 1960).

Crawfurd, Andrew, *The Cairn of Lochwinnoch Mannuscripts*, 'compiled by Dr Andrew Crawfurd, of Johnshill, between 1827 and the year of Victoria's accession, 1837, consists in the main of his own handwritten notes often derived from interviews with village people with the addition of some newspaper cuttings'. Librarian's note, Paisley Central Library.

Cunningham, Noble E. Jr, *In Pursuit of Reason: The Life of Thomas Jefferson*, Louisiana State University Press (Baton Rouge and London, 1987)

Daiches, David, 'Style Périodique and Style Coupé: Hugh Blair and the Scottish Rhetoric of American Independence', in *Scotland and America in the Age of the Enlightenment* (Edinburgh, 1990), pp. 209-26.
'John Witherspoon, James Wilson and the Influence of Scottish Rhetoric, on America', in *Sociability and Society in Eighteenth-Century Scotland*, edited by John Dwyer and Richard B. Sher, (Edinburgh, 1993), pp. 163-80.

Dakin, A., *Calvinism*, Duckworth (London, 1949).

Devine, T. M., *The Scottish Nation 1700-2000*, Penguin Books (Harmondsworth, 2000).
Scotland's Empire 1600-1815, Penguin Books (London, 2003).

Diamond, Peter J., 'Witherspoon, William Smith and the Scottish Philosophy in Revolutionary America', in *Scotland and America in the Age of Enlightenment,* (Edinburgh, 1990), pp. 115-32.

Dix, William S., *The Princeton University Library in the Eighteenth Century*, (Princeton, 1978).

Donaldson, Gordon, *Scottish Historical Documents*, Scottish Academic Press (Edinburgh and London, 1974).

Donovan, Robert Kent, 'The Popular Party of the Church of Scotland and the American Revolution', in *Scotland and America in the Age of the Enlightenment*, (Edinburgh, 1990), pp. 81-99.

'Evangelical Civic Humanism in Glasgow: The American War Sermons of William Thom', in *The Glasgow Enlightenment*, edited by Andrew Hook and Richard B. Sher (East Linton, 1995), pp. 227-45.

Dwyer, John and Richard B. Sher, ed., *Sociability and Society in Eighteenth-Century Scotland*, Mercat Press (Edinburgh, 1993).

Emerson, Roger, 'The Contexts of the Scottish Enlightenment', in *The Cambridge Companion to The Scottish Enlightenment*, ed. by Andrew Broadie, (Cambridge, 2003), pp. 9-30.

Erskine, John, 'Of Laws in General', in *The Scottish Enlightenment, An Anthology*, ed. Alexander Broadie, (Edinburgh, 1997), pp. 598-613.

Falcone, Joseph J., *New Jersey Books 1698-1800*, Joseph J. Falcone Inc. (Princeton, 1992).
New Jersey Books 1801-1860, Joseph J. Falcone Inc. (Princeton, 1996). Note. These two books contain a catalogue of books published in or associated with New Jersey, and are part of the Joseph J. Falcone Collection, in Princeton Public Library.

Fénelon, Francois De, *Telemachus, son of Ulysses*, edited by and translated by Patrick Riley, Cambridge University Press (Cambridge, 1994).
Aventures De Télémaque suivies *Du Recueil Des Fables, Composées pour l'education de Mgr le Duc de Bourgorgue*, par Fénelon, Archevé De Cambrai Maison Didot, Firmin - Didot Et Cie, Editeurs, Imprimeurs de L'Instut, Rue Jacob, 56, Paris. [undated].

Fergusson, James, *John Fergusson 1727-1750*, Jonathan Cape (London, 1948).

Findlay, Bill, ed., *A History of Scottish Theatre*, Edinburgh University Press (Edinburgh, 1998).

Fischer, David Hackett, *Washington's Crossing*, (Oxford, 2004).

Fleischacker, Samuel, 'The impact on America: Scottish philosophy and the American founding', in *The Cambridge Companion to the Scottish Enlightenment*, (Cambridge, 2003), pp. 316-37.

Ford, Philip J., *George Buchanan: Prince of Poets*, Aberdeen University Press (Aberdeen, 1982).

Fry, Michael, *The Scottish Empire*, Tuckwell Press and Birlinn Ltd. (East Lothian, and Edinburgh, 2002).
'Bold, Independent, Unconquer'd and Free': How the Scots Made America Safe for Democracy and Capitalism, Fort Publishing Ltd (Ayr, 2003).

Gaskill, Howard,   ed., *The Poems of Ossian and Related Works*, with an
                Introduction by Fiona Stafford, Edinburgh University Press
                (Edinburgh, 1996).

Gerard, Alexander, *An Essay on Genius*, (London and Edinburgh, 1774).

Godechot, Jacques, *France and the Atlantic Revolution of the Eighteenth
                Century, 1770-1799*, Translated by Herbert H. Rowen, The
                Free Press, New York, Collier Macmillan Publishers London
                (London, 1965).

Green, Ashbel,   *The Life of the Revd. John Witherspoon D.D., LL.D.*, ed.
                Henry Littleton Savage, (Princeton, 1973).

Harrison, Richard A., *Princetonians 1776-1788: A Biographical Dictionary*,
                Princeton University Press (Princeton, 1981).

Hart, D. G. and Muether, John, 'Turning Points in American Presbyterian
                History, Part 4: A National Presbyterian Church 1789', a
                paper produced for the Orthodox Presbyterian Church,
                Reprinted from *New Horizons*, April 2005.

Herman, Arthur,   *The Scottish Enlightenment: The Scots' Invention of the
                Modern World*, Fourth Estate (London, 2003).

Hervey, James,   *Meditations and Contemplations*, (London, 1855).

Hoeveeler, Jr, J. David, *James McCosh and the Scottish Intellectual Tradition:
                From Glasgow to Princeton*, Princeton University Press
                (Princeton, 1981).

Hickie, W. J.,   *Greek-English Lexicon to the New Testament*, Macmillan
                (London, 1945).

Hook, Andrew,   ed., *The History of Scottish Literature, Volume 2, 1660-
                1800*, Aberdeen University Press (Aberdeen, 1989).

Hook, Andrew, and Richard B. Sher, editors, *The Glasgow Enlightenment*,
                Tuckwell Press (East Linton, 1995).

Isaacson, Walter, *Benjamin Franklin: An American Life*, Simon & Schuster
                Paperbacks (New York, 2004).

Johnson, Abel,   *Notes on the History Lectures of John Witherspoon, by Abel
                Johnson*, (Class of 1784), in Princeton University Library.

Keane, John,   *Tom Paine: A Political Life*, (London, 1996).

Kennedy, Thomas D., 'William Leechman, Pulpit Eloquence and the Glasgow
                Enlightenment', in *The Glasgow Enlightenment*, (East
                Linton, 1995), pp. 56-72.

Landsman, Ned C., 'Witherspoon and the Problem of Provincial Identity in
                Scottish Evangelical Culture', in *Scotland and America in
                the Age of the Enlightenment*, (Edinburgh, 1990), pp. 29-45.
                'Liberty, Piety and Patronage: The Social Context of
                Contested Clerical Calls in Eighteenth-Century Glasgow', in
                The Glasgow Enlightenment, (East Linton, 1995).

BIBLIOGRAPHY

'Presbyterians and Provincial Society: The Evangelical Enlightenment in the West of Scotland, 1740-1775', in *Sociability and Society in Eighteenth-Century Scotland*, edited by John Dwyer and Richard B. Sher, The Mercat Press (Edinburgh, 1993), pp. 194-209.

ed.*, Nation and Province in the First British Empire: Scotland and the Americas, 1600-1800*, Published in Association with the Eighteenth-Century Scottish Studies Society (London, 2001).

Lathrop, John,   *Innocent Blood Crying to God. From the Streets of Boston. A Sermon occasioned by the horrid murder of Messieurs Samuel Gray, Samuel Maverick, James Caldwell and Crispus Attucks, with Pattrick Carr since dead and Christopher Monk judged irrecoverable and several others badly wounded, by a party of troops under the command of Captain Preston. On the 5th of March, 1770 and Preached on the Lord's day following*; By John Lathrop A.M. Pastor of the 2nd Church in Boston. *'Cursed be their anger, for it was fierce and their wrath, for it was cruel'. Gen. xlix .7. 'The remainder of their wrath thou shalt restrain'. Psal. lxxvi.* London, Printed. Boston: Reprinted and sold by Edes and Gill, opposite the new Court House in Queen Street, M,DCC,LXXI.

Lenman, Bruce,   *The Jacobite Risings in Britain 1689-1746*, Scottish Cultural Press (Aberdeen, 1995).
    The Jacobite Clans of the Great Glen 1650-1784, Scottish Cultural Press (Aberdeen, 1995).

Locke, John,   *An Essay Concerning Human Understanding*, abridged and edited by Raymond Wilburn, J. M. Dent & Sons Ltd. (London, 1948).
    An Essay Concerning Human Understanding, abridged and edited with an introduction by John Yolton, J. M. Dent & Sons Ltd. (London, 1961).
    Two Treatises of Civil Government, Introduction by Professor W. S. Carpenter, J. M. Dent & Sons Ltd. (London, 1955).

McGinty, J. Walter, *Robert Burns and Religion*, Ashgate (Aldershot and Burlington, 2003).

McIntosh, John R., *Church and Theology in Enlightenment Scotland: The Popular Party, 1740-1800,* Tuckwell Press (East Linton, 1998).

Macintyre, Gordon, *Dugald Stewart: The Pride and Ornament of Scotland*, Sussex Academic Press (Brighton, 2003).

BIBLIOGRAPHY

Macrone, Michael, *It's Greek to Me!,* Pavillion Books Ltd. (London, 1992).
Macquarrie, John, *Twentieth Century Religious Thought*, SCM Press Ltd.
        (London, 1963).
Malthus, Thomas. R., *An Essay on Population,* 2 vols J. M. Dent & Sons Ltd.
        (London, 1952)
Miller, Edward, and Frederick P. Wells, *History of Ryegate, Vermont: From its*
        Settlement by the Scotch-American Company of Farmers to
        Present Time, with Genealogical Records of Many Families,
        St. Johnsbury Vt., The Caledonian Company, 1913.
Miller, Thomas P., 'Witherspoon, Blair and the Rhetoric of Civic Humanism',
        in *Scotland and America in the Age of the Enlightenment*,
        (Edinburgh, 1990), pp. 100-14.
        'Francis Hutcheson and the Civic Humanist Tradition', in
        The Glasgow Enlightenment, (East Linton, 1995), pp. 40-55.
Morrison, Jeffry H., *John Witherspoon and The Founding Of The American*
        Republic, University of Notre Dame Press (Indiana, 2005)
Newton, Isaac, *The Principia*, Translated by Andrew Motte, Prometheus
        Books (New York, 1995).
Oliver, Neil *A History of Scotland*, Phoenix (London, 2010). first
        published Weidenfield & Nicolson (London 2009).
Oz-Salzberger, Fania, 'The Political Theory of the Scottish Enlightenment', in
        The Cambridge Companion to the Scottish Enlightenment,
        ed., Alexander Broadie, (Cambridge, 2003), pp. 157-77.
Paine, Thomas, *Agrarian Justice*, Penguin Books (London, 2004).
        Common Sense, Penguin Books (London, 2004)
Pascal, Blaise, *Pascal's Pensées*, Translated by W. F. Trotter, Introduction
        by T. S. Eliot, J. M. Dent & Sons Ltd. (London, 1956).
Paterson, James, *History of the County of Ayr with a Genealogical Account of*
        the Families of Ayrshire, Vol. I, John Dick (Ayr, 1847).
Peterson, Charles E., 'Robert Smith, Philadelphia Builder-Architect: From
        Dalkeith to Princeton', in *Scotland and America in the* Age
        of the *Enlightenment*, (Edinburgh, 1990), pp. 274-99.
Rabelais, François, *The Histories of Gargantua and Pantagruel*, Translated and
        with an Introduction by J. M. Cohen, Penguin Books
        (Harmondsworth, 1957)
Reid, J. M., *Kirk and Nation*, Skeffington & Son Ltd. (London, 1960).
Reid, Thomas, *An Inquiry into the Human Mind, On the Principles of*
        Common Sense, Thoemmes Antiquarian Books Ltd., 4th
        edition 1785 (Bristol, 1990).
Ross, Ian Simpson, *The Life of Adam Smith*, OUP (Oxford, 1995).
Russell, Bertrand, *History of Western Philosophy*, Unwin (London, 1979).
Scotch American Farmers, *A Plan agreed upon by a great many FARMERS and*
        OTHERS, in the shires of Dumbarton, Clydesdale and

Renfrew &c. for purchasing and improving lands within his
Majesty's Dominions in North America, in such Manner as
is, or shall be, conformable to the Laws and Privileges of his
Majesty's Subjects in Great Britain. Paisley. Printed in the
year MDCCLXXII. Price Three Pence. In Volume 4 of
Pamphlets in the John Witherspoon Collection, Princeton
University

Scott, Hew,   *Fasti Ecclesiae Scoticana: The Succession of ministers of the*
Church of Scotland from the Reformation, New Edition,
Volume III, Oliver and Boyd (Edinburgh, 1920).

Scott, William Robert, *Francis Hutcheson: His Life, Teaching and Position in*
the History of Philosophy, Thoemmes Press, A reprint of the
1900 edition (Bristol, 1992).

Scullion, Adrienne, 'The Eighteenth Century', in *A History of Scottish Theatre*,
ed. by Bill Findlay, (pp. 80-136)

Selden, William K., *Women of Princeton*, (Princeton University, 2000).

Sher, Richard B., *Church and University in the Scottish Enlightenment: The*
Moderate Literati of Edinburgh, Edinburgh University Press
(Edinburgh, 1985).
'Witherspoon's Dominion of Providence and the Scottish
Jeremiad Tradition', in *Scotland and America in the Age of*
the Enlightenment, (Edinburgh, 1990), pp. 46-64.
'Literature and the Church of Scotland', in *The History of*
Scottish Literature Volume 2 1660-1800 edited by Andrew
Hook, (Aberdeen, 1989) pp. 259-71.

Sher, Richard B. and Jeffrey R. Smitten, *Scotland and America in the Age of the*
*Enlighte*nment, Edinburgh University Press (Edinburgh,
1990).

Shreiner, Samuel A., *A Place Called Princeton*, Arbor House (New York,
1984).

Sloane, William Milligan, ed., *The Life of James McCosh: A record Chiefly*
Autobiographical, T. and T. Clark (Edinburgh, 1896)

Smith, Samuel Stanhope, *A System of Moral Philosophy for the Students of*
Nassau Hall, by Samuel Stanhope Smith. A set of lectures 1-
4 and 5-10. In two soft cover, parchment bound notebooks,
in *The Samuel Stanhope Smith Collection*, Princeton
University Library.

Smith, Adam,   *Lectures on Rhetoric and Belles Lettres*, ed. J. G. Bryce,
Liberty Fund (Indianapolis, 1985).
Considerations Concerning the First Formation of
Languages and the Different Genius of original and
compounded Languages is appended to this volume.

BIBLIOGRAPHY

The Theory of Moral Sentiments, edited by D. D. Raphael and A. L. Macfie, Liberty Fund (Indianapolis, 1982).

The Wealth of Nations: Books I-III, Introduction by Andrew Skinner, Penguin (Harmondsworth, 1986).

Sterne, Laurence, *The Life and Opinions of Tristram Shandy, Gentleman*, Penguin Books (Harmondsworth, 1986).

Tait, L. Gordon, *The Piety of John Witherspoon, Pew, Pulpit, and Public Forum*, Geneva Press (Louisville, 2001).

The Concise Dictionary of National Biography: From earliest times to 1985, 3 vols The Softback Preview edition by arrangement from Oxford University Press (Oxford, 1995).

The Confession of Faith, containing: *The Confession of Faith, The Larger Catechism, The Shorter Catechism, The Directory for Public Worship, The Form of Presbyterial Church Government with References to The Proofs From The Scripture*. William Blackwood & Sons Ltd. (Edinburgh and London, 1959).

The Constitution of the Presbyterian Church in the United States of America, containing: *The Confession of Faith, The Catechisms, The Government and Discipline* and *The Directory for the Worship of God*. Ratified and adopted by the Synod of New York and Philadelphia, May the 16th and 18th, 1788 and continued by adjournment until the 28th of the same Month. Philadelphia: Printed by Thomas Bradford. In front street fourth door below Market Street, MDCCLXXXIX. Authors note: This particular copy has on its frontispiece a number, '127' and a signature that appears to be that of John Witherspoon.

The Good News Bible, The Bible Societies (London, 1976).

The Holy Bible, King James Version, Collins (Glasgow, 1949).

The Interlinear Greek-English New Testament, The Nestle Greek Text with a Literal English Translation by the Reverend Alfred Marshall D. Litt., Samuel Bagster & Sons Ltd. (London, 1958).

The New English Bible, Oxford University Press (Oxford, 1970).

The Pennsylvania Magazine or American Monthly Museum, MDCCLXXV, Volume 1, Philadelphia: Printed and sold by R. Aitken, Printer and Bookseller opposite the London Coffee House Front Street.

The Scots Magazine, Vol. 15, 1753; Vols 30-37, 1768-1775, printed by A. Murray and J. Cochrane, Edinburgh.

The Statistical Account of Scotland 1791-1799, edited by Sir John Sinclair, Volume VI, Ayrshire, with a new introduction by John Strawhorn, General Editors: Donald J. Withrington and Ian R. Grant, E P Publishing Ltd. (Wakefield, 1982)

Walker, Williston, *A History of the Christian Church*, T. & T. Clark
(Edinburgh, 1953).

Ward, Harry M., *The American Revolution: Nationhood Achieved, 1763-
1788*, St. Martin's Press (New York, 1995).

Warnock, G. J., *Berkeley*, Penguin Books (Harmondsworth, 1953).

Watson, Roderick, *The Literature of Scotland*, Macmillan (London, 1984).

Weintraub, Stanley, *Iron Tears*, Simon and Schuster (London, 2005).

Whitelaw, James, 'The Journal of James Whitelaw', in *History of Ryegate,
Vermont*, by Edward Miller and Frederick P. Wells, (St.
Johnsbury Vt., 1913).

Williams, Merryn, ed., *Revolutions 1775-1830*, Penguin Books
(Harmondsworth, 1971).

Witherspoon, John, *Essays on Important Subjects* Volumes I-IV, (Edinburgh,
1805).

The Works of John Witherspoon 9 vols (Edinburgh, 1805).

The Works of the Rev. John Witherspoon D.D. LL.D., 3 vols
(Philadelphia, 1800).

*Sermons on Practical Subjects to which is added a Farewell
Discourse delivered at Paisley in April and May 1768*
(Glasgow, 1768).

*Lectures on Moral Philosophy and Eloquence By the Rev.
John Witherspoon D.D. LL.D.* from the Woodward Third
Edition, (Philadelphia, 1810). Authorised facsimile by
Tylers Green, High Wycombe, England, a Xerox Company.

Lectures on Moral Philosophy, 1795. General Manuscript
[Bound] (1840) CO 199 No. 32 Princeton University
Library. Student notes of James Agnew, of the Class of
1795. Certified by his father Daniel Agnew to be in his son's
handwriting.

Notes by Abel Johnson, (Class of 1784) on the *History
Lectures of John Witherspoon*, in the John Witherspoon
Collection, Box 1 Folder 40.

*Essay on the Connection between the Doctrine of
Justification by the Imputed Righteousness of Christ, and
Holiness of Life; with some reflections upon the Reception
which that Doctrine hath generally met with in the World*,
(Glasgow, 1756).

A Practical Treatise on Regeneration, within a damaged
volume: *Treatises on Justification and Regeneration by J.
Witherspoon D.D. with an introductory essay by William
Wilberforce, Esq. Author of a Practical View of Christianity,*
(Glasgow, 1824). *Treatise on Regeneration* first published
1764.

BIBLIOGRAPHY

Christian Magnanimity, A Sermon Preached at Princeton, Sept. 1775 The Sabbath preceding the Annual Commencement: and again with Additions, September 23 1787 to which is added *An Address to the Senior Class* who were to receive the degree of Bachelor of Arts, By John Witherspoon D.D., President of the College of New Jersey (Princeton, 1787 and reprinted at Paisley, 1788).

Scots Anticipation or A Summary of the Debate containing the Substance of some of the Principal Speeches that are to be delivered in the G- A-y of the C-h of S-d upon an Overture transmitted by the P-l S-d of G- and A. relating to Popery, (Edinburgh, 1779) by Anon "A fellow labourer".

A Charge of Sedition and Faction Against Good Men, especially faithful Ministers considered and accounted for. A *Sermon preached in the Abbey Church of Paisley on Thursday Sept. 7th 1758* (Glasgow, 1758)

Four letters on Education By John Witherspoon D.D. (Glasgow, 1799).

The Dominion of Providence over the Passions of Men. A sermon preached at Princeton on 17th May 1776. Being the General Fast appointed by the Congress throughout the United Colonies. To which is added *An Address to the Natives of Scotland, residing in America, By John Witherspoon D.D. President of the College of New Jersey.* The second edition with Elucidating Remarks (Philadelphia), reprinted Glasgow, 1777.

Ecclesiastical Characteristics or The Arcana of Church Policy. Being an humble Attempt to open up the Mystery of Moderation wherein is shewn: A plain and easy way to the Character of a Moderate Man, as at present in repute in the Church of Scotland, The Third Edition Corrected and Enlarged. (Glasgow, 1754).

Serious Enquiry into the Nature and Effects of the Stage. Being an attempt to show that contributing to the Support of a Public Theatre is inconsistent with the Character of a Christian. By John Witherspoon M.A., Ministerof the Gospel in Beith (Glasgow, 1757).

John Witherspoon Collection, Firestone Library, Princeton University. Papers and Correspondance Boxes 1 and 2.

Disputatio Philosophica, De Mentis Immortalitate by Joannes Wederspan (Edinburgh, 1739).

Sermons by the Late John Witherspoon SSTP, President of the College of New Jersey. A Supplementary Volume

including such sermons as are not already published in his works. To which is added: The History of a Corporation of Servants and Other Tracts (Edinburgh, 1798).
Manuscript Notebook of John Witherspoon's for 1763, incorporated in *The Universal Scots Almanack for the year of our Lord MDCCLXIII Being the third year after leap year*. (Edinburgh). In Princeton University Library.
Almanack and Memorandum Book of Dr. John Witherspoon, 1768. In Princeton University Library.

Woods, David Walker, *John Witherspoon*, Fleming H. Revell Company, Legacy Reprint Series, First published New York, 1906.

Wrenn, Laurence G., *John Witherspoon and Church Law*, A Dissertation submitted in Partial Fulfillment of the Requirements for the Degree of Doctor of Canon Law. 1979. Pontifica Universitas Lateranensis, Institutum Utrisque Iuris. Theses ad Lauream in Iure Canonico.

Yeats, Y. B., *Y. B. Yeats Selected Poetry*, edited and with an Introduction by A. Norman Jeffares, Macmillan (London, 1979).

Young, Robert, *Analytical Concordance to the Holy Bible*, Lutterworth Press (London, 1961).

***

Index

INDEX

Church, John 331, 333
Cicero 4, 167, 171, 175, 176, 180, 188, 189, 284, 290, 356
Civil laws 121, 157, 158, 159
Clarke, Dr Samuel 124-126, 129, 179, 183, 184
Cleghorn, Gulielmus, *Analogia & Philosophia Prima* 185
Clow, James 168
Coercive Acts 193
Cohen, J. M. 11
College of New Jersey 72-103, 1, 10, 115, 176, 177, 180, 231, 248, 250,
      253, 256, 277, 284, 291, 292, 315, 332, 340, 348, 350, 351, 353, 358,
      362, 363, 369
      fees 97
      hospitality 275
      library 76, 81, 86, 90-96
      Memorial of the College of New Jersey 100
      Prospectus 75, 177
      student life 96-103
      students's revolutionary activity 200
      war damage 277
Collins, Varnum Lansing, *President Witherspoon, A Biography* 1, 6, 7, 64,
      77, 79, 88, 90, 96, 200, 208, 220, 235, 240, 241, 246, 270, 271, 272
Committee of Correspondence 87, 102, 185, 200, 224, 282, 296, 302, 353
Committee on Foreign Affairs 220, 221, 223, 236, 238, 239, 268, 348, 352
Committee of Secret Correspondence 220, 224, 236, 239, 342
Common Sense by Thomas Paine 210, 215, 219-222, 229-231, 267-269
Common Sense Philosophy 19, 86, 130, 155, 156, 168, 283, 370
Concord 193, 199, 322, 363
Condillac, Abbé Étienne bonnet de, *Essai sur l'origine des connaissances
      humaines* 174
Confederacy 191, 212, 233, 234, 241, 242, 311
Confession of Faith (Westminster) 4, 12, 18, 43, 49, 67, 116, 217, 218,
      307-314
Considerations on the First Formation of Languages by Adam Smith 173,
      174
Continental Congress 97, 115, 193, 199, 201, 202, 206, 224, 244, 347, 349,
      350, 360
Court of Session 30, 343, 344
Crawfurd, Dr Andrew 8, 9
Cromwell, Oliver 228, 294, 303
Cunningham, Alexander 253
Cunningham, Noble E. Jnr, *In Pursuit of Reason: The Life of Thomas
      Jefferson* 359
Curling 9, 30, 272, 275

INDEX

INDEX

INDEX

INDEX

INDEX

INDEX

INDEX

INDEX

Lightning Source UK Ltd.
Milton Keynes UK
UKOW030934290712

196743UK00002B/14/P